# Cognition and Emotion

# Cognition and Emotion
## Reviews of Current Research and Theories

Edited by Jan De Houwer and
Dirk Hermans

 Psychology Press
Taylor & Francis Group
HOVE AND NEW YORK

Published in 2010
by Psychology Press
27 Church Road, Hove, East Sussex BN3 2FA

Simultaneously published in the USA and Canada
by Psychology Press
270 Madison Avenue, New York, NY 10016

*Psychology Press is an imprint of the Taylor & Francis Group,
an informa business*

© 2010 Psychology Press

Typeset in Chennai by Datapage (India) Private Limited
Printed and bound in Great Britain by TJ International Ltd, Padstow, Cornwall
Cover design by Anú Design

This publication has been produced with paper manufactured to
strict environmental standards and with pulp derived from
sustainable forests.

*British Library Cataloguing in Publication Data*
A catalogue record for this book is available from the British Library

*Library of Congress Cataloging in Publication Data*
Cognition and emotion: reviews of current research and theories /
edited by Jan De Houwer and Dirk Hermans.
      p. cm.
  Includes bibliographical references and index.
  ISBN 978-1-84169-871-7 (hb)
  1. Emotions and cognition. 2. Cognition. 3. Emotions. I. De Houwer, Jan.
II. Hermans, Dirk.
  BF311.C54773 2010
  152.4—dc22
                                              2009042746

ISBN: 978-1-84169-871-7 (hbk)

# Contents

# Contributors

**Isabelle Blanchette**, Université du Québec a Trois-Rivières, CP500, Trois-Rivières (Québec), Canada, G9A 5H7.

**Tobias Brosch**, University of Geneva, 7 Rue de Battoirs, HE-1205 Geneva, Switzerland.

**Jan De Houwer**, Ghent University, Henri Dunantlaan 2, B-9000 Ghent, Belgium.

**Robin S. Edelstein**, University of Michigan, 530 Church Street, Ann Arbor, Michigan 48109, USA.

**Dirk Hermans**, University of Leuven, Tiensestraat 102, B-3000 Leuven, Belgium.

**Sander L. Koole**, Vrije Universiteit Amsterdam, van der Boechorststraat 1, NL-1081 BT, Amsterdam, The Netherlands.

**Linda J. Levine**, University of California, Irvine, 3340 Social Ecology II, Irvine, CA 92697-7085, USA.

**Iris B. Mauss**, University of Denver, Denver, CO 80208, USA.

**Agnes Moors**, Ghent University, Henri Dunantlaan 2, B-9000 Ghent, Belgium.

**Gilles Pourtois**, Ghent University, Henri Dunantlaan 2, B-9000 Ghent, Belgium.

**Anne Richards**, Birkbeck College, Malet Street, London WC1E 7HX, UK.

**Michael D. Robinson**, North Dakota State University, PO Box 6050, Fargo, ND 58108-6050, USA.

**David Sander**, University of Geneva, 7 Rue de Battoirs, HE-1205 Geneva, Switzerland.

**Jenny Yiend**, Institute of Psychiatry, King's College London, London SE5 8HF, UK.

# Introduction

Emotions are complex and multifaceted phenomena. This is reflected in the multitude of perspectives from which emotions are studied. Theories have focused on physiological, developmental, social, cultural, differential, behavioural and many other aspects of our emotional life. Within this variety of approaches, the study of the cognition–emotion interaction has always taken a rather unique position. Though the relationship between cognition and emotion has been the fascination of many philosophers and other great thinkers, empirically oriented researchers have considered them an odd couple for a long time, and have mostly studied them separately. Even after the advent of new experimental techniques for studying cognitive processes like attention, perception and memory in the early 1970s, emotions were seldom included as an object of study.

Since the 1980s, research on cognition and emotion has expanded and, more importantly, differentiated. Researchers started to investigate interactions between emotion and attention, memory, learning, judgements, decisions and other cognitive processes. Others translated these findings and insights to the study of emotional pathologies with an emphasis on anxiety and depression. The growing evidence on, for instance, attentional and memory biases in these disorders lay at the basis of a domain that is now also known as "experimental psychopathology". Other lines of research focus on cognitive aspects of emotion regulation and emotion elicitation, and the biological underpinnings of the cognition–emotion interaction. Particularly, the causal status of cognitive processes in the elicitation of emotions has been (and continues to be) one of the major domains in this area.

Research on the relation between cognition and emotion is booming. So many studies on this topic are being published that it is difficult if not impossible to keep track of all the relevant evidence. There is thus a great need for papers that review the existing evidence on particular aspects of the interplay between cognition and emotion. The aim of the present book is to provide researchers and students with a collection of state-of-the-art reviews of the most important research topics in cognition and emotion research. All of the review papers in this book (except our own) have recently been published in the journal *Cognition & Emotion*. By bringing these reviews together, we can provide a unique overview of the knowledge that has been generated in the past decades about the many and complex ways in which cognition and emotion interact.

About two years ago, we started asking a number of upcoming researchers to review the existing literature on one aspect of the interplay between cognition and emotion. We selected the following topics: Emotion theories, feeling and thinking, the perception of emotion, the expression of emotion, emotion regulation, emotion and memory, and emotion and attention. Each contributor was asked to write a review paper that would give the reader a good idea of (a) the kind of issues addressed in the literature on that specific topic, (b) the main theories, findings, and conclusions, and (c) the most important challenges for the future. At the same time, we indicated that the paper should be more than a summary. Each contributor was asked to impose a structure on the literature that clarifies (a) how the different research topics are related, (b) what the similarities and differences are between the most important theoretical views, and (c) how these views relate to the existing evidence. Given the size of the literature on each of these topics, it is inevitable that the authors selected and highlighted certain topics, theories, and studies. However, the authors were asked to be as fair and objective as possible in their selection and discussion of the literature. Their ultimate aim was to provide a structured review that researchers and students alike can use as a jumping board to learn more about a specific topic.

In order to guarantee the quality of the papers, each paper was submitted to a very thorough review process. For each paper, we asked three leading experts to provide critical but constructive comments. Each paper underwent at least two rounds of reviews. The entire process required a tremendous amount of work from the authors but also from the reviewers. Writing a good review paper is an extremely difficult enterprise. Apart from the sheer magnitude of the work involved in reading and summarising the relevant literature, it is almost inevitable that authors and reviewers have different views on what are the main findings and theories in the literature and on how the literature is best structured. We were very fortunate that all of the authors and reviewers were extremely constructive. The authors were willing to take into account the many critical comments of the reviewers even if it required them to rethink and reorganise the entire manuscript. The reviewers were willing to look for ways to improve the paper even if they had clear differences of opinion with the authors. Without so much benevolence, the review papers would never have reached their current high quality. Hence, we are convinced that the review papers of this book will provide useful tools for students and researchers alike and will stimulate further research on the interplay between cognition and emotion.

Jan De Houwer
Dirk Hermans
*July 2009*

# 1 Theories of emotion causation: A review

**Agnes Moors**
*Ghent University, Ghent, Belgium*

In this paper I review a selection of emotion theories. I propose a framework in which various theories can be placed and compared. The framework is organised around the question of emotion causation. The aim is to highlight what theories of emotion causation have in common and where they move apart. Before looking at the explanations for emotion provided by various theories, I briefly consider what it is that these theories try to explain. As I illustrate in the first section, disagreement among emotion theories already starts here.

## DEFINING EMOTION

Asked about a definition of emotions, many theorists start by listing a number of components that they consider as being part of a prototypical emotional episode. I use the term emotional episode to indicate anything starting from the stimulus to the later components or the immediate consequences of the emotion. The notion of emotional episode is thus potentially broader than the notion of emotion. Examples of components are: (a) a cognitive component; (b) a feeling component, referring to emotional experience; (c) a motivational component, consisting of action tendencies or states of action readiness (e.g., tendencies to flee or fight); (d) a somatic component, consisting of central and peripheral physiological responses; and (e) a motor component, consisting of expressive behaviour (e.g., fight and flight and facial and vocal expressions). These components correspond to functions such as: (a) stimulus evaluation or appraisal; (b) monitoring (which may serve the further function of control or regulation); (c) preparation and support of action; and (d) action. Table 1.1 depicts these components with their corresponding functions.

It should be noted that within this list of components, the definitions of the terms cognition and feeling is not unitary. The meaning of the term cognition seems to shift depending on the category with which it is contrasted. Cognition can be understood in the broad sense of the mental when it is contrasted with somatic and motor responses. Several scholars

*Table 1.1* Examples of components and corresponding functions

| Components | Functions |
| --- | --- |
| Cognitive | Stimulus evaluation/appraisal |
| Feeling | Monitoring → regulation |
| Motivational ⎱ | |
| Somatic   ⎰ | Preparation and support of action |
| Motor | Action |

define mental processes as those that are mediated by representations. Representations are functional notions invoked to explain variable stimulus–response relations. They come into the picture when a stimulus does not invariably lead to the same response (with the same quality and intensity) at different points in time and in different contexts (Bermudéz, 1995; Moors, 2007). Cognition is understood in a more narrow sense when it is contrasted with other mental concepts such as motivation and feeling. It has been argued that goals are mentally represented but that they have special dynamic qualities that are not shared by other kinds of representations (e.g., the activation of goal representations accumulates over time and persists in the face of obstacles; Bargh & Barndollar, 1996). Thus, when contrasted with motivation, cognition can be defined as based on non-dynamic representations. When contrasted with feeling, cognition can be defined in the narrow philosophical sense of the Intentional[1] part of the mental (Green, 1996). Feeling corresponds to the phenomenal part of the mental. A mental state is Intentional by virtue of being directed at or about something. It is phenomenal by virtue of having irreducible qualia that are entirely subjective (e.g., Block, 1995; Nagel, 1974).[2] It is worth noting that there exist other narrow views of cognition. One narrow view is that cognitive processes are mediated by propositional representations (as opposed to perceptual ones, see below). Another narrow view is that cognitive processes are non-automatic (as opposed to automatic). A final narrow view is that cognitive processes are rule based (as opposed to associative). In sum, the cognitive component can be understood in the broad sense of mental or in the more narrow sense of non-dynamic, Intentional, propositional, non-automatic, or rule based.

The component of feeling or emotional experience is sometimes understood in the narrow sense of the phenomenal part of the mental (see above)

---

1 Following Searle (1983), I write Intentionality in philosophical use with a capital I and intentionality in ordinary use with a lower case i.

2 A state can be directed at something by forming a representation of it. Thus, in this view, cognitive processes also correspond to representation-mediated processes. Note that according to this view, the mental is broader than the representational; it also includes phenomenal states that are non-representational.

and sometimes in the broader sense of conscious experience, with both a phenomenal and an Intentional aspect. Some authors even argue that emotional experience only has an Intentional aspect. According to them, emotional experience is about the other components in the emotional episode (appraisal, action tendencies, and somatic and motor responses).

Emotion theorists disagree about the exact number and nature of the components they include in the emotional episode. The definition of components is one source of disagreement. For example, inclusion of a cognitive component is more likely when cognition is defined in a broad than in a narrow sense (cf. Lazarus, 1982, versus Zajonc, 1980). Needless to say, there are many other sources of disagreement about the components to include (cf. the special issue edited by Frijda, 2007, in *Social Science Information*).

Emotion theorists not only disagree about the components that they include in the emotional episode, but also about the component(s) that they include in or identify with the emotion (Prinz, 2004). Some theorists isolate one (or a few) component(s) from the emotional episode and call it emotion. For example, James (1890) equated emotion with the feeling component. Frijda (1986) singled out the motivational component as the phenomenon to be explained, equating emotions with states of action readiness. Several theorists include all or most components of the emotional episode in their definition of emotion (Clore & Centerbar, 2004; Scherer, 2005). It may be noted that some theorists treat the motor component as a consequence of emotion rather than as a part of it. Others distinguish between spontaneous and planned behaviour, treating the former as a part of emotion and the latter as a consequence.

Further, emotion theorists disagree about whether the components in the emotional episode occur sequentially, and, if so, whether they occur in a fixed order. Among those that accept a fixed order, there is disagreement about the particular order proposed. Theorists who assume a fixed order and who equate emotion with one component often consider the other components in the episode as causes and consequences of the emotion. Theorists who assume a fixed order and who equate emotion with the entire emotional episode can still split the emotional episode in an antecedent and a consequent part. It may be noted that the relation between sequentiality and causality is an asymmetric relation. Causality implies sequentiality (causes precede their effects), but sequentiality does not imply causality (early parts precede late parts, but do not necessarily cause them).

Essential for a definition of emotion is that it demarcates emotions from phenomena that are not emotions. I list a number of demarcation criteria that have turned up in the literature. Some theorists exclude from the class of emotions phenomena that lack one of the components that they consider essential for emotions or the emotional episode. For example, reflexes (e.g., startle reflex) have been refused the status of emotions because they do not have a cognitive component or because they bypass stimulus evaluation (cf. Leventhal & Scherer, 1987). Sensory experiences such as feeling cold or pain are not considered emotions because they are pure feelings that lack Intentionality (they lack a cognitive component, defined in the philosophical sense of the term). Attitudes and preferences have been excluded from the class of emotions because they lack clear somatic and motor correlates (Lang, 1985; Scherer, 2005).

It may be true that some components are necessary for emotion, yet no component seems to be unique (Frijda, 2007; Parrott, 2007). Indeed, cognition, feeling, motivation, and somatic and motor responses may be present (even all at once) in phenomena that are not emotions. To illustrate this, Frijda (2007) mentioned the example of a piece of soap that slips through one's fingers under the shower and that leads to a shift in action tendency, manifested in feeling, somatic responses, and the action of groping for the soap. All the components are there, yet many authors will be unlikely to categorise this as an emotional episode. Theorists have therefore proposed additional criteria that may help set the boundaries of the class of emotions. Some additional criteria have to do with the content of components. One criterion specifies the content of the appraisal component. Appraisal theorists have argued that emotions occur when a stimulus is appraised as relevant and/or (in)congruent to a central goal (Frijda, 1986; Lazarus, 1991; Oatley & Johnson-Laird, 1987; Moors, 2007; Scherer, 2005). In the soap example, the event may be relevant only to a goal of minor importance. Some theorists (even some appraisal theorists) have left the possibility open that emotions arise when the stimulus is appraised as positive or negative, independent of current goals (Frijda, 2007; Scherer, 2005, takes this to be the case for the emotion disgust and for emotions elicited by music). A second content criterion specifies the content of the experience component. Many theorists have argued that the experience of an emotion must have a positive or negative flavour (e.g., Ortony & Turner, 1990), thereby excluding neutral states such as surprise and interest. Other additional criteria are based on quantitative features. For example, Scherer (1984, 1993b) proposed that a phenomenon can be called an emotion when all (or most) components are recruited in a co-ordinated and synchronised manner. A final set of criteria has been proposed to delineate emotions from moods. These include duration (emotions: short; moods: long), intensity (emotions: high; moods: low), and the presence or absence of a specific target (emotions: present; moods: absent).

Emotion theorists not only disagree about the boundaries of the class of emotions, they also disagree about how they think the class of emotions or emotional phenomena should be internally structured. A first group of theorists takes a limited set of emotions with a special status, called basic emotions, as the building blocks of emotional life. Basic emotions can be recombined or elaborated to form non-basic emotions. Members of this group of theorists vary with regard to the number and identity of the emotions they enumerate as basic. This is because they rely on different criteria for inclusion and discrimination within this set. Examples of criteria are that each basic emotion has a unique neural signature (Darwin, 1872/1965; Ekman, 2007; Izard, 1977; Panksepp, 1982, 1998, 2000), a unique pattern of appraisal values (e.g., Roseman, 1991), a unique action tendency (Frijda, 1986), a unique physiological response pattern (Ekman, Levenson, & Friesen, 1983), a unique facial expression (Ekman, 1984), and a unique experiental quality (Oatley & Johnson-Laird, 1987). A second group of theorists takes a small set of sub-emotional variables as the building blocks of emotional life. Members of this group vary with regard to the number and nature of the variables they postulate. For example, several appraisal theorists put forward six or more appraisal variables (e.g., novelty, valence, goal relevance, goal congruence, coping potential, and agency). These variables are conceived of as dimensional by some authors (e.g., Scherer, 1984, 1994) and as discrete by others (e.g., Lazarus, 1991; see Roseman & Smith, 2001). The combination of values on discrete/dimensional appraisal variables gives rise to a large/infinite number of specific emotions. For another example, Russell (2003) put forward the dimensional variables of valence and arousal. These are variables of experience and neurophysiological activity. Contrary to the appraisal variables mentioned above, however, Russell's building blocks do not combine to form specific emotions (see below).

Given the many ways in which emotion theories can differ, there are many ways in which an overview of them can be organised. I choose to organise theories according to their views of emotion causation, and, related to this, the order in which they place emotional components within an emotional episode. This means that I discuss only theories that have an explicit, unique view of emotion causation. It also means that I compare the selected theories especially with regard to their view of emotion causation. There are, of course, other ways in which to organise an overview of emotion theories. One could compare theories with regard to the way in which they structure the class of emotional phenomena (into discrete emotions versus sub-emotional variables; see above). One could also compare theories with regard to their preferred research method. It is good to keep in mind that different principles for organising overviews can lead to different groupings of theories.

## EMOTION CAUSATION

The question about the cause of emotions is a question about what is happening between the stimulus (the input) and the emotion (the output) or between the stimulus and the consequent part of the emotional episode. Ideally, an emotion theory that is concerned with emotion causation should explain the observation that some but not all stimuli in the environment elicit an emotion. I dub this "the elicitation problem" (Q1; Power &

Dalgleish, 2007, called it "the event problem"). This problem subsumes two subquestions. The first subquestion (Q1A) asks which stimuli elicit an emotion and which stimuli do not. The second subquestion (Q1B) asks how the organism determines this. It is a question about the mechanisms (and representations) responsible for selecting the stimuli that elicit an emotion.

What else should a theory concerned with emotion causation explain, besides the presence or absence of an emotion? It should also explain certain characteristics of the emotion. As mentioned above, emotion theorists have different definitions of emotion. They are thus likely to disagree about the to-be-explained characteristics of emotion. One way to escape from this impasse is to look for very general characteristics that all or most emotion theorists would agree on. I think that, at the very least, emotion theorists agree that an emotion (as many other natural and artificial phenomena) has quantity and quality. The quantity aspect refers to the intensity of an emotion and varies from no intensity (and hence no emotion) to very high intensity. The quality aspect, in a broad sense, refers to the valence (positive/negative) of an emotion, and, in a narrow sense, to specific emotions such as anger, fear, sadness, and joy (to name just a few). Theories concerned with emotion causation should ideally explain variations in quantity and quality. I refer to the quantity issue as "the intensity problem" (Q2), and to the quality issue as "the differentiation problem" (Q3). The intensity problem subsumes two subquestions: A first subquestion (Q2A) asks which stimuli elicit weak emotions and which elicit strong ones. A second subquestion (Q2B) asks about the mechanisms (and representations) that determine the intensity of the ensuing emotion. It may be noted that the elicitation problem can be seen as part of the intensity problem. The presence or absence of an emotion can be considered as a matter of intensity: The absence of an emotion can be situated at one extreme end of the intensity scale. The differentiation problem can also be split into two subquestions: A first subquestion (Q3A) asks which stimuli elicit positive emotions and which elicit negative ones or (for theories that distinguish more specific emotions) which stimuli elicit specific emotion such as anger, fear, sadness, and joy. A second subquestion (Q3B) asks about the mechanisms (and representations) that determine the quality of the ensuing emotion, the mechanisms that are charged with differentiation in the broad or the narrow sense.

Relying on Marr's (1982) proposal that processes can be described at different levels of analysis, one can say that the set of subquestions about stimuli (Q1A, Q2A, Q3A) and the set of subquestions about mechanisms and representations (Q1B, Q2B, Q3B) are *both* concerned with the process involved in emotion elicitation. They just deal with a different level of process description. Marr (1982) taught us that processes can be described at three levels of analysis. At the first, functional level, a process is described as a relation between input and output; it is specified what the process does. At this level can also be described the conditions under which the process operates. At the second, algorithmic level, a process is described in terms of the mechanisms that translate input into output. At this level can also be specified the format of the representations (or codes) on which the mechanisms operate. At the third, implementational level, the physical realisation of the process in the brain is specified. This level deals with the neurological structures, circuits, or networks involved. The subquestions about the stimuli that elicit emotions (Q1A, Q2A, and Q3A) can be said to deal with the functional level of process understanding: Stimuli are the input; emotions are the output. The subquestions about the underlying mechanisms and representations (Q1B, Q2B, and Q3B) can be said to address the algorithmic level. One could argue that a complete theory of emotion causation should also address the third level of process understanding, and several theories have addressed this level. In the present overview, however, the focus is mostly (but not exclusively) on the first two levels (see Table 1.2). Theories concerned with emotion causation can differ in two important ways. First, they can diverge on the set of questions (A, B, C) and hence the level of process description (functional, algorithmic, implementational) that they address. Second, they can address the same set of questions but provide radically different answers.

I review a selection of emotion theories (some are families) that have made claims about the causation of emotion. Because of the growing interdisciplinary contacts among psychologists and philosophers, I have chosen not to restrict the overview to well-known psychological theories, but to also include dominant philosophical theories.[3] The theories discussed are: (T1) James' (1890) theory; (T2) Schachter's (1964) theory; (T3) appraisal theories; (T4) network theories; (T5) affect program theory; (T6) Barrett's (2006b) conceptual act theory; (T7) philosophical cognitivism; and (T8) philosophical perceptual theories.[4] The order in which these

3 In the present paper, the distinction between philosophical and psychological theories is based on the background of their authors and on a difference in approach that can be traced back to a difference in starting point. Philosophers often start from the structure of language in the hope of learning something about the structure of reality. Psychologists often start from the observation of reality. I further wish to note that I use the term theory in a liberal sense to indicate any internally coherent collection of hypotheses, regardless of whether these hypotheses have been submitted to empirical testing.

4 The theories of Schachter (1964) and Barrett (2006b) have often been grouped together in the family of two-factor or constructivist theories, and James' (1890) theory has sometimes been added as the precursor of this tradition. In the present paper, I chose to discuss these theories separately because they occupy radically different positions on the criteria that I have set out to organise this review. James can indeed be considered as a precursor of Schachter, but both propose different components for the differentiation of emotions. Barrett's theory is undeniably a two-factor theory like Schachter's, but Barrett also builds on insights developed by appraisal theories. As a result, the processes that Barrett proposes for the elicitation of emotions differ from those proposed by Schachter in several important respects (see below).

Table 1.2 Overview of questions that should be addressed by theories of emotion causation, linked to Marr's levels of analysis

| | Problems related to emotion causation | | |
| --- | --- | --- | --- |
| *Marr's levels of process description* | *Question 1: Elicitation* | *Question 2: Intensity* | *Question 3: Differentiation* |
| A. Functional level: Relation between input and output | Question 1A:<br><br>Which stimuli elicit emotions and which do not?<br><br>What are the conditions under which emotions are elicited | Question 2A:<br><br>Which stimuli elicit weak versus strong emotions? | Question 3A:<br><br>Which stimuli elicit positive versus negative emotions? (anger, fear, sadness, joy, etc.) |
| B. Algorithmic level: Mechanisms and format of representations (codes) | Question 1B:<br><br>What are the mechanisms and representations that determine emotion elicitation? | Question 2B:<br><br>What are the mechanisms and representations that determine the intensity of emotions? | Question 3B:<br><br>What are the mechanisms and representations that determine the quality of emotions? |
| C. Implementational level: Neurological structures or routes | Question 1C:<br><br>What is the neurological basis of emotion elicitation? | Question 2C:<br><br>What is the neurological basis of emotion intensity? | Question 3C:<br><br>What is the neurological basis of emotion differentiation? |

*Note:* The C-questions are not discussed in the present paper.

theories are discussed is partly determined by historical considerations (because later theories build on the insights developed by older theories and sometimes present solutions to problems of older theories) but not entirely so (several theories developed more or less in parallel, and most of them have early roots).

Examination of these theories shows that most of them assume that some kind of processing is involved in emotion elicitation. Theories differ with regard to the kind of processing that they propose. In this respect, it is worth pointing at three differences. A first difference has to do with the *conditions* under which they think emotion-eliciting processes can operate. Some theories (e.g., T2 and T7) assume that the processes involved in emotion causation are non-automatic (i.e., conscious, controlled, non-efficient, and/or slow) whereas others (e.g., T3, T4, T5, T6, and T8) emphasise that they can also be automatic (i.e., unconscious, uncontrolled, efficient, and/or fast). As argued by Bargh (e.g., 1989; see also Moors & De Houwer, 2006a, 2006b) automaticity has to do with the conditions under which a process is able to operate. A process is automatic when it operates under suboptimal conditions (such as when there is subliminal stimulus input, no goal to engage in the process, a goal to counteract the process, a lack of attentional capacity, and/or a lack of time); a process is non-automatic when it only operates under optimal conditions (such as when there is supraliminal stimulus input, the goal to engage in the process, no goal to counteract the process, abundant attentional capacity, and/or abundant time).

A second difference among theories of emotion causation has to do with the *format of the representations* they put forward. Some theories (e.g., T7) hold that emotions are elicited by mechanisms operating on propositional representations whereas others (e.g., T3, T4, T5, T6, and T8) argue that they can also be elicited by mechanisms operating on perceptual representations. It is important to note that various authors have characterised the distinction between propositional and perceptual representations in different ways. Some authors state that propositional representations are verbal-like or abstract whereas perceptual representations are image-like in that they contain concrete modality-specific sensory features (e.g., Barrett, 2006b). Others state that propositional representations are mental contents to which one ascribes truth value, whereas perceptual representations are mental contents that one entertains without necessarily believing them (Charland, 1997). Still others stress that propositional, but not perceptual, representations have a similar compositional structure as propositions. Propositions are composed of meaningful parts that can be recombined to form new propositions (e.g., Fodor, 1980; but see Bermudéz, 1995).

A third difference among theories of emotion causation has to do with the *object or input* of the emotion-eliciting process. In most theories, the input of the crucial process is the stimulus. In the theories of James (1890) and

Schachter (1964), however, the input of the crucial process is the physical responses of the person to the stimulus. Barrett's (2006b) theory gives equal weight to one process that has the stimulus as its input and another process that has the output of the other process (i.e., an experience) as its input.

As mentioned, theories of emotion causation not always propose different kinds of processes; they sometimes just differ with regard to the levels of process understanding that they address. Many theories are concerned with the algorithmic level (T3, T4, and T6, and to some extent T7 and T8) and some with the implementational level (T1, T5, and T6, and some theories in T3 and T4). Only few theories (T3, and to some extent T7) seriously address the functional level. In the next sections, the selected theories are discussed one by one. The aim is to identify the components that theories invoke to solve the problems of elicitation (Q1), intensity (Q2), and differentiation (Q3), and to report on the order in which they place components within a prototypical emotional episode. Another aim is to detail the above claim that theories differ with regard to the kind of processing they propose (i.e., *conditions, format of representations,* and *object*) and the levels of process description they address (functional, algorithmic, and implementational).

It is worth reiterating that theories of emotion causation differ with regard to the component(s) that they identify with the emotion and hence the phenomenon they set out to explain. Some theories equate emotion with a single component, such as the feeling component (T1 and T2) or the cognitive component (members of T7 and T8). Other theories take emotion to be a syndrome composed of several components such as feelings, cognition, motivation, somatic and/or motor responses (most members of T3, T4, and T5).

## JAMES' THEORY

According to James (1884, 1890) a stimulus activates the sensory cortex, which directly (or in some unspecified way) elicits peripheral somatic and/or motor responses. Feedback of these bodily responses returns to the sensory cortex where it produces emotional experience (Figure 1.1). Emotional experience is nothing but the conscious experience of bodily responses. James equated emotion with emotional experience (i.e., the

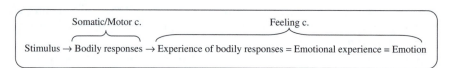

*Figure 1.1* Order of components in James' theory.

feeling component) so his theory has been called a feeling theory. James' theory was revolutionary at the time because it turned around the conventional order of events within an emotional episode. Whereas folk theory assumed that emotional experience precedes bodily responses ("we run/tremble because we feel afraid"), James postulated that bodily responses precede emotional experience ("we feel afraid because we run/tremble"). It is fair to note that before James, Descartes (1644/1998) had already proposed this order of events to occur within an emotional episode.

In James' (1890) theory, both the intensity (Q2A) and the quality (Q3A) of emotions are determined by the intensity and quality of the bodily responses (i.e., the somatic and motor components) that occur in response to the stimulus. The quality of the emotion is determined by the specific response pattern elicited by the stimulus. Each specific emotion has its own response signature. An important shortcoming is that James does not explain how bodily responses are produced in the first place. In other words, he does not address the elicitation problem (Q1).

James' (1890) theory has been criticised on empirical and theoretical grounds. On the empirical side, Cannon (1927) argued: (a) that the autonomous responses that accompany specific emotions lack specificity (e.g., both anger and fear come with increased heart rates); (b) that artificial induction of physical arousal (e.g., by injection of adrenalin) does not produce real emotions; and (c) that disconnection of peripheral organs from the central nervous system (disrupting feedback) does not eliminate emotions. After Cannon, renewed interest has arisen for each of these issues, but there is currently no consensus (Cacioppo, Berntson, Larsen, Poehlmann, & Ito, 2000; Christie & Friedman, 2004; Chwalisz, Diener, & Gallagher, 1988; Ekman, Levenson, & Friesen, 1983; Levenson, 1992; Levenson, Ekman, & Friesen, 1990; see Barrett, 2006a,b; Cornelius, 1996; Niedenthal, Krauth-Gruber, & Ric, 2006, for reviews; see also, e.g. the rise of neo-Jamesian theories, Damasio, 1994; Prinz, 2004). The theoretical criticism was that James (1890) reduced emotions to experiences of bodily responses and therefore failed to account for the fact that emotions have Intentional objects (e.g., Solomon, 1976). For example, sadness is not just the experience of a pattern of bodily responses. It is also about something, for example, about the fact that something valuable is lost forever.

## SCHACHTER'S THEORY

Schachter (1964) reconciled James' (1890) notion that somatic responses precede emotional experience with Cannon's (1927) criticism that these responses lack specificity and are therefore not capable of bringing forth specific emotions. Schachter's theory is a two-factor or two-step theory. In the first step, stimulus input produces an undifferentiated state of physiological arousal.[5] In the second step, the arousal is interpreted in light of the characteristics of that input. It is this cognitive process of attribution of arousal to the presumed cause of the arousal that produces a specific emotional experience (see Figure 1.2). Like James, Schachter equated emotion with emotional experience (i.e., the feeling component).

The degree of arousal (i.e., the somatic component) determines the intensity of the emotion (Q2) whereas the additional element of attribution (i.e., the cognitive component) provides the quality of the emotion (Q3). Attribution of arousal to different eliciting events produces different emotions. Initially, the confrontation with a dangerous dog and the reunion with a beloved person cause similar physical arousal. It is only after attribution of this arousal to the danger versus the reunion that an emotion of fear versus joy is elicited. Schachter and Singer (1962) supported their view with an experiment in which injections of adrenaline (causing physical arousal) led to joy versus anger depending on whether they were in the presence of a happy versus angry bystander. It was assumed that the bystander's emotion led participants to interpret their own arousal as joy versus anger.

Within the prevailing scientific climate, Schachter's (1964) cognitive attribution process was conceived of as a conscious process, as if physical arousal can be coloured in an arbitrary manner by conscious thoughts. Although Schachter built in a cognitive component in charge of emotion differentiation, he did not specify a component that determines which stimuli lead to arousal in the first place. The cognitive component does not precede arousal and therefore cannot determine which stimuli elicit arousal (and hence an emotion) and which do not. In other words, the theory fails to address the elicitation problem (Q1).

Critics have challenged the empirical evidence for Schachter's theory (see Reisenzein, 1983, for a review) as well as the theory itself (Zajonc, 1980). Zajonc argued against Schachter's (1964) idea that cognition is a necessary cause of emotions. Kunst-Wilson and Zajonc (1980) demonstrated that mere (repeated) exposure to stimuli led to an increase in liking of those stimuli, even when the stimuli were presented subliminally so that conscious identification of them was not possible. This and other arguments led Zajonc to conclude that cognition is unnecessary for affect.[6]

---

5 Two different meanings of the term arousal circulate in emotion literature. In the first sense, arousal refers to physical arousal (i.e., the somatic component). In the second sense, arousal refers to intensity (activation–deactivation) and can be a property of several components (e.g. the feeling component).

6 Zajonc (1980) claimed that cognition is unnecessary for affect (by which he meant raw positive–negative quality or valence), but not that cognition is unnecessary for full-blown specific emotions. His data are nevertheless relevant for theories concerned with emotion causation, at least for those theories that conceive of affect as a minimal form of emotion or as an early step in emotion causation (e.g., Barrett, 2005; Scherer, 1984).

*Figure 1.2* Order of components in Schachter's theory.

Appraisal theories of emotion envisaged another solution for the problem raised by the data of Kunst-Wilson and Zajonc. These theories are discussed in the next section.

## APPRAISAL THEORIES

Appraisal theories of emotion (e.g., Arnold, 1960; Frijda, 1986; Lazarus, 1966, 1991; Oatley & Johnson-Laird, 1987; Ortony, Clore, & Collins, 1988; Roseman, Antoniou, & José, 1996; Scherer, 1984; Smith & Ellsworth, 1985) retained Schachter's (1964) idea that cognition is an antecedent of emotion, but they no longer equated cognition with conscious cognition. These theorists suggested that much of the cognitive work involved in the elicitation of emotion is unconscious or otherwise automatic (e.g., Arnold, 1960; Scherer, 2001, 2004). Kunst-Wilson and Zajonc's (1980) data showed that conscious cognition is unnecessary for emotion or affect, but not that unconscious cognition is unnecessary. Arnold (1960) coined the term appraisal to refer to the cognitive process involved in emotion elicitation, and, accordingly, theories in this tradition have been dubbed appraisal theories.

Appraisal theories also differ from Schachter (1964) in that they place the cognitive component at the very onset of the emotional episode (after the stimulus), prior to bodily responses. Thus, the cognitive component can be invoked as the one that determines which stimuli lead to an emotion and which do not (cf. elicitation problem, Q1). This component also determines which emotion should be produced (cf. differentiation problem, Q3) and how intense it should be (cf. intensity problem, Q2; see below). Further, appraisal theories shift Schachter's conscious attribution process to the end of the emotion episode. Thus, unconscious appraisal of stimuli takes place prior to the emotion whereas conscious attribution of the emotion to a cause and/or labelling of the emotion (e.g., as fear or anger) takes place after the emotion. It is important to note that the crucial distinction between emotion-antecedent appraisal and emotion-consequent attribution is not so much the nature of the cognitive operations involved (appraisal can include causal attribution, cf. the appraisal variable of agency) or the degree to which they are conscious (both can probably be conscious or unconscious), but the object or input of these processes. In the case of emotion-antecedent appraisal, the input is the stimulus; in the case of emotion-consequent attribution, the input is the emotion.

It is somewhat precarious to detail the order of the remaining components within the emotional episode because there is divergence among appraisal theories. By way of illustration, I present a much-cited order (see Figure 1.3). Appraisal of the stimulus causes an action tendency (i.e., the motivational component). The action tendency can be manifested in physiological responses (i.e., the somatic component), which prepare and support the occurrence of behaviour (i.e., the motor component). Emotional experience (i.e., the feeling component) is often considered as the totality of the traces that all the other components leave in consciousness. Thus, it is difficult to picture emotional experience as a separate phase in the emotional episode.

Contemporary appraisal theorists (e.g., Scherer, 2001) have proposed refinements to the sequence of components presented above. I mention three refining assumptions. First, organisms always occupy some value on the components proposed. Thus, a sequence of components is actually a sequence of *changes* in these components. Second, the processes involved in one component need not be entirely completed before they can initiate changes in subsequent components. For example, partial completion of the appraisal component can already trigger changes in the components of action tendencies, responses, and experience. Third, the changes caused in subsequent components feed back into prior components. This is called recurrence. For example, changes in response components feed back into the appraisal component, causing re-appraisal. It may be noted that these refinements are not incompatible with the sequence of components presented above. Despite the fact that at any point in time, several recurrent cycles are running simultaneously so that the processes in several components occur in parallel, the order within each cycle is fixed. In each cycle, stimuli must be appraised before they lead to action tendencies and responses.

Appraisal theories have traditionally focused on the first subquestion of the problems of elicitation, intensity, and differentiation. They have addressed the questions of which stimuli elicit an emotion versus no emotion (Q1A), which stimuli elicit weak versus strong emotions (Q2A),

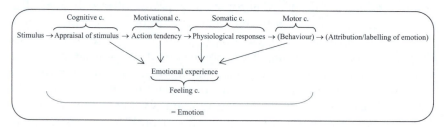

*Figure 1.3* Order of components in appraisal theories.

and which stimuli elicit which specific emotions (Q3A). Several appraisal theories have also addressed the second subquestion about the mechanisms and representations involved in the elicitation (Q1B), intensity (Q2B), and differentiation (Q3B) of emotions. In trying to develop hypotheses regarding the A-Questions, appraisal theorists have quickly come to the conclusion that it is impossible to make a fixed list of stimuli that elicit an emotion (or an emotion of the same intensity and quality) in all people or on all occasions. They have emphasised that there are few if any one-to-one relations between specific stimuli and specific emotions (Roseman & Smith, 2001). The same emotion can be produced by very different stimuli, and the same stimulus can lead to different emotions in different individuals or on different occasions. For example, anger can be produced by an insult, a computer crash, or by accidentally hitting one's head against the kitchen cabinet. A computer crash can lead to anger in one person or on one occasion, but to fear or panic in another person or on another occasion. Appraisal theorists have tried to discover the commonalities among stimuli that elicit emotions (or the same ones) and the differences among stimuli that do and stimuli that do not elicit emotions (or different ones). As a result of this exercise, they have come up with a set of appraisal variables. Each variable deals with one aspect of the encounter. The values on these variables combine to form an appraisal pattern. It is assumed that each specific emotion is caused by a unique appraisal pattern. I now turn to a discussion of a few important appraisal variables.

A first variable is goal relevance. A stimulus elicits an emotion when it is goal relevant, that is when it provides information about the satisfaction status of a goal or concern. Emotions are reliably caused by constellations of stimuli and goals. For example, hearing a noise in the hall at night is not inherently emotion provoking; it is only so because it is relevant for one's goal for physical safety (it might indicate that a violent robber is trying to break into the house). The variable of goal relevance is also responsible for the intensity of emotions. The more important the goal at stake, the stronger the ensuing emotion. A second variable is goal congruence. Specific emotions are not evoked by specific classes of stimuli but instead by specific classes of constellations of stimuli and goals. A constellation of a match between a stimulus and a goal leads to a positive emotion whereas a constellation of a mismatch leads to a negative emotion, irrespective of the specific stimuli or the specific goals at stake. A noise in the hall elicits a negative emotion when it constitutes a mismatch with one's goal for physical safety, but so does any stimulus that constitutes a mismatch with some goal. Appraisal theorists have identified a number of other variables such as certainty, coping potential, and agency/blame for the further breakdown of positive and negative emotions into more specific emotions such as joy, hope, pride, anger, fear, and sadness. Examples of hypotheses developed by appraisal theorists are that anger and sadness are elicited by an actual mismatch, whereas fear occurs in response to a pending mismatch

(Arnold, 1960), that events are more easy to cope with in the case of anger than in the cases of fear and sadness (Scherer, 1988), and that anger occurs when the mismatch is caused by an animate agent, especially when it was on purpose (Lazarus, 1991; but see Berkowitz & Harmon-Jones, 2004). In sum, the appraisal variable of goal relevance is appraisal theory's solution to the problems of elicitation (Q1A) and intensity (Q2A). The remaining appraisal variables (goal congruence, coping potential, agency/blame) provide a solution to the differentiation problem (Q3A).

Despite a fair degree of overlap, individual appraisal theories disagree about the precise number and identity of the appraisal variables that they include. According to Scherer (1999), part of the disagreement stems from differences in the number and identity of the emotions that appraisal theories set out to explain. A theory that tries to explain anger, fear, sadness, and joy needs less appraisal variables than a theory that also tries to explain surprise, disgust, shame, jealousy, pride, and guilt. Scherer ascribes another part of the disagreement to methatheoretical choices. Some theories put emphasis on parsimony, restricting their list of variables to the necessary and sufficient ones (or even the typical ones); others put emphasis on exhaustivity, trying to explain the greatest variety within emotion categories, such as different shades of anger and fear. There is also disagreement about the precise appraisal patterns that they postulate for each emotion. For example, some appraisal theorists consider the appraisal variable of agency/blame as necessary for anger (e.g., Lazarus, 1991) whereas others do not (e.g., Frijda & Zeelenberg, 2001).

Appraisal researchers have investigated hypotheses about the relation between specific appraisal patterns and specific emotions, using self-report methods as their primary source (e.g., Roseman, 1991; Scherer, 1993b, 1997; Smith & Ellsworth, 1985; Smith & Lazarus, 1993). Participants have been asked, for instance, to recall how they appraised a particular emotion-evoking event or to imagine which emotion they would feel given certain appraisals. The use of self-report for discovering appraisals involved in emotion causation has been the target of severe criticism (e.g., Davidson, 1992; Parkinson & Manstead, 1992). Apart from the limited evidential value of correlative studies for causal relations, self-report data have been characterised as an unreliable source for gaining insight in automatic processes. Given the assumption that appraisal is assumed to be automatic most of the time, it is unlikely that it would be available for self-report. Appraisal theorists (e.g., Frijda, 1993; Frijda & Zeelenberg, 2001; Lazarus, 1991; Scherer, 1993a) are aware of the limitations of self-report studies. They acknowledge that self-report data are an unreliable source for tracing the actual appraisal variables involved in emotion causation. They suspect instead that the appraisal patterns found in their studies reveal the structure of the content of emotional experience (e.g., Frijda, 1993; Scherer, 1993a) or that they reflect post hoc causal attributions (Nisbet & Wilson, 1977; Parkinson & Manstead, 1992; Rimé, Philippot, & Cisamolo, 1990;

Robinson & Clore, 2002). Such attributions are often based on stereotypic scripts about the relation between appraisals and emotions. Participants may be particularly encouraged to draw from stereotypic scripts because of the fact that self-report studies make use of emotion words. Asked about the cause of an emotion labelled as fear, participants may mention an event appraised as dangerous (threatening the goal of safety) because they make use of the stereotypic script according to which fear occurs in response to danger (Frijda & Zeelenberg, 2001; Izard, 1993). To break out of this circularity, several authors have proposed to abandon the use of emotion words and to change the dependent variable from emotional experience to action tendencies (Frijda & Zeelenberg, 2001), physiological response patterns (Pecchinenda, 2001), or behavioural responses (such as vocal and facial expressions; Johnstone, van Reekum, & Scherer, 2001; Kaiser & Wehrle, 2001). These other correlates of emotions have the advantage that they are logically independent of appraisal and that they suffer less from the influence of stereotypic scripts (Frijda & Zeelenberg, 2001).

As pointed out above, appraisal theories address the functional level of process understanding. Their aim is to understand the relation between specific appraisal patterns and specific emotions. They are guided by the question of which information is minimally or typically processed before specific emotions occur. Several appraisal theorists have also ventured hypotheses about the algorithmic level of process understanding (B-Questions). Most of them propose a dual-mode (or multi-mode) model. They put forward two (sometimes three) mechanisms for emotion elicitation: one is rule based, the other is associative (e.g., Clore & Ortony, 2000; Smith & Kirby, 2000, 2001; Teasdale, 1999; van Reekum & Scherer, 1997; see Smith & Neumann, 2005, for a review). Rule based mechanisms compute the values for individual appraisal variables and combine them in order to select the appropriate emotion. The associative mechanism corresponds to the retrieval or reinstatement of previously computed and stored appraisal patterns. Some theorists add a third mechanism: the activation of innate sensory-motor connections (Leventhal & Scherer, 1987). A limited set of stimuli (e.g., faces, loud noise, and sudden loss of support) is thought to have the innate capacity to elicit emotional responses. Other theorists refuse to stretch the notion of appraisal so that it includes the activation of sensory-motor connections.

Advocates of multi-mode models have made a priori assumptions about (a) the format of the representations that serve as the input to these mechanisms and (b) the conditions under which these mechanisms can operate. The rule based mechanism is said to operate on propositional representations and the associative mechanism on perceptual representations (Leventhal & Scherer, 1987; but see Smith & Kirby, 2001). Sensory-motor connections can be triggered by sensory features that are not yet integrated into a perceptual representation. To the extent that the sensory-motor mechanism is not mediated by representations, it falls out of the cognitive realm. The rule based mechanism is said to be flexible but non-automatic; the activation of learned and innate stimulus–emotion connections is said to be rigid (and hence more error prone) but automatic (Clore & Ortony, 2000; Smith & Kirby, 2001; but see Moors, 2008). For example, when processing conditions are optimal, hearing an insulting remark may cause a person to weigh the implications of the event for her/his goals and the possibilities for taking action. When processing conditions are suboptimal, however, the person has to rely on memory recordings of previous insults and the associated appraisal pattern. The associative mechanism that figures in multi-mode models of emotion causation is highly reminiscent of the mechanism for emotion elicitation proposed by network theories of emotion. It is to network theories that I now turn.

## NETWORK THEORIES

Network theories of emotion (e.g., Berkowitz, 1990; Bower, 1981; Lang, 1985; Leventhal, 1980, 1984) have their roots in associative models from the conditioning literature and semantic network models from the memory literature. Common to all network theories is the assumption that emotions are recorded in memory and that activation of these recordings is the principal cause of emotions (Q1). Network models assume that initially only a handful of biologically relevant stimuli elicit unconditioned emotional responses and that the range of stimuli that evoke these emotional responses is progressively elaborated through conditioning procedures (Martin & Levey, 1978). When an emotional episode takes place, information about the stimulus, action tendencies, and responses (in all models), as well as about conceptual meaning and emotional experience (in some models) is encoded in memory in distinct nodes. For each specific emotion, these nodes are organised in a schema (Leventhal, 1980) or a network structure (Bower, 1981; Lang, 1985). A newly encountered, neutral stimulus acquires emotion-eliciting power through repeated pairings with a stimulus that was already represented in memory as part of an emotional schema. The (consistent) co-occurrence in time and space of the new stimulus with the old stimulus is sufficient for the new stimulus to become associated with the same schema (i.e., learning). In this way, existing schemata are elaborated. On a later occasion, when the new stimulus is encountered in isolation, the associated schema is activated (i.e., retrieval) and an emotion ensues.

Schemata may be triggered by stimuli that are either identical or similar to the ones represented in the schema (i.e., generalisation). Another characteristic of schemata or networks is that they may be activated via different entry points. An emotion schema can be activated via stimuli, but also via responses, for instance, when emotion-specific facial expressions are mimicked (e.g., Lang, 1994; cf. facial feedback hypothesis). Note that if responses are to trigger the schema for one specific emotion in an unambiguous way, there must be a unique response pattern for that emotion. The debate about the existence of emotion-specific response patterns is thus also important for network theories (at least for their assumption that schemas can be activated via responses).

There is no consensus about whether, during *learning* or acquisition, the creation of an associative link between the old and the new stimulus requires anything beyond the mere co-occurrence in time and space of these stimuli. Some investigators claim that persons must also be aware of this co-occurrence (e.g., Pleyers, Corneille, Luminet, & Yzerbyt, 2007; Shanks & Dickinson, 1990) whereas others posit that awareness is not always required (Baeyens, Eelen, & Van den Bergh, 1990). With respect to *retrieval* or *deployment*, on the other hand, there is general consensus that both the activation of an emotion schema and the further spreading of activation among the nodes within the schema can take place in an unconscious (and otherwise automatic) fashion. The content of a node becomes conscious when the strength of activation in this node exceeds a certain threshold.

Network activation is regarded as a form of cognition (if cognition is understood in the broad sense of representation-mediated processing). Thus, in network theories, emotions are elicited by the cognitive component (cf. elicitation problem, Q1). The quality of the emotion is also delivered by the cognitive component (cf. differentiation problem, Q3). A stimulus activates the stored emotional schema of a previously encountered stimulus to which it is most similar. The intensity of the emotion is determined by the strength of activation of the schema (cf. intensity problem, Q2). Network activation is a mechanism (i.e., an associative mechanism), to be situated on the algorithmic level of process understanding. In other words, network theories address the second subquestion of the problems of elicitation (Q1B), intensity (Q2B), and differentiation (Q3B). They are less concerned with the first subquestion of these problems, which is to know which stimuli elicit emotions (Q1A), which stimuli elicit strong versus weak emotions (Q2A), and which stimuli lead to which specific emotions (Q3A). From a purely associative point of view, each stimulus should be capable of eliciting any emotion (except perhaps a limited set of unconditioned stimuli; Öhman & Mineka, 2001). Whether or not a stimulus elicits an emotion, and which one, is entirely dependent on the other stimuli with which the stimulus was previously paired. This does not seem very plausible. Purely associative models probably meet their limits here. Most network theories (e.g., Lang, 1994; Teasdale, 1999) therefore leave room for a rule based mechanism that computes the values of stimuli on a number of variables, much like the variables proposed in appraisal theories. They thus present a multi-mode view similar to that discussed in the section on appraisal theories (see also the joint publication of Leventhal and Scherer, 1987).

At the time that network theories of emotion were first developed, the computational metaphor of the mind ruled. Recent theories of emotion elicitation that are based on the connectionist or dynamic systems metaphor of the mind (e.g., Lewis, 2005) can be considered modern variants of network theory. In both classic and new network theories, the central mechanism for emotion elicitation is associative. In classic networks models, an emotion is represented as a schema, in which each constitutive component has a separate localist representation (i.e., a node). The assumption that the schema can be activated via different entry points (stimulus side, response side) gives the impression that network activation is a sequential affair. In network models inspired by connectionism or dynamic systems theory, components are represented in distributed form and multiple components can be activated in parallel. These components constrain each other mutually (with numerous feedback loops) until a stable solution emerges.

## AFFECT PROGRAM THEORY

Emotion causation has to do with the part ranging from the stimulus to the emotion or the consequent part of the emotion. This part can further be subdivided in a part in which evaluation of the stimulus takes place and a part in which evaluation of the stimulus is translated into the (other) components of the emotion (see also Reisenzein, 2001). The first part is the traditional territory of appraisal theories. Affect program theory (e.g., Ekman, 1992, 2007; Izard, 1977; Panksepp, 1998, 2000; Tomkins, 1962) proposes a hypothesis about the second part, a hypothesis that is situated, moreover, on the implementational level. The hypothesis is that each basic emotion has a unique neural circuit (or other neural signature). These circuits are said to be installed by evolution to serve specific adaptational functions. For example, the neural circuit of fear serves survival whereas the neural circuit of anger serves territorial concerns. A neural circuit is triggered when it receives an input of a certain nature. Specification of the nature of this input is left to other theories (or it is similar to what other theories have proposed). Ekman (1992), for example, accepts that neural circuits are triggered by prior appraisals (in the multi-modal sense). In the default case, once the neural circuit of a specific emotion is triggered, it runs to completion and gives rise to specific action tendencies, specific responses, and specific emotional experience. The default case obtains when activation of the neural circuit exceeds a certain threshold and when counteracting influences are either absent or not strong enough (cf. Ekman, 1992). Affect program theory is intrinsically dedicated to the view that basic emotions are the building blocks of emotional life (the principle for inclusion and discrimination being the existence of a unique neural substrate; see above).

Evidence adduced in support of affect program theory is either direct or indirect (see Ortony & Turner, 1990, for a review). Direct evidence is neurological evidence for the existence of emotion-specific neural circuits (e.g., Panksepp, 1998, 2000). Examples of indirect evidence are: (a) evidence for the existence of emotion-specific responses (e.g., facial expressions and physiological response patterns; e.g., Ekman, 1972; Ekman, Levenson, & Friesen, 1983); (b) evidence that these emotion-specific responses are universal (Ekman, 1972); and (c) evidence for a high degree of co-ordination among the various components of each specific emotion. It may be noted that in the case of indirect evidence, research on the consequent part of emotions is used to support assumptions about the antecedent part.

Affect program theory only speaks about the implementational level of the second part of emotion causation. It is therefore in principle compatible with the previous theories discussed. James' (1890) notion of emotion-specific response patterns is easily reconcilable with affect programs (cf. Damasio's, 1999, neo-Jamesian theory). Appraisal theorists could agree that specific appraisal patterns trigger specific affect programs. Network theorists could agree that some associations in the network are hard-wired whereas others are added as a result of learning (e.g., Lewis, 2005). On the other hand, these other theories are also compatible with the alternative view that the neural circuitry underlying emotions is not organised into emotion-specific modules, but rather into structures that are specific to sub-emotional variables (Ortony & Turner, 1990). These brain structures are not developed uniquely for emotions but are shared with other psychological functions. For example, certain brain structures are involved in approach and avoidance behaviour, regardless of whether this behaviour is emotional or not. According to some appraisal theories (e.g., Scherer, 2001), appraisal variables induce parts of action tendencies, leading to parts of physiological response patterns and parts of expressive behaviour. James and classic network theories assume that each emotion has a unique response pattern. This does not force them, however, to accept that the number of response patterns—and hence the number of emotions—is limited to six.

## BARRETT'S CONCEPTUAL ACT THEORY

Barrett's (2006b) conceptual act theory builds on Russell's (2003) core affect theory. Russell contested the assumption held by affect program theory that basic emotions are the building blocks of emotional life, casting doubt on both direct and indirect evidence for the existence of affect programs (e.g., Russell, 1994; see also Barrett, 2006b; Russell & Barrett, 1999). Instead, he put forward the sub-emotional variables of valence and arousal as the building blocks of emotional life. These variables can be considered as properties of stimuli, properties of neurophysiological states, and properties of conscious experience. Stimuli vary on the dimensional variables of valence and arousal. The combination of values on both variables is called "affective quality". The affective quality of stimuli causes in the person a state called "core affect", which has both a neurophysiological side (i.e., valence and arousal are associated with distinct neural systems) and a mental side (i.e., the conscious experience of affective quality; Russell & Barrett, 1999). Thus, the building blocks of emotional life combine to form core affect but not specific emotions. According to Russell, what traditional theories call specific emotions is nothing but the categorisation of core affect into one of the so-called emotion categories (e.g., anger, fear, sadness, and joy). These categories are not given in nature (i.e., natural kinds) but are socio-cultural constructions (i.e., artefacts). Russell's theory has accordingly been dubbed a constructivist theory. It may be noted that Russell not only rejects that individual basic emotions are natural kinds, but also that the entire class of specific emotions is a natural kind.

Barrett (2006b) agrees with Russell (2003) that basic emotions and the class of specific emotions are not natural kinds. She disagrees, however, with Russell's premise that a phenomenon merits explanation only when it is filed as a natural kind. Even if specific emotions are artefacts, they still require an explanation. In line with Russell, Barrett proposes a two-factor theory. In one factor, stimuli elicit core affect; in another factor, core affect is categorised. Unlike Russell, however, Barrett does not picture the categorisation of core affect as something that happens after experience, but rather as something that helps shape the experience (see Figure 1.4). In Barrett's theory, the end result is a specific emotional experience.

Barrett conceives of the categorisation of core affect as a form of perception. She emphasises that perception is influenced by previously acquired conceptual knowledge. This is why she sometimes uses the term conceptual act to refer to the categorisation of core affect. Barrett draws an analogy between the categorisation process in emotion perception and colour perception. The retina registers light of different wave lengths. The spectrum of wave lengths is a continuum. Yet people perceive categories of colours (red, green, yellow, blue) depending on previously acquired

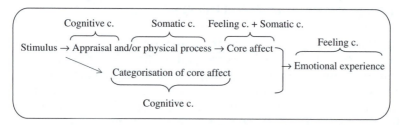

*Figure 1.4* Order of components in Barrett's theory.

conceptual knowledge. The same happens with emotion. Whether people categorise an episode of core affect as anger, fear, or sadness depends on acquired conceptual knowledge (emotion scripts).

Barrett (2006b) describes the mechanisms involved in the two factors of her theory (Q1B). Core affect can be generated by multiple mechanisms (in line with multi-mode models proposed by appraisal theories and network theories), such as rule based computation, activation of learned and innate associations, and even purely physical mechanisms (e.g., being tired can cause low arousal and negative valence; see also Izard, 1993). The subsequent categorisation of core affect can also be obtained with rule based or associative mechanisms, but emphasis is on the associative mechanism. The associative mechanism in Barrett's theory resembles the complex associative mechanism proposed by connectionist and dynamic systems models. It is governed by principles of constraint satisfaction. That is, various sources of information (the stimulus and previous knowledge) constrain each other mutually until a stable solution (i.e., an emotion category) emerges.

Category representations are not propositional[7] or static, but perceptual, embodied, and situated (Barsalou, 1999). They are perceptual in that they have modality-specific sensory/perceptual features. They are called embodied because they also have motor features so that activation of them leads to partial re-enactment or simulation of previous instances of the category (see Damasio, 1994, for a similar proposal). Situated representations have content that is context dependent. A person may have different scripts of anger and the context determines which script becomes activated. For example, anger may be manifested in fighting in the context of a playground, in shouting in the context of traffic, and in biting one's lip in the context of a waiting room. Barrett further assumes that the processes in both factors (core affect and categorisation) are often completed in an automatic way. In addition, she does not conceive of the two factors as sequential steps but as two sources of influence that constrain each other until they reach a stable solution. Given that the factors of core affect and categorisation are not separated in time and that they can rely on similar mechanisms, one may wonder about the basis for keeping a distinction between them. One possibility is that core affect is obligatory and ubiquitous, whereas categorisation is optional.

Like network theories, Barrett (2006b) addresses the second (but not the first) subquestion of the problems of elicitation (Q1B), intensity (Q2B), and differentiation (Q3B). The mechanisms involved in producing core affect are responsible for the elicitation, intensity, and raw positive–negative

---

7 It is potentially confusing to say, on the one hand, that category knowledge is conceptual, and on the other hand, that it is not stored in propositional form. Other scholars tend to group conceptual and propositional representations.

differentiation of emotions. The mechanisms involved in the categorisation of core affect are responsible for the further differentiation of emotional quality, leading to experiences of anger, fear, and sadness. An important question is which criteria are used as a basis for categorisation. The bodily correlates of core affect are (according to Barrett) insufficiently differentiated to fulfil this role. One option is that categorisation is based on the stimulus or its deep structure (i.e., appraisal). Suppose a person loses a valued object and feels bad (i.e., core affect). The person's conceptual knowledge that in his/her culture, the loss of a valued object is associated with sadness could be sufficient for categorising the bad feeling as a sad feeling.

This raises the question of how to distinguish Barrett's theory from appraisal theories. A possible answer is that appraisal theories assume that the loss of a valued object produces sadness regardless of one's learning history (influenced by culture). According to these theories, a person's learning history can determine which objects he/she considers as valued and hence which events he/she appraises as losses, but it does not determine which relations hold between appraisals and emotions. In Barrett's view, there are no intrinsic relations between appraisals and emotions. The loss of something valued is not intrinsically bound up with sadness, and danger is not intrinsically bound up with fear. These relations exist only in people's minds, and activation of these relations determines the narrow quality of the emotion.[8]

Another difference between Barrett and appraisal theories concerns the role of emotion categories (e.g., anger, fear, sadness). For Barrett, emotion categories are an intrinsic part of emotional experience. They are used to endow (low-specific) core affect with specificity. For appraisal theories, emotion categories tend to come into the picture consequent upon emotional experience. They can be used to label emotions or emotional components that are already specific. The specificity of these components stems from the appraisals that caused them.

Emotional experience is the only component in Barrett's theory that has specificity in the narrow sense. It is therefore tempting to consider this theory as a feeling theory (i.e., a theory that equates emotion with emotional experience) like the theories of James (1890) and Schachter (1964).

Like Schachter (1964) and Russell (2003), Barrett (2006b) has a two-factor theory. The output of the first factor is less differentiated than that of the second factor. In addition to this obvious similarity, the three theories have other similarities and differences. First, in Schachter's theory, the first

---

8 Barrett's (2006b) theory can explain but does not predict cultural variation. If research could reveal that fear is universally linked to danger, this would demonstrate that this link exists in the conceptual knowledge of all individuals of all cultures.

factor results in a state of undifferentiated arousal, whereas in the theories of Russell and Barrett, the first factor results in core affect, which is a state in which valence and arousal are combined. Thus, in Schachter's theory, the first factor only delivers intensity whereas in the theories of Russell and Barrett, the first factor delivers intensity and raw positive–negative quality. Second, Barrett and Russell, but not Schachter, allow cognitive processes to intervene in the first factor. Third, Schachter conceived of the process in the second factor as conscious; Barrett takes it to be unconscious (and otherwise automatic) most of the time. Fourth, according to Schachter and Barrett, the result of the second factor is emotional experience. The process in this factor (attribution or categorisation) shapes the emotional experience. According to Russell, however, the categorisation in the second factor is a cold cognitive affair that comes after experience. Unlike Schachter and Barrett, Russell does not consider the product of the second factor as the phenomenon to be explained.

I now turn to the philosophical theories. Philosophers are less concerned with questions of causation and mechanics, but more with questions of ontology (What kind of a thing is an emotion? Is it feeling feeling, or a cognition, a perception?) and rationality (cf. de Sousa, 1987). Nevertheless, philosophical theories can be examined according to the criteria put forward in this review.

## PHILOSOPHICAL COGNITIVISM

Cognitivist philosophers (e.g., Lyons, 1980; Nussbaum, 1990; Solomon, 1976) reacted against James' (1890) proposal to identify emotions with feelings. In doing so, these philosophers relied on a narrow meaning of feeling as the purely phenomenal part of the mental, the part that is not about something and that cannot be captured in representational form. To do justice to the Intentionality of emotions, cognitivist philosophers proposed that emotions are caused by or identical to cognitions, more in particular, judgements of the stimulus. In discussing this proposal, philosophers elaborated on the kind of representations that judgements are but they neglected the mechanisms that operate on or produce these representations. Thus, they addressed only part of the algorithmic level of process understanding (QB). Judgements are propositional representations, understood here as mental contents to which one ascribes truth value.

Cognitivism comes in two varieties. In a first variety, emotion is equated with cognition (Nussbaum, 1990; Solomon, 1976). In this variety, bodily components (somatic and motor responses) are either neglected or placed near the end of the emotional episode (see Figure 1.5, top panel). Some proponents of this variety add that emotion is a special type of judgement. For example, Nussbaum (1990) argued that emotions are judgements that are relevant to the person's concerns (cf. appraisal theories). In a second

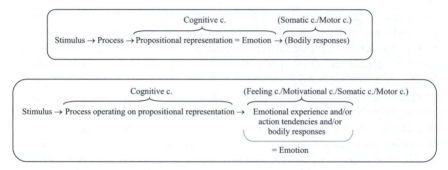

*Figure 1.5* Order of components in cognitivist theories.

variety, emotion is caused by but not identical to cognition (e.g., Lyons, 1980). Proponents of this variety equate emotion with one or several other components (such as feeling, motivation, and somatic and/or motor responses; see Figure 1.5, bottom panel).

The cognitive component is responsible for the elicitation of emotions (Q1; at least in the second variety) and the differentiation of emotions (Q3; in both varieties). Emotions differ when the content of their judgements differs. For example, anger corresponds to the judgement that one has purposefully been harmed, fear to the judgement that one is in danger, and sadness to the judgement that one has lost something valued forever. Hypotheses about the relation between judgements and emotions can be situated on the functional level of process understanding (Q1A, Q3A). They are often similar to the hypotheses put forward by appraisal theorists about the relation between appraisals and emotions.

Critics of cognitivism have argued that babies and animals cannot form judgements or propositional representations, yet they seem to have emotions. Another criticism is the "fear-of-flying" objection (de Sousa, 2007). One can judge that flying is the safest means of transportation (based on statistical information) but still experience fear of flying. Thus, the judgement that one is in danger does not seem necessary for the emotion of fear. A final criticism is that the first variety of cognitivism disregards the somatic aspects of emotion and reduces emotions to cold thoughts (see Scarantino, in press, for a more elaborate set of criticisms).

## PHILOSOPHICAL PERCEPTUAL THEORIES

Perceptual theorists of emotion (e.g., Clarke, 1986; de Sousa, 1987; Goldie, 2000) argued that emotions need not be identified with propositional representations but can also be identified with perceptual representations of the stimulus (see Figure 1.6). Here also, the distinction between propositional and perceptual is seen as a matter of truth evaluability. Propositional

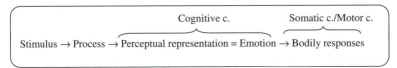

*Figure 1.6* Order of components in perceptual theories.

representations are those that one holds to be true whereas perceptual representations are those that one entertains without necessarily believing them. To become scared, it is sufficient to see or construe a situation as dangerous, without believing it for a fact. Perceptual theorists reacted against the cognitivist view that emotion is a form of judgement. As de Sousa (2007) put it, emotions are not so much judgements but ways of seeing. Perceptual theorists proposed that processes involved in emotion have more in common with those involved in perception than those involved in judgement. For one thing, both emotion and perception arise automatically. That is, they arise instantly, unintentionally, and efficiently (i.e., with minimal use of attentional capacity), and they are difficult to counteract. People lack control over their emotions in a similar way as they lack control over their perceptions. One cannot choose to be angry or frightened (i.e., perceive a stimulus as irritating or frightening) just as one cannot choose to perceive an apple as an apple. For another thing, so-called irrational emotions (i.e., emotions that run counter to one's beliefs, e.g., fear of flying, fear of spiders) show resemblance to perceptual illusions. Perceptual illusions appear real and compelling, yet the person knows (rationally—from propositional knowledge) that they are not; the person does not necessarily believe what he/she sees. Likewise, irrational emotions do not arise from judgements in the sense that a person believes that he/she is in danger, yet he/she cannot escape seeing or construing the stimulus as dangerous (cf. Goldie, 2000).

The opposition between perception and cognition evoked in this literature stems from a narrow view of cognition. Cognitive processes are restricted to those that operate on propositional representations (see above). Many contemporary scholars, however, entertain a broader definition of cognition. They argue that processes are cognitive when they are mediated by representations, irrespective of the format of these representations (cf. Moors, 2007). This view of cognition is broad enough to include processes that operate on or produce perceptual representations. It is also broad enough to include automatic processes. Thus, it turns out that philosophical perceptual theories have a lot in common with contemporary psychological theories that assign an important role to cognition (e.g., appraisal theories, network theories, and Barrett's, 2006b, theory).

Some scholars (e.g., Charland, 1997) have called James' (1890) theory a perceptual theory and have grouped it together with philosophical perceptual theories (Charland, 1997). The central process in James' theory is the experience of bodily responses. And it is often argued that the experience of bodily responses is a form of (self-)perception. It is important to note, however, that the perception in philosophical perceptual theories has a different object or input than the perception in James' theory. In the former, the input of perception is the stimulus; in the latter, it is the person's bodily responses to the stimulus. Put differently, even if one would argue that the feeling in James's theory is not purely phenomenal and has an Intentional aspect, it must still be stressed that the feeling in his theory is about bodily responses and not about the meaning of the stimulus.

An obvious similarity between Barrett's (2006b) theory and philosophical perceptual theories is that both emphasise the role of perceptual representations. The meaning of the term perceptual representation, however, is somewhat different in both theories. Barrett emphasises the sensory (image-like) properties of perceptual representations. Philosophical perceptual theories stress that perceptual representations have content that one entertains without necessarily believing it. Such content can still be coded in a verbal-like format.

## CONCLUSION

I have presented an overview of theories concerned with emotion causation selected from both the psychological and philosophical literature. I have used psychological terminology to draw similarities and indicate differences among these theories. Five sources of variation among theories were identified.

A first source of variation is the definition of emotion endorsed. Most emotion theories have a list of components that they consider part of an emotional episode. Individual theories differ with regard to the number and nature of the components that they include in the emotional episode as well as the components that they identify with the emotion. Part of the disagreement about the explanation of emotion stems from disagreement about what to count as emotion. Theories further disagree about the building blocks of emotional life (basic emotions versus sub-emotional variables), about the status they confer to the class of specific emotions (natural kind versus artefact) and about the boundaries of this class.

A second source of variation has to do with the components that theories invoke to solve the problems of elicitation (Q1), intensity (Q2), and differentiation (Q3). These are three problems that I think theories of emotion causation should address. The theories of James (1890) and Schachter (1964) put forward the somatic component to account for the intensity of emotion. Differentiation in James' (1890) theory is accounted for by the somatic component; in Schachter's (1964) theory it is accomplished by a cognitive component. James and Schachter both fail to address the elicitation problem. Appraisal theories and network theories take cognition to account for elicitation, intensity, and differentiation of emotions. In both theories, however, there is room for the activation of direct stimulus–response connections that count as non-cognitive according to most views of cognition. In Barrett's theory, elicitation, intensity, and raw positive–negative differentiation of emotions can be accounted for by cognitive as well as purely physical processes. The further differentiation into specific emotional experiences is a matter of cognition (i.e., categorisation process). The two philosophical theories discussed take the cognitive component to be responsible for the elicitation and differentiation of emotions, at least if cognition is understood in a broad representation-mediated sense.

The problems of elicitation, intensity, and differentiation can be considered at the functional level, the algorithmic level, and the implementational level. A third source of variation among theories is the levels of process description that they address. At the functional level, it can be asked which stimuli elicit emotions versus no emotions (Q1A), which stimuli elicit weak emotions versus strong ones (Q2A), and which stimuli elicit which emotions (positive versus negative ones, or specific ones; Q3A). These questions have received most attention from appraisal theories, and to some extent, from philosophical cognitivist theories. Another question that can be situated on the functional level concerns the conditions (optimal versus suboptimal) under which emotion-eliciting processes occur. Many of the theories discussed have taken position with regard to this question (appraisal theories; network theories; Barrett, 2006b; perceptual theories) and some have been ascribed a position (Schachter, 1964; cognitivist theories). At the algorithmic level, it can be asked which mechanisms (rule based versus associative) and which formats of representation (propositional versus perceptual) are involved in the elicitation (Q1B), intensity (Q2B), and differentiation (Q3B) of emotions. Appraisal theories, network theories, and Barrett (2006b) have discussed mechanisms and formats of representation. The two philosophical theories have only discussed formats of representation. At the implementational level, it can be asked which neurological structures or circuits are involved in the elicitation (Q1C), intensity (Q2C), and differentiation (Q3C) of emotions. The unique contribution of affect program theory to the issue of emotion causation can be situated on this level. This is not to say that other theories have neglected this level (see James, 1890; Barrett, 2006b, Scherer & Peper, 2001).

A fourth source of variation has to do with the kind of process that emotion theories hold responsible for emotion elicitation. Some theories have different assumptions about the *conditions* (optimal versus suboptimal) under which this process can operate. In philosophical cognitivist theories and Schachter's theory, the cognitive process that causes emotions is most likely conceived of as a conscious process. In most other theories, the emotion-antecedent process is assumed to be unconscious (and otherwise automatic) most of the time. Theories sometimes propose a different *format* for the *representations* involved in emotion causation. Cognitivist theories choose representations with a propositional format; perceptual theories appraisal theories, network theories, and Barrett (2006b) leave room for representations with a perceptual format. Theories may also differ with regard to the *mechanisms* that they put forward. Some of the theories discussed do not provide details about mechanisms (James, 1890; Schachter, 1964; philosophical theories), but it is unlikely that they all envisage the same mechanism. The theories that do elaborate on mechanisms seem to be largely in agreement with each other. Appraisal theories, network theories, and Barrett all agree that stimulus evaluation can be accomplished by multiple mechanisms: rule based, associative, sensory-motor, and (for some) purely physical mechanisms. In most theories, it seems that the associative mechanism plays the leading part. The associative mechanism that figures in older versions of network theory and appraisal theory have localist representations and seem to be activated in a sequential manner. The associative mechanism that figures in Barrett's theory and in modern versions of network theory (e.g., Lewis, 2005) and appraisal theory (e.g., Scherer, 2000) is modelled after the complex associative mechanism proposed in connectionist or dynamic systems models.

A fifth and final source of disagreement is the order in which emotion theories place the components of the emotional episode. James (1890) placed the somatic component prior to the feeling component. Schachter (1964) kept James' order of events except that he interposed a cognitive component between the somatic and the feeling components. In appraisal theories, the cognitive component occurs prior to the motivational component. This motivational component is followed by the components of somatic responses and behaviour. Each of these components is logically prior to the feeling component. Network theories do not prioritise one specific order of components. Cognition may precede somatic responses, but somatic responses may also precede cognition. Unlike Schachter (1964) and Russell (2003), Barrett (2006b) does not suppose that the two factors in her theory (core affect and categorisation) happen sequentially. They are triggered simultaneously and constrain each other mutually. Given the embodied nature of the representations in her theory, there is not a strict separation between somatic and cognitive components. The sharp distinction between mind and body is eluded.

In addition to disagreement, the above summary also reveals that there is a great deal of agreement among theories. For one thing, all the theories discussed can be fitted into the componential mould. Several theories even agree on the majority of the components that they include. For another, several theories assume that emotion-antecedent processing is cognitive (at least in a broad representation-mediated sense), that it can be automatic, and that multiple mechanisms and representations can be involved. Finally, the overview shows that there is an evolution from assumptions of non-automatic, propositional, and step-wise processing toward assumptions of more automatic, perceptual, and parallel processing. This evolution corresponds to evolutions in other domains of psychology. In conclusion, the proposed framework brings to the surface differences as well as similarities among theories of emotion causation. This may be helpful in reducing confusion and in pointing out new directions for future research. By relativising superficial differences among theories, there is more energy left to concentrate on the fundamental ones and to move the field forward. It is my hope that the present framework will also prove useful for the comparison of emotion theories that were not discussed in the present paper and for emotion theories that will be proposed in the future.

## REFERENCES

Arnold, M. B. (1960). *Emotion and personality*. New York: Columbia University Press.

Baeyens, F., Eelen, P., & Van den Bergh, O. (1990). Contingency awareness in evaluative conditioning: A case for unaware affective-evaluative learning. *Cognition and Emotion, 4*, 3–18.

Bargh, J. A. (1989). Conditional automaticity: Varieties of automatic influence in social perception and cognition. In J. S. Uleman & J. A. Bargh (Eds.), *Unintended thought* (pp. 3–51). New York: Guilford Press.

Bargh, J. A., & Barndollar, K. (1996). Automaticity in action: The unconscious as repository of chronic goals and motives. In P. M. Gollwitzer & J. A. Bargh (Eds.), *The psychology of action: Linking cognition and motivation to behavior* (pp. 457–481). New York: Guilford Press.

Barrett, L. F. (2005). Feeling is perceiving: Core affect and conceptualization in the experience of emotion. In L. F. Barrett, P. Niedenthal, & P. Winkielman (Eds.), *Emotion and consciousness* (pp. 255–284). New York: Guilford Press.

Barrett, L. F. (2006a). Are emotions natural kinds? *Perspectives on Psychological Science, 1*, 28–58.

Barrett, L. F. (2006b). Solving the emotion paradox: Categorization and the experience of emotion. *Personality and Social Psychology Review, 10*, 20–46.

Barsalou, L. W. (1999). Perceptual symbol systems. *Behavioral and Brain Sciences, 22*, 577–660.

Berkowitz, L. (1990). On the formation and regulation of anger and aggression: A cognitive-neoassociationistic analysis. *American Psychologist, 45*, 494–503.

Berkowitz, L., & Harmon-Jones, E. (2004). Toward an understanding of the determinants of anger. *Emotion, 4*, 107–130.

Bermudéz, J. L. (1995). Nonconceptual content: From perceptual experience to subpersonal computational states. *Mind and Language, 10*, 333–369.

Block, N. (1995). On a confusion about a function of consciousness. *Behavioral and Brain Sciences, 18*, 227–287.

Bower, G. H. (1981). Mood and memory. *American Psychologist, 36*, 129–148.

Cacioppo, J. T., Berntson, G. G., Larsen, J. T., Poehlmann, K. M., & Ito, T. A. (2000). The psychophysiology of emotion. In M. Lewis & J. M. Haviland-Jones (Eds.), *Handbook of emotions* (2nd ed., pp. 173–191). New York: Guilford Press.

Cannon, W. B. (1927). The James–Lange theory of emotions: Critical examinations and an alternative theory. *American Journal of Psychology, 39,* 106–124.

Charland, L. C. (1997). Reconciling cognitive and perceptual theories of emotion: A representational proposal. *Philosophy of Science, 64,* 555–579.

Christie, I. C., & Friedman, B. H. (2004). Autonomic specificity of discrete emotions and dimensions of affective space: A multivariate approach. *International Journal of Psychophysiology, 51,* 143–153.

Chwalisz, K., Diener, E., & Gallagher, D. (1988). Autonomic arousal feedback and emotional experience: Evidence from the spinal cord injured. *Journal of Personality and Social Psychology, 54,* 820–828.

Clarke, S. G. (1986). Emotions: Rationality without cognitivism. *Dialogue, 25,* 663–674.

Clore, G. L., & Centerbar, D. (2004). Analyzing anger: How to make people mad. *Emotion, 4,* 139–144.

Clore, G. L., & Ortony, A. (2000). Cognition in emotion: Always, sometimes, or never? In R. D. Lane & L. Nadel (Eds.), *Cognitive neuroscience of emotion* (pp. 24–61). New York: Oxford University Press.

Cornelius, R. R. (1996). *The science of emotion: Research and tradition in the psychology of emotion.* Upper Saddle River, NJ: Prentice-Hall.

Damasio, A. R. (1994). *Descartes' error: Emotion, reason, and the human brain.* New York: Putnam.

Damasio, A. (1999). *The feeling of what happens: Body and emotion in the making of consciousness.* New York: Harcourt.

Davidson, R. J. (1992). Prolegomenon to the structure of emotion: Gleanings from neuropsychology. *Cognition and Emotion, 6,* 245–268.

Darwin, C. (1965). *The expression of the emotions in man and animals.* Chicago: University of Chicago Press. (Original work published 1872)

de Sousa, R. (1987). *The rationality of emotion.* Cambridge, MA: MIT Press.

de Sousa, R. (2007). Emotion. In E. N. Zalta (Ed.). *The Stanford encyclopedia of philosophy.* (Available at: http://plato.stanford.edu/archives/sum2007/entries/emotion/)

Descartes, R. (1998). The passions of the soul. In J. Cottingham, R. Stoothoff, & D. Murdoch (Eds.). *Selected philosophical writings of René Descartes.* Cambridge, UK: Cambridge University Press. (Original work published 1644)

Ekman, P. (1972). Universals and cultural differences in facial expressions of emotion. In J. Cole (Ed.), *Nebraska symposium on motivation 1971* (Vol. 19, pp. 207–283)). Lincoln, NE: University of Nebraska Press.

Ekman, P. (1984). Expression and the nature of emotion. In K. R. Scherer & P. Ekman (Eds.), *Approaches to emotion* (pp. 319–343). Hillsdale, NJ: Lawrence Erlbaum Associates, Inc.

Ekman, P. (1992). An argument for basic emotions. *Cognition and Emotion, 6,* 169–200.

Ekman, P. (2007). The directed facial action task. In J. A. Coan & J. J. B. Allen (Eds.), *Handbook of emotion elicitation and assessment* (pp. 47–53). Oxford, UK: Oxford University Press.

Ekman, P., Levenson, R. W., & Friesen, W. V. (1983). Autonomic nervous system activity distinguishes among emotions. *Science, 221*(4616), 1208–1210.

Fodor, J. A. (1980). *Representations: Essays on the foundations of cognitive science.* Cambridge, MA: MIT Press.

Frijda, N. H. (1986). *The emotions.* New York: Cambridge University Press.

Frijda, N. H. (1993). The place of appraisal in emotion. *Cognition and Emotion, 7,* 357–387.

Frijda, N. H. (2007). What emotions might be? Comments on the comments. *Social Science Information, 46,* 433–443.

Frijda, N. H., & Zeelenberg, M. (2001). What is the dependent? In K. R. Scherer, A. Schorr, & T. Johnstone (Eds.), *Appraisal processes in emotion* (pp. 141–155). New York: Oxford University Press.

Goldie, P. (2000). *The emotions: A philosophical exploration.* Oxford, UK: Oxford University Press.

Green, C. D. (1996). Where did the word "cognitive" come from anyway? *Canadian Psychology, 37,* 31–39.

Izard, C. E. (1977). *Human emotions.* New York: Plenum Press.

Izard, C. E. (1993). Four systems of emotion activation: Cognitive and noncognitive processes. *Psychological Review, 100,* 68–90.

James, W. (1884). What is an emotion? *Mind, 9,* 188–205.

James, W. (1890). *The principles of psychology.* New York: Dover.

Johnstone, T., van Reekum, C. M., & Scherer, K. R. (2001). Vocal correlates of appraisal processes. In K. R. Scherer, A. Schorr, & T. Johnstone (Eds.), *Appraisal processes in emotion* (pp. 271–284). New York: Oxford University Press.

Kaiser, S., & Wehrle, T. (2001). Facial expressions as indicators of appraisal processes. In K. Scherer, A. Schorr, & T. Johnstone (Eds.), *Appraisal processes in emotion.* Oxford, UK: Oxford University Press.

Kunst-Wilson, W. R., & Zajonc, R. B. (1980). Affective discrimination of stimuli that cannot be recognized. *Science, 207,* 557–558.

Lang, P. J. (1985). The cognitive psychophysiology of fear and anxiety. In A. H. Tuma & J. D. Maser (Eds.), *Anxiety and the anxiety disorders* (pp. 131–170). Hillsdale, NJ: Lawrence Erlbaum Associates, Inc.

Lang, P. J. (1994). The motivational organization of emotion: Affect–reflex connections. In S. H. M. Van Goozen, N. E. Van de Poll, & J. A. Sergeant (Eds.), *Emotions: Essays on emotion theory* (pp. 61–92). Hillsdale, NJ: Lawrence Erlbaum Associates, Inc.

Lazarus, R. S. (1966). *Psychological stress and the coping process.* New York: McGraw-Hill.

Lazarus, R. S. (1982). Thoughts on the relations between emotion and cognition. *American Psychologist, 37,* 1019–1024.

Lazarus, R. S. (1991). *Emotion and adaptation.* New York: Oxford University Press.

Levenson, R. W. (1992). Autonomic nervous system differences among emotions. *Psychological Science, 3,* 23–27.

Levenson, R. W., Ekman, P., & Friesen, W. V. (1990). Voluntary facial action generates emotion-specific autonomic nervous system activity. *Psychophysiology, 27,* 363–384.

Leventhal, H. (1980). Toward a comprehensive theory of emotion. In L. Berkowitz (Ed.), *Advances in experimental social psychology* (Vol. 13, pp. 139–197). New York: Academic Press.

Leventhal, H. (1984). A perceptual-motor theory of emotion. In L. Berkowitz (Ed.), *Advances in experimental social psychology* (Vol. 17, pp. 117–182). New York: Academic Press.

Leventhal, H., & Scherer, K. R. (1987). The relationship of emotion to cognition: A functional approach to a semantic controversy. *Cognition and Emotion, 1*, 3–28.

Lewis, M. D. (2005). Bridging emotion theory and neurobiology through dynamic system modeling. *Behavioral and Brain Sciences, 28*, 169–194.

Lyons, W. (1980). *Emotion.* Cambridge, MA: Cambridge University Press.

Marr, D. (Ed.). (1982). *Vision: A computational investigation into the human representation and processing of visual information.* New York: Freeman.

Martin, I., & Levey, A. B. (1978). Evaluative conditioning. *Advances in Behaviour Research and Therapy, 1*, 57–102.

Moors, A. (2007). Can cognitive methods be used to study the unique aspect of emotion: An appraisal theorist's answer. *Cognition and Emotion, 21*, 1238–1269.

Moors, A. (2008). *Automatic constructive appraisal as a candidate cause of emotion.* Manuscript submitted for publication.

Moors, A., & De Houwer, J. (2006a). Automaticity: A theoretical and conceptual analysis. *Psychological Bulletin, 132*, 297–326.

Moors, A., & De Houwer, J. (2006b). Problems with dividing the realm of cognitive processes. *Psychological Inquiry, 17*, 199–204.

Nagel, T. (1974). What is it like to be a bat? *Philosophical Review, 83*, 435–450.

Niedenthal, P. M., Krauth-Gruber, S., & Ric, F. (2006). *Psychology of emotion: Interpersonal, experiential, and cognitive approaches.* New York: Psychology Press.

Nisbet, R. E., & Wilson, T. D. (1977). Telling more than we can know: Verbal reports on mental processes. *Psychological Review, 84*, 231–259.

Nussbaum, M. (1990). *Love's knowledge.* Oxford, UK: Oxford University Press.

Oatley, K., & Johnson-Laird, P. N. (1987). Towards a cognitive theory of emotions. *Cognition and Emotion, 1*, 29–50.

Öhman, A., & Mineka, S. (2001). Fears, phobias, and preparedness: Toward an evolved module of fear and fear learning. *Psychological Review, 108*, 483–826.

Ortony, A., Clore, G. L., & Collins, A. (1988). *The cognitive structure of emotions.* Cambridge, UK: Cambridge University Press.

Ortony, A., & Turner, T. J. (1990). What's basic about basic emotions? *Psychological Review, 97*, 315–331.

Panksepp, J. (1982). Toward a general psychobiological theory of emotions. *Behavioral and Brain Sciences, 5*, 407–467.

Panksepp, J. (1998). *Affective neuroscience: The foundations of human and animal emotions.* New York: Oxford University Press.

Panksepp, J. (2000). Emotions as natural kinds within the mammalian brain. In M. Lewis & J. M. Haviland-Jones (Eds.), *Handbook of emotions* (2nd ed., pp. 137–156). New York: Guilford Press.

Parkinson, B., & Manstead, A. S. R. (1992). Appraisal as a cause of emotion. In M. S. Clark (Ed.), *Review of personality and social psychology* (Vol. 13, pp. 122–149). Newbury Park, CA: Sage.

Parrott, G. W. (2007). Components and the definition of emotion. *Social Science Information, 46,* 419–423.

Pecchinenda, A. (2001). The psychophysiology of appraisals. In K. R. Scherer, A. Schorr, & T. Johnstone (Eds.), *Appraisal processes in emotion: Theory, Methods, Research* (pp. 301–318). Oxford, UK: Oxford University Press.

Pleyers, G., Corneille, O., Luminet, O., & Yzerbyt, V. (2007). Aware and (dis)liking: Item-based analyses reveal that valence acquisition via evaluative conditioning emerges only when there is contingency awareness. *Journal of Experimental Psychology: Learning, Memory, and Cognition, 33,* 130–144.

Power, M., & Dalgleish, T. (2007). *Cognition and emotion: From order to disorder* (2nd ed.). Hove, UK: Psychology Press.

Prinz, J. J. (2004). *Gut reactions: A perceptual theory of emotion.* Oxford, UK: Oxford University Press.

Reisenzein, R. (1983). The Schachter theory of emotion: Two decades later. *Psychological Bulletin, 94,* 239–264.

Reisenzein, R. (2001). Appraisal processes conceptualized from a schema-theoretic perspective: Contributions to a process analysis of emotions. In K. R. Scherer, A. Schorr, & T. Johnstone (Eds.), *Appraisal processes in emotion* (pp. 187–201). New York: Oxford University Press.

Rimé, B., Philippot, P., & Cisamolo, D. (1990). Social schemata of peripheral changes in emotion. *Journal of Personality and Social Psychology, 59,* 38–49.

Robinson, M. D., & Clore, G. L. (2002). Belief and feeling: Evidence for an accessibility model of emotional self-report. *Psychological Bulletin, 128,* 934–960.

Roseman, I. J. (1991). Appraisal determinants of discrete emotions. *Cognition and Emotion, 5,* 161–200.

Roseman, I. J., Antoniou, A. A., & José, P. E. (1996). Appraisal determinants of emotions: Constructing a more accurate and comprehensive theory. *Cognition and Emotion, 10*(3), 241–277.

Roseman, I. J., & Smith, C. A. (2001). Appraisal theory: Overview, assumptions, varieties, controversies. In K. R. Scherer, A. Schorr, & T. Johnstone (Eds.), *Appraisal processes in emotion* (pp. 3–34). New York: Oxford University Press.

Russell, J. A. (1994). Is there universal recognition of emotion from facial expression? A review of the cross-cultural studies. *Psychological Bulletin, 115,* 102–141.

Russell, J. A. (2003). Core affect and the psychological construction of emotion. *Psychological Review, 110,* 145–172.

Russell, J. A., & Barrett, L. F. (1999). Core affect, prototypical emotional episodes; and other things called emotion: Dissecting the elephant. *Journal of Personality and Social Psychology, 76,* 805–819.

Scarantino, A. (in press) Insights and blindspots of the cognitivist theory of emotions. *British Journal for the Philosophy of Science.*

Schachter, S. (1964). The interaction of cognitive and physiological determinants of emotional state. In L. Berkowitz (Ed.), *Advances in experimental social psychology* (Vol. 1, pp. 49–80). New York: Academic Press.

Schachter, S., & Singer, J. (1962). Cognitive, social, and physiological determinants of emotional state. *Psychological Review, 69,* 379–399.

Scherer, K. R. (1984). On the nature and function of emotions: A component process approach. In K. R. Scherer & P. Ekman (Eds.), *Approaches to emotion* (pp. 293–317). Hillsdale, NJ: Lawrence Erlbaum Associates, Inc.

Scherer, K. R. (1988). Criteria for emotion-antecedent appraisal: A review. In V. Hamilton, G. H. Bower, & N. H. Frijda (Eds.), *Cognitive perspectives on emotion and motivation* (pp. 89–126). Dordrecht, The Netherlands: Kluwer.

Scherer, K. R. (1993a). Neuroscience projections to current debates in emotion psychology. *Cognition and Emotion, 7,* 1–41.

Scherer, K. R. (1993b). Studying the emotion-antecedent appraisal process: An expert system approach. *Cognition and Emotion, 7,* 325–355.

Scherer, K. R. (1994). Toward a concept of "modal emotions". In P. Ekman & R. J. Davidson (Eds.), *The nature of emotion: Fundamental questions* (pp. 25–31). Oxford, UK: Oxford University Press.

Scherer, K. R. (1997). Profiles of emotion-antecedent appraisals: Testing theoretical predictions across cultures. *Cognition and Emotion, 11,* 113–150.

Scherer, K. R. (1999). Appraisal theory. In T. Dalgleish & M. Power (Eds.), *Handbook of cognition and emotion* (pp. 637–661). Chichester, UK: Wiley.

Scherer, K. R. (2000). Emotions as episodes of subsystem synchronization driven by nonlinear appraisal processes. In M. D. Lewis & I. Granic (Eds.), *Emotion, development, and self-organization: Dynamic systems approaches to emotional development* (pp. 70–99). Cambridge, UK: Cambridge University Press.

Scherer, K. R. (2001). Appraisal considered as a process of multilevel sequential checking. In K. R. Scherer, A. Schorr, & T. Johnstone (Eds.), *Appraisal processes in emotion* (pp. 92–120). New York: Oxford University Press.

Scherer, K. R. (2004). Feelings integrate the central representation of appraisal-driven response organization in emotion. In A. S. R. Manstead, N. H. Frijda, & A. H. Fischer (Eds.), *Feelings and emotions: The Amsterdam symposium* (pp. 136–157). Cambridge, UK: Cambridge University Press.

Scherer, K. R. (2005). What are emotions? And how can they be measured? *Social Science Information, 44,* 695–729.

Scherer, K. R., & Peper, M. (2001). Psychological theories of emotion and neuropsychological research. In F. Boller & J. Grafman (Eds.), *Handbook of neuropsychology* (Vol. 5, pp. 17–48). Amsterdam: Elsevier.

Searle, J. R. (1983). *Intentionality: An essay in the philosophy of mind.* Cambridge, UK: Cambridge University Press.

Shanks, D. R., & Dickinson, A. (1990). Contingency awareness in evaluative conditioning: A comment on Baeyens, Eelen, and Van den Bergh. *Cognition and Emotion, 4,* 19–30.

Smith, C. A., & Ellsworth, P. C. (1985). Patterns of cognitive appraisal in emotion. *Journal of Personality and Social Psychology, 48,* 813–838.

Smith, C. A., & Kirby, L. D. (2000). Consequences require antecedents: Towards a process model of emotion elicitation. In J. P. Forgas (Ed.), *Feeling and thinking: The role of affect in social cognition* (pp. 83–106). Cambridge, UK: Cambridge University Press.

Smith, C. A., & Kirby, L. D. (2001). Toward delivering on the promise of appraisal theory. In K. R. Scherer, A. Schorr, & T. Johnstone (Eds.), *Appraisal processes in emotion* (pp. 121–138). New York: Oxford University Press.

Smith, C. A., & Lazarus, R. S. (1993). Appraisal components, core relational themes, and the emotions. *Cognition and Emotion, 7,* 233–269.

Smith, E. R., & Neumann, R. (2005). Emotion processes considered from the perspective of dual process models. In P. Niedenthal, L. Feldman-Barrett, & P. Winkielman (Eds.), *The unconscious in emotion* (pp. 287–311). New York: Guilford Press.

Solomon, R. C. (1976). *The passions: Emotions and the meaning of life.* New York: Doubleday.

Teasdale, J. D. (1999). Multi-level theories of cognition–emotion relations. In T. Dalgleish & M. Power (Eds.), *Handbook of cognition and emotion* (pp. 665–682). Chichester, UK: Wiley.

Tomkins, S. S. (1962). *Affect, imagery, consciousness: Vol. 1: The positive affects.* New York: Springer.

van Reekum, C. M., & Scherer, K. R. (1997). Levels of processing in emotion-antecedent appraisal. In G. Matthews (Ed.), *Cognitive science perspectives on personality and emotion* (pp. 259–300). Amsterdam: Elsevier Science.

Zajonc, R. B. (1980). Feeling and thinking: Preferences need no inferences. *American Psychologist, 3,* 151–175.

Correspondence should be addressed to: Agnes Moors, Department of Psychology, Ghent University, Henri Dunantlaan 2, B-9000 Ghent, Belgium. E-mail: agnes.moors@ugent.be

Agnes Moors is a fellow of the Scientific Research Foundation – Flanders (FWO).

I thank Klaus Scherer who acted as a reviewer for the valuable comments and suggestions.

# 2 Do feelings have a mind of their own?

Jan De Houwer
*Ghent University, Belgium*

Dirk Hermans
*University of Leuven, Belgium*

In 1979, Robert B. Zajonc was awarded the Distinguished Scientific Contribution Award by the American Psychological Association, for which occasion he was invited to give a lecture. On such events, honoured scientists often review the awarded research and present a personal view on future developments in the field of interest. Zajonc, however, chose to present a "richly provoking" (Rachman, 1981, p. 279) paper describing his views on the relation between affect and cognition.

At the time Zajonc presented his paper, it was generally accepted that affective reactions depend upon prior cognitive processing. Different existing models of affect and emotion agreed on one thing: Affective reactions can be observed only after considerable information processing has taken place (e.g., Lazarus, Averill, & Optin, 1970; Mandler, 1975). In other words, no affect without cognition. Zajonc's presentation was nothing less than a frontal attack on the cognitive analysis of the affect–cognition relation. He questioned the core of cognitive models by arguing that affective reactions may occur prior to and without the participation of cognitive processing. Whereas cognitive models postulate the primacy of cognition, Zajonc argued for the primacy of affect. Or, as stated in the title of his presentation (which was later published in *American Psychologist*; Zajonc, 1980): Preferences (affect) need no inferences (cognition).

Zajonc's (1980) paper and the debate that it evoked had a huge impact on emotion research. The fact that in May 2009, this paper was cited more than 2100 times gives some indication of its importance. The true impact of the paper, however, is evidenced by the wealth of studies that it has directly or indirectly inspired over the past 30 years. In this chapter, we present a brief overview of debate surrounding Zajonc's paper and the legacy of this debate in emotion research. Our aim is not to reopen the debate but to show how it provided the impetus for an explosion of research on automatic affective processing. In the first part of this chapter, we summarise the arguments that Zajonc and his opponents exchanged. We point out that the debate highlighted a number of important questions about the relation between cognition and emotion, questions that were addressed in subsequent research. In the second part of our chapter, we present a brief overview of this research. Our review of the evidence is not meant to be exhaustive but does aim to provide a useful summary of the main insights that were gained as a result of the research that was inspired by the debate.

Throughout this chapter, we will define the term "affective processing" as the mental act of evaluating the affective properties of a stimulus. Affective reactions are defined as those reactions that are caused by the outcome of affective processing, that is, by the affective properties of stimuli as evaluated by the organism. There is no general agreement on which properties can be regarded as affective or emotional (see Moors, this volume), but they include the properties of valence (good–bad) and arousal (active–passive). The vast majority of the studies on automatic affective processing have, however, focused on the processing of evaluative stimulus properties (see Eder & Rothermund, in press, for a recent exception). Our use of the term "affect" also does not overlap with the term "attitude" because the latter is typically used to refer only to the evaluative properties of stimuli (e.g., Fazio, 1986). Affective processing can be studied by examining the conditions under which affective reactions occur. The question regarding the relation between affect and cognition thus boils down to the question of whether affective reactions can arise without the involvement of cognitive processes.

## AN OVERVIEW OF THE DEBATE

### Preferences need no inferences

The arguments that Zajonc (1980) put forward in support of the *primacy of affect* hypothesis can be grouped into four categories (see Eder, Hommel, & De Houwer, 2007, for a related analysis). A first group of arguments draws upon how we, as humans, experience affective reactions at a *phenomenological level*. In daily life, we seem to have little control over our feelings. Affective reactions often arise involuntary and once present, they cannot easily be dismissed on logical grounds. Even if we know that the experienced affective reaction is inappropriate, we often cannot stop it. It is also hard to persuade someone into believing that (s)he likes something if that person actually dislikes it. People may doubt their beliefs, but they will never doubt their feelings. To summarise, affective reactions seem to defy reason and logic.

In a second section, Zajonc (1980) discussed some *behavioural data*, which, he claimed, support the primacy of affect hypothesis. He mainly drew upon his own work on the mere exposure effect. In mere exposure research, it has been shown that the liking of a stimulus will increase if the stimulus is repeatedly presented (Zajonc, 1968; see Bornstein, 1989, for a review). Importantly, participants will show increased liking of a repeatedly presented stimulus even if they do not recognise the stimulus as being previously presented. The strongest evidence for this claim comes from studies in which stimuli were presented only briefly. It was observed that the liking of presented stimuli increased even though participants could not consciously recognise the stimuli that were presented (e.g., Bornstein & D'Agostino, 1992; Kunst-Wilson & Zajonc, 1980). This suggests that liking does not depend upon cognitive processes such as conscious recognition.

A third group of arguments is based on *neurological evidence*. Zajonc (1980) pointed to studies that suggested that affective reactions depend more upon activity in the right hemisphere whereas cognitive reactions are mediated by the left hemisphere. This supports the hypothesis that affect and cognition rely upon separate systems. In order to show that an independent affective system is not neuroanatomically implausible, Zajonc proposed the locus coeruleus as the subcortical structure that might be involved in such a system.

Finally, Zajonc (1980) presented *evolutionary arguments* to support his position. First, he argued that both phylogenetically and ontogentically, affect precedes language and thinking. Affective reactions can be observed in phylogentically lower organisms, but also in infants of more complex species (such as humans) despite severe limitations in (or absence of) cognitive capabilities. Second, he pointed out that the limbic system, which underlies affective reactions in lower organisms, developed long before the cortex, which underlies cognitive capabilities. It is hard to imagine that upon development of the cortex, the limbic affective system lost its autonomy in the sense that all affective expressions would necessarily be cognitively (i.e., cortically) mediated. Third, from an evolutionary point of view, it would be counter-adaptive to make all affective reactions dependent upon cognitive analysis. Often the adaptive value of affective reactions depends upon the speed with which they occur. For instance, when an animal is confronted with a predator, it has no time to engage in elaborate cognitive processing. It needs to react as quickly as possible. In such cases, a fast, pre-cognitive affective reaction is adaptive.

Based on these four groups of arguments, Zajonc postulated the existence of an independent affective system that requires only minimal sensory input in order to be activated. This system will always generate an affective reaction immediately following sensory input and before other cognitive activities such as recognition or discrimination can occur. However, it is possible that cognitive processing will influence affective reactions. Often, cognitive processing will override the initial affective reactions. Nevertheless, automatic affective reactions will always precede cognitive reactions. To summarise, affect is primary.

## Feelings need inferences

Seldom has a theoretical paper aroused so many direct responses as Zajonc (1980). As was mentioned earlier, this can be attributed mainly to the fact that his views were diametrically opposed to generally accepted beliefs. Another reason is that, as Zajonc (1980, p. 171) elegantly admitted, his conclusions were "stronger than can be justified by the logic or weight of the evidence" that was present at the time. As such, Zajonc's paper was an easy target.

Some commentaries focused on one or more of Zajonc's arguments and questioned either their empirical basis or underlying logic (e.g., Birnbaum, 1981; Hassan & Ward, 1991; Mellers, 1981; O'Malley, 1981). Instead of evaluating each single counterargument, we will discuss only the most common and fundamental criticism. Many commentators (Baars, 1981; Greenberg & Safran, 1984; Kleinginna & Kleinginna, 1985; Lazarus, 1981, 1982, 1984; Merckelbach & Jansen, 1986; Parrot & Sabini, 1989; Plutchik, 1985; Tsal, 1985; Watts, 1983) correctly pointed out that Zajonc did not distinguish between conscious, controlled cognition and automatic cognition. At the time of Zajonc's presentation, evidence was accumulating on the existence of such automatic cognitive processes. These processes were characterised as involuntary, effortless, rapid, rigid, uncontrollable and unconscious (e.g., Posner & Snyder, 1975; Shiffrin & Schneider, 1977). Many of Zajonc's (1980) arguments related to cognition in the sense of conscious, controlled cognition. For instance, Zajonc argued that affect often seems to contradict reason and logic. However, reason and logic refer to conscious cognitive activities. The seemingly irrational nature of affect, therefore, only suggests that affect may be independent of conscious cognition. It says nothing about the possible involvement of automatic cognition in the generation of affect. If we experience affect as involuntary, effortless, and inescapable, this might well be because affect depends upon automatic cognitive processes that are in nature involuntary, effortless, and inescapable. Also the behavioural data that Zajonc (1980) mentioned, as well as the neurological and evolutionary arguments, at best allow for the conclusion that affective reactions can occur independently of controlled cognition. Hence, most commentators reaffirm their believe in the primacy of cognition.

## On the primacy of affect

In a number of papers, Zajonc (1981, 1984, 2000; Zajonc & Markus, 1984, 1985; Zajonc, Pietromonaco, & Bargh, 1982) responded to these objections. Most importantly, Zajonc clarifies his definition of cognition:

> My definition of cognition (Zajonc, 1980, p. 154) required some form of transformation of a present or past sensory input. "Pure" sensory input, untransformed according to a more or less fixed code, is not cognition. Cognition need not be deliberate, rational or conscious, but it must involve some minimum "mental work". This "mental work" may consist of operations on sensory input that transform that input

into a form that may become subjectively available, or it may consist of
the activation of items from memory. (Zajonc, 1984, p. 118)

The definition makes clear that Zajonc does distinguish between controlled
cognition and automatic cognition. He adopts a broad mentalist definition
(see Moors, 2007) that equates cognition to the (controlled or automatic)
transformation of sensory input through the generation, activation, or
transformation of internal representations. Because cognition is defined as a
"nonsensory process that transforms sensory input and produces or recruits
representations ... the question of cognitive participation in affect is
reduced to the presence of representational processes" (Zajonc & Markus,
1982, p. 127).

Importantly, Zajonc (1984; Zajonc & Markus, 1982, 1985) reaffirmed
his belief that affect can be primary to both controlled and automatic
cognition. He explicitly acknowledged that cognitive processes may always
be involved in deliberate and intentional affective reactions such as
evaluative judgements (Zajonc et al., 1982). Therefore, when Zajonc claimed
that affect can be primary to cognition, he actually meant that automatic
affective reactions can occur without the involvement of cognitive processes.

In order to substantiate the primacy of (automatic) affect, Zajonc (1984)
repeated some of the arguments that were put forward in his original
publication (Zajonc, 1980), this time with more emphasis on phylo- and
ontogenetic, and neuroanatomical evidence. He also presented additional
behavioural data for the primacy of affect. Zajonc acknowledged that
opponents might again argue that the affective phenomena he was
discussing involved some form of hidden automatic cognition. He intelli-
gently responded that if these and all other automatic affective reactions
were based on hidden cognition, the involvement of such cognition should
be demonstrated rather than assumed. It does not suffice to reject affective
phenomena that reveal no clear involvement of cognition as evidence for the
primacy of affect, solely based on the argument that some hidden cognition
must be involved. Arguments can only be rejected if it can be demonstrated
that cognition is involved or if it can be shown what representations need to
be activated (Zajonc, 1984; Zajonc & Markus, 1985). He urged cognitive
researchers to demonstrate how cognition is involved in the generation of
"true" affect: "It is a critical question for cognitive theory and for theories of
emotions to determine just what is the minimal information process that is
required for emotion" (Zajonc, 1984, p. 122).

## The legacy of the debate

After Zajonc's response to the comments on his original paper, the debate was
evaluated in a number of subsequent papers (e.g., Kleinginna & Kleinginna,
1985; Leventhal & Scherer, 1987; Merckelbach & Jansen, 1986; Plutchik,
1985). It was noted that the debate had stranded on definitional issues, and

that, depending upon how the terms "cognition" and "affect" are inter-preted, one could either defend the primacy of affect or the primacy of cognition based on the same body of evidence (Kleinginna & Kleinginna, 1985; Leventhal & Scherer, 1987). Nevertheless, Zajonc's (1980) work played an important role in renewing the interest in affective behaviour (Kitayama & Howard, 1994; Niedenthal & Halberstadt, 1995). As such, Zajonc had achieved one of the main goals that motivated him to write his 1980 paper, namely: "to appeal for a more concentrated study of affective phenomena that have been ignored for decades" (Zajonc, 1984, p. 117).

His work not only gave impetus but also direction to this new interest in affective behaviour by highlighting two research questions. Most impor-tantly, Zajonc's (1980) analysis stimulated cognitive researchers to recog-nise the importance of automatic affective processing, that is, affective processing that is not mediated by controlled cognitive processes. Many influential cognitive theories of affect and emotion that have been published since then acknowledge the important role played by automatic affective processing (e.g., Bargh & Chartrand, 1999; Fazio, 1986; Gawronski & Bodenhausen, 2006; Öhman, 1987; Sherer, 1993; Williams, Watts, Ma-cLeod, & Mathews, 1988). Inspired by these theories and new conceptua-lisations of the term "automaticity" (e.g., Bargh, 1992; Moors & De Houwer, 2006), researchers started to examine the properties of automatic affective processing, the variables that moderate the presence and outcome of this type of processing, the different effects that automatic affective processing can have, and the (cognitive) processes on which automatic affective processing might be based. Finally, some researchers also addressed Zajonc's claim that, at least in some cases, automatic affective reactions can occur independently of automatic cognitive processes. In the remainder of this chapter, we will present a brief overview of the research on automatic affective processing in which these issues were addressed.

## A BRIEF REVIEW OF RESEARCH ON AUTOMATIC AFFECTIVE PROCESSING

### Properties of automatic affective processing

At the time that Zajonc (1980, 1984) drew attention to the importance of automatic affective processing, the dominant view was that there are two sets of mutually exclusive cognitive processes, one being non-automatic or controlled processes and the other being automatic processes. According to this view, which is known as the all-or-none view of automaticity, all non-automatic processes have the same features (e.g., unconscious, intentional, controlled, effortful, and slow) whereas all automatic processes have the opposite features (e.g., unconscious, unintentional, uncontrolled, effortless, and fast). It has become clear, however, that this all-or-none view is incorrect. Studies have demonstrated that most processes possess features typical of non-automatic processes but also features typical of automatic processes. Evidence from Stroop studies, for instance, suggests that the processing of word meaning is automatic in that it does not depend on intention, resources, or time, but at the same time occurs only when attention is directed toward the word (see Logan, 1985, 1989, for reviews). An important implication of this conclusion is that one cannot simply characterise a process as automatic or non-automatic. Rather, it is necessary to always specify the sense in which a process is automatic, that is, to specify which automaticity features it possesses and which automaticity features it does not posses. Research has shown that affective processing can possess several features of automaticity. Much of this evidence comes from studies on affective priming (Fazio, Sanbonmatsu, Powell, & Kardes, 1986; Hermans, De Houwer, & Eelen, 1994). In a typical study on affective priming, a prime word is presented briefly before a target word appears. Participants are asked to evaluate the target word, that is, to determine whether the word refers to something good or something bad. Results typically show that participants respond more quickly when the target and the prime share the same valence (e.g., HAPPY–SUNSHINE; congruent trials) than when they differ in valence (e.g., HAPPY–CANCER; incongruent trials). This paradigm has often been used to study affective processing because the presence of an affective priming effect (e.g., faster responses on congruent than on incongruent trials) allows one to infer that the valence of the prime has been processed. This is because the congruence between the valence of the prime and the valence of the target can have an effect only if the valence of the prime has been processed. Hence, if one observes an affective priming effect under certain conditions, one can conclude that affective processing (of the prime) can take place under those conditions. We will now provide a brief overview of the conditions under which affective priming (and thus affective processing) can take place.

## Can affective processing be unconscious?

Evidence suggests that affective processing can be unconscious in at least two respects. First, several studies have revealed affective priming effects even when the primes were presented subliminally, that is, when participants were not aware of the presentations of the primes (e.g., Abrams, Klinger, & Greenwald, 2002; Draine & Greenwald, 1998; Hermans, Spruyt, De Houwer, & Eelen, 2003b; Klauer, Eder, Greenwald, & Abrams, 2007). Second, novel stimuli, the affective properties of which were created in the laboratory, can lead to affective priming effects even when participants are not aware of how they acquired their liking for the stimuli (e.g., Olson & Fazio, 2002). Hence, people can affectively process stimuli even when they are unaware of the stimuli that they process and even when they do not consciously know why they like or dislike the stimuli.

## Can affective processing be efficient?

Hermans, Crombez, and Eelen (2000) asked participants to perform an affective priming task while simultaneously reciting a series of digits. They found that the magnitude of the affective priming effect was unaffected by the degree of mental load imposed by the secondary task, which suggests that affective processing is relatively independent of available processing resources and thus efficient (see Klauer & Teige-Mocigemba, 2007, for more recent evidence).

## Can affective processing be fast?

There is ample evidence showing affective priming effects even when there is little time to process the primes. For instance, Klauer, Rossnagel, and Musch (1997; also see Hermans, De Houwer, & Eelen, 2001) found affective priming effects when the onset of the prime occurred 100 ms before or simultaneously with the onset of the target. Affective priming has been observed even when the onset of the prime occurs after the onset of the target (e.g., Fockenberg, Koole, & Semin, 2006). Such results indicate that the affective properties of the primes can be processed within a few hundred milliseconds after the presentation of the prime.

## Can affective processing be goal independent?

A first question in this context is whether affective processing of a particular stimulus can occur in an involuntary manner, that is, in the absence of the goal to affectively process that stimulus. The fact that affective priming can be found when participants are unaware of the prime stimulus already provides evidence for involuntary affective processing because awareness of the stimulus does seem to be a prerequisite for having a conscious goal to process that stimulus affectively. A second line of studies examined whether affective processing of a particular stimulus can occur in the absence of a goal to affectively process any stimulus in the environment. The results of these studies support the conclusion that affective processing can indeed be goal independent in this way. Most importantly, affective priming effects have been found in tasks that do not require the participants to adopt the goal to evaluate stimuli (e.g., task that require the participant to read or name the target, to determine the lexical status or semantic category of the target, or to compare the prime and target with regard to a non-affective feature such as colour; see Bargh, Chaiken, Raymond, & Hymes, 1996; Klauer & Musch, 2002; Spruyt, Hermans, De Houwer, & Eelen, 2002; but see Klauer & Musch, 2001).

Note, however, that this evidence is not entirely conclusive because there never was a direct test of whether participants (implicitly) adopted the goal to evaluate stimuli. Even when participants are not asked to evaluate stimuli, or even when the affective dimension is not mentioned by the experimenter, the mere presence of affectively valenced stimuli might be sufficient to induce an affective processing goal. What is certain is that affective priming effects are stronger when participants have the goal to evaluate stimuli than when they have the goal to process non-affective features of the stimuli (e.g., Spruyt, De Houwer, & Hermans, 2009a; Spruyt, De Houwer, Hermans, & Eelen, 2007).

*Conclusions*

Affective priming studies have confirmed that affective processing does have many of the features of automatic processes. It can occur even when participants: (1) are unaware of the stimulus that is processed affectively; (2) are unaware of why they like or dislike the stimulus; (3) are engaged in other effortful tasks and thus have little mental resources available for the affective processing of the stimulus; (4) have little time to process the stimulus affectively; (5) do not have the conscious goal to process the stimulus affectively; or (6) do not have the conscious goal to evaluate other stimuli. Recent evidence suggests, however, that affective processing is not completely unconditional. For instance, the presence of a goal to process non-affective features of a stimulus seems to reduce the probability of affective processing (e.g., Spruyt et al., 2009a).

## What determines the presence of automatic affective processing?

Now that we know more about the *way* in which affective processing can be automatic, we can examine *when* affective processing is automatic. This can be done by studying variables that moderate the presence of automatic affective reactions. We will distinguish two sets of moderators: Properties of the stimuli that evoke the automatic affective reactions and properties of the individual who shows the automatic affective reactions.

*Properties of the stimuli*

Fazio (1986) put forward the hypothesis that automatic affective reactions will be evoked only when the affective properties of the evoking stimulus are highly accessible. As a measure of accessibility, participants were asked to determine as quickly as possible whether a stimulus (e.g., a word or a picture) referred to something good (e.g., the word HAPPY) or something bad (e.g., the word CANCER). Stimuli that were evaluated quickly were said to have highly accessible affective properties. Fazio et al. (1986) found affective priming effects (and thus evidence for automatic affective processing) only when the affective properties of the primes were highly accessible. Moreover, manipulations of accessibility (e.g., training participants to access the affective properties of certain stimuli) also influenced the strength of the automatic affective reactions as captured by the affective-priming effect. Nevertheless, there is still some debate about the impact of accessibility on automatic affective processing. Most importantly, Bargh, Chaiken, Govender, and Pratto (1992; also see Bargh et al., 1996) failed to replicate the finding that affective priming was moderated by the accessibility of affective information. Moreover, the results of several studies suggest that the affective properties of recently learned stimuli can evoke automatic affective reactions even though the affective properties of these stimuli are probably difficult to access (e.g., De Houwer, Hermans, & Eelen, 1998; Hermans, Baeyens, & Eelen, 2003a).

*Properties of the individual*

Hermans et al. (2001) found that affective priming effects were stronger for participants who scored high on the "need to evaluate" scale than for those who had a low score on this scale. This suggests that individuals who are chronically engaged in consciously evaluating objects and situations, also show stronger automatic affective reactions. Hermans et al. argued that this relation might be mediated by the accessibility of affective information. Because accessibility depends on how often the affective properties of stimuli have been evaluated in the past, accessibility will on average be higher for individuals with a high need for evaluation, that is, individuals who constantly evaluate the affective properties of objects and situations in the environment.

A second line of studies that is relevant in this context concerns the impact of alexithymia on affective priming. Alexithymia refers to a lack in the capacity to identify and describe emotions. Vermeulen, Luminet, and Corneille (2006) observed smaller affective priming effects in participants high in alexithymia than in participants low in alexithymia. Finally, there are also indications that working-memory capacity (Klauer & Teige-Mocigemba, 2007) and the level of trait anxiety (Maier, Berner, & Pekrun, 2003) can modulate affective priming effects. In sum, research suggests that there are stable differences in the propensity of people to show automatic affective reactions.

## What determines the outcome of automatic affective processing?

In this section, we will consider those variables that determine the automatic evaluation of the affective properties of a stimulus, for instance whether a stimulus is automatically evaluated as being positive or negative. Although genetic factors undoubtedly also have an impact, the outcome of automatic affective processing is determined primarily by the nature of prior experiences with stimuli and on the nature of the context in which the stimuli are presented. Hence, we will focus on those two determinants.

### Prior experiences

Research has shown that automatic affective reactions toward an object can result from direct experiences with that object. We have already discussed studies on mere exposure, which showed that the repeated presentation of a stimulus can change the liking of that stimulus even when people are not aware of those presentations (e.g., Kunst-Wilson & Zajonc, 1980). Research on evaluative conditioning is also relevant in this context. Evaluative conditioning studies have shown that stimuli that often co-occur with positive stimuli (e.g., the aftershave of a loved one) tend to be liked more than those that often go together with negative stimuli (e.g., the aftershave of an enemy; see De Houwer, Thomas, & Baeyens, 2001; De Houwer, in press, for reviews). Such direct experiences have been shown to influence not only non-automatic affective reactions such as self-reported liking but also automatic evaluative reactions such as captured by affective priming effects (e.g., Hermans et al., 2003a). Automatic affective reactions can result also from indirect experiences with an object, that is, from information about the object that is communicated via verbal instruction or picked up via observation. For instance, simply telling people that members of a (fictitious) social group called "niffites" tend to behave in a bad manner will result in automatic negative reactions toward the members of that social group (Gregg, Seibt, & Banaji, 2006; see also De Houwer et al., 1998). The fact that a single instruction can lead to automatic affective reactions contradicts the common assumption that automatic reactions (affective or otherwise) are acquired slowly as the result of many experiences. It also raises important questions about whether or how automatic affective reactions that result from instructions differ from those that result from repeated direct experiences.

### Current context

The outcome of affective processing is highly dependent on the context in which stimuli are presented (see Blair, 2002, for a review). For instance, the same Black person might automatically evoke a negative reaction in the context of a backstreet alley but a positive reaction in the context of a basketball game (e.g., Wittenbrink, Judd, & Park, 2001). Automatic affective responses also depend on the goals that we have at a particular moment in time. For instance, food automatically evokes a much more positive reaction when we are hungry than after eating a large meal (e.g., Seibt, Häfner, & Deutsch; 2007; see also Ferguson & Bargh, 2004; Moors & De Houwer, 2001). In sum, contrary to the idea that automatic affective reactions are fixed and inflexible, many results have shown that automatic affective reactions are highly malleable.

## What are the effects of automatic affective processing?

Research has shown that the outcome of automatic affective processing (e.g., whether a stimulus is evaluated as positive or negative) can have multiple effects on behaviour. We will make a distinction between direct and indirect effects, that is, effects that are not (direct) or are (indirect) assumed to be mediated by other cognitive or affective processes.

### Direct effects

Stimuli that are evaluated as being positive tend to be approached whereas stimuli that are evaluated as negative tend to be avoided. There is evidence showing that such effects arise even when participants do not have the goal to evaluate stimuli and when little time is available (e.g., Chen & Bargh, 1999; Solarz, 1960). Such evidence has been interpreted as revealing a direct impact of automatic affective processing on (approach or avoidance) behaviour (e.g., Chen & Bargh, 1999). There is, however, some debate about whether this link is mediated by cognitive processes (see Eder & Rothermund, 2008; Krieglmeyer, Deutsch, De Houwer, & De Raedt, in press). For instance, Eder and Rothermund (2008) argued that positive (negative) stimuli automatically activate responses if and only if they are mentally encoded as being positive (negative). They showed that changes in the mental coding of responses (e.g., telling participants that pulling a joystick towards the body is actually moving the joystick downwards) also changed the way in which positive and negative stimuli activated those responses. Recent results by Krieglmeyer et al., however, suggest that in some cases, approach and avoid responses are activated by positive and negative stimuli irrespective of how they are cognitively represented.

### Indirect effects

Automatic affective processing can also influence behaviour in an indirect way. First, studies have shown that affective stimuli attract attention, even when people do not have the intention to evaluate the stimuli affectively nor the intention to attend to those stimuli (see Yiend, this volume, for a review). There is some indication that the attentional effects of automatic affective processing are driven primarily by the evaluation of the arousal level of the stimuli rather than the evaluation of valence (e.g., Vogt, De Houwer, Koster, Van Damme, & Crombez, 2008). The fact that automatic affective processing has an effect on attention in its turn allows for a host of additional, downstream effects. For instance, the increase in the amount of attention that is assigned to (certain) affective stimuli is likely to increase the impact of those stimuli on current behaviour and to improve memory for those stimuli.

Second, automatic affective processing can also influence behaviour through the effects it has on mood. For instance, Chartrand, van Baaren, and Bargh (2006), showed that the subliminal presentation of positive stimuli results in a positive mood, which, in its turn, leads to a more superficial processing of stimuli in the environment. Such findings show that automatic affective processing cannot only have immediate, short-term effects on cognition and behaviour (e.g., via the activation of approach or avoidance responses), but also more global and long-lasting effects.

*"Implicit measures" of automatic affective reactions*

Given the important impact that automatic affective reactions can have on behaviour, researchers started looking for ways to measure individual differences in automatic affective reactions in an attempt to better predict and understand individual differences in behaviour. For instance, Fazio, Jackson, Dunton, and Williams (1995) found that an affective priming measure of automatic affective reactions to faces of Black persons predicted subtle aspects of how participants interact with a Black person. Findings such as these have led to an explosion of research on implicit measures, that is, measures of automatic (affective) reactions. It is beyond the scope of this chapter to review all of these studies (see De Houwer, Teige-Mocigemba, Spruyt, & Moors, 2009; Fazio & Olson, 2003, for reviews). Nevertheless, the sheer number of studies on this topic shows how important the topic of automatic affective processing has become in modern psychology.

## On which cognitive processes is automatic affective processing based?

The core assumption of the cognitive approach in psychology is that the impact of the environment on behaviour is mediated by the activation and transformation of mental representations that encode information about stimuli in the environment. Cognitive models of automatic affective processing thus postulate that automatic affective reactions to stimuli in the environment occur only when mental representations about the affective properties of those stimuli have been activated or formed. Different cognitive theories differ in their assumptions about the nature of the intervening representations and the processes by which these representations are formed and transformed. Three classes of models can be distinguished based on the type of representation that they postulate: Symbolic network models, exemplar models, and subsymbolic network (or connectionist) models. We will briefly discuss each class of models as they relate to automatic affective processing. Finally, we will also discuss models that focus on the relation between automatic and non-automatic affective reactions.

## Symbolic network models

The first class of models is based on the idea that knowledge is represented in a semantic network of symbolic nodes. Each node is symbolic in that it is assumed to represent a certain stimulus or concept. The properties and meaning of a concept are reflected in the associations in which the corresponding node is involved. For instance, the fact that birds typically have wings can be represented by the presence of an association between the node that represents the concept "bird" and a node that represents the concept "wings" (e.g., Collins & Quinlan, 1972). Likewise, symbolic network models of automatic affective processing postulate that certain nodes represent the affective properties of stimuli. For instance, the fact that cancer is something bad could be represented by means of an association between the node representing "cancer" and a node representing "bad" (e.g., Bower, 1981; Fazio, 1986). Automatic affective reactions are attributed to the fact that evaluative associations can be activated automatically, that is, in the absence of awareness, cognitive resources, time, or certain goals.

Different symbolic network models of automatic affective processing differ with regard to their assumptions about the processes by which evaluative associations can be activated or about the number and content of the evaluative associations. For instance, Fazio (1986) postulated that only strong, easily accessible, evaluative associations can be activated automatically. Others dispute this assumption (e.g., Bargh et al., 1992, 1996). Moreover, whereas some models incorporate the assumption that all affective information about a concept is summarised into a single evaluative association (e.g., Fazio, 1986), others postulate the existence of multiple evaluative associations (e.g., Petty, Briñol, & DeMarree, 2007; Wilson, Lindsey, & Schooler, 2000).

## Exemplar models

A second class of models in cognitive psychology is called exemplar models (e.g., Hintzman, 1986; Medin & Schaffer, 1978; Nosofsky & Palmeri, 1997). Like symbolic network models, these models postulate the existence of symbolic representations. However, rather than assuming the existence of nodes that represent concepts, exemplar models assume the existence of exemplars that represent concrete past events. Each separate event is encoded in a different exemplar. The information from different events is not integrated at the time when the events are encountered but only at the time when information is retrieved from memory.

In the context of automatic affective reactions, it can be assumed that different events that contain information about the affective properties of a stimulus (e.g., the experience of pleasant flavour when eating a strawberry; someone telling you how nice strawberries are) are each stored in separate exemplars. The next time that the stimulus is presented, different exemplars that contain information about the stimulus will be automatically activated from memory. The automatic affective reaction will reflect the summary of all affective information that is retrieved from memory upon the presentation of the stimulus (e.g., Klauer, 2008). One could say that one's evaluation of the affective properties of a stimulus is not retrieved from memory but rather constructed on the spot, based on the information that is at that point in time retrieved from memory. Because the activation of exemplars from memory is assumed to be a function of the similarity between the current situation and the past situations stored in the exemplars, the retrieval of information will depend very much on the detailed properties of the current situation. This could explain why automatic affective reactions are very much context dependent (e.g., Schwarz, 2007). Note, however, that network models also contain a number of mechanisms by which context effects can be explained by network models (see Fazio, 2007; Gawronksi & Bodenhausen, 2006).

Exemplar models are clearly superior to symbolic network models in the capacity to account for the embodiment of affective processing. Affective processing is not only associated with a variety of bodily and neural responses, it also seems to causally depend on the presence of specific bodily and neural responses (e.g., Niedenthal, Barsalou, Winkielman, Krauth-Gruber, & Ric, 2005). For instance, participants are less accurate in judging the emotional nature of disgust- and joy-related words when they are prevented from activating facial muscles that are typically involved in facial expressions of disgust and joy (Niedenthal, Winkielman, Mondillon, & Vermeulen, 2009). Such results are difficult to explain on the basis of symbolic network models in which information is typically represented in an abstract, modality-independent manner. They can be explained on the basis of exemplar models if it is assumed that exemplar representations also contain information about embodied responses that were present in the encoded event.

*Subsymbolic network models*

The third class of cognitive models postulates the existence of subsymbolic networks (e.g., McClelland & Rumelhart, 1986). Like symbolic network models, subsymbolic network models postulate that knowledge is represented in a network of interconnected nodes. The crucial difference is that the nodes in a subsymbolic network do not symbolise stimuli, concepts, or events. Instead, knowledge is represented as patterns of activation across a large number of nodes. For instance, the concept "bird" is not symbolised by a specific node but by a specific pattern of activation. The affective properties of a concept can be seen as part of the pattern of activation that is evoked by stimuli related to that concept. Given that stimuli in the environment automatically give rise to patterns of activation in the network, the evaluation of the affective properties of a stimulus arises automatically as an aspect of the activation pattern that the stimulus evokes. Although subsymbolic network models are thus compatible with the idea that affective reactions can arise automatically, they have received little attention in research on (automatic) affective processing (see Conrey & Smith, 2007, for an exception).

*Models about the relation between automatic and non-automatic affective reactions*

Cognitive models of affective processing have focused not only on how automatic affective reactions come about but also on how these reactions relate to non-automatic affective reactions. Most models allow for the possibility of inconsistent automatic and non-automatic affective reactions even though they differ in their assumptions about how such dissociations can arise. So called dual-attitude models postulate that both types of affective reactions can be determined by different representations in memory. For instance, Wilson et al. (2000) put forward the idea that a single concept in a symbolic network can be involved in two evaluative associations that contradict each other (e.g., an association between "smoking" and "good" and between "smoking" and "bad"). Dissociations can arise when automatic and non-automatic affective reactions are based on different evaluative associations. Dual-process models, on the other hand, postulate that non-automatic affective reactions can be influenced by processes that do not impact on automatic affective reactions (e.g., Fazio, 1986; Gawronski & Bodenhausen, 2006; Petty et al., 2007). For instance, Fazio (1986) argued that automatic affective reactions are a direct function of the automatic activation of evaluative associations in memory whereas non-automatic affective reactions are modulated by controlled reasoning processes that people engage in when they have the motivation and opportunity to do so. Dual-process models have been especially successful in predicting when automatic and non-automatic affective reactions will overlap (see Gawronski & Bodenhausen, 2006; Fazio & Olson, 2003, for reviews).

## Does automatic affective processing (always) depend on cognitive processes?

The different cognitive models of (automatic) affective processing that we have discussed in the previous section incorporate different ideas about how automatic affective processing *could* depend on the (automatic) activation and transformation of mental representations. Despite the existence of these theories and despite the challenge that was formulated by Zajonc (1984), relatively little research has been directly aimed at testing whether particular cognitive processes and representations *do* underlie automatic affective reactions. There are a number of findings that strongly suggest that automatic affective reactions do at least sometimes depend on the activation and transformation of mental representations. This does not imply, however, that automatic affective reactions always depend on cognitive processes. In the remainder of this chapter, we will provide a brief overview of studies that directly examined the question of whether cognitive processes mediate automatic affective reactions. In line with Zajonc (1984), we define cognition as the formation and transformation of mental representations.

## Mere exposure effects

A first set of studies relates to the mere exposure effect, that is, the finding that the liking of a stimulus can change as the result of the repeated exposure of that stimulus. The observation that mere exposure effects do not depend on a conscious recognition of the presented stimulus was one of the corner stones of Zajonc's (1980) claim that affect does not need cognition. More recent findings, however, strongly suggest that mere exposure does depend on automatic cognitive processes, more precisely, the automatic activation of memory traces (e.g., Bonanno & Stillings, 1986; Mandler, Nakamura, & Van Zandt, 1987; Reber, Winkielman, & Schwarz, 1998; Rotteveel & Phaf, 2007). As is known from memory research (e.g., Hintzman & Curran, 1994), automatic activation of memory traces will result in a sense of familiarity or perceptual fluency. If it is assumed that familiarity or perceptual fluency results in an increase in liking, one can explain that repeatedly presented (and thus more familiar) stimuli will be liked more than those that were not previously presented. Memory research has also demonstrated that familiarity or fluency is not always sufficient to support conscious recognition (e.g., Mandler, 1980). Therefore, increases in familiarity, and thus in liking, could be observed even if conscious recognition fails.

## Context effects

Studies on the context specificity of automatic affective reactions also provide support for the idea that automatic affective reactions depend on cognitive processes. We have already noted that the context in which a stimulus is presented (e.g., a Black person in a backstreet alley or on a basketball court) determines the outcome of automatic affective processing. This implies that the automatic affective reaction is not simply a function of certain "sub-cognitive" features of the stimulus (e.g., the "preferanda" that according to Zajonc, 1980, determine affect) but depends on a combination of features of the stimulus and the context in which the stimulus occurs. Other studies show that also a non-physical, motivational context can modulate automatic affective reactions. For instance, the same stimulus can evoke a positive automatic affective reaction when it signals the achievement of a goal and a negative automatic affective reaction when it signals the failure to achieve a goal (e.g., Moors & De Houwer, 2001). It is difficult to imagine how the physical and motivational context can have such a dramatic impact without the intervention of cognitive processes.

*Dissociations between affect and cognition*

There are, however, also findings that seem to reveal cognitively unmediated affective reactions, that is, affective reactions that do not involve the formation or transformation of mental representations. Most of these findings have in common that they demonstrate effects of the affective properties of a stimulus in the absence of effects of non-affective properties of the stimulus. Assuming that mental representations always encode non-affective properties, such dissociations could be interpreted as evidence for affective reactions under conditions in which mental representations of the stimulus were absent. A first example of such a dissociation comes from studies conducted by Murphy and Zajonc (1993; Murphy, Monahan, & Zajonc, 1995). On each trial, they presented a photograph of a human face that expressed either a positive or negative emotion (e.g., happiness, fear, anger). Immediately following presentation of the facial expression, a Chinese ideograph was shown. Participants were asked to indicate how much they liked the ideograph. When facial expressions were presented for 4 ms—which was too brief to allow for a conscious recognition of the face—ideographs that were preceded by positive expressions were liked more than those preceded by negative expressions. No effects were found when faces were presented for 1000 ms, in which case they could be clearly perceived. Murphy and Zajonc (1993) found the opposite pattern of results when other, which they called "cognitive", attributes of the ideographs had to be rated. Judgements of "cognitive" attributes such as size, symmetry, or gender were not influenced by the size, symmetry, or gender of the preceding stimuli when the preceding stimuli were presented briefly (4 ms), but judgements were influenced when the preceding stimuli were presented long enough to be detected (1000 ms).

Murphy and Zajonc (1993, Experiment 6; see Dijksterhuis & Aarts, 2003, for related findings) observed also a second type of dissociation between the effects of affective and non-affective stimulus properties. On each trial, they presented for 4 ms a picture of a man or woman who expressed a positive or negative emotion. After an interval of 1000 ms, during which a pattern mask was presented, participants were shown the briefly presented face on one side of a screen and a face that was not presented on the other side. They were asked to indicate which of the two faces had been presented before the mask. If the not presented (incorrect) alternative was a face expressing an emotion of a different valence than the presented face, choice performance was more accurate than when both faces expressed an emotion of the same valence. However, performance did not depend upon whether gender was consistent. Hence, there were effects of the affective properties of faces under conditions that did not seem to allow for effects of non-affective properties of those faces.

A third and final set of dissociation data comes from studies conducted by Klauer and Musch (2002). On each trial, they presented two words that had the same (e.g., HAPPY–RAINBOW) or a different valence (e.g., SMILE–CANCER). Independently of the match in valence, the stimuli also matched or mismatched on a non-affective stimulus dimension (e.g., they had the same or a different colour). When participants had to decide whether the stimuli matched on the non-affective dimension (e.g., "Do the words have the same or a different colour?"), reaction times were influenced by the (task-irrelevant) match in valence (e.g., faster responses to HAPPY–RAINBOW than to SMILE–CANCER when the words had the same colour; vice versa for when the words had a different colour). When the match in valence was relevant, however, the (task-irrelevant) match on the non-affective dimension had no impact on performance. Hence, again there was an impact of affective stimulus properties (i.e., match in valence) under conditions where there was no impact of non-affective stimulus properties (e.g., match in colour).

## Limitations of dissociations

Although dissociations between the effects of affective and non-affective stimulus properties are intriguing, they should be interpreted with care (e.g., Dunn & Kirsner, 2003). In order to interpret these dissociations as evidence for affect without cognition, one needs to assume that the null effects of the non-affective stimulus properties demonstrate the complete absence of mental representations of the stimulus (i.e., the absence of cognition). It is, however, possible that non-affective stimulus properties are represented mentally but do not influence responding. For instance, the failure of Murphy and Zajonc (1993; Murphy et al., 1995) to observe effects of non-affective stimulus properties with short (4 ms) stimulus presentations does not necessarily imply that those properties were not processed under those conditions. As Marcel (1983a, 1983b) pointed out, some stimulus properties have better access to consciousness and can thus influence conscious judgements under conditions that eliminate the influence of other types of information. It is possible that affective information has better access to consciousness than information about "cognitive" properties such as size, symmetry, or gender. Hence, both might have been processed even when only effects of affective properties were observed. However, arguments like these render the hypothesis that automatic affective reactions depend on automatic cognition unfalsifiable. When there is no evidence for cognitive processing under conditions that do show evidence for affective processing, one can always argue that cognitive processing did occur but could not be observed for one reason or another. Rather than relying on such post hoc arguments, cognitive researchers should conduct additional studies to test whether automatic cognition is involved.

Such additional studies, conducted with regard to dissociation, have been reported by Klauer and Musch (2002). Spruyt, De Houwer, Hermans, Everaert, and Moors (2009b) noted that Klauer and Musch always asked participants to respond in a positive, affirmative manner when stimuli matched on the relevant dimension and to respond in a negative, disconfirming manner when stimuli mismatched on that dimension. The mere fact that the responses were affectively laden could have increased the salience of the affective properties of the stimuli and thus the probability that these properties influenced performance even when they were task irrelevant. To test this idea, they conducted a new experiment in which participants responded by saying the name of one colour (e.g., "blue") for words that matched on the task-relevant dimension and by saying the name of another colour (e.g., "green") when the words mismatched on that dimension. Under these conditions, a task-irrelevant match in colour did influence responses. This shows that a task-irrelevant match on a non-affective dimension can have an impact on performance. Hence, the dissociation that was observed by Klauer and Musch appears to be due to the nature of the responses that they used rather than to differences in the conditions under which affective and non-affective stimulus properties are processed.

*Neuropsychological evidence*

Since the publication of Zajonc's (1980) seminal paper, there has been an explosion in neuropsychological research about the brain structures that are involved in the processing of affective and non-affective stimulus properties. It is beyond the scope of this chapter to review all of this evidence. Recent reviews of the relevant literature (e.g., Duncan & Feldman Barrett, 2007; Storbeck & Clore, 2007) point to the conclusion that affective and non-affective processing is fundamentally intertwined. In those limited cases where some results could be interpreted as evidence for affective reactions that are unmediated by cognitive processes, additional studies showed that such reactions occur only under very limited conditions. For instance, LeDoux (1990) observed conditioned emotional responses to the presence of a tone in animals whose auditory cortex was removed. However, he also found that cortical areas do play an indispensable role in the establishment of conditioned emotional responses to tones of a particular frequency. It seems only logical that cortical areas have this function. Automatic affective reactions depend very much on the visual details of a stimulus. For instance, perceptually similar words such as "luck" and "lock" are likely to evoke very different automatic affective reactions. In order for a system to generate different affective responses to different stimuli, it must be able to differentiate between the stimuli. Although subcortical pathways may be sufficient to discriminate between clearly different, isolated perceptual stimuli, it is unlikely that more complex, multifeatured stimuli can be differentiated at this level (LeDoux, 1990). Rather, substantial cognitive processing is required to differentiate complex stimuli. It therefore makes sense that cognitive processes precede the automatic affective reactions evoked by complex stimuli (also see Storbeck & Clore, 2007).

## SUMMARY AND CONCLUSIONS

Until Zajonc's (1980) seminal publication, cognitive researchers mainly focused on deliberate, consciously controlled affective judgements but ignored spontaneous, automatic affective reactions. Zajonc made clear that automatic affective reactions do occur and are an important aspect of affective behaviour. Subsequent research confirmed the existence and importance of automatic affective processing. During the past 30 years, much has been learned about the way in which automatic affective processing is automatic, the conditions under which automatic affective processing can occur, the variables that determine the outcome of automatic affective processing, the effects that it has on behaviour, the possible cognitive processes on which automatic affective processing is based, and whether cognitive processes actually underlie automatic affective processing. In fact, the literature on automatic affective processing that has accumulated over the past 30 years is so large that we could only briefly summarise some of the most important insights that have been reached.

Although a lot has been learned about automatic affective processing, many issues still need to be addressed in future research. For instance, it is still not clear whether affective processing occurs only in the presence of certain goals. Moreover, there is disagreement about whether certain stimuli (e.g., those with highly accessible attitudes) are more likely to evoke automatic affective reactions than other stimuli. Only a very limited number of studies has examined whether there are interindividual differences in the propensity to show automatic affective reactions. Although we know that automatic affective reactions can result from both direct and indirect experiences with stimuli, it still needs to be examined whether the source of an automatic affective reaction determines its properties (e.g., the way in which it is automatic). More research is also needed on how automatic affective reactions impact on behaviour. Measures of automatic affective reactions need to be perfected. Existing models of automatic affective reactions are relatively unsophisticated. They incorporate ideas about the cognitive processes and representations that could produce these reactions but give few details about the way in which affective reactions can be automatic or about how direct and indirect experiences can shape these reactions. Finally, too few studies have directly examined the possibility that affective reactions can occur prior to or in the absence of cognitive processing. Despite these remaining issues of dispute, there is general agreement about the importance of automatic affective processing as a determinant of human behaviour. We are therefore confident that future research will continue to shed new light on this important phenomenon.

## REFERENCES

Abrams, R. L., Klinger, M. R., & Greenwald, A. G. (2002). Subliminal words activate semantic categories (not automated motor responses). *Psychonomic Bulletin and Review, 9*, 100–106.

Baars, B. J. (1981). Cognitive versus inference. *American Psychologist, 36*, 223–224.

Bargh, J. A. (1992). The ecology of automaticity. Toward establishing the conditions needed to produce automatic processing effects. *American Journal of Psychology, 105*, 181–199.

Bargh, J. A., Chaiken, S., Govender, R., & Pratto, F. (1992). The generality of the attitude activation effect. *Journal of Personality and Social Psychology, 62*, 893–912.

Bargh, J. A., Chaiken, S., Raymond, P., & Hymes, C. (1996). The automatic evaluation effect: Unconditional automatic activation with a pronunciation task. *Journal of Experimental Social Psychology, 32*, 104–128.

Bargh, J. A., & Chartrand, T. L. (1999). The unbearable automaticity of being. *American Psychologist, 54*, 462–479.

Birnbaum, M. H. (1981). Thinking and feeling: A sceptical review. *American Psychologist, 36*, 99–101.

Blair, I. V. (2002). The malleability of automatic stereotypes and prejudice. *Personality and Social Psychology Review, 6*, 242–261.

Bonanno, G. A., & Stillings, N. A. (1986). Preference, familiarity, and recognition after repeated brief exposures to random geometric shapes. *American Journal of Psychology, 99*, 403–415.

Bornstein, R. F. (1989). Exposure and affect: Overview and meta-analysis of research 1968–1987. *Psychological Bulletin, 106*, 265–289.

Bornstein, R. F., & D'Agostino, P. R. (1992). Stimulus recognition and the mere exposure effect. *Journal of Personality and Social Psychology, 63*, 545–552.

Bower, G. H. (1981). Mood and memory. *American Psychologist, 36*, 129–148.

Chartrand, T. L., van Baaren, R., & Bargh, J. A. (2006). Linking automatic evaluation to mood and information processing style: Consequences for experienced affect, information processing, and stereotyping. *Journal of Experimental Psychology: General, 135*, 70–77.

Chen, M., & Bargh, J. A. (1999). Consequences of automatic evaluation: Immediate behavioral predispositions to approach or avoid the stimulus. *Personality and Social Psychology Bulletin, 25*, 215–224.

Collins, A. M., & Quinlan, M. R. (1972). How to make a language user. In E. Tulving & W. Donaldson (Eds.), *Organisation of memory* (pp. 310–351). New York: Academic Press.

Conrey, F. R., & Smith, E. R. (2007). Attitude representation: Attitudes as patterns in a distributed connectionist representational system. *Social Cognition, 25*, 718–735.

De Houwer, J. (in press). A review of the procedural knowledge about and mental process models of evaluative conditioning. In T. Schachtman & Steve Reilly (Eds.), *Applications of learning and conditioning.* Oxford, UK: Oxford University Press.

De Houwer, J., Hermans, D., & Eelen, P. (1998). Affective and identity priming with episodically associated stimuli. *Cognition and Emotion, 12*, 145–169.

De Houwer, J., Teige-Mocigemba, S., Spruyt, A., & Moors, A. (2009). Implicit measures: A normative analysis and review. *Psychological Bulletin, 135*, 347–368.

De Houwer, J., Thomas, S., & Baeyens, F. (2001). Associative learning of likes and dislikes: A review of 25 years of research on human evaluative conditioning. *Psychological Bulletin, 127*, 853–869.

Dijksterhuis, A., & Aarts, H. (2003). On wildebeests and humans: The preferential detection of negative stimuli. *Psychological Science, 14*, 14–18.

Draine, S. C., & Greenwald, A. G. (1998). Replicable unconscious semantic priming. *Journal of Experimental Psychology: General, 127*, 286–303.

Duncan, S., & Feldman Barrett, L. (2007). Affect is a form of cognition: A neurobiological analysis. *Cognition and Emotion, 21*, 1184–1211.

Dunn, J. C., & Kirsner, K. (2003). What can we infer from double dissociations? *Cortex, 39*, 1–7.

Eder, A. B., Hommel, B., & De Houwer, J. (2007). How distinctive is affective processing? On the implications of using cognitive paradigms to study affect and emotion. *Cognition and Emotion, 21*, 1137–1154.

Eder, A. B., & Rothermund, K. (2008). When do motor behaviors (mis)match affective stimuli? An evaluative coding view of approach and avoidance reactions. *Journal of Experimental Psychology: General, 137*, 262–281.

Eder, A. B., & Rothermund, K. (in press). Automatic influence of arousal information on evaluative processing: Valence–arousal interactions in an affective Simon task. *Cognition and Emotion.*

Fazio, R. H. (1986). How do attitudes guide behavior? In R. M. Sorrentino & E. T. Higgins (Eds.), *Handbook of motivation and cognition* (Vol. 1, pp. 204–243). New York: Guilford Press.

Fazio, R. H. (2007). Attitudes as object-evaluation associations of varying strength. *Social Cognition, 25*, 603–637.

Fazio, R. H., Jackson, J. R., Dunton, B. C., & Williams, C. J. (1995). Variability in automatic activation as an unobtrusive measure of racial attitudes: A bona fide pipeline? *Journal of Personality and Social Psychology, 69*, 1013–1027.

Fazio, R. H., & Olson, M. A. (2003). Implicit measures in social cognition research: Their meaning and use. *Annual Review of Psychology, 54*, 297–327.

Fazio, R. H., Sanbonmatsu, D. M., Powell, M. C., & Kardes, F. R. (1986). On the automatic activation of attitudes. *Journal of Personality and Social Psychology*, *50*, 229–238.

Ferguson, M. J., & Bargh, J. A. (2004). Liking is for doing: The effects of goal pursuit on automatic evaluation. *Journal of Personality and Social Psychology*, *87*, 557–572.

Fockenberg, D., Koole, S. L., & Semin, G. R. (2006). Backward affective priming: Even when the prime is late, people still evaluate. *Journal of Experimental Social Psychology*, *42*, 799–806.

Gawronski, B., & Bodenhausen, G. V. (2006). Associative and propositional processes in evaluation: An integrative review of implicit and explicit attitude change. *Psychological Bulletin*, *132*, 692–731.

Greenberg, L. S., & Safran, J. D. (1984). Integrating affect and cognition: A perspective on the process of therapeutic change. *Cognitive Therapy and Research*, *8*, 559–578.

Gregg, A. P., Seibt, B., & Banaji, M. R. (2006). Easier done than undone: Asymmetry in the malleability of implicit preferences. *Journal of Personality and Social Psychology*, *90*, 1–20.

Hassan, A. M., & Ward, P. S. (1991). On the primacy of the brain. *Current Psychology: Research and Reviews*, *10*, 103–111.

Hermans, D., Baeyens, F., & Eelen, P. (2003a). On the acquisition and activation of evaluative information in memory: The study of evaluative learning. In J. Musch & K. C. Klauer (Eds.), *The psychology of evaluation: Affective processes in cognition and emotion* (pp. 139–168). Mahwah, NJ: Lawrence Erlbaum Associates, Inc.

Hermans, D., Crombez, G., & Eelen, P. (2000). Automatic attitude activation and efficiency: The fourth horseman of automaticity. *Psychologica Belgica*, *40*, 3–22.

Hermans, D., De Houwer, J., & Eelen, P. (1994). The affective priming effect: Automatic activation of evaluative information in memory. *Cognition and Emotion*, *8*, 515–533.

Hermans, D., De Houwer, J., & Eelen, P. (2001). A time course analysis of the affective priming effect. *Cognition and Emotion*, *15*, 143–165.

Hermans, D., Spruyt, A., De Houwer, J., & Eelen, P. (2003b). Affective priming with subliminally presented pictures. *Canadian Journal of Experimental Psychology*, *57*, 97–114.

Hintzman, D. L. (1986). Schema abstraction in a multiple-trace memory model. *Psychological Review*, *93*, 328–338.

Hintzman, D. L., & Curran, T. (1994). Retrieval dynamics of recognition and frequency judgements: Evidence for separate processes of familiarity and recall. *Journal of Memory and Language*, *33*, 1–18.

Kitayama, S., & Howard, S. (1994). Affective regulation of perception and comprehension: Amplification and semantic priming. In P. M. Niedenthal & S. Kitayama (Eds.), *The heart's eye: Emotional influences in perception and attention* (pp. 41–65). San Diego, CA: Academic Press.

Klauer, K. C. (2008). Spontaneous evaluations. In F. Strack & J. Förster (Eds.), *Social cognition: The basis of human interaction* (pp. 199–217). New York: Psychology Press.

Klauer, K. C., Eder, A. B., Greenwald, A. G., & Abrams, R. L. (2007). Priming of semantic classifications by novel subliminal prime words. *Consciousness and Cognition, 16*, 63–83.

Klauer, K. C., & Musch, J. (2001). Does sunshine prime loyal? Affective priming in the naming task. *Quarterly Journal of Experimental Psychology, 54A*, 727–751.

Klauer, K. C., & Musch, J. (2002). Goal-dependent and goal-independent effects of irrelevant evaluations. *Personality and Social Psychology Bulletin, 28*, 802–814.

Klauer, K. C., Rossnagel, R., & Musch, J. (1997). List–context effects in evaluative priming. *Journal of Experimental Psychology: Learning, Memory, and Cognition, 23*, 246–255.

Klauer, K. C., & Teige-Mocigemba, S. (2007). Controllability and resource dependence in automatic evaluation. *Journal of Experimental Social Psychology, 43*, 648–655.

Kleinginna, P. R., Jr., & Kleinginna, A. M. (1985). Cognition and affect: A reply to Lazarus and Zajonc. *American Psychologist, 40*, 470–471.

Krieglmeyer, R., Deutsch, R., De Houwer, J., & De Raedt, R. (in press). Being moved: Valence activates approach-avoidance behavior independent of evaluation and approach-avoidance intentions. *Psychological Science*.

Kunst-Wilson, W. R., & Zajonc, R. B. (1980). Affective discrimination of stimuli that cannot be recognized. *Science, 207*, 557–558.

Lazarus, R. S. (1981). A cognitivist's reply to Zajonc on emotion and cognition. *American Psychologist, 36*, 222–223.

Lazarus, R. S. (1982). Thoughts on the relations between emotion and cognition. *American Psychologist, 37*, 1019–1024.

Lazarus, R. S. (1984). On the primacy of cognition. *American Psychologist, 39*, 124–129.

Lazarus, R. S., Averill, J. R., & Optin, E. M. (1970). Towards a cognitive theory of emotion. In M. B. Arnold (Ed.), *Feeling and emotion* (pp. 207–232). New York: Academic Press.

LeDoux, J. E. (1990). Information flow from sensation to emotion: Plasticity in the neural computation of stimulus value. In M. Gabriel & J. Moore (Eds.), *Learning and computational neuroscience: Foundations of adaptive networks* (pp. 3–51). Cambridge, MA: MIT Press.

Leventhal, H., & Scherer, K. (1987). The relationship of emotion to cognition: A functional approach to a semantic controversy. *Cognition and Emotion, 1*, 3–28.

Logan, G. D. (1985). Skill and automaticity: Relations, implications, and future directions. *Canadian Journal of Psychology, 39*, 367–386.

Logan, G. D. (1989). Automaticity and cognitive control. In J. S. Uleman & J. A. Bargh (Eds.), *Unintended thought: Limits of awareness, intention, and control* (pp. 52–74). New York: Guilford Press.

Maier, M. A., Berner, M. P., & Pekrun, R. (2003). Directionality of affective priming: Effects of trait anxiety and activation level. *Experimental Psychology, 50*, 116–123.

Mandler, G. (1975). *Mind and emotion*. New York: Wiley.

Mandler, G. (1980). Recognizing: The judgement of previous occurrence. *Psychological Review, 87*, 252–271.

Mandler, G., Nakamura, Y., & Van Zandt, B. J. (1987). Non-specific effects of exposure on stimuli that cannot be recognized. *Journal of Experimental Psychology: Learning, Memory, and Cognition, 13*, 646–648.

Marcel, A. J. (1983a). Conscious and unconscious perception: Experiments on visual masking and word recognition. *Cognitive Psychology, 15,* 197–237.

Marcel, A. J. (1983b). Conscious and unconscious perception: An approach to the relation between phenomenal experience and perceptual processes. *Cognitive Psychology, 15,* 238–300.

McClelland, J. L., & Rumelhart, D. E. (1986). *Parallel distributed processing: Explorations in the microstructure of cognition* (Vol. II). Cambridge, MA: MIT Press.

Medin, D. L., & Schaffer, M. M. (1978). Context theory of classification learning. *Psychological Review, 85,* 207–238.

Mellers, B. (1981). Feeling more than thinking. *American Psychologist, 36,* 802–803.

Merckelbach, H., & Jansen, A. (1986). Emotie, cognitie en het ontstaan van fobieën [Emotions, cognition, and the origins of phobia]. *Gedragstherapie, 19,* 145–160.

Moors, A. (2007). Can cognitive methods be used to study the unique aspect of emotion: An appraisal theorist's answer. *Cognition and Emotion, 21,* 1238–1269.

Moors, A., & De Houwer, J. (2001). Automatic appraisal of motivational valence: Motivational affective priming and Simon effects. *Cognition and Emotion, 15,* 749–766.

Moors, A., & De Houwer, J. (2006). Automaticity: A conceptual and theoretical analysis. *Psychological Bulletin, 132,* 297–326.

Murphy, S. T., Monahan, J. L., & Zajonc, R. B. (1995). Additivity of nonconscious affect: Combined effects of priming and exposure. *Journal of Personality and Social Psychology, 69,* 589–602.

Murphy, S. T., & Zajonc, R. B. (1993). Affect, cognition, and awareness: Affective priming with suboptimal and optimal stimulus. *Journal of Personality and Social Psychology, 64,* 723–739.

Niedenthal, P. M., Barsalou, L., Winkielman, P., Krauth-Gruber, S., & Ric, F. (2005). Embodiment in attitudes, social perception, and emotion. *Personality and Social Psychology Review, 9,* 184–211.

Niedenthal, P., & Halberstadt, J. B. (1995). The acquisition and structure of emotional response categories. *The Psychology of Learning and Motivation, 33,* 23–64.

Niedenthal, P., Winkielman, P., Mondillon, L., & Vermeulen, N. (2009). Embodiment of emotion concepts. *Journal of Personality and Social Psychology, 96,* 1120–1136.

Nosofsky, R. M., & Palmeri, T. J. (1997). An exemplar-based random walk model of speeded classification. *Psychological Review, 104,* 266–300.

Öhman, A. (1987). The psychophysiology of emotion: An evolutionary-cognitive perspective. *Advances in Psychophysiology, 2,* 79–127.

Olson, M. A., & Fazio, R. H. (2002). Implicit acquisition and manifestation of classically conditioned attitudes. *Social Cognition, 20,* 89–104.

O'Malley, M. (1981). Feeling without thinking? Reply to Zajonc. *The Journal of Psychology, 108,* 11–15.

Parrot, W. G., & Sabini, J. (1989). On the "emotional" qualities of certain types of cognition: A reply to arguments for the independence of cognition and affect. *Cognitive Therapy and Research, 13,* 49–65.

Petty, R. E., Briñol, P., & DeMarree, K. G. (2007). The meta-cognitive model (MCM) of attitudes: Implications for attitude measurement, change, and strength. *Social Cognition, 25,* 657–686.

Plutchik, R. (1985). On emotion: The chicken-and-egg problem revisited. *Motivation and Emotion, 9,* 197–200.

Posner, M. I., & Snyder, C. R. R. (1975). Attention and cognitive control. In R. L. Solso (Ed.), *Information processing and cognition: The Loyola symposium* (pp. 55–85). Hillsdale, NJ: Lawrence Erlbaum Associates, Inc.

Rachman, S. (1981). The primacy of affect: Some theoretical implications. *Behaviour Research and Therapy, 19,* 279–290.

Reber, R., Winkielman, P., & Schwarz, N. (1998). Effects of perceptual fluency on affective judgments. *Psychological Science, 9,* 45–48.

Rotteveel, M., & Phaf, R. H. (2007). Mere exposure in reverse: Mood and motion modulate memory bias. *Cognition and Emotion, 21,* 1323–1346.

Schwarz, N. (2007). Attitude construction: Evaluation in context. *Social Cognition, 25,* 638–656.

Seibt, B., Häfner, M., & Deutsch, R. (2007). Prepared to eat: How immediate affective and motivational responses to food cues are influenced by food deprivation. *European Journal of Social Psychology, 37,* 359–379.

Sherer, K. R. (1993). Neuroscience projections to current debates in emotion psychology. *Cognition and Emotion, 7,* 1–42.

Shiffrin, R. M., & Schneider, W. (1977). Controlled and automatic human information processing: II. Perceptual learning, automatic attending, and a general theory. *Psychological Review, 84,* 127–190.

Solarz, A. K. (1960). Latency of instrumental responses as a function of compatibility with the meaning of eliciting verbal signs. *Journal of Experimental Psychology, 59,* 239–245.

Spruyt, A., De Houwer, J., & Hermans, D. (2009a). Modulation of semantic priming by feature-specific attention allocation. *Journal of Memory and Language, 61,* 37–54.

Spruyt, A., De Houwer, J., Hermans, D., & Eelen, P. (2007). Affective priming of non-affective semantic categorization responses. *Experimental Psychology, 54,* 44–53.

Spruyt, A., De Houwer, J., Hermans, D., Everaert, T., & Moors, A. (2009b). *Salience effects in automatic affective and nonaffective stimulus processing.* Manuscript in preparation.

Spruyt, A., Hermans, D., De Houwer, J., & Eelen, P. (2002). On the nature of the affective priming effect: Affective priming of naming responses. *Social Cognition, 20,* 225–254.

Storbeck, J., & Clore, G. L. (2007). On the interdependence of cognition and emotion. *Cognition and Emotion, 21,* 1212–1237.

Tsal, Y. (1985). On the relationship between cognitive and affective processes: A critique of Zajonc and Markus. *Journal of Consumer Research, 12,* 358–362.

Vermeulen, N., Luminet, O., & Corneille, O. (2006). Alexithymia and the automatic processing of affective information: Evidence from the Affective Priming Paradigm. *Cognition and Emotion, 20,* 64–91.

Vogt, J., De Houwer, J., Koster, E. H. W., Van Damme, S., & Crombez, G. (2008). Allocation of spatial attention to emotional stimuli depends upon arousal and not valence. *Emotion, 8,* 880–885.

Watts, F. N. (1983). Affective cognition: A sequel to Zajonc and Rachman. *Behaviour Research and Therapy, 21*, 89–90.

Williams, J., Watts, F., MacLeod, C., & Mathews, A. (1988). *Cognitive psychology and emotional disorders.* Chichester, UK: Wiley.

Wilson, T. D., Lindsey, S., & Schooler, T. Y. (2000). A model of dual attitudes. *Psychological Review, 107*, 101–126.

Wittenbrink, B., Judd, C. M., & Park, B. (2001). Spontaneous prejudice in context: Variability in automatically activated attitudes. *Journal of Personality and Social Psychology, 81*, 815–827.

Zajonc, R. B. (1968). Attitudinal effects of mere exposure. *Journal of Personality and Social Psychology: Monograph, 9*(1, Part 2), 1–28.

Zajonc, R. B. (1980). Feeling and thinking. Preferences need no inferences. *American Psychologist, 35*, 151–175.

Zajonc, R. B. (1981). A one-factor mind about mind and emotion. *American Psychologist, 36*, 102–103.

Zajonc, R. B. (1984). On the primacy of affect. *American Psychologist, 39*, 117–123.

Zajonc, R B. (2000). Feeling and thinking: Closing the debate over the independence of affect. In J. P. Forgas (Ed.), *Feeling and thinking: The role of affect in social cognition* (pp. 31–58). Cambridge, UK: Cambridge University Press.

Zajonc, R. B., & Markus, H. (1982). Affective and cognitive factors in preferences. *Journal of Consumer Research, 9*, 123–131.

Zajonc, R. B., & Markus, H. (1984). Affect and cognition: The hard interface. In C. E. Izard, J. Kagan, & R. B. Zajonc (Eds.), *Emotions, cognition, and behavior* (pp. 73–102). Cambridge, UK: Cambridge University Press.

Zajonc, R. B., & Markus, H. (1985). Must all affect be mediated by cognition? *Journal of Consumer Research, 12*, 363–364.

Zajonc, R. B., Pietromonaco, P., & Bargh, J. (1982). Independence and interaction of affect and cognition. In M. S. Clark & S. T. Fiske (Eds.), *Affect and cognition* (pp. 211–227). Hillsdale, NJ: Lawrence Erlbaum Associates, Inc.

Correspondence should be addressed to: Jan De Houwer, Ghent University, Henri Dunantlaan 2, B-9000 Ghent, Belgium. E-mail: Jan.DeHouwer@UGent.be

Preparation of this chapter was supported by GOA Grant BOF/GOA2006/001 and Methusalem Grant BOF09/01M00209 of Ghent University to JDH.

We thank Andreas Eder and Adriaan Spruyt for comments on an earlier draft of this chapter.

# 3 The perception and categorisation of emotional stimuli: A review

Tobias Brosch
*University of Geneva, Geneva, Switzerland*

Gilles Pourtois
*University of Geneva, Geneva, Switzerland, and Ghent University, Ghent, Belgium*

David Sander
*University of Geneva, Geneva, Switzerland*

## INTRODUCTION

In order to successfully move about in the world and respond to its permanent challenges, we have to rapidly make sense of our multifarious and fast-changing environment. To do so, we create an internal mental representation of the stimuli that are immediately present in our surroundings. Any given external object in the environment, the *distal stimulus* (e.g., a stone) is not processed as such, but is represented in the organism as a physical stimulation pattern on the senses, the *proximal stimulus* (e.g., the pattern of light on the retina reflected by the stone). Perception is the transformation of the proximal stimulus into a *percept*, the accessible, subjective, reportable experience that takes the form of an activation of a certain category in the mind (e.g., the accessible visual experience of the stone). How we perceive our environment is thus profoundly shaped by categorisation. When we categorise a stimulus, we group certain objects or concepts as equivalent or analogous, thereby reducing the information complexity of the external world. At the same time, a lot of information about the stimulus is inferred due to its association with a category. The act of categorisation is therefore critical to cognition (see Harnad, 2005) and allows us to give meaning to the world.

Sometimes we are confronted with classes of stimuli that have more direct relevance for our well-being and survival than others. For instance, some stimuli may signal danger or threat, such as predators or enemies, whereas other stimuli signal chances for growing and expansion, such as potential mates or food sources. Such stimuli require rapid adaptive responses, such as evading the threat or approaching the positive stimulus. One might expect that, given the high importance of such "emotional" stimuli for the organism, the perceptual processing of these stimuli should be prioritised to allow for a rapid appraisal of the situation and consequently the rapid preparation of an appropriate behavioural response. In line with this, many everyday examples suggest that the perception of emotional stimuli is somewhat special, or heightened, relative to non-emotional stimuli. Smiling people, cute babies, erotic scenes, but also poisonous snakes or scenes of war and mutilations seem to catch one's eye more easily than emotionally "neutral" stimuli. Moreover, as the process of categorisation is crucial for the organisation of perception, one may furthermore expect that extremely relevant stimuli are categorised into special emotion categories, which may differ in some respects from other categories. In line with this, a lot of empirical evidence illustrates how people make use of such special categories to guide their perception of the environment. For example, it has been shown that people are able to rapidly and accurately classify emotional expressions into emotional categories, even when the sender has a cultural background different from their own.

In this paper, we will examine the special role of emotional stimuli in perception and categorisation. We will first discuss some fundamental aspects of perception in general, with an emphasis on the central cognitive process of categorisation. By introducing general principles of perception and categorisation, we will be able to investigate whether similar principles apply to the perception and categorisation of emotional and neutral stimuli, or if different mechanisms may be involved. We will then tackle the question "What is an emotional stimulus?" taking into account various definitions from different theories of emotion, and review different suggestions of how the emotional categories we use to classify and label highly relevant stimuli are determined, learned, and eventually used to guide our perception. Afterwards, we will illustrate the preferential perception of emotional stimuli by reviewing some of the key findings from the empirical literature. We will address two main lines of research, (i) research focusing on *qualitative* effects of emotional stimuli, i.e., research addressing the question of how people are able to categorise different stimuli into emotional categories, and (ii) research focusing on *quantitative* effects of emotional stimuli, i.e., research addressing the question of how the emotionality of a stimulus can modulate and sometimes even transform perception, independent of whether people are asked to (consciously) categorise them. We will conclude with some reflections on how research on the perception of emotional stimuli can contribute to some current debates in psychology, namely (i) about the role of bottom-up vs. top-down factors in emotional processing and experience, and (ii) about the nature of the relationship between cognition and emotion.

A review on a topic as large as "perception and categorisation of emotional stimuli" necessarily has to be selective. For example, we will restrict ourselves to research using relatively simple stimuli, such as emotional words, pictures of emotional scenes, or emotional expressions conveyed by face, body, or voice. We will not survey more complex emotional behaviours, behaviour descriptions or emotional events and their effect on people's inferences of emotions, traits, competences, or status and power characteristics. There is a large literature in social and clinical psychology on these topics (see, e.g., Augoustinos, Walker, & Donaghue, 2006, for a review). Furthermore, perception does not always involve a conscious subjective experience and we do not intend to reduce categorisation to conscious experience. Research on "unconscious perception" shows that under certain conditions such as degraded stimulus input or lapse of attention or awareness, stimuli can nonetheless be categorised to some extent, be partly processed and eventually have an impact on behaviour without being consciously experienced (Merikle & Daneman, 1998; Winkielman, Berridge, & Wilbarger, 2005; Zajonc, 1980). Here, however, we focus on the perception of emotional stimuli, when the categorised percept of these stimuli presumably enters awareness.

## PERCEPTION AS A FUNDAMENTAL CATEGORISATION PROCESS

### What is categorisation?

How do we perceive and categorise objects? Which fundamental psychological mechanisms underlie this ability? These questions have been central to psychology for many decades (see Cohen & Lefebvre, 2005; Palmeri & Gauthier, 2004, for reviews). In fact, perception and object recognition sometimes are considered the crucial issues that research on human cognition has to explain (Kourtzi & DiCarlo, 2006), as a deeper insight into these processes will also substantially further the understanding of downstream higher-order cognitive processes such as memory, language, or consciousness. Many scholars have stressed that perception profoundly depends on the process of top-down categorisation (Barrett, 2006b; Davidoff, 2001; Palmeri & Gauthier, 2004; Rosch, 1975; Rosch, Mervis, Gray, Johnson, & Boyes-Braem, 1976). How we perceive our environment is thus shaped by categorisation processes that guide and constrain the organisation of incoming stimulus information and thus make a conscious representation and identification of this information possible. This principle is supposed to hold for all kinds of categories, no matter whether the perceived content is colour, certain objects, faces, facial expressions of emotion, emotional feeling or any other attribute (Barrett, 2006b; Cohen & Lefebvre, 2005; Davidoff, 2001).

During categorisation, a continuously changing stimulus is identified against discrete and pre-existing categories or conceptual boundaries. This can be experienced, for example, when we are watching a rainbow. Even though a rainbow is composed of a continuous range of varying wavelengths, we perceive chunks of colours rather than a gradual continuum of changing colours. Due to the influence of top-down information about colour categories, the linear physical changes of the distal and proximal stimuli have non-linear effects on the percept.

Categorisation allows us to structure stimuli by grouping or classifying them according to certain principles, such as perceptual similarities (Rosch, 1978), semantic rules or theories (Murphy & Medin, 1985), implications for goal states (Barsalou, 1983) or evoked emotional responses (Niedenthal, Halberstadt, & Innes-Ker, 1999). By categorising a stimulus we give meaning to it, as categorisation allows us to make inferences, analogies, and predictions about a stimulus and to communicate about the stimulus with people who share our concepts (Niedenthal et al., 1999).

Object categorisation occurs very rapidly (Thorpe, Fize, & Marlot, 1996). An efficient categorisation process allows us to constrain, guide and summarise the processing of stimuli encountered in the environment with minimal cognitive effort. When a stimulus is categorised, a large amount of relevant information related to the category is activated and made available, whereas irrelevant distinctions within categories are omitted for the sake of cognitive economy (McClelland & Rumelhart, 1985; Rosch, 1978; Rosch et al., 1976). Ultimately, categorisation operates as a strong filter, which drastically reduces the information content available in the external world by grouping certain objects as equivalent. Categorisation furthermore facilitates rapid object discrimination. It is easier to discriminate two colours of different shades when they cross colour category boundaries than when they are within the same category, even though the differences in wavelength are identical for the two pairs (Bornstein & Korda, 1984). Similar results have been obtained, e.g., for the differentiation of speech phonemes (Liberman, Harris, Hoffman, & Griffith, 1957) and the discrimination of familiar faces (Beale & Keil, 1995). This effect, basically enhancing perceived between-category differences and reducing perceived within-category differences, was coined the *categorical perception effect* (Harnad, 1987).

## How are categories determined?

How exactly categories and their boundaries are determined is a matter of debate. Even for a rather simple domain such as colour categories, the theoretical positions that have been advanced span all the space between *universalistic* (categories are determined by perceptual factors based on the properties of colour-coding neurons; Berlin & Kay, 1969) and *relativistic* views (categories are arbitrarily set based on language and cultural conventions about concepts of colour; Whorf, 1956). Strong support for the universalistic view came from evidence showing that the Dani, a remote branch of a hunter-gatherer tribe, showed the same cognitive organisation of colour as speakers of English, even though they only used two basic terms for the whole range of visible colours (Rosch Heider, 1972). This was interpreted as showing that a certain categorical organisation of colours may be found universally in humans and may be predetermined genetically. On the other hand, results showing that the possession of certain linguistic colour terms influences the organisation of categories suggested that it is mostly language and semantic concepts that shape the organisation of incoming stimulus information (Roberson, Davies, & Davidoff, 2000). In this view, the placement of the boundaries between categories is not considered to be based on pre-existing universals, but rather on conventions within a cultural group.

As will be outlined in the next section, a similar debate exists for emotional categories (see also Boster, 2005). Theoretical suggestions on how emotional categories are defined go from the universalistic perspective that there are biologically based universal emotion categories, the "basic emotions"[1] (Ekman, 1992; Izard, 2007; Panksepp, 1998), to the notion that multicomponent patterns of emotional responses that occur with a relatively high frequency are categorised into "modal emotions" (Scherer, 1994b), and finally to the constructivist perspective that emotional experience is based on the categorisation of a raw affective quality into emotional categories, which are considered to be man-made concepts (Barrett, 2006a).

## EMOTIONAL CATEGORIES

### What is an emotional stimulus?

When comparing the role of emotional and non-emotional stimuli in perception, an important issue that needs to be tackled is the definition of "emotional stimulus": Why is a stimulus perceived or categorised as "emotional" at all? One way to address this question is to find a definition based on functional considerations. Following this line, one can begin by asking why "emotional stimuli"—which constitute a group of rather heterogeneous stimuli—should be categorised together and treated in a preferential manner by the organism. To this end, we will briefly review how different influential psychological theories of emotion provide important clues to what actually renders a stimulus emotional. One should keep in mind that, generally, theories of emotion are concerned with the

---

1 In this context, one finds frequent analogies between perceptual and emotional categories. For example, according to Izard (2007), "it is possible to argue by analogy that the capacity to discriminate among basic-emotion feeling states, like discriminating among basic tastes, is innate and invariant across the lifespan" and "the data relating to the underlying neural and behavioral processes suggest that the emergence of discriminable basic emotion feelings is analogous to that for basic tastes" (see Sander, 2008).

elicitation of emotional responses (see also Moors, 2009), but less with the definition of "emotional stimulus" or the processes involved in the perception of such stimuli. However, these issues are highly intertwined, as, very often, the perception of a stimulus as "emotional" will subsequently elicit an emotional response. Thus, it should be possible to draw some conclusions about the conditions under which a stimulus is perceived as "emotional" (and another one is not) based on the different theoretical approaches. In addition to the distinction between emotional and non-emotional stimuli, different theoretical views furthermore allow us to gain insight on the actual cognitive processes involved in the perception and categorisation of emotional stimuli. In reviewing the different theoretical approaches, we will first outline the main points of agreement and disagreement between the theories. Afterwards, we will discuss some of the issues about which the different approaches disagree in the light of the empirical evidence on the perception and categorisation of emotional stimuli.

Most emotion theories agree that emotional stimuli represent a special type of stimulus as they possess high relevance for the survival and well-being of the observer. For instance, some stimuli may signal threats, such as predators or enemies, whereas other stimuli signal chances for growing and expansion, such as potential mates or food sources. Such stimuli require rapid responses, like evading the threat or approaching the positive stimulus. Emotional responses are adaptive responses to an eliciting stimulus, including action tendencies, bodily responses, behavioural responses and a change in subjective feeling. They prepare the organism for action, while allowing for some flexibility in terms of the response, as an emotional stimulus is not associated reflex-like with a specific response, but an emotion primes an arsenal of potential adaptive responses (Frijda, 2007; Scherer, 1994a). In the context of adaptive responding, it appears furthermore functional to assume that the perceptual processing of emotional stimuli is prioritised to allow for a more rapid computation and situation analysis.

Whereas most theories of emotion agree that emotions serve to organise adaptive responses to stimuli that are important for the survival and well-being of the organism, different theories disagree with regards to the mechanisms underlying this adaptive function.

*Basic emotion theories* assume a number of distinct basic emotions, including, e.g., anger, fear, sadness, happiness, disgust or surprise. In this tradition, the term "basic" is used to express three postulates (Ekman, 1992): First, it conveys the notion that "there are a number of separate emotions which differ from one another in important ways", second, it indicates that "evolution played an important role in shaping both the unique and the common features which these emotions display as well as their current function", finally, the term refers to the notion that the existence of non-basic emotions can be explained by combinations of the basic emotions. Basic emotions are defined as affect programmes that are triggered by appropriate eliciting events to produce emotion-specific response patterns such as prototypical facial expressions and physiological reactions (Ekman, 1992), driven by specific neural response systems (Panksepp, 1998). According to basic emotion theories, perceptual processing of emotional stimuli is assumed to be essentially organised in a categorical manner, with innate categories being universally found in humans. Some theorists suggest a special role for the basic emotion of fear (Öhman & Mineka, 2001). Due to evolutionary reasons, fear/threat-related stimuli such as angry facial expressions, snakes or spiders are thought to be attended to, perceived, recognised, remembered and associated with adaptive behavioural output faster or more readily than any other emotional stimulus.

*Appraisal theories of emotion* suggest that emotional processes are elicited as the individual continuously appraises objects, behaviours, events and situations with respect to their relevance for his/her needs, goals, values, and general well-being (Ellsworth & Scherer, 2003). Emotions are elicited and differentiated on the basis of the subjective evaluation of a stimulus or event on a set of standard criteria or objectives such as novelty, intrinsic pleasantness, goal conduciveness, and normative significance, as well as the coping potential of the organism. Appraisal is subjective and thus a function of the individual and the specific situation/context, therefore allowing for differences between, e.g., species, age groups, personal dispositions, and cultural contexts. The outcome of the appraisals of these different criteria is predicted to directly drive response patterning of physiological reactions, motor expression, and action preparation (Scherer, 2001). With regards to emotion categories, it has been suggested that the subjective experience of the response patterning ("qualia") is categorised into "modal emotions" (Scherer, 1994b), reflecting the relatively frequent occurrence of some patterns of responses that are associated with core concerns or core relational themes (Smith & Kirby, 2009; Smith & Lazarus, 1990).

*Dimensional theories of emotion* emphasise the role of a few key dimensions, usually valence and arousal, in the organisation and categorisation of emotional stimuli. The dimensional approach allows us to distinguish between negative and positive emotions of different intensities, which reflects two basic motivational systems, the appetitive and the aversive systems that underlie approach and withdrawal behaviour, respectively (Davidson & Irwin, 1999; Lang, 1995; Schneirla, 1959). According to Russell (2003), *core affect*, the primary, consciously accessible internal emotional state, consists exclusively of an integral blend of valence and arousal. The affective quality of a stimulus is the capacity of this stimulus to change core affect.

*Constructivist theories of emotion* emphasise the role of culture, language, and high-level cognition in the emergence of emotional experience.

Barrett (2006a,b) recently adapted Schachter's theory of emotion (see also Moors, 2009) to propose a *conceptual act approach* based on the core affect notion put forward by Russell (2003). According to this view, emotion categories are not natural entities, but man-made concepts. The experience of emotions is based on a process that categorises a readout of core affect into language-based emotion categories. According to this relativistic view, language provides conceptual categories, which in turn constrain the process that attributes meaning to stimuli, including emotional ones, and thus biases perception. Thus, the perception of a stimulus as emotional should depend heavily on the language context of the observer (Barrett, Lindquist, & Gendron, 2007b).

To summarise, different theories of emotion differ in the way they conceptualise how stimuli are categorised as emotional. Basic emotion theories claim that certain classes of stimuli trigger predefined affect programmes, which then elicit specific response patterns. In contrast to this rather inflexible mechanism, which is mainly based on a schema evaluation or a pattern-matching process between a stimulus and a template, appraisal theories emphasise the importance of the subjective evaluation of the stimulus according to its importance for the individual. This allows for a greater amount of flexibility and individual adjustment of person, situation and what is perceived as emotional. Dimensional theories propose a very general, economical mechanism linking stimulus processing to an evaluation that basically distinguishes between positive and negative stimuli and between stimuli leading to different degrees of activation. Finally, constructivist theories emphasise the constraining role of language context on the mapping of these dimensions into emotion categories. Thus, different theories of emotion differ with regards to how much emphasis they put on bottom-up mechanisms and top-down mechanisms determining what makes a stimulus emotional, how it is categorised and how it is perceived, with basic emotion theories arguing that it is mainly (but not always) stimulus driven bottom-up processes, appraisal theories suggesting a more flexible and dynamic mechanism taking into account the interaction of stimulus and the needs and goals of the observer, and constructivist theories mainly focusing on the constraining top-down effects of mental representations and language knowledge.

## How are emotion categories determined?

Whereas the previous section mainly focused on theoretical issues regarding the distinction between emotional and non-emotional stimuli, now we will address the related question of how our internal emotional categories, i.e., the categories we use to classify and label emotions and emotionally relevant stimuli, are determined, and to which extent these categories may be similar to or different from non-emotional categories.

Across many languages we find a large variety of categories that we use to describe our emotional experiences (e.g., "fear") or the elicitors of such experiences (e.g., "threats"). According to basic emotion theories, the basic emotions constitute innate categories, which are shaped by evolutionary pressures. However, as will be outlined in more detail in a later section of this paper, there are several lines of argumentation that go against the notion of universal or innate emotional categories.

If emotion categories like "fear" or "anger" are not innate, they may be learned, just like other categories such as "birds" or "furniture". In this context, it has been argued that the boundaries of emotion categories are not well-defined,[2] but that membership in an emotion category is based on the extent of resemblance to a prototype (prototype theory of emotion; Russell & Fehr, 1987). States elicited by a certain event or stimulus are perceived to be instances of fear, anger, or happiness to the extent that they resemble certain ideal cases. Category membership, thus, is a matter of degree rather than all-or-nothing (*internal structure*), and no sharp boundaries separate category members from non-members (*fuzzy boundaries*). Based on early theoretical work by Rosch and colleagues (1976), emotion categories (and the category "emotion") have been suggested to be hierarchically organised, with positive and negative emotions as superordinate categories, categories such as anger, fear, or happiness at the basic level, and subordinate categories such as wrath, rage, fury, annoyance (Russell & Fehr, 1987; Shaver, Schwartz, Kirson, & O'Connor, 1987).

Many prototype categories we use in daily life are created based on the correlational structure of properties that observers perceive in the world. Properties of objects do not occur randomly, but some combinations tend to co-occur frequently (such as "feathers" and "wings"), whereas some other combinations rarely occur together (such as "fur" and "wings"). Although atypical cases do exist, in general different stimuli sharing some common properties can be put into discrete categories (e.g., "birds") to simplify the organisation of the environment (Rosch, 1978; Rosch et al., 1976). Similar processes might be involved in the development of emotion categories, concepts, schemas, or scripts. An event that interrupts goal attainment might frequently be paired with a subjective experience of frustration and arousal, behavioural attempts at overcoming the blockage, and typical facial and vocal expression patterns (Hess, Philippot, & Blairy, 1998), all of which might then be integrated into a semantic network representing the *anger* concept, which guides the categorisation of emotional expressions (Russell, 1991).

---

2   In well-defined categories, category membership can be defined by one or more individually necessary and jointly sufficient features, as is the case for example for "square" or "grandfather".

In addition to categories based on the correlational structure of the environment, other categorical grouping mechanisms have been proposed. For example, it has been suggested that facial expressions of emotion are examples of *goal-derived categories*, optimised to reach the goal of emotion communication, rather than *taxonomic categories*, which help to economically describe the environment (Barsalou, 1985; Horstmann, 2002). When participants were asked to choose typical examples of facial emotion expressions out of several exemplars with different expression intensities, they chose the most extreme version (Horstmann, 2002). Thus, the facial expressions of emotion that are perceived as "most typical" are not the ones that are encountered frequently, but the ones that are most suitable to communicate a certain emotion (see also Smith, Cottrell, Gosselin, & Schyns, 2005). This suggests that the basic emotion categories may have been created to maximise communicative goal attainment.

Furthermore, the psychological concept of *core relational themes* (Smith & Kirby, 2009; Smith & Lazarus, 1990) is of particular interest with respect to its categorical function. Core relational themes are categorical conceptualisations of emotion-eliciting appraisals. Each core relational theme is specific to a given emotion and refers to a combination of a set of appraisal outputs (e.g., high importance, high undesirability and other-accountability define the core relational theme of "other-blame", which may elicit "anger"). Therefore, each core relational theme may be seen as a functional category that has the potential to elicit a specific emotion.

The subjective emotional feeling elicited by a stimulus may be a further central feature in determining category membership. Stimuli that evoke the same emotional response may thus be grouped together and treated as equivalent things, even when they are perceptually, functionally and theoretically different. When participants had to categorise triads of concepts that shared both emotional and non-emotional relations (e.g., *joke*, *speech*, and *sunbeam*), participants for whom affective information was made salient by experiencing a positive or negative mood used emotional response categories (i.e., grouped together *joke* and *sunbeam*), whereas participants in a neutral mood grouped the concepts into non-emotional categories (*joke* and *speech*), indicating that the evoked subjective emotional feeling can be a category-defining property (Niedenthal et al., 1999).

To sum up, empirical evidence and theoretical considerations indicate that emotion categories are not principally determined universally or biologically, but are learned and continuously adjusted in a flexible way. Grouping of different stimuli into an emotional category can be based on a number of different principles, reflecting the correlational structure of the environment, the optimisation of communicative goal attainment, the combination of a set of appraisal outputs, or the subjective emotional feeling elicited by a stimulus. Emotion categories thus can be considered as adaptive and flexible emotion scripts, integrating aspects of emotion elicitation (appraisal, core relational themes) and of the emotional response toward the emotional stimulus (bodily responses, motor responses, action tendencies, and subjective feeling). Some aspects of these may be relatively hard-wired (e.g., a simple response like a startle reflex), others mainly determined by culture (e.g., a more complex appraisal of norm compatibility). Together, the integrated emotion category then may guide the perception and categorisation of emotional stimuli, as will be outlined in the remainder of this paper.

## EMPIRICAL STUDIES ON THE PERCEPTION AND CATEGORISATION OF EMOTIONAL STIMULI

The theoretical considerations reviewed in the first part of this paper point to important questions that can be addressed in empirical research on how people actually perceive emotional stimuli. For example, as discussed above, a crucial prediction of basic emotion theories is the universal and presumably innate organisation of fixed emotion categories, whereas other theories emphasise the flexibility, malleability, versatility, and context-dependency of emotional processing. Thus, in the next section, we will discuss what empirical research on the perception of emotional stimuli can contribute to the question of the relative contribution of bottom-up and top-down factors in emotional processing. Furthermore, we will evaluate empirical results showing how perception actually profits from having some stimuli tagged as emotional and others not, and we will discuss how such studies can help to answer the question of what actually defines an emotional stimulus, essentially by taking into consideration what kind of emotional stimuli are prioritised in perception. To shed some light on these questions, we will discuss primarily two broad lines of research: (i) research focusing on *qualitative* effects of emotional stimuli, addressing the question of how people categorise different stimuli into emotional categories, and (ii) research focusing on *quantitative* effects of emotional stimuli, referring to how the emotionality of a stimulus may modulate and transform perception.

## Qualitative effects of emotion on perception: The categorisation of stimuli as emotional

### Is there universality in emotional categorisation?

A central tenet of basic emotion theories is the assumption that emotional stimuli, especially facial emotional expressions, are universally perceived in a categorical manner. In two very influential lines of research, Ekman (1972, 1992; Ekman & Friesen, 1975) and Izard (1971) have investigated the universality of the recognition of emotional facial expressions. In their studies, they asked participants to categorise facial displays of emotion into several basic emotion categories. For example, participants were shown a photograph of a person expressing prototypical facial configuration of fear, and then were given a number of response alternatives such as "fear", "happiness", "anger" or "disgust" to choose from. Alternatively, they were asked to freely describe the emotion they recognised in the picture without being given labels. Ekman and Izard both found that their participants were able to correctly categorise the facial expressions into a number of basic emotions. This was the case even when the receiver (the participant asked to categorise the expression) was from a different culture than the sender (the person posing for the photograph) and was in fact never exposed to the sender's culture. These results have been confirmed in a more recent meta-analysis showing that facial expressions of emotion are correctly categorised across cultures with an accuracy of 58% (Elfenbein & Ambady, 2002). Similar results have been reported for the categorisation of vocal emotional expressions. Another meta-analysis (Juslin & Laukka, 2003) showed that vocalisations of emotions are correctly categorised across cultures with largely above-chance accuracy. Other studies have furthermore demonstrated above-chance categorisation of bodily expressions of emotion (Atkinson, Dittrich, Gemmell, & Young, 2004; de Gelder, 2006). High intraindividual correlations have been observed for correct identification of different emotional signals in facial, prosodic and lexical channels. People who excel at correctly categorising facial expressions of emotion perform similarly highly using other channels, leading to the suggestion that an amodal system might be involved in perceptual identification of various emotional expressions in different communication channels (Borod et al., 2000).

People are not only able to label emotional expressions with categories, but the actual percept of emotional expression seems to be influenced by category boundaries. Just as top-down category information transforms the gradually changing continuum of wavelengths in a rainbow into the perception of chunks of different colours (categorical perception effect; Harnad, 1987), instances of emotional facial expressions that are morphed into each other along a continuum between two emotions (e.g., from happiness to fear), are perceived as belonging to discrete categories (either happiness or fear). Moreover, pairs of emotional faces that differ from each other by a given physical amount on such a continuum can be discriminated more accurately when the pairs belong to two different emotion categories than when they belong to the same category (Calder, Young, Perrett, Etcoff, & Rowland, 1996; Etcoff & Magee, 1992; Young et al., 1997). Similar evidence has been provided for a categorical perception of vocal emotion expression (Laukka, 2005). These effects illustrate that, even though the participants' task is not to assign the faces or voices to emotional categories, the incoming information on facial and vocal emotion expression seems to be automatically transformed into categories. Furthermore, these results allow some conclusions about the actual *percept* of the perceived stimuli, namely that there is a qualitative difference in how similar expressions actually appear to a perceiver depending on whether or not they belong to the same emotional category: two facial expressions that differ by an exact physical amount on a continuum between two expressions appear more distinct from each other when they cross a category boundary, but more similar when they do not cross such a boundary.

Results on the categorisation of emotional expression have provoked a great amount of debate (see, e.g., Ekman, 1994; Izard, 1994; Russell, 1994, 1995). Main criticisms stemmed from some methodological aspects of the conducted research. For example, the caricatural nature of facial expression stimuli used in the research was questioned, which mainly showed extreme versions of facial expressions, which are rarely observed in daily life (Carroll & Russell, 1997). Furthermore, people make more errors when they are not given forced-choice response alternatives, but have to respond freely. This suggests that available language-based emotion categories drive the answer in a top-down manner. A third point of criticism concerns the fact that, even though there is still above-chance accuracy when sender and receiver come from different cultures, accuracy is reliably higher when both come from the same culture (Elfenbein & Ambady, 2002; Juslin & Laukka, 2003), suggesting that emotional categories are to some extent shaped by cultural factors and language-based representations.

Thus, consistent with the predictions of basic emotion theories, it has been shown that humans are able to categorise prototypical facial, vocal and bodily expressions of emotion into discrete emotion categories with above-chance accuracy. However, consistent with theoretical approaches emphasising the role of culture- and language-based top-down factors, cultural knowledge has been shown to further improve performance on categorisation tasks, leading to the conclusion that emotional categories are no innate universals, but (at least to some extent) shaped by top-down cultural factors.

## The role of context and top-down effects in emotional categorisation

Alternative approaches to facial expression and its recognition have been developed based on dimensional theories of emotion, predicting that facial expressions are not categorised directly into specific basic categories, but convey values of valence and arousal, which are subsequently used to attribute an emotion to the face (Russell, 1997), and on appraisal theories of emotion, emphasising the link between appraisal outcomes and facial expression patterns (e.g., Scherer, 1992). According to the latter view, the facial expression of a given emotion expresses a differential sequential and cumulative response pattern based on a series of appraisal outcomes. Decoders should thus be able to recognise a facial expression of emotion from the outcomes of the pattern of cognitive appraisals that have produced the emotion. Sander, Grandjean, Kaiser, Wehrle, and Scherer (2007) tested the hypothesis that operations involved in orienting the focus of attention (e.g., gaze direction) and operations concerned with evaluation of events would interact in the decoding of facial emotions. They found that the perceived specificity and intensity of fear and anger depended on gaze direction (direct gaze for anger and averted gaze for fear; see also Adams & Kleck, 2003; Sander, Grafman, & Zalla, 2003). Using a judgement paradigm, Scherer and Grandjean (2008) had people assign pictures of facial expressions of emotions to underlying patterns of appraisal ("something unexpected has happened", "I am in a dangerous situation and I don't know how to get out of it") and to basic emotion labels ("surprise", "fear") and demonstrated similarly high success rates both for the appraisal criteria categories and the basic emotion categories.

Constructivist theories of emotion, appraisal theories and, to a lesser extent, also dimensional theories underline the importance of context in determining why and how a stimulus is perceived as emotional. Confirming the important role of context, it has been shown that the same facial expression can be interpreted as showing different emotional states (e.g., fear or anger, surprise or happiness)—and thus classified into different emotion categories—depending on the situational context that has been given to the observer (Carroll & Russell, 1996; Kim, Somerville, Johnstone, Alexander, & Whalen, 2003; Kim et al., 2004; Russell & Fehr, 1987; Wallbott & Ricci-Bitti, 1993). For example, if a participant is shown a prototypical expression of anger, together with the information that this person has just been in a frightening situation, the face will be categorised as fearful. Contextual information influences perception already at very early perceptual levels. When subjects judged a facial expression of disgust presented in an anger context, not only did they drop substantially in their categorisation accuracy (from 87% to 13% compared to a disgust context), but their early eye movements followed the visual scan path usually elicited by facial expressions of anger (Aviezer et al., 2008). Furthermore, perceptual memory encoding has been shown to be influenced by conceptual knowledge: When participants viewed ambiguous facial stimuli (morphed faces depicting a blend of two emotion categories) while category knowledge about one of the emotions was made more accessible, participants later remembered the face stimuli in line with the conceptual knowledge that was active during encoding (Halberstadt & Niedenthal, 2001). These results highlight the role of contextual information in the perceptual categorisation of emotional stimuli.

To summarise, research has shown that when people are asked to classify expressions of emotion, they are able to do so with high accuracy. Similarly good performance is observed whether the classification is based on basic emotion categories (Elfenbein & Ambady, 2002), a dimensional system (Bradley & Lang, 1994; Russell & Fehr, 1987), or appraisal criteria (Scherer & Grandjean, 2008). Thus, even though results from categorisation or classification tasks are frequently taken as main evidence supporting basic emotion theory, they seem not to be unequivocally in favour of any theoretical approach, but rather compatible with several of them.

However, what can be concluded from the empirical results reviewed here is that contextual top-down effects are extremely important for the categorisation of a stimulus as emotional. Contextual or cultural information strongly influence the outcome of categorisation. Contextual effects do not just modulate late, high-level interpretation processes, but impact at the most basic levels of visual processing. It is nevertheless possible that there is some innate or universal core that plays a role in the definition of the extension of emotion categories. For example, with regards to facial expressions of emotion there may be aspects that are conserved genetically due to their high adaptive functionality. It has been demonstrated that when subjects show facial expressions of fear, they have a larger visual field, allowing for a more efficient scanning of the environment for threats, whereas when they pose expressions of disgust, nasal volume and air velocity during inspiration are reduced, lowering the intake of potentially repulsive substances (Susskind et al., 2008). Such features may be universal parts of the definition of the extension of emotion categories, and one can speculate that they may contribute to the above-chance performance in categorisation tasks that is not due to methodological artefacts and cultural facilitation. However, emotional categories and emotional categorisation are also to a large extent shaped by top-down contextual and cultural factors determined by language. Emotion categorisation serves as a rapid and reliable mechanism for complexity reduction and response preparation, however, it is highly sensitive to situational and contextual factors.

## Quantitative effects of emotion on perception: The perception of emotional stimuli

So far we have considered studies where participants are asked to make direct/explicit categorisations of emotional stimuli, mainly expressions of emotion in different modalities. Whereas such results may shed light on emotion categories, their boundaries, how they are defined and how people use them when they are asked to, they do not address a crucial question, maybe the most important one: What is the advantage of having special emotion categories, how does perception profit from having some stimuli tagged as emotional and others not? In summarising some of the theoretical and empirical work reviewed above, one can conclude that categorisation serves complexity reduction, whereas emotions serve the optimisation of adaptive behaviour towards stimuli that are relevant for the needs, goals and well-being of the organism. The role of emotion in perception and categorisation thus should ultimately be related to a perceptual prioritisation of categories of relevant stimuli in order to facilitate further processing and response preparation.

In the next part of the paper, we thus focus on quantitative effects of emotional stimuli in perception, investigating how the emotionality of a stimulus can modulate and transform perception, even when people are not consciously categorising the stimulus as emotional. Thus, we will consider studies where participants' explicit task is not a categorisation task, but, for example, to search for a specific picture in a display, or to identify rapidly presented words. Nevertheless, the tasks require some implicit form of emotional categorisation and contain emotional and neutral stimuli. In these paradigms, the emotionality of the stimuli modulates the efficiency with which the task is performed, suggesting interaction between emotion and perception. By integrating these studies in our review, we will be able to provide a more targeted overview of the diversity of subprocesses and effects involved in perceptual processing of emotional stimuli. Furthermore, studies on the categorisation of emotion usually employ facial (or less often vocal and bodily) expressions of emotion, whereas the studies we are going to present now also use other kinds of stimuli, such as emotional words and affective pictures of scenes or objects.

## How does perception profit from having stimuli tagged as emotional?

In the *visual search task* participants are instructed to search for a target within a search grid containing the target as well as a varying number of distracter stimuli, which may or may not share some similarities with the target stimulus. The task is either to indicate whether all stimuli belong to the same object category or not (thus a categorisation task, but not an explicit categorisation of "emotional" vs. "neutral") or to search for a predefined target. Typically, faster detection times are obtained when the target has some emotional value, such as an angry face among neutral faces (Hansen & Hansen, 1988; Öhman, Lundqvist, & Esteves, 2001b) or a snake among flowers (Öhman, Flykt, & Esteves, 2001a), indicating that the emotional target is either identified in a preattentive manner or that processing resources are very rapidly allocated toward its position. The search advantage for emotional stimuli was originally interpreted as a parallel search leading to a "pop out" effect (Öhman et al., 2001a; Treisman & Gormican, 1988). However, there is now increasing consensus that the search process for emotional stimuli is essentially serial, but characterised by smaller increases in response time when more distractors are added (see, e.g., Horstmann, 2007). Emotional stimuli have been shown both to speed up the orienting of attention and to prolong the disengagement of attention (Fox, Russo, & Dutton, 2002; Koster, Crombez, Van Damme, Verschuere, & De Houwer, 2004); faster detection of an emotional target among neutral distractors (compared with detection of a neutral target among emotional distractors) may thus be due to either faster orienting of attention to the target or faster disengagement from the neutral distracters. Studies using a full factorial design (including, e.g., threatening targets and threatening distractors) suggest that both attention capture and disengagement prolongation by emotional stimuli contribute to the search advantage for emotional stimuli in the visual search task (Flykt, 2005).

In the *attentional blink paradigm* (Raymond, Shapiro, & Arnell, 1992), participants are presented with a series of stimuli such as words or pictures at high presentation rates (rapid serial visual presentation, RSVP, around 10 stimuli per second). Participants then have to identify one or more of these targets. Any single target can be reported accurately, but reporting a second target is considerably impaired when the two targets are presented within a short interval (200–500 ms). Impaired performance is thought to reflect capacity limitations which restrict access to awareness (Shapiro, Arnell, & Raymond, 1997). It has been shown that the deficit in performance is greatly attenuated for emotional stimuli, which can be reported with higher accuracy than neutral stimuli when appearing as second target (Anderson, 2005). Conversely, the deficit in performance may increase for a neutral target that follows an emotional stimulus. These results indicate that emotional stimuli are selected preferentially from a perceptual temporal stream, thus facilitating processes leading to stimulus awareness.

Increased processing of emotional stimuli was furthermore demonstrated in a *perceptual identification task* (Zeelenberg, Wagenmakers, & Rotteveel, 2006), where emotional words were presented for around 25 ms and masked immediately. Afterwards, subjects had to indicate the word they had seen by choosing between two words. Word recognition was increased for both positive and for negative emotional words compared to neutral words. Interestingly, in a similar task, when people were asked to recognise rapidly presented and masked images of snakes and spiders, recognition rates were correlated with individual disgust sensitivity, whereas individual fear of spider correlated with the tendency to falsely report having perceived spiders (Wiens, Peira, Golkar, & Öhman, 2008), showing that individual differences in emotional sensitivity measures can influence perception both objectively (improved perception) and subjectively (increased misperceptions).

Taken together, these results show that the emotional quality of a diverse range of stimuli (such as words, pictures, or faces) can be extracted rapidly under suboptimal processing conditions and facilitate the further perceptual processing of the stimulus (Phelps, 2006; Vuilleumier, 2005).

## What is the defining "emotionality" criterion for perceptual prioritisation?

Although some basic emotion theories state that rapid perceptual processing is specific for threat stimuli that are evolutionarily prepared (Öhman & Mineka, 2001), it has repeatedly been shown that ontogenetically acquired threatening stimuli (such as guns or knives) show similar effects (Blanchette, 2006; Brosch & Sharma, 2005; Fox, Griggs, & Mouchlianitis, 2007).

Furthermore, even though the visual search paradigm is frequently cited to support preferential detection of threat-related stimuli, and some early visual search studies found faster detection of threatening information when comparing symbolic happy and angry faces ("smilies" and "frownies"; e.g., Eastwood, Smilek, & Merikle, 2001), recently it has been argued that the finding of preferential attention capture by angry compared to happy faces is due to the lower relevance of happy faces compared to angry faces, but that attention capture as such is driven by stimulus relevance in general, not by fear-relevance (Brosch, Sander, Pourtois, & Scherer, 2008; Brosch, Sander, & Scherer, 2007).

With regard to the empirical evidence for a potential threat specificity in the visual search paradigm, results are quite mixed (Wolfe & Horowitz, 2004). Some studies report a search advantage for angry faces, that is sometimes driven exclusively by the eye region (Fox & Damjanovic, 2006), sometimes by the mouth region (Horstmann & Bauland, 2006). Other studies report a search advantage both for angry and happy faces (Williams, Moss, Bradshaw, & Mattingley, 2005), or for happy compared to angry faces (Juth, Lundqvist, Karlsson, & Öhman, 2005). Furthermore, faster detection of animals is not specific to threat-related animals such as snakes or spiders (Öhman et al., 2001a), but has also been observed for cute, positively valenced animals (Tipples, Young, Quinlan, Broks, & Ellis, 2002). Generally, the results from visual search studies for emotional stimuli do not indicate a faster detection specific to threat stimuli, but rather seem to support the notion of a faster detection of emotional stimuli in general (see Frischen, Eastwood, & Smilek, 2008, for a similar argumentation). Similarly, the attenuation of the attentional blink has been demonstrated both for negative and for positive high-arousing stimuli (Anderson, 2005; Anderson & Phelps, 2001; Keil & Ihssen, 2004; Most, Smith, Cooter, Levy, & Zald, 2007).

Taken together, the empirical evidence indicates that increased perception is not restricted to fear-relevant stimuli, but is observed for stimuli with both positive and negative valence, consistent with the assumption of a perceptual prioritisation of highly relevant information (Brosch et al., 2008).

*Is increased perception due to emotional effects or basic stimulus characteristics?*

Most researchers studying the preferential perception of emotional stimuli assume that the prioritisation of the stimuli is due to the emotional quality of the stimulus as assessed by the individual. Nevertheless, one cannot exclude that the effects are due to associated characteristics of stimulus or task (e.g., spatial frequencies, low level perceptual correlates) and not direct effects of the stimulus emotionality (see, e.g., Cave & Batty, 2006). It has been shown, for example, that the degree of attentional capture by an emotional stimulus does not always correspond to the strength of affective evaluations for the same stimulus when measured by implicit tests such as affective priming (Purkis & Lipp, 2007). However, in other tasks, ratings of emotional intensity correlate with degree of response facilitation (Brosch et al., 2007). A role of emotional processes is also supported by the findings that attentional biases can be modulated by individual state and trait differences related to emotion. For example, attentional bias toward threatening information is often enhanced in people with specific phobia: attention is directed faster to pictures of snakes than spiders in snake phobics, but vice versa in spider phobics (Öhman et al., 2001a). Such individual differences strongly suggest that prioritised attention is determined by an appraisal of the emotional meaning and personal relevance of a stimulus, rather than just salient sensory features. Furthermore, it is important to consider that the emotionality of a stimulus may actually be conveyed by some very simple perceptual features, such as the v-shape of the eyebrows in a threatening facial expression (Aronoff, Barclay, & Stevenson, 1988) or the basic configuration of the baby schema (Lorenz, 1943).

### Are there differences between the effects of emotional words and emotional pictures?

The various studies reviewed in this paper used emotional and neutral words as well as images of emotional or neutral scenes or expressions. With regard to the activation of emotion concepts, it would be interesting to know whether there are fundamental processing differences between emotional words and non-verbal displays of emotion. One might assume, for example, that words activate emotion concepts more easily than other emotional stimuli, and thus lead to stronger top-down effects on processing. On the other hand, one may argue that pictures represent stronger or ecologically more valid stimuli than words, and thus may lead to stronger concept activation. The studies reviewed so far do not give any definitive answers on this question. For example, studies investigating the attentional blink have found rapid attentional prioritisation of both emotional words (Anderson, 2005) and emotional pictures (Most et al., 2007), but no study has compared the perceptual effects of the two types of stimuli. Linguistic studies in general find that pictures allow access to semantic information more rapidly than words, as the latter have to go through phonological processing first; only after a word string has been recognised as a word will its semantic properties be accessed (see Glaser, 1992, for a review). Some more direct evidence for stronger or more automatic concept activation by emotional pictures than words comes from studies showing that the emotionality of a picture interferes with the affective categorisation of words, whereas the emotionality of words does not (or only to a lesser extent) interfere with the affective categorisation of pictures (Beall & Herbert, 2008; De Houwer & Hermans, 1994).

*Which mechanisms underlie the prioritised perception of emotional stimuli?*

The increased perception of emotional stimuli, shown across a wide range of paradigms and methods, may depend both on memory-based processes and an online evaluation of the stimulus. Emotional stimuli such as words or objects may have stronger memory representations than neutral ones (LaBar & Cabeza, 2006; Phelps & Sharot, 2008), probably due to the higher implicit or explicit goal relevance of such stimuli for the organism (see Levine & Edelstein, 2009). The emotional significance of a stimulus enhances the formation of long-term memory traces, shown by better memory performance for emotional than neutral stimuli (Hamann, Ely, Grafton, & Kilts, 1999). The stronger memory representation may lead to a facilitated activation of the representations, which accounts for findings such as the preferential identification of masked emotional words compared to neutral words (Zeelenberg et al., 2006) or the facilitated selection of emotional words from a temporal stream of rapidly presented words (Anderson, 2005). Furthermore, memory representations of emotional stimuli, either on the basis of individual stimuli or on the basis of emotional stimulus categories, may already include emotional information in the sense of evaluation results, i.e., one might already know from earlier interactions with a stimulus that it has high relevance, both via explicit knowledge (e.g., when I see the face of a person that I don't like because I am aware that he has been mean to me) and via implicit pathways (e.g., when I smell a food for which I have a taste aversion). In this sense the stored information acts as an evaluation shortcut, so that no new elaborate evaluation is necessary. Other forms of affective evaluation cannot solely rely on memory processes. Context-sensitive processes need to take into account the current situation as well as the need or goal state of the organism and match it with the properties of the stimulus. This kind of processing needs an online appraisal (see, e.g., Moors, in press). Both kinds of processes may play a role in the evaluation of the affective value of a stimulus.

## DISCUSSION

### Why do we need emotional stimulus categories?

The research that we have reviewed here shows that emotion is a strong incentive for perception and that emotionally relevant words or images may produce both qualitative and quantitative changes in the speed and amount of what is eventually perceived by the individual. People are able to categorise stimuli into emotional categories, be they based on basic emotions, dimensional approaches, or appraisal criteria. The category boundaries affect the actual percept of emotional stimuli, as shown by the *categorical perception effect*. Furthermore, independent of any categorisation task, emotional stimuli are perceived preferentially.

A special role for emotional stimuli in perception is obviously useful, as emotional stimuli, i.e., stimuli that possess high relevance for the survival and well-being of the observer, usually require rapid behavioural responses, a preferential perception being the first step in the co-ordination of such an adaptive response. Emotional categories allow the organism to rapidly organise the processing of environmental information based on the relevance of the information with regards to current needs and goals. Just as one main function of categorisation in general is the rapid access to and retrieval of a lot of information about the incoming stimulus, a function of emotional categorising seems to be the rapid access to and retrieval of information that makes a quick adaptive response possible. Emotional categorisation thus can be conceptualised as an automatic, adaptive "tag for high priority processing" (see Yantis & Johnson, 1990).

## How do we categorise emotional stimuli: On the influence of bottom-up and top-down mechanisms

One central, frequently reoccurring debate in research on the processing, perception and categorisation of emotional stimuli is centred around the question of the relative importance of universal, biological bottom-up factors, as emphasised, e.g., by adherents of basic emotion theories, versus culturally and socially determined top-down factors, as emphasised especially by constructivist theories. This question has recently returned to the attention of emotion psychology due to a debate in *Perspectives in Psychological Sciences* (Barrett, 2006a; Barrett et al., 2007a; Izard, 2007; Panksepp, 2007, 2008). Based mainly on the argument that there is a lack of human neurophysiological evidence for discrete response patterning, Barrett promotes a constructivist approach claiming that emotion categories are not natural entities, but man-made concepts. The experience of emotions is understood as the categorisation of core affect, an internal state describable only in terms of valence and arousal, into language-based emotion categories (Barrett, 2006a). In contrast, based on a large amount of animal data showing discrete emotional response systems for a number of fundamental behaviours (e.g., FEAR, RAGE, PLAY; Panksepp, 1998), Panksepp rejects the extreme constructivist position and suggests that human emotion researchers need to take into account cross-species data indicating basic emotional systems to understand the "primal sources of human emotional feelings" (Panksepp, 2007, 2008).

What can the study of the perception of emotional objects contribute to this hotly debated issue? Some of the principal claims of the debate can be evaluated under the light of the empirical data and conceptual arguments that we discuss here. The data on categorisation tasks leave very little doubt about the fact that the claim of a strong universality of emotion categories put forward in support of basic emotion theories is not supported by the empirical evidence. The data rather indicate a large role of culture and context in an ongoing and flexible development of the categories that we use to carve our environment. Emotion categories seem to be learned and refined over time by integrating emotion-related information that frequently occurs together. This may nevertheless include some biological bottom-up aspects, such as adaptive responses like the opening of the eyes in a fear expression (Susskind et al., 2008), but furthermore includes culture-specific, socially determined aspects. Emotional categorisation is furthermore based to a great extent on available information about the current situational context.

Thus, whether and how a stimulus is perceived as emotional is not static, fixed or invariant, but critically depends on and fluctuates according to the person's particularities (such as the current mood or motivations) and specific context (e.g., situation, time, culture). Hence, a given stimulus can be emotional for one person, while being perceived as carrying less or even lacking any emotional meaning by another individual. Furthermore, the emotional meaning of a given stimulus may fluctuate for the exact same individual according to the specific context (situation and time) in which this stimulus is encountered. It is mainly for that reason that it is not easily possible to compile a fixed list of "emotional stimuli" that elicit an emotional effect in all people and on all occasions. A given stimulus becomes emotional for a person due to the individual interaction of that stimulus with the perceiving organism, assessing the individual emotional relevance of the stimulus for the person. To put it simply, a snake by itself is not an emotional stimulus, nor does it guarantee the elicitation of an emotion, but it takes a snake and somebody who is afraid of snakes to have an emotion. There might be some stimuli that elicit highly similar emotional responses across all persons, for example a strong fear-eliciting stimulus such as a painful electric prickling. However, even such extreme cases should be conceptualised as reflecting an interaction between the person and the stimulus, as demonstrated by interindividual differences in pain perception related to factors such as race, sex, catastrophism or anxiety level (Ploghaus et al., 2001; Sheffield, Biles, Orom, Maixner, & Sheps, 2000).

Thus, categorisation, while acting as an efficient mechanism for rapid complexity reduction, takes into account situational and contextual factors. The outcomes of the rapid categorisation mechanisms should not be mistaken for a modular mechanism for emotional processing, which is restricted to a few basic categories. Whereas the perception of emotional stimuli can be easily described in terms of basic categories or dimensions, the actual process that renders a stimulus emotional must be conceived of as more complex, highly flexible and context dependent. To explain the perception and categorisation of emotional stimuli, it is thus not sufficient to rely on a few basic, inflexible, hardwired categories. Emotional categorisation is modulated by our language capacities and available labels, and emotional categories seem to be similar to non-emotional categories in that they reflect correlational structures that we experience in our environment. They may be different from non-emotional categories, however, in that they integrate information about the different components of emotions, such as appraisal, action tendencies, bodily responses, behavioural responses and changes in subjective feeling, and in that emotional categorisation functions as a tag for high priority processing in the service of adaptive response preparation toward relevant stimuli.

It is furthermore doubtful that a purely constructivist position can account for results obtained in research on the perception of emotional stimuli. Especially in tasks where multiple stimuli are presented or stimuli are presented in a rapid visual stream with one stimulus every 100 ms or less, it is not clear how a preferential processing of emotional stimuli can be accounted for when the only emotional quality that is available for guiding perception is an unspecified internal core affect reflecting changes in a "neurophysiological barometer" (Barrett, 2006a). As constructivist theories mainly focus on the mechanisms underlying the subjective experience of emotions, they do not formulate relevant predictions or explanations about the topic of automatic perceptual prioritisation of emotional stimuli.

Componential appraisal theories of emotion (e.g., Scherer, 2009) focus on the effects of stimulus appraisal on the response patterning of physiological reactions, motor expression, and action preparation, which then may be integrated into an emotion category that can be used to structure the environment, guide perception, and give rise to a subjective feeling. Like constructivist approaches, appraisal theory can thus account for the richness and flexibility of the extension of the emotional categories, as appraisal is not hard wired, but takes into account individual particularities and specific contexts (e.g., Frijda, 2007). Unlike constructivist approaches, however, it postulates more specific mechanisms that give rise to the emotional quality that is categorised (core affect in the case of Barrett, 2006a, *versus* a response pattern of appraisal results, physiological reactions, motor expression, and action preparation, in the case of Scherer, 2009). From this perspective, effects like the rapid prioritisation of emotional stimuli by the perceptual system thus can be understood as embedded in the patterning of appraisal processes, action preparation and physiological orienting responses, and may serve to optimise perception even before a conscious categorisation has occurred.

## The relation of perception/cognition and emotion

Another important psychological debate is centred on the question of whether separate mechanisms exist for a dedicated processing of emotional stimuli or whether emotional and non-emotional stimuli are processed by the same cognitive mechanisms (Duncan & Barrett, 2007; Eder, Hommel, & De Houwer, 2007; Lazarus, 1984; Leventhal & Scherer, 1987; Pessoa, 2008; Storbeck, Robinson, & McCourt, 2006; Zajonc, 1980). If emotion and cognition are treated as separate or dissociable psychological processes, researchers would gain little insight on emotional perception by studying cognitive mechanisms of perception and categorisation. If, however, emotional stimuli are a special class of stimuli, which are processed by the same cognitive mechanisms as "neutral" stimuli, one can investigate cognitive mechanisms to elucidate a special role of emotional stimuli in perception in the sense of preferential treatment within cognitive processing (Moors, 2007).

The so-called "trilogy of the mind" (Hilgard, 1980), separating cognition, emotion and motivation into distinct entities, still seems to be very influential in the current literature. However, in most theories, the question of whether affective processes are dissociated from cognitive processes (such as Zajonc's, 1980, strong claim that "preferences need no inferences") can be reduced to the question of whether sensory processes are considered as cognitive in nature or not (see also Parrott & Schulkin, 1993). If one defines with Neisser (1967) cognitive processes as those processes "by which the sensory input is transformed, reduced, elaborated, stored, recovered, and used", it would still remain to be shown that sensory input alone can indeed elicit emotion without any kind of transformation.

The evidence reviewed in this article shows that perceptual and emotional processing are highly intertwined. In contrast to the view that perception is an encapsulated process that is not influenced by top-down influences such as expectations or prior knowledge (Pylyshyn, 1999), the evidence suggests that perception is a highly dynamic, proactive process, which influences and is reciprocally influenced by other processes, including emotional processes, through dynamic interactions. The perception of an emotional stimulus is both stimulus driven and concept driven, i.e., the result is shaped by sensory information as well as by memory-based conceptual information and online evaluation capacities. In extreme cases, emotional top-down concepts may even bias the perception of non-emotional stimuli. For example, in one study participants were shown ambiguous figures that could be interpreted as a "B" or as a "13" and were told that if they saw a "B" they would be assigned to a condition where they would taste orange juice, whereas if they saw a "13" they would taste a green, foul-smelling vegetable smoothie. Participants tended to report having seen the version that later would assign them to the favoured outcome (Balcetis & Dunning, 2006). Perception can be conceived as an interaction of bottom-up sensory signals that are processed and integrated by the sensory pathways, and top-down knowledge systems already present in the observer, which are used to structure and understand the new incoming information (Bar, 2004, 2007; Yantis, 1992). The emotional meaning of the stimulus emerges from interactions between the stimulus content and the actual state of the individual, during a proactive process. This conclusion is consistent with a recent analysis of neuroimaging studies suggesting that a segregation of the brain into "emotional" and "cognitive" areas is not supported by the empirical evidence (Pessoa, 2008).

The current review thus suggests that the perception of emotional stimuli does not seem to require special dedicated kinds of "emotional" processing mechanisms. The emotional quality of a stimulus rather seems to trigger a high-priority processing mode inside an integrated cognitive–affective system.

## CONCLUSIONS

In the present paper, we have shed some light on the perception and categorisation of emotional stimuli, by integrating theoretical perspectives on what makes a stimulus emotional and on how emotional categories are formed, as well as empirical data illustrating how stimuli are categorised as emotional as well as how the perception of emotional stimuli[3] is prioritised.

Emotional categorisation is a very important mechanism by which we structure our environment. Emotion is a strong incentive for perception, and emotional stimuli may produce both qualitative and quantitative changes in the speed and amount of what is eventually perceived by the individual. People classify facial, vocal and bodily expressions of emotion with high accuracy, allowing them to rapidly assess the emotional state of interaction partners. This classification can occur according to "basic" emotion categories, dimensions such as valence or arousal, and appraisal criteria such as relevance or coping potential. Furthermore, emotional stimuli in general are prioritised in perception, are detected more rapidly and gain access to conscious awareness more easily than non-emotional stimuli.

Emotion categories are not determined universally or biologically, but are flexible and continuously adjusted. Like other categories, they reflect correlational structures experienced in the environment. However, they are special in that they integrate different aspects of the emotional response toward a stimulus (such as appraisal components, core relational themes, action tendencies, bodily responses, behavioural responses, subjective feeling). Furthermore, contextual top-down information is extremely

---

3 One should be aware that "emotional stimuli" as used in the studies presented here only very rarely elicit a full-blown emotion with an intense subjective feeling component. Reading the word "snake" will probably not very often be linked with experiencing strong feelings of fear. However, as shown by the evidence reviewed in this article, the perceptual processing of the word may still be increased compared to emotionally neutral words.

important for the categorisation of a stimulus as emotional. This flexibility in categorisation helps to rapidly and economically perceive the environment by focusing on relevant information, but nevertheless allows for adjusting the definition of what is relevant at a given moment, congruent with the view of emotion as a highly flexible interface between stimulus input and adaptive response.

## REFERENCES

Adams, R. B. Jr., & Kleck, R. E. (2003). Perceived gaze direction and the processing of facial displays of emotion. *Psychological Science, 14,* 644–647.

Anderson, A. K. (2005). Affective influences on the attentional dynamics supporting awareness. *Journal of Experimental Psychology: General, 134,* 258–281.

Anderson, A. K., & Phelps, E. A. (2001). Lesions of the human amygdala impair enhanced perception of emotionally salient events. *Nature, 411,* 305–309.

Aronoff, J., Barclay, A. M., & Stevenson, L. A. (1988). The recognition of threatening facial stimuli. *Journal of Personality and Social Psychology, 54,* 647–655.

Atkinson, A. P., Dittrich, W. H., Gemmell, A. J., & Young, A. W. (2004). Emotion perception from dynamic and static body expressions in point-light and full-light displays. *Perception, 33,* 717–746.

Augoustinos, M., Walker, I., & Donaghue, N. (2006). *Social cognition: An integrated introduction.* London: Sage.

Aviezer, H., Hassin, R. R., Ryan, J., Grady, C., Susskind, J., Anderson, A., et al. (2008). Angry, disgusted, or afraid? Studies on the malleability of emotion perception. *Psychological Science, 19,* 724–732.

Balcetis, E., & Dunning, D. (2006). See what you want to see: Motivational influences on visual perception. *Journal of Personality and Social Psychology, 91,* 612–625.

Bar, M. (2004). Visual objects in context. *Nature Reviews Neuroscience, 5,* 617–629.

Bar, M. (2007). The proactive brain: Using analogies and associations to generate predictions. *Trends in Cognitive Sciences, 11,* 280–289.

Barrett, L. F. (2006a). Are emotions natural kinds? *Perspectives on Psychological Science, 1,* 28–58.

Barrett, L. F. (2006b). Solving the emotion paradox: Categorization and the experience of emotion. *Personality and Social Psychology Review, 10,* 20–46.

Barrett, L. F., Lindquist, K. A., Bliss-Moreau, E., Duncan, S., Gendron, M., Mize, J., et al. (2007a). Of mice and men: Natural kinds of emotions in the mammalian brain? A response to Panksepp and Izard. *Perspectives on Psychological Science, 2,* 297–311.

Barrett, L. F., Lindquist, K. A., & Gendron, M. (2007b). Language as context for the perception of emotion. *Trends in Cognitive Sciences, 11,* 327–332.

Barsalou, L. W. (1983). Ad hoc categories. *Memory & Cognition, 11,* 211–227.

Barsalou, L. W. (1985). Ideals, central tendency, and frequency of instantiation as determinants of graded structure in categories. *Journal of Experimental Psychology: Learning, Memory, and Cognition, 11,* 629–654.

Beale, J. M., & Keil, F. C. (1995). Categorical effects in the perception of faces. *Cognition, 57,* 217–239.

Beall, P. M., & Herbert, A. M. (2008). The face wins: Stronger automatic processing of affect in facial expressions than words in a modified Stroop task. *Cognition and Emotion, 22,* 1613–1642.

Berlin, B., & Kay, P. (1969). *Basic color terms: Their universality and evolution.* Berkeley, CA: University of California Press.

Blanchette, I. (2006). Snakes, spiders, guns, and syringes: How specific are evolutionary constraints on the detection of threatening stimuli? *Quarterly Journal of Experimental Psychology, 59,* 1484–1504.

Bornstein, M. H., & Korda, N. O. (1984). Discrimination and matching within and between hues measured by reaction times: Some implications for categorical perception and levels of information processing. *Psychological Research, 46,* 207–222.

Borod, J. C., Pick, L. H., Hall, S., Sliwinski, M., Madigan, N., Obler, L. K., et al. (2000). Relationships among facial, prosodic, and lexical channels of emotional perceptual processing. *Cognition and Emotion, 14,* 193–211.

Boster, J. (2005). Emotion categories across languages. In H. Cohen & C. Lefebvre (Eds.), *Handbook of categorization in cognitive science.* Amsterdam: Elsevier.

Bradley, M. M., & Lang, P. J. (1994). Measuring emotion: The self-assessment manikin and the semantic differential. *Journal of Behavioural Therapy and Experimental Psychiatry, 25,* 49–59.

Brosch, T., Sander, D., Pourtois, G., & Scherer, K. R. (2008). Beyond fear: Rapid spatial orienting towards positive emotional stimuli. *Psychological Science, 19,* 362–370.

Brosch, T., Sander, D., & Scherer, K. R. (2007). That baby caught my eye. Attention capture by infant faces. *Emotion, 7,* 685–689.

Brosch, T., & Sharma, D. (2005). The role of fear-relevant stimuli in visual search: A comparison of phylogenetic and ontogenetic stimuli. *Emotion, 5,* 360–364.

Calder, A. J., Young, A. W., Perrett, D. I., Etcoff, N. L., & Rowland, D. (1996). Categorical perception of morphed facial expressions. *Visual Cognition, 3,* 81–118.

Carroll, J. M., & Russell, J. A. (1996). Do facial expressions signal specific emotions? Judging emotion from the face in context. *Journal of Personality and Social Psychology, 70,* 205–218.

Carroll, J. M., & Russell, J. A. (1997). Facial expressions in Hollywood's portrayal of emotion. *Journal of Personality and Social Psychology, 72,* 164–176.

Cave, K. R., & Batty, M. J. (2006). From searching for features to searching for threat: Drawing the boundary between preattentive and attentive vision. *Visual Cognition, 14,* 629–646.

Cohen, H., & Lefebvre, C. (Eds.). (2005). *Handbook of categorization in cognitive science.* Amsterdam: Elsevier.

Davidoff, J. (2001). Language and perceptual categorisation. *Trends in Cognitive Sciences, 5,* 382–387.

Davidson, R. J., & Irwin, W. (1999). The functional neuroanatomy of emotion and affective style. *Trends in Cognitive Science, 3,* 11–21.

de Gelder, B. (2006). Towards the neurobiology of emotional body language. *Nature Reviews Neuroscience, 7,* 242–249.

De Houwer, J., & Hermans, D. (1994). Differences in the affective processing of words and pictures. *Cognition and Emotion, 8,* 1–20.

Duncan, S., & Barrett, L. F. (2007). Affect is a form of cognition: A neurobiological analysis. *Cognition & Emotion, 21,* 1184–1211.

Eastwood, J. D., Smilek, D., & Merikle, P. M. (2001). Differential attentional guidance by unattended faces expressing positive and negative emotion. *Perception & Psychophysics, 63,* 1004–1013.

Eder, A. B., Hommel, B., & De Houwer, J. (2007). How distinctive is affective processing? On the implications of using cognitive paradigms to study affect and emotion. *Cognition & Emotion, 21,* 1137–1154.

Ekman, P. (1972). Universals and cultural differences in facial expressions of emotion. In J. K. Cole (Ed.), *Nebraska symposium on motivation* (pp. 207–283). Lincoln, NE: University of Nebraska Press.

Ekman, P. (1992). An argument for basic emotions. *Cognition and Emotion, 6,* 169–200.

Ekman, P. (1994). Strong evidence for universals in facial expressions: A reply to Russell's mistaken critique. *Psychological Bulletin, 115,* 268–287.

Ekman, P., & Friesen, W. V. (1975). *Unmasking the face.* Englewood Cliffs, NJ: Prentice-Hall.

Elfenbein, H. A., & Ambady, N. (2002). On the universality and cultural specificity of emotion recognition: A meta-analysis. *Psychological Bulletin, 128,* 203–235.

Ellsworth, P. C., & Scherer, K. R. (2003). Appraisal processes in emotion. In R. J. Davidson, H. H. Goldsmith, & K. R. Scherer (Eds.), *Handbook of affective sciences* (pp. 572–595). Oxford, UK: Oxford University Press.

Etcoff, N. L., & Magee, J. J. (1992). Categorical perception of facial expressions. *Cognition, 44,* 227–240.

Flykt, A. (2005). Visual search with biological threat stimuli: Accuracy, reaction times, and heart rate changes. *Emotion, 5,* 349–353.

Fox, E., & Damjanovic, L. (2006). The eyes are sufficient to produce a threat superiority effect. *Emotion, 6,* 534–539.

Fox, E., Griggs, L., & Mouchlianitis, E. (2007). The detection of fear-relevant stimuli: Are guns noticed as quickly as snakes? *Emotion, 7,* 691–696.

Fox, E., Russo, R., & Dutton, K. (2002). Attentional bias for threat: Evidence for delayed disengagement from emotional faces. *Cognition and Emotion, 16,* 355–379.

Frijda, N. H. (2007). *The laws of emotion.* Mahwah, NJ: Lawrence Erlbaum Associates, Inc.

Frischen, A., Eastwood, J. D., & Smilek, D. (2008). Visual search for faces with emotional expressions. *Psychological Bulletin, 134,* 662–676.

Glaser, W. R. (1992). Picture naming. *Cognition, 42,* 61–105.

Halberstadt, J. B., & Niedenthal, P. M. (2001). Effects of emotion concepts on perceptual memory for emotional expressions. *Journal of Personality and Social Psychology, 81,* 587–598.

Hamann, S. B., Ely, T. D., Grafton, S. T., & Kilts, C. D. (1999). Amygdala activity related to enhanced memory for pleasant and aversive stimuli. *Nature Neuroscience, 2,* 289–293.

Hansen, C. H., & Hansen, R. D. (1988). Finding the face in the crowd: An anger superiority effect. *Journal of Personality and Social Psychology, 54,* 917–924.

Harnad, S. (1987). *Categorical perception: The groundwork of cognition*. Cambridge, UK: Cambridge University Press.

Harnad, S. (2005). To cognize is to categorize: Cognition is categorization. In H. Cohen & C. Lefebvre (Eds.), *Handbook of categorization in cognitive science*. Amsterdam: Elsevier.

Hess, U., Philippot, P., & Blairy, S. (1998). Facial reactions to emotional facial expressions: Affect or cognition? *Cognition & Emotion, 12*, 509–531.

Hilgard, E. R. (1980). The trilogy of mind: Cognition, affection, and conation. *Journal of the History of Behavioral Sciences, 16*, 107–117.

Horstmann, G. (2002). Facial expressions of emotion: Does the prototype represent central tendency, frequency of instantiation, or an ideal? *Emotion, 2*, 297–305.

Horstmann, G. (2007). Preattentive face processing: What do visual search experiments with schematic faces tell us? *Visual Cognition, 15*, 799–833.

Horstmann, G., & Bauland, A. (2006). Search asymmetries with real faces: Testing the anger-superiority effect. *Emotion, 6*, 193–207.

Izard, C. E. (1971). *The face of emotion*. New York: Appleton-Century-Crofts.

Izard, C. E. (1994). Innate and universal facial expressions: Evidence from developmental and cross-cultural research. *Psychological Bulletin, 115*, 288–299.

Izard, C. E. (2007). Basic emotions, natural kinds, emotion schemas, and a new paradigm. *Perspectives on Psychological Science, 2*, 260–280.

Juslin, P. N., & Laukka, P. (2003). Communication of emotions in vocal expression and music performance: different channels, same code? *Psychological Bulletin, 129*, 770–814.

Juth, P., Lundqvist, D., Karlsson, A., & Öhman, A. (2005). Looking for foes and friends: Perceptual and emotional factors when finding a face in the crowd. *Emotion, 5*, 379–395.

Keil, A., & Ihssen, N. (2004). Identification facilitation for emotionally arousing verbs during the attentional blink. *Emotion, 4*, 23–35.

Kim, H., Somerville, L. H., Johnstone, T., Alexander, A. L., & Whalen, P. J. (2003). Inverse amygdala and medial prefrontal cortex responses to surprised faces. *Neuroreport, 14*, 2317–2322.

Kim, H., Somerville, L. H., Johnstone, T., Polis, S., Alexander, A. L., Shin, L. M., et al. (2004). Contextual modulation of amygdala responsivity to surprised faces. *Journal of Cognitive Neuroscience, 16*, 1730–1745.

Koster, E., Crombez, G., Van Damme, S., Verschuere, B., & De Houwer, J. (2004). Does imminent threat capture and hold attention? *Emotion, 4*, 312–317.

Kourtzi, Z., & DiCarlo, J. J. (2006). Learning and neural plasticity in visual object recognition. *Current Opinion in Neurobiology, 16*, 152–158.

LaBar, K. S., & Cabeza, R. (2006). Cognitive neuroscience of emotional memory. *Nature Reviews Neuroscience, 7*, 54–64.

Lang, P. (1995). The emotion probe: Studies of motivation and attention. *American Psychologist, 50*, 372–385.

Laukka, P. (2005). Categorical perception of vocal emotion expressions. *Emotion, 5*, 277–295.

Lazarus, R. S. (1984). On the primacy of cognition. *American Psychologist, 39*, 124–129.

Leventhal, H., & Scherer, K. R. (1987). The relationship of emotion to cognition: A functional approach to a semantic controversy. *Cognition and Emotion, 1*, 3–28.

Levine, L. J., & Edelstein, R. S. (2009). Emotion and memory narrowing: A review and goal relevance approach. *Cognition and Emotion, 23*, 833–875.

Liberman, A. M., Harris, K. S., Hoffman, H. S., & Griffith, B. C. (1957). The discrimination of speech sounds within and across phoneme boundaries. *Journal of Experimental Psychology, 54*, 358–368.

Lorenz, K. (1943). Die angeborenen Formen möglicher Erfahrung [The innate forms of potential experience]. *Zeitschrift für Tierpsychologie, 5*, 233–519.

McClelland, J. L., & Rumelhart, D. E. (1985). Distributed memory and the representation of general and specific information. *Journal of Experimental Psychology: General, 114*, 159–188.

Merikle, P. M., & Daneman, M. (1998). Psychological investigations of unconscious perception. *Journal of Consciousness Studies, 5*, 5–18.

Moors, A. (2007). Can cognitive methods be used to study the unique aspect of emotion: An appraisal theorist's answer. *Cognition and Emotion, 21*, 1238–1269.

Moors, A. (2009). A review of theories concerned with emotion causation. *Cognition and Emotion, 23*, 625–662.

Moors, A. (in press). Automatic constructive appraisal as a candidate cause of emotion. *Emotion Review*.

Most, S. B., Smith, S. D., Cooter, A. B., Levy, B. N., & Zald, D. H. (2007). The naked truth: Positive, arousing distractors impair rapid target perception. *Cognition and Emotion, 21*, 964–981.

Murphy, G. L., & Medin, D. L. (1985). The role of theories in conceptual coherence. *Psychological Review, 92*, 289–316.

Neisser, U. (1967). *Cognitive psychology*. New York: Appleton-Century-Crofts.

Niedenthal, P. M., Halberstadt, J. B., & Innes-Ker, A. H. (1999). Emotional response categorization. *Psychological Review, 106*, 337–361.

Öhman, A., Flykt, A., & Esteves, F. (2001a). Emotion drives attention: Detecting the snake in the grass. *Journal of Experimental Psychology: General, 130*, 466–478.

Öhman, A., Lundqvist, D., & Esteves, F. (2001b). The face in the crowd revisited: A threat advantage with schematic stimuli. *Journal of Personality and Social Psychology, 80*, 381–396.

Öhman, A., & Mineka, S. (2001). Fears, phobias, and preparedness: Toward an evolved module of fear and fear learning. *Psychological Review, 108*, 483–522.

Palmeri, T. J., & Gauthier, I. (2004). Visual object understanding. *Nature Reviews Neuroscience, 5*, 291–303.

Panksepp, J. (1998). *Affective neuroscience: The foundations of human and animal emotions*. New York: Oxford University Press.

Panksepp, J. (2007). Neurologizing the psychology of affects: How appraisal-based constructivism and basic emotion theory can coexist. *Perspectives on Psychological Science, 2*, 281–295.

Panksepp, J. (2008). Cognitive conceptualism: Where have all the affects gone? Additional corrections for Barrett et al. (2007). *Perspectives on Psychological Science, 3*, 305–308.

Parrott, W. G., & Schulkin, J. (1993). What sort of system could an affective system be? A reply to LeDoux. *Cognition and Emotion, 7*, 65–69.

Pessoa, L. (2008). On the relationship between emotion and cognition. *Nature Reviews Neuroscience, 9*, 148–158.

Phelps, E. A. (2006). Emotion and cognition: Insights from studies of the human amygdala. *Annual Review of Psychology, 57,* 27–53.

Phelps, E. A., & Sharot, T. (2008). How (and why) emotion enhances the subjective sense of recollection. *Current Directions in Psychological Science, 17,* 147–152.

Ploghaus, A., Narain, C., Beckmann, C. F., Clare, S., Bantick, S., Wise, R., et al. (2001). Exacerbation of pain by anxiety is associated with activity in a hippocampal network. *Journal of Neuroscience, 21,* 9896–9903.

Purkis, H. M., & Lipp, O. V. (2007). Automatic attention does not equal automatic fear: Preferential attention without implicit valence. *Emotion, 7,* 314–323.

Pylyshyn, Z. (1999). Is vision continuous with cognition? The case for cognitive impenetrability of visual perception. *Behavioral and Brain Sciences, 22,* 341–423.

Raymond, J. E., Shapiro, K. L., & Arnell, K. M. (1992). Temporary suppression of visual processing in an RSVP task: An attentional blink? *Journal of Experimental Psychology: Human Perception and Performance, 18,* 849–860.

Roberson, D., Davies, I., & Davidoff, J. (2000). Color categories are not universal: Replications and new evidence from a stone-age culture. *Journal of Experimental Psychology: General, 129,* 369–398.

Rosch, E. (1975). Cognitive representations of semantic categories. *Journal of Experimental Psychology: General, 104,* 192–233.

Rosch, E. (1978). Principles of categorization. In E. Rosch & B. B. Lloyd (Eds.), *Cognition and categorization* (pp. 27–48). Hillsdale, NJ: Lawrence Erlbaum Associates, Inc.

Rosch, E., Mervis, C., Gray, W. D., Johnson, D. M., & Boyes-Braem, P. (1976). Basic objects in natural categories. *Cognitive Psychology, 8,* 382–439.

Rosch Heider, E. (1972). Universals in color naming and memory. *Journal of Experimental Psychology, 93,* 10–20.

Russell, J. A. (1991). Culture and the categorization of emotions. *Psychological Bulletin, 110,* 426–450.

Russell, J. A. (1994). Is there universal recognition of emotion from facial expressions? A review of the cross-cultural studies. *Psychological Bulletin, 115,* 102–141.

Russell, J. A. (1995). Facial expressions of emotion: What lies beyond minimal universality? *Psychological Bulletin, 118,* 379–391.

Russell, J. A. (1997). Reading emotions from and into faces: Resurrecting a dimensional contextual perspective. In J. A. Russell & J. M. Fernandez-Dols (Eds.), *The psychology of facial expressions* (pp. 295–320). New York: Cambridge University Press.

Russell, J. A. (2003). Core affect and the psychological construction of emotion. *Psychological Review, 110,* 145–172.

Russell, J. A., & Fehr, B. (1987). Relativity in the perception of emotion in facial expressions. *Journal of Experimental Psychology: General, 116,* 223–237.

Sander, D. (2008). Basic tastes and basic emotions: Basic problems, and perspectives for a nonbasic solution [commentary]. *Behavioral and Brain Sciences, 31,* 88.

Sander, D., Grafman, J., & Zalla, T. (2003). The human amygdala: An evolved system for relevance detection. *Reviews in the Neurosciences, 14,* 303–316.

Sander, D., Grandjean, D., Kaiser, S., Wehrle, T., & Scherer, K. R. (2007). Interaction effects of perceived gaze direction and dynamic facial expression:

Evidence for appraisal theories of emotion. *European Journal of Cognitive Psychology, 19,* 470–480.

Scherer, K. R. (1992). What does facial expression express? In K. Strongman (Ed.), *International review of studies on emotion* (Vol. 2, pp. 139–165). Chichester, UK: Wiley.

Scherer, K. R. (1994a). Emotion serves to decouple stimulus and response. In P. Ekman & R. J. Davidson (Eds.), *The nature of emotion: Fundamental questions* (pp. 127–130). New York: Oxford University Press.

Scherer, K. R. (1994b). Toward a concept of "modal emotions". In P. Ekman & R. J. Davidson (Eds.), *The nature of emotion: Fundamental questions* (pp. 25–31). New York: Oxford University Press.

Scherer, K. R. (2001). Appraisal considered as a process of multilevel sequential checking. In K. R. Scherer, A. Schorr, & T. Johnstone (Eds.), *Appraisal processes in emotion: Theory, methods, research* (pp. 92–120). New York: Oxford University Press.

Scherer, K. R. (2009). The dynamic architecture of emotion: Evidence for the component process model. *Cognition and Emotion, 27,* 1307–1351.

Scherer, K. R., & Grandjean, D. (2008). Facial expressions allow inference of both emotions and their components. *Cognition and Emotion, 22,* 789–801.

Schneirla, T. (1959). An evolutionary and developmental theory of biphasic processes underlying approach and withdrawal. In *Nebraska Symposium on Motivation* (pp. 1–42). Lincoln: Nebraska Press.

Shapiro, K. L., Arnell, K. M., & Raymond, J. E. (1997). The attentional blink. *Trends in Cognitive Sciences, 1,* 291–296.

Shaver, E., Schwartz, J., Kirson, D., & O'Connor, C. (1987). Emotion knowledge: Further exploration of a prototype approach. *Journal of Personality and Social Psychology, 52,* 1061–1086.

Sheffield, D., Biles, P. L., Orom, H., Maixner, W., & Sheps, D. S. (2000). Race and sex differences in cutaneous pain perception. *Psychosomatic Medicine, 62,* 517–523.

Smith, C. A., & Kirby, L. D. (2009). Core relational themes. In D. Sander & K. R. Scherer (Eds.)., *The Oxford companion to emotion and the affective sciences.* Oxford, UK: Oxford University Press.

Smith, C. A., & Lazarus, R. S. (1990). Emotion and adaptation. In L. A. Pervin (Ed.), *Handbook of personality: Theory and research* (pp. 609–637). New York: Guilford Press.

Smith, M. L., Cottrell, G. W., Gosselin, F., & Schyns, P. G. (2005). Transmitting and decoding facial expressions. *Psychological Science, 16,* 184–189.

Storbeck, J., Robinson, M. D., & McCourt, M. E. (2006). Semantic processing precedes affect retrieval: The neurological case for cognitive primacy in visual processing. *Review of General Psychology, 10,* 41–55.

Susskind, J. M., Lee, D. H., Cusi, A., Feiman, R., Grabski, W., & Anderson, A. K. (2008). Expressing fear enhances sensory acquisition. *Nature Neuroscience, 11,* 843–850.

Thorpe, S., Fize, D., & Marlot, C. (1996). Speed of processing in the human visual system. *Nature, 381,* 520–522.

Tipples, J., Young, A. W., Quinlan, P., Broks, P., & Ellis, A. W. (2002). Searching for threat. *Quarterly Journal of Experimental Psychology, 55A,* 1007–1026.

Treisman, A., & Gormican, S. (1988). Feature analysis in early vision: Evidence from search asymmetries. *Psychological Review, 95*, 15–48.

Vuilleumier, P. (2005). How brains beware: Neural mechanisms of emotional attention. *Trends in Cognitive Sciences, 9*, 585–594.

Wallbott, H. G., & Ricci-Bitti, P. (1993). Decoders' processing of emotional facial expression: A top-down or bottom-up mechanism? *European Journal of Social Psychology, 23*, 427–443.

Whorf, B. L. (1956). The relation of habitual thought and behavior to language. In J. B. Carroll (Ed.), *Language, thought and reality: Essays by B. L. Whorf.* Cambridge, MA: MIT Press.

Wiens, S., Peira, N., Golkar, A., & Öhman, A. (2008). Recognizing masked threat: Fear betrays, but disgust you can trust. *Emotion, 8*, 810–819.

Williams, M. A., Moss, S. A., Bradshaw, J. L., & Mattingley, J. B. (2005). Look at me, I'm smiling: Visual search for threatening and nonthreatening facial expressions. *Visual Cognition, 12*, 29–50.

Winkielman, P., Berridge, K. C., & Wilbarger, J. L. (2005). Unconscious affective reactions to masked happy versus angry faces influence consumption behavior and judgments of value. *Personality and Social Psychology Bulletin, 31*, 121–135.

Wolfe, J. M., & Horowitz, T. S. (2004). What attributes guide the deployment of visual attention and how do they do it? *Nature Reviews Neuroscience, 5*, 495–501.

Yantis, S. (1992). Multielement visual tracking: Attention and perceptual organization. *Cognitive Psychology, 24*, 295–340.

Yantis, S., & Johnson, D. N. (1990). Mechanisms of attentional priority. *Journal of Experimental Psychology: Human Perception and Performance, 16*, 812–825.

Young, A. W., Rowland, D., Calder, A. J., Etcoff, N. L., Seth, A., & Perrett, D. I. (1997). Facial expression megamix: Tests of dimensional and category accounts of emotion recognition. *Cognition, 63*, 271–313.

Zajonc, R. B. (1980). Feeling and thinking: Preferences need no inferences. *American Psychologist, 35*, 151–175.

Zeelenberg, R., Wagenmakers, E. J., & Rotteveel, M. (2006). The impact of emotion on perception: Bias or enhanced processing? *Psychological Science, 17*, 287–291.

Correspondence should be addressed to: Tobias Brosch, Swiss Centre for Affective Sciences, University of Geneva, 7, Rue des Battoirs, 1205 Geneva, Switzerland. E-mail: tobias.brosch@unige.ch

The preparation of this article was supported by the National Centre of Competence in Research for Affective Sciences, financed by the Swiss National Science Foundation.

# 4 Measures of emotion: A review

Iris B. Mauss
*University of Denver, Denver, CO, USA*
Michael D. Robinson
*North Dakota State University, Fargo, ND, USA*

From an intuitive layperson perspective, it should be easy to determine whether someone is experiencing a particular emotion. However, scientific evidence suggests that measuring a person's emotional state is one of the most vexing problems in affective science. To organise our review of research relevant to this question, we take as our starting point a consensual, componential model of emotion (see Figure 4.1). In this model, an emotional response begins with appraisal of the personal significance of an event (Lazarus, 1991; Scherer, 1984; Smith & Ellsworth, 1985), which in turn gives rise to an emotional response involving subjective experience, physiology, and behaviour (Frijda, 1988; Gross, 2007; Lang, 1988; Larsen & Prizmic-Larsen, 2006). The present review examines whether emotion-evocative stimuli are associated with discrete patterns of responding in each system, how such responses seem to be structured, and if such responses converge (i.e., are co-ordinated or correlated) with one another.

Because the literatures that are relevant to the questions examined here are extensive, the present review must be selective. In our review, we concentrate on studies involving non-clinical human adult samples rather than children, animals, or clinical populations. We focus on the response components depicted in Figure 4.1 rather than on cognitive antecedents and correlates of emotion. To further constrain the scope of our review, we focus on emotional states rather than emotion-related traits such as extraversion and neuroticism (see Matthews & Gilliland, 1999; Robinson & Neighbors, 2006; Rusting, 1998, for relevant reviews). Finally, we focus our review on the most commonly used measures for each response system.

Throughout our review, we examine findings from both dimensional and discrete perspectives. According to the dimensional perspective, there are a few fundamental dimensions that organise emotional responses. The most commonly assumed dimensions are valence, arousal (sometimes referred to as activation), and approach–avoidance (Davidson, 1999; Lang, Bradley, & Cuthbert, 1997; Russell & Barrett, 1999; Schneirla, 1959; Watson, Wiese, Vaidya, & Tellegen, 1999). The valence dimension contrasts states of pleasure (e.g., happy) with states of displeasure (e.g., sad), and the arousal

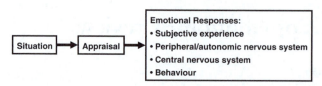

*Figure 4.1* A consensual component model of emotional responding.

dimension contrasts states of low arousal (e.g., quiet) with states of high arousal (e.g., surprised). Approach motivation is characterised by tendencies to approach stimuli (e.g., as would likely be facilitated by excitement), whereas avoidance motivation is characterised by tendencies to avoid stimuli (e.g., as would likely be facilitated by anxiety).

Researchers disagree to some extent about which dimensional scheme should be used and how different dimensions relate to each other. For example, some theorists state that positive and negative emotions are inversely related (Russell, 1980), but others favour the view that positive and negative emotions are relatively independent of each other (Larsen, McGraw, & Cacioppo, 2001; Tellegen, Watson, & Clark, 1999). In addition, some argue that approach and avoidance are more or less synonymous with positive and negative emotional states, respectively (Watson et al., 1999). However, as we outline below, some emotional states such as anger pose problems for this view, in that they suggest a dissociation of valence and approach–avoidance (Harmon-Jones & Allen, 1998). More generally, our review will make it clear that different measures of emotion are particularly sensitive to different dimensions; thus, for different measures different dimensional schemes are most appropriate. Although dimensional frameworks disagree in some of their specifics, they agree that emotional states can be organised in terms of a limited number of underlying dimensions.

In contrast, the discrete emotions perspective contends that each emotion (e.g., anger, sadness, contempt) corresponds to a unique profile in experience, physiology, and behaviour (Ekman, 1999; Panksepp, 2007). It is possible to reconcile dimensional and discrete perspectives to some extent by proposing that each discrete emotion represents a combination of several dimensions (Haidt & Keltner, 1999; Smith & Ellsworth, 1985). For example, anger could be characterised by negative valence, high arousal, and approach motivation, whereas fear could be characterised by negative valence, high arousal, and avoidance motivation. Despite these considerations, dimensional and discrete perspectives differ in how they conceptualise and describe emotional states (Barrett, 2006b). For this reason, we contrast such perspectives in our review.

To guide the reader, Table 4.1 presents an overview of the measures reviewed for each response system depicted in the consensual model of Figure 4.1. Table 4.1 also summarises our conclusions concerning the

*Table 4.1* Overview of response systems, measures, and emotional states to which they are sensitive

| Response system | Measure | Sensitivity |
| --- | --- | --- |
| Subjective experience | Self-report | Valence and arousal |
| Peripheral physiology (ANS) | Autonomic nervous system (ANS) measures | Valence and arousal |
| Affect-modulated startle | Startle response magnitude | Valence, particularly at high levels of arousal |
| Central physiology (CNS) | EEG | Approach and avoidance |
| | fMRI, PET | Approach and avoidance |
| Behaviour | Vocal characteristics: Amplitude, pitch | Arousal |
| | Facial behaviour: Observer ratings | Valence; some emotion specificity |
| | Facial behaviour: EMG | Valence |
| | Whole body behaviour: Observer ratings | Some emotion specificity |

aspects of emotional state best captured by each measure. We begin by reviewing self-report measures of emotion.

## SELF-REPORT MEASURES OF EMOTION

In our view, the validity of self-reports of emotion is too often seen as an all-or-none phenomenon. Here, we follow Robinson and Clore (2002), who concluded that the degree to which self-reports are valid varies by the type of self-report (see also Robinson & Sedikides, in press). Specifically, self-reports of current emotional experiences are likely to be more valid than are self-reports of emotion made somewhat distant in time from the relevant experience (Robinson & Clore, 2002). In a very interesting study, for example, Barrett, Robin, Pietromonaco, and Eyssell (1998) asked men and women to report on their emotional traits "in general" as well as on their emotional reactions to events in daily life. Sex differences in emotional traits were prominent and large, whereas sex differences in daily experience were quite meagre and inconsistent, suggesting that trait reports of emotion are more biased (in this case by gender stereotypes) than reports made directly after an event. Conceptually similar findings have been reported when asking individuals to estimate their past or likely future responses to emotional events (e.g., Mitchell, Thompson, Peterson, & Cronk, 1997) On the basis of such evidence for bias, Robinson and Clore concluded that self-reports of one's current experience ("online") are likely to be more valid than self-reports concerning past, future, or trait-related experiences of emotion.

However, there are concerns that even "online" reports of emotion can be biased among certain groups of individuals. For example, it is thought that individuals high in social desirability may be less willing and/or capable of reporting negative emotional states (Paulhus & Reid, 1991; Welte & Russell, 1993). Although this suggestion has proven somewhat controversial (Shedler, Mayman, & Manis, 1993; Taylor, Lerner, Sherman, Sage, & McDowell, 2003), there are still concerns that individuals high in social desirability may give less valid reports of their emotions (Paulhus & John, 1998). A second relevant individual-difference variable is alexithymia. It has been suggested that individuals high in alexithymia react to emotional stimuli, but are less capable of conceptualising their emotional experiences in a manner conducive to self-report (Lane, Ahern, Schwartz, & Kaszniak, 1997). In sum, there are individual differences in awareness of and willingness to report on emotional states that potentially compromise even online reports of emotional experience.

Finally, one purpose of our review is to compare dimensional and discrete perspectives of emotional responding. In the domain of self-reported emotional states, it is quite clear that dimensions such as valence and arousal (Russell & Barrett, 1999) or tendencies toward approach and avoidance (Watson et al., 1999) capture the lion's share of variance. Indeed, the dimensional nature of self-reported emotional responses is so substantial that it has been suggested that the dimensional correlates of self-reported emotion be examined first before there is any legitimate claim to emotion specificity (Watson, 2000).

*Summary*

Self-reports of emotion are likely to be more valid to the extent that they relate to currently experienced emotions. Even in this case, though, there are concerns that not all individuals are aware of and/or capable of reporting on their momentary emotional states. Finally, Table 4.1 follows from our review of this literature in suggesting that dimensional frameworks, relative to discrete ones, better capture this measure of emotion.

## AUTONOMIC MEASURES OF EMOTION

The autonomic nervous system (ANS) is a general-purpose physiological system responsible for modulating peripheral functions (Öhman, Hamm, & Hugdahl, 2000). This system consists of sympathetic and parasympathetic branches, which are generally associated with activation and relaxation, respectively. Because of the general-purpose nature of the ANS, its activity is not exclusively a function of emotional responding, but rather encompasses a wide variety of other functions related to digestion, homeostasis, effort, attention, and so forth (Berntson & Cacioppo, 2000). This is an important point because it is often not clear whether activity in the ANS reflects emotional processes or, perhaps instead, other functions subserved by the ANS (Obrist, Webb, Sutterer, & Howard, 1970; Stemmler, 2004).

The most commonly assessed indices of ANS activation are based on electrodermal (i.e., sweat gland) or cardiovascular (i.e., blood circulatory system) responses. Electrodermal responding is typically quantified in terms of skin conductance level (SCL) or short-duration skin conductance responses (SCRs). The most commonly used cardiovascular measures include heart rate (HR), blood pressure (BP), total peripheral resistance (TPR), cardiac output (CO), pre-ejection period (PEP), and heart rate variability (HRV). Each of these measures varies in terms of whether it primarily reflects sympathetic activity, parasympathetic activity, or both. For example, SCL and PEP predominantly reflect sympathetic activity, HR and BP reflect a combination of sympathetic and parasympathetic activity, and HRV has been closely linked to parasympathetic activity (Cacioppo, Berntson, Larsen, Poehlmann, & Ito, 2000).

James (1884) was among the first psychologists to suggest that different emotional states (e.g., sadness, anger, fear) involve specific patterns of ANS activation. James's speculations have been central to many important theories of emotion (Ellsworth, 1994; Lang, 1994), though Ellsworth cautions that it would be a mistake to equate James's theory with peripheral ANS responding considered alone. Nonetheless, much of the research inspired by James's theory of emotion has focused on ANS measures. One reason for the continued scientific interest in autonomic specificity is that people generally believe that their emotions involve discrete patterns of ANS activation (such as the presumed link between anxiety and increased heart rate: Scherer & Wallbott, 1994). However, the validity of such beliefs is suspect because perceptions of ANS responses are generally not predictive of actual ANS responses (Mauss, Wilhelm, & Gross, 2004; Pennebaker, 1982).

Furthermore, although some evidence for autonomic specificity has been reported (Christie & Friedman, 2004; Ekman, Levenson, & Friesen, 1983; Stemmler, Heldmann, Pauls, & Scherer, 2001), a recent meta-analysis has characterised such effects as inconsistent (Cacioppo et al., 2000). In this meta-analysis, only a small set of the 37 ANS measures reviewed reliably differentiated discrete emotions and replicable findings were specific to particular comparisons (e.g., finger temperature decreases less in anger than in fear, but finger temperature does not differentiate other discrete emotions). Also, although there were mean differences in some ANS responses across emotions, results were highly inconsistent across studies. By contrast, different induction methods (e.g., directed facial expressions versus film clips) have much more reliable effects on ANS measures than different emotions, again highlighting the paucity of support for the autonomic specificity hypothesis (Cacioppo et al., 2000).

Given these considerations, it may be best to view ANS responding in terms of broader dimensions such as arousal (Cacioppo et al., 2000; Duffy, 1962; Malmo, 1959). In support of this point, Peter Lang and colleagues have shown, in a number of studies (e.g., Bradley & Lang, 2000b; Lang, Greenwald, Bradley, & Hamm, 1993), that SCL increases systematically and linearly according to the rated arousal of emotional stimuli (e.g., slides). Moreover, the same studies have found that relations between stimulus arousal and SCL activity are independent of stimulus valence, emotion induction method, and, indeed, which specific emotion is targeted by the induction. Such findings are consistent with theories contending that ANS activity indexes the arousal level of the emotional state rather than its discrete emotional basis (Arnold, 1960; Cannon, 1931; Duffy, 1962).

However, not all measures of ANS responding map onto a single dimension. According to the principle of "directional fractionation" (Lacey, 1967), different measures of ANS activity can operate independently or even in opposition to each other. For example, HR decreases can co-occur with increases in sympathetic activity as assessed by other ANS measures (Bradley & Lang, 2000b; Lang et al., 1997; Libby, Lacey, & Lacey, 1973). To explain such fractionation of the ANS system, at least one additional dimension must be taken into consideration (Cacioppo et al., 2000; Russell & Barrett, 1999). Konorski, and later Lang (Konorski, 1967; Lang, Bradley, & Cuthbert, 1990; Lang et al., 1997) proposed appetitive and aversive systems as the second important dimension of ANS responding; others have proposed a similar valence dimension (Cacioppo et al., 2000; Russell & Barrett, 1999). For example, Cacioppo and colleagues' meta-analysis (2000) revealed that blood pressure, cardiac output, heart rate, and skin conductance response duration respond to emotional valence.

Although individual ANS measures appear responsive to dimensions rather than discrete emotional states, the joint consideration of multiple ANS measures may support a greater degree of autonomic specificity (Cacioppo et al., 2000; Stemmler, 2004). For example, Stemmler reports that anger and fear, despite being matched in terms of valence and arousal, could be differentiated by a combination of cardiovascular and respiratory measures. Similarly, Kreibig, Wilhelm, Roth, and Gross (2007) found that eleven ANS measures, jointly considered, differentiated responses to fear-inducing versus sadness-inducing film clips (matched on valence and arousal) with 85% accuracy. Thus, combinations of multiple ANS measures may yield better predictions of discrete emotional states. However, data of this type often capitalise on sample-specific findings and should be viewed as tentative in the absence of replications.

Recall, also, that ANS measures serve multiple masters including perceived and actual task demands, coping appraisals, and motor behaviour (Obrist et al., 1970; Stemmler, 2004). For this reason, it may be problematic to view *any* ANS pattern as a straightforward reflection of the emotional state of the individual. Such considerations are particularly problematic for views emphasising an invariant, unmediated influence of emotion on physiological responding (Panksepp, 1999; Tompkins, 1995). By contrast, if one views emotions as inextricably linked to task demands, coping, and motor behaviour (Ekman, 1999; Larsen, Berntson, Poehlmann, Ito, & Cacioppo, 2008; Levenson, 2003; Stemmler, 1989), then it is less of a concern that ANS activity responds to both emotional states and non-emotional factors.

*Summary*

The idea that discrete emotions have distinct autonomic signatures has not faired well in the literature. Instead, relevant studies often point to relationships among dimensions, particularly those of valence and arousal, and ANS responses. It is possible that considering patterns of multiple ANS measures will lead to autonomic specificity in the future, but more work is needed before coming to firm conclusions. Table 4.1 thus reinforces our central conclusion that ANS measures primarily respond to dimensional aspects of emotional states.

## STARTLE RESPONSE MAGNITUDE AS A MEASURE OF EMOTION

Startle in response to a sudden, intense stimulus is a universal reflex that involves multiple motor actions, including tensing of the neck and back muscles and an eye blink (Landis & Hunt, 1939). The startle response serves a protective function, guarding against potential bodily injury (particularly of the eye) and serving as a behavioural interrupt that is thought to facilitate vigilance in relation to a possible threat (Graham, 1979). In support of this hypothesis, the amygdala, which is a brain structure centrally involved in vigilance and threat detection (Whalen, 1998), plays a key role in modulating the startle response in threatening contexts (Davis, 1989; Koch & Schnitzler, 1997). Because the startle response thus lies at the intersection of several response systems (ANS, CNS, and behaviour), we describe it in a separate section.

The most robust component of the behavioural cascade that constitutes the startle reflex is the eye blink. Therefore, the amplitude of the eye blink is usually used to index startle magnitude among human participants. Such procedures involve an electromyogram (EMG) measurement in which muscle activity is assessed from electrodes placed over the orbicularis oculi muscle, just beneath the lower eyelid. The most commonly used startle-eliciting stimulus is the so-called "startle probe", a brief (50 ms) burst of white noise within the 95–110 decibel range.

Building to some extent on the work of Davis (1989), Lang (1995) made a strong case for the utility of startle amplitude as a measure of emotion. The logic here is that when the avoidance system is activated by a negative emotional state, then defensive responses (including the startle reflex) should be primed and thus increased relative to during neutral states. Conversely, higher levels of approach motivation likely inhibit tendencies toward a defensive orientation and should thus be associated with a lesser startle response magnitude relative to neutral states. Lang (1995) maps approach and avoidance onto positive and negative emotional states and thus hypothesises an inverse linear relationship between the valence of a person's emotional state and the startle response magnitude.

Lang's (1995) hypothesis has been strongly supported. Multiple studies have shown that when startle probes are delivered in the context of pictures and sounds that vary in valence, the magnitude of the startle response is larger in the context of unpleasant stimuli and smaller in the context of pleasant stimuli, both relative to neutral stimuli (Bradley, Cuthbert, & Lang, 1993; Bradley & Lang, 2000a; Vrana, Spence, & Lang, 1988). Such effects have been linked to emotional valence rather than to discrete emotional states (Lang, 1995). Convergent support for the startle response as a measure of emotional valence comes from the clinical literature. Phobic individuals should exhibit greater negative emotion and thus larger startle responses to phobic stimuli, and this result has been reported (Cook & Turpin, 1997). Conversely, individuals meeting criteria for psychopathy are thought to be deficient in threat processing. Consistent with this idea, such individuals, relative to non-psychopathic individuals, have been shown to exhibit smaller startle responses to threatening stimuli (Patrick, 1994).

Two important points qualify the general formulation that startle indexes emotional valence. First, it has been shown that startle magnitude is only sensitive to valence in the context of high-arousal stimuli (Cuthbert, Bradley, & Lang, 1996; Lang, 1995). Second, the startle appears to be particularly useful for understanding reactivity to perceived stimuli such as emotional pictures relative to other induction methods such as conditioning or imagery (Mallan & Lipp, 2007; Miller, Patrick, & Levenston, 2002; Sabatinelli, Bradley, & Lang, 2001). Within emotion-perception tasks, though, several potential confounds have been ruled out, including stimulus novelty, attentional factors, and sensory modality (Bradley, Cuthbert, & Lang, 1990; Bradley et al., 1993; Hawk & Cook, 1997; Lang et al., 1990 Lang et al., 1997).

### Summary

Together, the results summarised here suggest that the startle response is a marker of the valence dimension of emotional states. Specifically, as summarised in Table 4.1, the startle response is reliably larger in the context of high-arousal negative stimuli and reliably smaller in the context of high-arousal positive stimuli. At the same time, the measure does not appear to assess discrete emotional states.

## BRAIN STATES AS A MEASURE OF EMOTION

Following early theorising by Cannon (1931) and Bard (1928), many investigators have proposed that the physiological correlates of discrete emotions are likely to be found in the brain rather than in peripheral physiological responses (Buck, 1999; Izard, 2007; Panksepp, 2007). Researchers have taken up this challenge using EEG and neuroimaging methods. Because these methods produce very different types of data, we review EEG and imaging results separately.

### Electroencephalography (EEG)

Although the temporal resolution of EEG is excellent, its spatial resolution is limited (Dale & Sereno, 1993). Thus, EEG measures typically contrast activation in fairly large regions of the brain, often anterior (i.e., front of brain) versus posterior (i.e., back of brain) in combination with the distinction between left-sided and right-sided hemispheric activation. The most common EEG measure of this type is alpha power (8–13 Hz band), which is thought to be inversely related to regional cortical activation (Allen, Urry, Hitt, & Coan, 2004). In our review, we focus on what is termed "frontal asymmetry", which contrasts alpha power in the left frontal region with alpha power in the right frontal region, as this asymmetry-based measure has been particularly important to the emotion literature (Davidson, 1999).

Early studies of frontal asymmetry linked it to emotional valence. For example, Tomarken, Davidson, and Henriques (1990) found that greater left-sided activation at baseline predicted more intense experiences of positive than negative emotion, using a trait measure of emotional experience (although only among those individuals with stable EEG asymmetry profiles over time). Along similar lines, Davidson, Ekman, Saron, Senulis, and Friesen (1990) found that the induction of positive emotions by film clips led to greater left-sided frontal activation subsequent to the induction. These data suggest that frontal asymmetry assesses, or at least predisposes people to, pleasant emotional experiences (Davidson, 1999).

Subsequent studies, however, have provided convincing evidence that the frontal EEG asymmetry measure reflects the relative balance of approach versus avoidance motivation to a greater extent than it reflects emotional valence (Davidson, 1999). For example, Sutton and Davidson (1997) found that greater left-sided activation predicted dispositional tendencies toward approach, whereas greater right-sided asymmetry predicted dispositional tendencies toward avoidance. In contrast, the frontal asymmetry measure did not predict dispositional tendencies toward positive or negative emotions, suggesting an association of frontal asymmetry with approach–avoidance rather than with valence.

Other sources of data converge on a similar model of frontal asymmetry. Of particular importance are studies that link anger, an unpleasant but approach-related emotion, to greater left-hemispheric activation (Harmon-Jones & Allen, 1998; Harmon-Jones, Lueck, Fearn, & Harmon-Jones, 2006). Also, tendencies toward worry, thought to be approach-motivated in the sense of being linked to problem solving, have been linked to relatively greater left-frontal EEG activity (Heller, Schmidtke, Nitschke, Koven, & Miller, 2002). Thus, the emerging consensus appears to be that frontal EEG asymmetry primarily reflects levels of approach motivation (left hemisphere) versus avoidance motivation (right hemisphere).

## Neuroimaging studies

Neuroimaging studies, using fMRI (functional magnetic resonance imaging) or PET (positron emission tomography) technologies, can locate activation in far more specific brain regions than EEG. For this reason, it has been proposed that neuroimaging methods may be better suited than EEG to reveal emotion specificity in the brain (Panksepp, 1998). fMRI measures the uptake of oxygen in the blood (the "blood oxygenation level dependent" or BOLD signal; Detre & Floyd, 2000). PET assesses metabolic activity in the brain through the injection of a radioactive isotope the concentrations of which can be measured by a positron-emitting radio-isotope (Volkow, Rosen, & Farde, 1997). In both technologies, the assumption is that a greater signal reflects greater blood flow to a particular brain region, which in turn is thought to reflect activation of that region. For the sake of convenience, then, we refer to both sources of data in terms of the "activation" of the relevant brain region.

At the outset, it must be mentioned that any complex reaction such as an emotional state is likely to involve circuits rather than any brain region considered in isolation (Kagan, 2007; LeDoux, 2000; Storbeck, Robinson, & McCourt, 2006). However, particular brain regions may play a relatively greater or lesser role within larger circuits; thus localisation studies are meaningful in identifying the key regions involved. Our review here follows from two meta-analyses examining whether fear, disgust, sadness, and happiness can be linked to activation in particular brain regions (Murphy, Nimmo-Smith, & Lawrence, 2003; Phan, Wager, Taylor, & Liberzon, 2002). The majority of the reviewed studies were included in both meta-analyses, but the two meta-analyses differed somewhat in their analytic approach and, indeed, in their conclusions, as documented next.

The strongest apparent relation in both meta-analyses is between fear stimuli and amygdala activation (Murphy et al., 2003; Phan et al., 2002). However, there are reasons to resist the idea that amygdala activation is a straightforward reflection of fear. The amygdala is particularly responsive to fearful images relative to other fear-induction methods, and may thus be more closely tied to emotional perception than emotional experience (Wager et al., 2008). Moreover, the amygdala primarily responds to uncertainty and ambiguity, even relative to expected and unambiguous fearful stimuli

(LeDoux, 1996; Pessoa, Padmala, & Ungerleider, 2005; Whalen, 1998). Additionally, other data have linked amygdala activation to negative emotions more generally (Cahill et al., 1996) and even to reward processing and positive emotional states (Canli, 2004; Murray, 2007). Finally, it has been shown that individuals with bilateral damage to the amygdala can experience negative emotions, including fear (Anderson & Phelps, 2001; Anderson & Phelps, 2002). The preponderance of evidence thus suggests that the amygdala primarily responds to unexpected inputs of motivational significance rather than the experience of fear or processing of fear-related stimuli per se (Barrett, 2006b; Berridge, 1999; Holland & Gallagher, 1999).

Both meta-analyses agree that disgust stimuli tend to be associated with insula activation. However, the meta-analysis of Phan et al. (2002) found that a wide variety of negative emotion inductions activated the insula as well. Thus, the idea that there is a specific link between insula activation and disgust appears problematic. Furthermore, the insula supports many psychological functions, including processing of taste information, implicit learning, procedural memory, and motor performance (e.g., Frank, O'Reilly, & Curran, 2006; Keele, Ivry, Mayr, Hazeltine, & Heuer, 2003; Kiefer & Orr, 1992). For these reasons, it is difficult to endorse the simple view that insula activation can be equated with disgust.

Considering sadness, Phan et al. (2002) reported that 60% of the studies they reviewed found activation in the medial prefrontal cortex (mPFC), but Murphy et al. (2003) reported the strongest localisation pattern in the supracallosal anterior cingulate cortex (ACC; with about 50% of studies manipulating sadness showing this effect). This may not be an important discrepancy because the supracallosal ACC is well connected to areas of the mPFC, and thus an ACC–mPFC circuit may be involved in sadness. However, Barrett (2006a) raised an important concern about such studies, namely that they typically relied on induction methods involving high cognitive demand such as recalling a past event that caused sadness. This is an important potential confound because Phan et al. reported that cognitively demanding emotion inductions activate rostral portions of the ACC to a greater extent than passive emotional processing tasks do. This presents a concern for claiming a 1-to-1 correspondence of sadness to activation of an ACC–mPFC circuit.

The neural correlates of anger and happiness have been even less robust than those discussed above (Murphy et al., 2003; Phan et al., 2002). Furthermore, for the correlates reported, there are potential confounds such as those pertaining to the induction method used (Barrett, 2006a; Wager et al., 2008). In addition, there are concerns that some of the studies reviewed in the two meta-analyses used methods that have limited spatiotemporal resolution. Thus, although there has been some progress in understanding the neural correlates of fear, disgust, and potentially sadness, the discrete-emotions perspective has yet to produce strong, replicable findings.

At the same time, meta-analyses provide support for a dimensional perspective on emotion and brain activity. Consistent with the EEG data reported above, approach-related emotional states appear to be left-lateralised in the brain (Murphy et al., 2003; Wager, Phan, Liberzon, & Taylor, 2003). In addition to these lateralised patterns, Wager et al. (2003) found systematic relations between approach-motivated states and anterior and rostral portions of the medial prefrontal cortex (PFC) as well as the nucleus accumbens. Wager et al. (2003) also found systematic relations between avoidance-motivated states and the amygdala (especially its lateral and basolateral nuclei) and the ACC. Thus, there is increasing evidence that emotional states related to approach and avoidance involve localisable brain circuits (Barrett & Wager, 2006; Wager et al., 2008).

*Summary*

EEG and neuroimaging studies converge in concluding that relative left-hemisphere activation is reflective of approach-related states, whereas relative right-hemisphere activation is reflective of avoidance-related states. Specific brain regions, too, appear to be linked to states of approach and avoidance, as reviewed in the section on neuroimaging studies. Table 4.1 thus concludes that CNS measures appear to be sensitive to the dimensions of approach and avoidance. That said, because emotional states are complex and likely to involve circuits, neuroimaging methods that examine interrelated activity among multiple brain regions may hold more promise for understanding whether and how emotional specificity is instantiated in the brain.

## BEHAVIOUR AS A MEASURE OF EMOTION

Darwin (1965) suggested that emotions serve an evolved communicative function and thus should prime behaviours that reveal one's emotional state to others (see Ekman, 1992, for a related view). Another set of theories links emotional states to action dispositions, such as the primed tendency toward flight in the case of fear (Frijda, 1986; Lang et al., 1997). According to these theories, it should be possible to infer a person's emotional state from vocal characteristics, facial displays, and whole-body behaviours. We next review progress in this area of research. Because the term "expression" implies that emotions *naturally* trigger a given behaviour, we refer to "behaviour" or "movement" rather than "expression".

## Vocal characteristics

People often report that they infer the emotional states of others from vocal characteristics (Planalp, 1998). Scientific studies have examined this intuition most commonly by decomposing the acoustic waveform of speech and then assessing whether such acoustic properties are associated with the emotional state of the speaker (Juslin & Scherer, 2005). In our review, we concentrate on the most common measures, namely voice amplitude (i.e., loudness) and pitch (also known as fundamental frequency or $F_0$). Although advances in the digital analysis of sound waveforms have made it increasingly feasible to measure other vocal characteristics such as minute changes of vocal-fold vibration (see Bachorowski & Owren, 1995; Protopapas & Lieberman, 1997, for reviews), work of this complex type is just beginning and much remains to be learned (Juslin & Scherer, 2005).

The most consistent association reported in the literature is between arousal and vocal pitch, such that higher levels of arousal have been linked to higher-pitched vocal samples (Bachorowski, 1999; Kappas, Hess, & Scherer, 1991; Pittam, Gallois, & Callan, 1990). For example, Scherer, Banse, Wallbott, and Goldbeck (1991) examined the acoustic features of emotional nonsense sentences spoken by actors. When the actors were depicting high-arousal emotions such as fear, joy, and anger, pitch was higher than when they were depicting lower-arousal emotions such as sadness. Similar findings have been reported in studies of vocal character-istics following success or failure feedback and in the context of naturalistic studies of emotion and vocal responses (Bachorowski & Owren, 1995).

Based on results of this type, Bachorowski and Owren (1995) suggested that vocal pitch can be used to assess the level of emotional arousal currently experienced by the individual. On the other hand, it has been more difficult to find vocal characteristics that are sensitive to valence (Bachorowski, 1999; Leinonen, Hiltunen, Linnankoski, & Laakso, 1997; Protopapas & Lieberman, 1997). For example, anger and joy are similar in emotional arousal, but different in valence, yet both emotions have been linked to comparable vocal pitch and vocal amplitude (Johnstone & Scherer, 2000).

In the most comprehensive study that we know of, Banse and Scherer (1996) examined relations between 14 induced emotions and 29 acoustic variables. The authors found that a combination of ten acoustic properties differentiated discrete emotions to a greater extent than could be attributed to valence and arousal alone. For example, elation was characterised by medium low frequency (LF) energy and an increase of pitch over time, whereas anger was characterised by low LF energy and a decrease of pitch over time. However, these links were complex and multivariate in nature, involving post hoc comparisons that were novel to the literature and in some cases perhaps not theoretically motivated. Thus, replications are crucial to having greater confidence in the findings reported in this study.

## Facial behaviour

Darwin (1965) reasoned that facial displays are closely tied to the likely behaviour of the organism (e.g., biting in the case of anger, which would result in exposed teeth). Darwin further contended that such emotion–behaviour links reflect biologically evolved mechanisms, in that they subserve survival-related actions and communication functions. Ekman built on Darwin's analysis and showed that prototypic facial behaviours of at least six "basic" emotions (anger, fear, disgust, happiness, sadness, and surprise) could be recognised cross-culturally (Ekman & Friesen, 1971; Ekman, Sorenson, & Friesen, 1969; Fridlund, Ekman, & Oster, 1987; Izard, 1971). It is a different question—and one more pertinent to our review—to consider whether people spontaneously display such prototypic facial behaviours when in a particular emotional state.

*Observer ratings*

To examine the latter question, we review emotion-induction studies that have sought to link an induced emotional state to facial behaviours displayed during or immediately after the induction. Many of the relevant studies have quantified facial behaviour using componential coding. In most componential coding systems, trained coders detect facial muscle movements—or "facial actions"—using reliable scoring protocols (see Cohn & Ekman, 2005; Ekman & Friesen, 1978, for a comprehensive review). The most widely used componential coding system is the Facial Action Coding System (FACS; Ekman & Friesen, 1978; Ekman, Friesen, & Hager, 2002). The FACS is an anatomically based, comprehensive measurement system that assesses 44 different muscle movements (e.g., raising of the brows, tightening of the lips). As such, it measures all possible combinations of movements that are observable in the face rather than just movements that have been theoretically postulated. Other coding schemes seek to streamline the coding efforts by focusing on facial muscle contractions that are thought to have emotional significance (e.g., Izard, 1971; Kring & Sloan, 2007).

Facial behaviours appear to reliably indicate the valence of a person's emotional state (Russell, 1994). For example, Duchenne ("non-social") smiles—involving wrinkling of the muscles around the eyes—have often been linked to experiences of positive emotion (Ekman, Davidson, & Friesen, 1990; Frank, Ekman, & Friesen, 1993; Hess, Banse, & Kappas, 1995; Keltner & Bonanno, 1997). By contrast, negative emotion inductions are often associated with a visible facial behaviour in which the eyebrows are lowered and brought closer together (Kring & Sloan, 2007). In a recent study using a more molar facial action coding system, Mauss, Levenson, McCarter, Wilhelm, and Gross (2005) found strikingly large correlations between valence and the person's facial behaviours, $rs > .80$.

The case for the emotion specificity of facial behaviour has been more problematic and, indeed, very few studies of this type have been reported. In one such study, Rosenberg and Ekman (1994) exposed participants to disgust- and fear-inducing film clips. Following each film clip, participants rated their experience of eight discrete emotions. Subsequently, videotaped facial behaviour was scored in terms of the same eight discrete emotions. The researchers then determined whether discrete experiences and facial behaviours co-occurred beyond chance level. This was the case, but such relationships were also weak and not very robust in nature (see Bonanno & Keltner, 2004, for additional results of this type).

Other results, though, present challenges for the entire enterprise of treating facial behaviours as a reflection of the person's emotional state, regardless of whether a dimensional or discrete perspective is adopted. For example, Schneider and Josephs (1991) found that children smiled more after failure feedback than after success feedback, clearly a problem for the assumption that smiles reflect positive emotional states. In addition, several studies have found that associations between positive emotional states and facial smiles are stronger—and perhaps exclusive to—contexts in which an audience is present (Fernandez-Dols & Ruiz-Belda, 1995; Fridlund, 1991; Kraut & Johnston, 1979). Such results comport with Darwin's (1965) analysis of the communicative function of facial behaviour. They also suggest that it may often be hazardous to assume that exhibited facial behaviour provides a "direct readout" of a person's emotional state.

*Electromyography (EMG)*

Facial behaviours potentially indicative of emotion can also be assessed with facial EMG, which involves measuring electrical potential from facial muscles via the placement of electrodes on the face. The two most frequently targeted muscle groups are the corrugator supercilii (associated with furrowing of the eyebrows) and the zygomatic muscle (associated with raising of the corners of the lips). Results from this literature have converged on the utility of these measures for assessing the valence of a person's emotional state, but are generally viewed as limited in understanding discrete emotional reactions (Cacioppo, Berntson, Klein, & Poehlmann, 1997; Larsen et al., 2008; but see Vrana, 1993). Corrugator muscle activity decreases linearly with the pleasantness of affective stimuli—responding to stimuli across the full valence spectrum, while zygomatic muscle activity increases linearly with the pleasantness of affective stimuli—responding to pleasant stimuli (see Bradley & Lang, 2000b; Lang et al., 1993; Larsen, Norris, & Cacioppo, 2003, for reviews). Cacioppo et al. suggested that facial EMG activity reflects implicit evaluation processes (Dimberg, Thunberg, & Elmehed, 2000), but more work of this type is warranted before coming to firm conclusions (Larsen et al., 2003).

## Whole-body behaviour

Darwin (1965) presented the idea that bodily behaviours are biologically evolved to communicate one's emotional state to conspecifics. Although research on bodily expressions of emotion is relatively sparse (Adolphs, 2002; Van den Stock, Righart, & de Gelder, 2007), the research that does exist points to the idea that at least certain emotional states may have distinct bodily behaviour signatures. In particular, pride and embarrassment have been linked to expansive and diminutive body postures, respectively. Stepper and Strack (1993) found that participants experienced greater pride if an elevated posture had been implicitly manipulated beforehand. Results from Tracy and Robins' research programme confirm the link between pride and an expansive body posture (Tracy & Matsumoto, 2008; Tracy & Robins, 2004; Tracy, Robins, & Lagattuta, 2005). Conversely, Keltner and Buswell (1997) have found that embarrassment is reflected in bodily postures associated with minimising one's spatial presence, a result consistent with ethological data on dominance–submission and resulting behavioural postures (Mazur, 2005).

Although embarrassment and pride have been linked to distinct body postures, they have not been linked to distinct facial behaviours (Keltner & Buswell, 1997; Tracy & Robins, 2004). App, McIntosh, and Reed (2007) presented a social-functional analysis in which they provided a rationale for why some emotions are primarily associated with facial behaviours, whereas other emotions are primarily associated with whole-body behaviours. They suggested that some emotions, namely anger, fear, disgust, happiness, and sadness, primarily serve individual-level adaptive functions and should therefore be linked to facial behaviours rather than whole-body behaviours, which are potentially disruptive of an individual's interactions with the environment. On the other hand, the authors suggested that emotions such as embarrassment, guilt, pride, and shame are centrally linked to a person's position within a social status hierarchy. These emotions, then, should be more systematically associated with behaviours that signal to larger groups of individuals one's current emotional state (i.e., whole-body behaviours). Functional analyses of this type appear promising for understanding links between emotions and behaviour, and more research is encouraged.

## Summary

The assessment of vocal characteristics appears to be especially useful in understanding levels of emotional arousal, with higher levels of pitch and amplitude associated with higher levels of arousal (Table 4.1). By contrast, attempts to link emotional valence or discrete emotions to vocal characteristics have been met with mixed success at best, although more sophisticated methods may be capable of doing so in the future. Thus, we conclude that vocal characteristics are primarily reflective of the dimension of emotional arousal.

By contrast, facial behaviours appear to be particularly sensitive to the valence of a person's emotional state (Table 4.1). An important caveat, though, is that a number of factors such as gender, culture, expressiveness, and the inferred presence of an audience, likely moderate relations between emotional states and facial behaviours. This may be true to such an extent that the absence of changes in facial behaviour should not be equated with the absence of an emotion, and vice versa.

Body posture has not received a great deal of attention as a measure of emotion. Yet, studies that have been conducted suggest that pride and embarrassment are associated with expansive versus diminutive postures, respectively (Table 4.1). App and colleagues' analysis suggests that such links may be specific to social-status-related emotions (Table 4.1). If this proves to be the case, body posture measures might be unique among the measures that we reviewed in supporting a discrete emotional perspective.

## GENERAL DISCUSSION

Having reviewed measures of the main components of emotional responding and their sensitivity to different aspects of emotional state, we now comment on two more general questions that cut across our review. The first question is whether dimensional or discrete approaches better capture the structure of emotional responses. The second question is whether multiple measures of emotion converge, as is suggested by the consensual model of Figure 4.1.

## Measures of emotional responding: Dimensional or discrete?

Emotions have been conceptualised in both dimensional and discrete terms. Dimensional perspectives argue that emotional states are organised by underlying factors such as valence, arousal, and motivational state (Barrett & Russell, 1999; Watson et al., 1999). Discrete emotion perspectives, by contrast, suggest that each emotion (e.g., anger, sadness, happiness) has unique experiential, physiological, and behavioural correlates.

Our review tended to support the dimensional perspective. For example, we reviewed evidence for the idea that emotion specificity has been difficult to establish in the domains of ANS activity, affect-modulated startle responses, and vocal characteristics. Even in relation to measures of emotion that are associated with a greater degree of specificity, such as facial behaviour, dimensional frameworks appear to have substantial explanatory value. Thus, one conclusion of our review is that dimensions appear to capture the lion's share of variance of emotional responses.

Dimensional and discrete perspectives can be reconciled to some extent by conceptualising discrete emotions in terms of combinations of multiple dimensions (e.g., anger = negative valence, high arousal, and high approach motivation) that *appear* discrete because they are salient (Carver, 2004; Haidt & Keltner, 1999). If discrete emotions are defined in this manner, there is no necessary antagonism between the two perspectives (Haidt &

Keltner, 1999). However, to the extent that dimensional perspectives are sufficient for capturing the essence of particular emotional states, such perspectives should be favoured because they are more parsimonious (Watson, 2000). In addition, the available data are incompatible with the notion that discrete emotional states are *categorically* different from one another, that is, that they are "natural kinds" (cf. Barrett, 2006a).

Of course, some data differentiate emotional states beyond the three factors of valence, arousal, and approach–avoidance (App et al., 2007; Banse & Scherer, 1996; DeSteno, Petty, Wegener, & Rucker, 2000; Lerner, Dahl, Hariri, & Taylor, 2007; Rosenberg & Ekman, 1994). It may be that investigations using more sophisticated methods (e.g., ANS approaches that take into account combinations of variables or fMRI approaches that examine activity in brain circuits rather than specific brain regions), will support the discrete emotions perspective beyond what has been shown so far.

## To what extent do different measures of emotion converge?

Our review focused on each measure of emotion individually. Thus, an important remaining question is the extent to which different measures of emotion converge in understanding a person's emotional state. The idea that the components of emotion *should* converge is consistent with theories invoking the idea of "affect programmes". When such programmes are activated, according to these theories, there should be convergent outputs in emotional experience, physiology, and behaviour (see Figure 4.1 for such a model).

This model has not been well supported in studies that have examined convergence of response systems. Correlations among multiple measures of emotion are moderate at best, small in typical studies, and inconsistent across studies (e.g., Cacioppo et al., 2000; Lang, 1988; Mauss et al., 2004). Psychometric factors could play some role in the lack of convergence typically observed. For example, any one measure of emotion is likely associated with variance unique to it, in turn rendering high levels of convergence difficult to find. Also, most prior studies have assessed coherence in terms of between-individual correlations, thus measuring whether individuals who respond strongly in one component also respond strongly in another. It has been noted that such between-individual analyses might not be the best test of response coherence but that within-individual associations of measures across time more closely denote response-system coherence as implied by the theories of emotion outlined above (Buck, 1980; Lacey, 1967; Stemmler, 1992).

Recent studies have addressed some of these psychometric limitations by using reliable and valid measures and by using within-subject designs (Mauss et al., 2005; Reisenzein, 2000; Ruch, 1995). These studies have found higher levels of convergence than prior studies, but the relevant correlations were still low to moderate in strength (e.g., Mauss et al., 2005). In sum, psychometric issues do not appear sufficient in understanding the low levels of convergence observed in studies of this type.

The typical lack of strong convergence among multiple measures of emotion has three important implications. First, it appears that the construct of "emotion" cannot be captured with any one measure considered alone (Lang, 1988; Mandler, 1975; Rachman, 1978). In other words, emotions are multiply determined rather than characterised by a one-dimensional process such as that depicted in Figure 4.1. Practically speaking, then, the more measures of emotion that are obtained and the better they are tailored to the particular context and research question, the more one will likely learn from a particular study (cf. Larsen & Prizmic-Larsen, 2006). Second, dissociations among different measures of emotion may be relatively normal rather than necessarily reflective of a dysregulated system. In this context, research that examines the mechanisms that mediate and explain particular response-system dissociations will be particularly useful. Third, there are likely to be moderator variables that affect convergence across measures of emotion (Fridlund, Schwartz, & Fowler, 1984; Lacey, Bateman, & Vanlehn, 1953; Picard, Vyzas, & Healey, 2001). If this is the case, then a more idiographic approach would be necessary to understand the nature of emotional response coherence (Malmo, Shagrass, & Davis, 1950).

## CONCLUSIONS

The present review examined whether emotional states are associated with specific and invariant patterns of experience, physiology, and behaviour. We suggest that measures of emotional responding appear to be structured along dimensions (e.g., valence, arousal) rather than discrete emotional states (e.g., sadness, fear, anger). Additionally, different measures of emotion appear sensitive to different dimensional aspects of state (e.g., facial EMG is sensitive to valence, whereas skin conductance is sensitive to arousal) and are not strongly related to one another. Practically speaking, then, there is no "gold standard" measure of emotional responding. For theories of emotion, this means that there is no "thing" that defines emotion, but rather that emotions are constituted by multiple, situationally and individually variable processes.

## REFERENCES

Adolphs, R. (2002). Recognizing emotion from facial expressions: Psychological and neurological mechanisms. *Behavioral and Cognitive Neuroscience Reviews*, *1*(1), 21–62.

Allen, J. J. B., Urry, H. L., Hitt, S. K., & Coan, J. A. (2004). The stability of resting frontal electroencephalographic asymmetry in depression. *Psychophysiology, 41*(2), 269–280.

Anderson, A. K., & Phelps, E. A. (2001). Lesions of the human amygdala impair enhanced perception of emotionally salient events. *Nature, 411*(6835), 305–309.

Anderson, A. K., & Phelps, E. A. (2002). Is the human amygdala critical for the subjective experience of emotion? Evidence of intact dispositional affect in patients with amygdala lesions. *Journal of Cognitive Neuroscience, 14*(5), 709–720.

App, B., McIntosh, D., & Reed, C. (2007). *A social-functional approach to emotion communication: "How" depends on "why".* Poster presented at the annual meeting of the Society for Personality and Social Psychology.

Arnold, M. B. (1960). *Emotion and personality.* New York: Columbia University Press.

Bachorowski, J.-A. (1999). Vocal expression and perception of emotion. *Current Directions in Psychological Science, 8*(2), 53–57.

Bachorowski, J.-A., & Owren, M. J. (1995). Vocal expression of emotion: Acoustic properties of speech are associated with emotional intensity and context. *Psychological Science, 6*(4), 219–224.

Banse, R., & Scherer, K. R. (1996). Acoustic profiles in vocal emotion expression. *Journal of Personality and Social Psychology, 70*(3), 614–636.

Bard, P. (1928). A diencephalic mechanism for the expression of rage with special reference to the sympathetic nervous system. *American Journal of Physiology, 84*, 490–515.

Barrett, L. F. (2006a). Are emotions natural kinds? *Perspectives in Psychological Science, 1*, 28–58.

Barrett, L. F. (2006b). Solving the emotion paradox: Categorization and the experience of emotion. *Personality and Social Psychology Review, 10*(1), 20–46.

Barrett, L. F., Robin, L., Pietromonaco, P. R., & Eyssell, K. M. (1998). Are women the "more emotional" sex? Evidence from emotional experiences in social context. *Cognition and Emotion, 12*(4), 555–578.

Barrett, L. F., & Russell, J. A. (1999). The structure of current affect: Controversies and emerging consensus. *Current Directions in Psychological Science, 8*(1), 10–14.

Barrett, L. F., & Wager, T. D. (2006). The structure of emotion: Evidence from neuroimaging studies. *Current Directions in Psychological Science, 15*(2), 79–83.

Berntson, G. G., & Cacioppo, J. T. (2000). From homeostasis to allodynamic regulation. In J. T. Cacioppo, L. G. Tassinary, & G. G. Berntson (Eds.), *Handbook of psychophysiology* (2nd ed., pp. 459–481). New York: Cambridge University Press.

Berridge, K. C. (1999). Pleasure, pain, desire, and dread: Hidden core processes of emotion. In D. Kahneman, E. Diener, & N. Schwarz (Eds.), *Well-being: The foundations of hedonic psychology* (pp. 525–557). New York: Russell Sage Foundation.

Bonanno, G. A., & Keltner, D. (2004). The coherence of emotion systems: Comparing "on-line" measures of appraisal and facial expressions, and self-report [Brief Report]. *Cognition and Emotion, 18*(3), 431–444.

Bradley, M. M., Cuthbert, B. N., & Lang, P. J. (1990). Startle reflex modification: Emotion or attention? *Psychophysiology, 27*(5), 513–522.

Bradley, M. M., Cuthbert, B. N., & Lang, P. J. (1993). Pictures as prepulse: Attention and emotion in startle modification. *Psychophysiology, 30*(5), 541–545.

Bradley, M. M., & Lang, P. J. (2000a). Affective reactions to acoustic stimuli. *Psychophysiology, 37*(2), 204–215.

Bradley, M. M., & Lang, P. J. (2000b). Measuring emotion: Behavior, feeling, and physiology. In R. D. Lane & L. Nadel (Eds.), *Cognitive neuroscience of emotion* (pp. 242–276). New York: Oxford University Press.

Buck, R. (1980). Nonverbal behavior and the theory of emotion: The facial feedback hypothesis. *Journal of Personality and Social Psychology, 38*(5), 811–824.

Buck, R. (1999). The biological affects: A typology. *Psychological Review, 106*(2), 301–336.

Cacioppo, J., Berntson, G. G., Klein, D. J., & Poehlmann, K. M. (1997). The psychophysiology of emotion across the lifespan. *Annual Review of Gerontology and Geriatrics, 17*, 27–74.

Cacioppo, J. T., Berntson, G. G., Larsen, J. T., Poehlmann, K. M., & Ito, T. A. (2000). The psychophysiology of emotion. In M. Lewis & J. M. Haviland-Jones (Eds.), *The handbook of emotion*. New York: Guildford Press.

Cahill, L., Haier, R., Fallon, J., Akire, M., Tang, C., Keator, D., et al. (1996). Amygdala activity at encoding correlated with long-term, free recall of emotional information. *Proceedings of the National Academy of Sciences, 93*, 8016–8321.

Canli, T. (2004). Functional brain mapping of extraversion and neuroticism: Learning from individual differences in emotion processing. *Journal of Personality, 72*(6), 1105–1132.

Cannon, W. B. (1931). Again the James–Lange and the thalamic theories of emotion. *Psychological Review, 38*(4), 281–295.

Carver, C. S. (2004). Self-regulation of action and affect. In R. F. Baumeister & K. D. Vohs (Eds.), *Handbook of self-regulation: Research, theory, and applications* (pp. 13–39). New York: Guilford Press.

Christie, I. C., & Friedman, B. H. (2004). Autonomic specificity of discrete emotion and dimensions of affective space: A multivariate approach. *International Journal of Psychophysiology, 51*(2), 143–153.

Cohn, J. F., & Ekman, P. (2005). Measuring facial action. In J. A. Harrigan, R. Rosenthal, & K. R. Scherer (Eds.), *The new handbook of methods in nonverbal behavior research* (pp. 9–64). New York: Oxford University Press.

Cook, E., III, & Turpin, G. (1997). Differentiating orienting, startle, and defense responses: The role of affect and its implications for psychopathology. In P. J. Lang, R. F. Simons, & M. T. Balaban (Eds.), *Attention and orienting: Sensory and motivational processes* (pp. 137–164). Mahwah, NJ: Lawrence Erlbaum Associates, Inc.

Cuthbert, B. N., Bradley, M. M., & Lang, P. J. (1996). Probing picture perception: Activation and emotion. *Psychophysiology, 33*(2), 103–111.

Dale, A. M., & Sereno, M. I. (1993). Improved localization of cortical activity by combining EEG and MEG with MRI cortical surface reconstruction: A linear approach. *Journal of Cognitive Neuroscience, 5*(2), 162–176.

Darwin, C. (1965). *The expression of the emotions in man and animals*. Chicago: The University of Chicago Press. (Original work published 1872)

Davidson, R. J. (1999). Neuropsychological perspectives on affective styles and their cognitive consequences. In T. Dalgleish & M. J. Power (Eds.), *Handbook of cognition and emotion* (pp. 103–123). New York: Wiley.

Davidson, R. J., Ekman, P., Saron, C. D., Senulis, J. A., & Friesen, W. V. (1990). Approach–withdrawal and cerebral asymmetry: Emotional expression and brain physiology I. *Journal of Personality and Social Psychology, 58*(2), 330–341.

Davis, M. (1989). Neural systems involved in fear-potentiated startle. *Annals of the New York Academy of Sciences, 563*, 165–183.

DeSteno, D., Petty, R. E., Wegener, D. T., & Rucker, D. D. (2000). Beyond valence in the perception of likelihood: The role of emotion specificity. *Journal of Personality and Social Psychology, 78*(3), 397–416.

Detre, J. A., & Floyd, T. F. (2000). Functional MRI and its applications to the clinical neurosciences. *Neuroscientist, 7*, 64–79.

Dimberg, U., Thunberg, M., & Elmehed, K. (2000). Unconscious facial reactions to emotional facial expressions. *Psychological Science, 11*(1), 86–89.

Duffy, E. (1962). *Activation and behavior*. New York: Wiley.

Ekman, P. (1992). Facial expressions of emotion: New findings, new questions. *Psychological Science, 3*, 34–38.

Ekman, P. (1999). Basic emotions. In T. Dalgleish & M. J. Power (Eds.), *Handbook of cognition and emotion* (pp. 45–60). New York: Wiley.

Ekman, P., Davidson, R. J., & Friesen, W. V. (1990). The Duchenne smile: Emotional expression and brain physiology II. *Journal of Personality and Social Psychology, 58*(2), 342–353.

Ekman, P., & Friesen, W. V. (1971). Constants across cultures in the face and emotion. *Journal of Personality and Social Psychology, 17*(2), 124–129.

Ekman, P., & Friesen, W. V. (1978). *Facial action coding system: A technique for the measurement of facial movement*. Palo Alto, CA: Consulting Psychologists Press.

Ekman, P., Friesen, W. V., & Hager, J. C. (2002). *The facial action coding system*. Salt Lake City, UT: Research Nexus eBook.

Ekman, P., Levenson, R. W., & Friesen, W. V. (1983). Autonomic nervous system activity distinguishes among emotions. *Science, 221*(4616), 1208–1210.

Ekman, P., Sorenson, E. R., & Friesen, W. V. (1969). Pan-cultural elements in facial displays of emotion. *Science, 164*(3875), 86–88.

Ellsworth, P. C. (1994). William James and emotion: Is a century of fame worth a century of misunderstanding? *Psychological Review, 101*(2), 222–229.

Fernandez-Dols, J. M., & Ruiz-Belda, M. A. (1995). Expression of emotion versus expressions of emotions: Everyday conceptions of spontaneous facial behavior. In *Everyday conceptions of emotion: An introduction to the psychology, anthropology and linguistics of emotion* (Vol. 81). New York: Kluwer Academic/Plenum Publishers.

Frank, M. G., Ekman, P., & Friesen, W. V. (1993). Behavioral markers and recognizability of the smile of enjoyment. *Journal of Personality and Social Psychology, 64*(1), 83–93.

Frank, M. J., O'Reilly, R. C., & Curran, T. (2006). When memory fails, intuition reigns: Midazolam enhances implicit inference in humans. *Psychological Science, 17*(8), 700–707.

Fridlund, A. J. (1991). Sociality of solitary smiling: Potentiation by an implicit audience. *Journal of Personality and Social Psychology, 60*(2), 229–240.

Fridlund, A. J., Ekman, P., & Oster, H. (1987). Facial expressions of emotion. In A. W. Siegman & S. Feldstein (Eds.), *Nonverbal behavior and communication* (2nd ed., pp. 143–223). Hillsdale, NJ: Lawrence Erlbaum Associates, Inc.

Fridlund, A. J., Schwartz, G. E., & Fowler, S. C. (1984). Pattern recognition of self-reported emotional state from multiple-site facial EMG activity during affective imagery. *Psychophysiology, 21*(6), 622–637.

Frijda, N. H. (1986). *The emotions.* Cambridge, UK: Cambridge University Press.

Frijda, N. H. (1988). The laws of emotion. *American Psychologist, 43*(5), 349–358.

Graham, F. K. (1979). Distinguishing among orienting, defense, and startle reflexes. In H. D. Kimmel, E. H. V. Olst, & J. F. Orlebeke (Eds.), *The orienting reflex in humans.* Hillsdale, NJ: Lawrence Erlbaum Associates, Inc.

Gross, J. J. (2007). *Handbook of emotion regulation.* New York: Guilford Press.

Haidt, J., & Keltner, D. (1999). Culture and facial expression: Open-ended methods find more expressions and a gradient of recognition. *Cognition and Emotion, 13*(3), 225–266.

Harmon-Jones, E., & Allen, J. J. B. (1998). Anger and frontal brain activity: EEG asymmetry consistent with approach motivation despite negative affective valence. *Journal of Personality and Social Psychology, 74*(5), 1310–1316.

Harmon-Jones, E., Lueck, L., Fearn, M., & Harmon-Jones, C. (2006). The effect of personal relevance and approach-related action expectation on relative left frontal cortical activity. *Psychological Science, 17*(5), 434–440.

Hawk, L. W., & Cook, E. W., III (1997). Affective modulation of tactile startle. *Psychophysiology, 34*(1), 23–31.

Heller, W., Schmidtke, J. I., Nitschke, J. B., Koven, N. S., & Miller, G. A. (2002). States, traits, and symptoms: Investigating the neural correlates of emotion, personality, and psychopathology. In D. Cervone & W. Mischel (Eds.), *Advances in personality science* (pp. 106–126). New York: Guilford Press.

Hess, U., Banse, R., & Kappas, A. (1995). The intensity of facial expression is determined by underlying affective state and social situation. *Journal of Personality and Social Psychology, 69*(2), 280–288.

Holland, P. C., & Gallagher, M. (1999). Amygdala circuitry in attentional and representational processes. *Trends in Cognitive Sciences, 3*(2), 65–73.

Izard, C. E. (1971). *The face of emotion.* East Norwalk, CT: Appleton-Century-Crofts.

Izard, C. E. (2007). Levels of emotion and levels of consciousness. *Behavioral and Brain Sciences, 30*(1), 96–98.

James, W. (1884). What is an emotion? *Mind, 9,* 188–205.

Johnstone, T., & Scherer, K. R. (2000). Vocal communication of emotion. In M. Lewis & J. M. Haviland-Jones (Eds.), *Handbook of Emotions* (pp. 220–235). New York: Guilford Press.

Juslin, P. N., & Scherer, K. R. (2005). Vocal expression of affect. In J. A. Harrigan, R. Rosenthal, & K. R. Scherer (Eds.), *The new handbook of methods in nonverbal behavior research* (pp. 65–135). New York: Oxford University Press.

Kagan, J. (2007). A trio of concerns. *Perspectives on Psychological Science, 2*(4), 361–376.

Kappas, A., Hess, U., & Scherer, K. R. (1991). Voice and emotion. In R. S. Feldman & B. Rime (Eds.), *Fundamentals of nonverbal behavior* (pp. 200–238). Cambridge, UK: Cambridge University Press.

Keele, S. W., Ivry, R., Mayr, U., Hazeltine, E., & Heuer, H. (2003). The cognitive and neural architecture of sequence representation. *Psychological Review*, *110*(2), 316–339.

Keltner, D., & Bonanno, G. A. (1997). A study of laughter and dissociation: Distinct correlates of laughter and smiling during bereavement. *Journal of Personality and Social Psychology*, *73*(4), 687–702.

Keltner, D., & Buswell, B. N. (1997). Embarrassment: Its distinct form and appeasement functions. *Psychological Bulletin*, *122*(3), 250–270.

Kiefer, S. W., & Orr, M. R. (1992). Taste avoidance, but not aversion, learning in rats lacking gustatory cortex. *Behavioral Neuroscience*, *106*(1), 140–146.

Koch, M., & Schnitzler, H.-U. (1997). The acoustic startle response in rats— Circuits mediating evocation, inhibition and potentiation. *Behavioural Brain Research*, *89*(1–2), 35–49.

Konorski, J. (1967). *Integrative activity of the brain*. Chicago: University of Chicago Press.

Kraut, R. E., & Johnston, R. E. (1979). Social and emotional messages of smiling: An ethological approach. *Journal of Personality and Social Psychology*, *37*(9), 1539–1553.

Kreibig, S. D., Wilhelm, F. H., Roth, W. T., & Gross, J. J. (2007). Cardiovascular, electrodermal, and respiratory response patterns to fear- and sadness-inducing films. *Psychophysiology*, *44*(5), 787–806.

Kring, A. M., & Sloan, D. M. (2007). The facial expression coding system (FACES): Development, validation, and utility. *Psychological Assessment*, *19*(2), 210–224.

Lacey, J. (1967). Somatic response patterning and stress: Some revisions of activation theory. In M. H. Appley & R. Trumbull (Eds.), *Psychological stress: Issues in research*. New York: Appleton-Century-Crofts.

Lacey, J. I., Bateman, D. E., & Vanlehn, R. (1953). Autonomic response specificity: An experimental study. *Psychosomatic Medicine*, *15*, 8–21.

Landis, C., & Hunt, W. (1939). *The startle pattern*. Oxford, UK: Farrar & Rinehart.

Lane, R. D., Ahern, G. L., Schwartz, G. E., & Kaszniak, A. W. (1997). Is alexithymia the emotional equivalent of blindsight? *Biological Psychiatry*, *42*(9), 834–844.

Lang, P. J. (1988). What are the data of emotion? In V. Hamilton, G. H. Bower, & N. H. Frijda (Eds.), *Cognitive perspectives on emotion and motivation* (pp. 173–191). New York: Kluwer Academic/Plenum Publishers.

Lang, P. J. (1994). The varieties of emotional experience: A meditation on James– Lange theory. *Psychological Review*, *101*(2), 211–221.

Lang, P. J. (1995). The emotion probe: Studies of motivation and attention. *American Psychologist*, *50*(5), 372–385.

Lang, P. J., Bradley, M. M., & Cuthbert, B. N. (1990). Emotion, attention, and the startle reflex. *Psychological Review*, *97*(3), 377–395.

Lang, P. J., Bradley, M. M., & Cuthbert, B. N. (1997). Motivated attention: Affect, activation, and action. In P. J. Lang, R. F. Simons, & M. T. Balaban (Eds.), *Attention and orienting: Sensory and motivational processes* (pp. 97–135). Mahwah, NJ: Lawrence Erlbaum Associates, Inc.

Lang, P. J., Greenwald, M. K., Bradley, M. M., & Hamm, A. O. (1993). Looking at pictures: Affective, facial, visceral, and behavioral reactions. *Psychophysiology*, *30*(3), 261–273.

Larsen, J. T., Berntson, G. G., Poehlmann, K. M., Ito, T. A., & Cacioppo, J. T. (2008). The psychophysiology of emotion. In M. Lewis, J. M. Haviland-Jones, & L. F. Barrett (Eds.)*The handbook of emotions* (3rd ed., pp. 180–195). New York: Guilford Press.

Larsen, J. T., McGraw, A. P., & Cacioppo, J. T. (2001). Can people feel happy and sad at the same time? *Journal of Personality and Social Psychology, 81*(4), 684–696.

Larsen, J. T., Norris, C. J., & Cacioppo, J. T. (2003). Effects of positive and negative affect on electromyographic activity over zygomaticus major and corrugator supercilii. *Psychophysiology, 40*(5), 776–785.

Larsen, R. J., & Prizmic-Larsen, Z. (2006). Measuring emotions: Implications of a multimethod perspective. In M. Eid & E. Diener (Eds.), *Handbook of multimethod measurement in psychology* (pp. 337–351). Washington, DC: American Psychological Association.

Lazarus, R. S. (1991). *Emotion and adaptation.* Oxford, UK: Oxford University Press.

LeDoux, J. E. (1996). *The emotional brain: The mysterious underpinnings of emotional life.* New York: Simon & Schuster.

LeDoux, J. E. (2000). Emotion circuits in the brain. *Annual Review of Neuroscience, 23,* 155–184.

Leinonen, L., Hiltunen, T., Linnankoski, I., & Laakso, M.-L. (1997). Expression of emotional-motivational connotations with a one-word utterance. *Journal of the Acoustical Society of America, 102*(3), 1853–1863.

Lerner, J. S., Dahl, R. E., Hariri, A. R., & Taylor, S. E. (2007). Facial expressions of emotion reveal neuroendocrine and cardiovascular stress responses. *Biological Psychiatry, 61*(2), 253–260.

Levenson, R. W. (2003). Blood, sweat, and fears: The autonomic architecture of emotion. In P. Ekman, J. J. Campos, R. J. Davidson, & F. B. M. de Waal (Eds.), *Emotions inside out: 130 years after Darwin's: The expression of the emotions in man and animals* (pp. 348–366). New York: New York University Press.

Libby, W. L., Lacey, B. C., & Lacey, J. I. (1973). Pupillary and cardiac activity during visual attention. *Psychophysiology, 10*(3), 270–294.

Mallan, K. M., & Lipp, O. V. (2007). Does emotion modulate the blink reflex in human conditioning? Startle potentiation during pleasant and unpleasant cues in the picture–picture paradigm. *Psychophysiology, 44*(5), 737–748.

Malmo, R. B. (1959). Activation: A neuropsychological dimension. *Psychological Review, 66*(6), 367–386.

Malmo, R. B., Shagrass, C., & Davis, F. H. (1950). Symptom specificity and bodily reactions during psychiatric interview. *Psychosomatic Medicine, 12,* 362–376.

Mandler, G. (1975). *Mind and emotion.* New York: Wiley.

Matthews, G., & Gilliland, K. (1999). The personality theories of H. J. Eysenck and J. A. Gray: A comparative review. *Personality and Individual Differences, 26*(4), 583–626.

Mauss, I. B., Levenson, R. W., McCarter, L., Wilhelm, F. H., & Gross, J. J. (2005). The tie that binds? Coherence among emotion experience, behavior, and physiology. *Emotion, 5*(2), 175–190.

Mauss, I. B., Wilhelm, F. H., & Gross, J. J. (2004). Is there less to social anxiety than meets the eye? Emotion experience, expression, and bodily responding. *Cognition and Emotion, 18*(5), 631–662.

Mazur, A. (2005). *Biosociology of dominance and deference*. Lanham, MD: Rowman & Littlefield.

Miller, M. W., Patrick, C. J., & Levenston, G. K. (2002). Affective imagery and the startle response: Probing mechanisms of modulation during pleasant scenes, personal experiences and discrete negative emotions. *Psychophysiology, 39*(4), 519–529.

Mitchell, T. R., Thompson, L., Peterson, E., & Cronk, R. (1997). Temporal adjustments in the evaluation of events: The "rosy view". *Journal of Experimental Social Psychology, 33*(4), 421–448.

Murphy, F. C., Nimmo-Smith, I., & Lawrence, A. D. (2003). Functional neuroanatomy of emotions: A meta-analysis. *Cognitive, Affective & Behavioral Neuroscience, 3*(3), 207–233.

Murray, E. (2007). The amygdala, reward and emotion. *Trends in Cognitive Sciences, 11*, 489–497.

Obrist, P. A., Webb, R. A., Sutterer, J. R., & Howard, J. L. (1970). The cardiac-somatic relationship: Some reformulations. *Psychophysiology, 6*(5), 569–587.

Öhman, A., Hamm, A., & Hugdahl, K. (2000). Cognition and the autonomic nervous system: Orienting, anticipation, and conditioning. In J. T. Cacioppo, L. G. Tassinary, & G. G. Berntson (Eds.), *Handbook of psychophysiology* (2nd ed., pp. 533–575). New York: Cambridge University Press.

Panksepp, J. (1998). *Affective neuroscience: The foundations of human and animal emotions*. New York: Oxford University Press.

Panksepp, J. (1999). Emotions as viewed by psychoanalysis and neuroscience: An exercise in consilience. *Neuro-Psychoanalysis, 1*(1), 15–38.

Panksepp, J. (2007). Neurologizing the psychology of affects: How appraisal-based constructivism and basic emotion theory can coexist. *Perspectives on Psychological Science, 2*(3), 281–295.

Patrick, C. J. (1994). Emotion and psychopathy: Startling new insights. *Psychophysiology, 31*(4), 319–330.

Paulhus, D. L., & John, O. P. (1998). Egoistic and moralistic biases in self-perception: The interplay of self-deceptive styles with basic traits and motives. *Journal of Personality, 66*(6), 1025–1060.

Paulhus, D. L., & Reid, D. B. (1991). Enhancement and denial in socially desirable responding. *Journal of Personality and Social Psychology, 60*(2), 307–317.

Pennebaker, J. W. (1982). Physical symptoms associated with blood pressure. *Psychophysiology, 19*(2), 201–210.

Pessoa, L., Padmala, S., & Ungerleider, L. G. (2005). Quantitative prediction of perceptual decisions during near-threshold fear detection. *Proceedings of the National Academy of Sciences of the United States of America, 102*(15), 5612–5617.

Phan, K. L., Wager, T. D., Taylor, S. F., & Liberzon, I. (2002). Functional neuroanatomy of emotion: A meta-analysis of emotion activation studies in PET and fMRI. *NeuoroImage, 16*, 331–348.

Picard, R. W., Vyzas, E., & Healey, J. (2001). Toward machine emotional intelligence: Analysis of affective physiological state. *IEEE Transactions Pattern Analysis and Machine Intelligence, 23*(10), 1172–1191.

Pittam, J., Gallois, C., & Callan, V. (1990). The long-term spectrum and perceived emotion. *Speech Communication, 9*(3), 177–187.

Planalp, S. (1998). Communicating emotion in everyday life: Cues, channels, and processes. In P. A. Andersen & L. K. Guerrero (Eds.), *Handbook of communication and emotion: Research, theory, applications, and contexts* (pp. 29–48). San Diego, CA: Academic Press.

Protopapas, A., & Lieberman, P. (1997). Fundamental frequency of phonation and perceived emotional stress. *Journal of the Acoustical Society of America, 101*(4, Pt. 1), 2267–2277.

Rachman, S. (1978). Human fears: A three systems analysis. *Scandinavian Journal of Behaviour Therapy, 7*(4), 237–245.

Reisenzein, R. (2000). Exploring the strength of association between the components of emotion syndromes: The case of surprise. *Cognition and Emotion, 14*(1), 1–38.

Robinson, M. D., & Clore, G. L. (2002). Episodic and semantic knowledge in emotional self-report: Evidence for two judgment processes. *Journal of Personality & Social Psychology, 83*(1), 198–215.

Robinson, M. D., & Neighbors, C. (2006). Catching the mind in action: Implicit methods in personality research and assessment. In M. Eid & E. Diener (Eds.), *Handbook of multimethod measurement in psychology* (pp. 115–125). Washington, DC: American Psychological Association.

Robinson, M. D., & Sedikides, C. (in press). Traits and the self: Toward an integration. In P. J. Corr & G. Matthews (Eds.), *Handbook of personality*. Cambridge, UK: Cambridge University Press.

Rosenberg, E. L., & Ekman, P. (1994). Coherence between expressive and experiential systems in emotion. *Cognition and Emotion, 8*(3), 201–229.

Ruch, W. (1995). Will the real relationship between facial expression and affective experience please stand up: The case of exhilaration. *Cognition and Emotion, 9*(1), 33–58.

Russell, J. A. (1980). A circumplex model of affect. *Journal of Personality and Social Psychology, 39*(6), 1161–1178.

Russell, J. A. (1994). Is there universal recognition of emotion from facial expressions? A review of the cross-cultural studies. *Psychological Bulletin, 115*(1), 102–141.

Russell, J. A., & Barrett, L. F. (1999). Core affect, prototypical emotional episodes, and other things called emotion: Dissecting the elephant. *Journal of Personality and Social Psychology, 76*(5), 805–819.

Rusting, C. L. (1998). Personality, mood, and cognitive processing of emotional information: Three conceptual frameworks. *Psychological Bulletin, 124*(2), 165–196.

Sabatinelli, D., Bradley, M. M., & Lang, P. J. (2001). Affective startle modulation in anticipation and perception. *Psychophysiology, 38*(4), 719–722.

Scherer, K. R. (1984). Emotion as a multicomponent process: A model and some cross-cultural data. *Review of Personality & Social Psychology, 5*, 37–63.

Scherer, K. R., Bance, R., Wallbott, H. G., & Goldbeck, T. (1991). Vocal cues in emotion encoding and decoding. *Motivation and Emotion, 15*, 123–148.

Scherer, K. R., & Wallbott, H. G. (1994). Evidence for universality and cultural variation of differential emotion response patterning. *Journal of Personality and Social Psychology, 66*, 310–328.

Schneider, K., & Josephs, I. (1991). The expressive and communicative functions of preschool children's smiles in an achievement-situation. *Journal of Nonverbal Behavior, 15*(3), 185–198.

Schneirla, T. C. (1959). An evolutionary and developmental theory of biphasic processes underlying approach and withdrawal. In M. R. Jones (Ed.), *Nebraska symposium on motivation, 1959* (pp. 1–42). Lincoln, NE: University of Nebraska.

Shedler, J., Mayman, M., & Manis, M. (1993). The illusion of mental health. *American Psychologist, 48*(11), 1117–1131.

Smith, C. A., & Ellsworth, P. C. (1985). Patterns of cognitive appraisal in emotion. *Journal of Personality and Social Psychology, 48*(4), 813–838.

Stemmler, G. (1989). The autonomic differentiation of emotions revisited: Convergent and discriminant validation. *Psychophysiology, 26*(6), 617–632.

Stemmler, G. (1992). *Differential psychophysiology: Persons in situations*. Berlin, Germany: Springer-Verlag.

Stemmler, G. (2004). Physiological processes during emotion. In P. Philippot & R. S. Feldman (Eds.), *The regulation of emotion* (pp. 33–70). Mahwah, NJ: Lawrence Erlbaum Associates, Inc.

Stemmler, G., Heldmann, M., Pauls, C. A., & Scherer, T. (2001). Constraints for emotion specificity in fear and anger: The context counts. *Psychophysiology, 38*(2), 275–291.

Stepper, S., & Strack, F. (1993). Proprioceptive determinants of emotional and nonemotional feelings. *Journal of Personality and Social Psychology, 64*, 211–220.

Storbeck, J., Robinson, M. D., & McCourt, M. E. (2006). Semantic processing precedes affect retrieval: The neurological case for cognitive primacy in visual processing. *Review of General Psychology, 10*(1), 41–55.

Sutton, S. K., & Davidson, R. J. (1997). Prefrontal brain asymmetry: A biological substrate of the behavioral approach and inhibition systems. *Psychological Science, 8*(3), 204–210.

Taylor, S. E., Lerner, J. S., Sherman, D. K., Sage, R. M., & McDowell, N. K. (2003). Are self-enhancing cognitions associated with healthy or unhealthy biological profiles? *Journal of Personality and Social Psychology, 85*(4), 605–615.

Tellegen, A., Watson, D., & Clark, L. A. (1999). On the dimensional and hierarchical structure of affect. *Psychological Science, 10*(4), 297–303.

Tomarken, A. J., Davidson, R. J., & Henriques, J. B. (1990). Resting frontal brain asymmetry predicts affective responses to films. *Journal of Personality and Social Psychology, 59*, 791–801.

Tompkins, S. S. (1995). *Exploring affect*. Cambridge, UK: Cambridge University Press.

Tracy, J. L., & Matsumoto, D. (2008). The spontaneous display of pride and shame: Evidence for biologically innate nonverbal displays. *Proceedings of the National Academy of Sciences, 105*, 11655–11660.

Tracy, J. L., & Robins, R. W. (2004). Show your pride: Evidence for a discrete emotion expression. *Psychological Science, 15*(3), 194–197.

Tracy, J. L., Robins, R. W., & Lagattuta, K. H. (2005). Can children recognize pride? *Emotion, 5*(3), 251–257.

Van den Stock, J., Righart, R., & de Gelder, B. (2007). Body expressions influence recognition of emotions in the face and voice. *Emotion, 7*(3), 487–494.

Volkow, N. D., Rosen, B., & Farde, L. (1997). Imaging the living human brain: Magnetic resonance imaging and positron emission tomography. *Proceedings of National Academy of Sciences of the United States of America, 94,* 2787–2788.

Vrana, S. R. (1993). The psychophysiology of disgust: Differentiating negative emotional contexts with facial EMG. *Psychophysiology, 30*(3), 279–286.

Vrana, S. R., Spence, E. L., & Lang, P. J. (1988). The startle probe response: A new measure of emotion? *Journal of Abnormal Psychology, 97*(4), 487–491.

Wager, T. D., Barrett, L. F., Bliss-Moreau, E., Lindquist, K., Duncan, S., Kober, H., et al. (2008). The neuroimaging of emotion. In M. Lewis, J. M. Haviland-Jones, & L. F. Barrett (Eds.), *Handbook of emotions* (pp. 249–271). New York: Guilford Press.

Wager, T. D., Phan, K. L., Liberzon, I., & Taylor, S. F. (2003). Valence, gender, and lateralization of functional brain anatomy in emotion: A meta-analysis of findings from neuroimaging. *NeuroImage, 19,* 513–531.

Watson, D. (2000). *Mood and temperament.* New York: Guildford Press.

Watson, D., Wiese, D., Vaidya, J., & Tellegen, A. (1999). The two general activation systems of affect: Structural findings, evolutionary considerations, and psychobiological evidence. *Journal of Personality and Social Psychology, 76*(5), 820–838.

Welte, J. W., & Russell, M. (1993). Influence of socially desirable responding in a study of stress and substance abuse. *Alcoholism: Clinical and Experimental Research, 17*(4), 758–761.

Whalen, P. J. (1998). Fear, vigilance, and ambiguity: Initial neuroimaging studies of the human amygdala. *Current Directions in Psychological Science, 7*(6), 177–188.

Correspondence should be addressed to: Iris B. Mauss, Department of Psychology, University of Denver, Denver, CO 80208, USA. E-mail: imauss@psy.du.edu

# 5 The psychology of emotion regulation: An integrative review

Sander L. Koole

*VU University Amsterdam, Amsterdam, The Netherlands*

Emotions are often portrayed as irresistible forces that exert a sweeping influence on behaviour. There is reason to believe, however, that people are much more flexible in dealing with their emotions. As it turns out, people can control virtually every aspect of emotional processing, including how emotion directs attention (Rothermund, Voss, & Wentura, 2008), the cognitive appraisals that shape emotional experience (Gross, 1998a), and the physiological consequences of emotion (Porges, 2007). These and other processes whereby people manage their own emotions are commonly referred to as *emotion regulation*. Emotion regulation has been linked to such important outcomes as mental health (Gross & Muñoz, 1995), physical health (Sapolsky, 2007), relationship satisfaction (Murray, 2005), and work performance (Diefendorff, Hall, Lord, & Strean, 2000). It thus seems vital to learn more about the psychology of emotion regulation.

The past decade has witnessed an explosion of emotion-regulation research (see Gross, 2007, for a comprehensive overview). Indeed, since the last review on this topic was published in *Cognition and Emotion* (Gross, 1999), more than 700 journal articles appeared with the term "emotion regulation" in the title or abstract, according to the PsycInfo database. The number of relevant publications becomes several times greater if one considers work on closely related topics such as mood regulation, affect regulation, and coping. The tremendous increase in research volume has rendered the study of emotion regulation one of the most vibrant areas in contemporary psychology. At the same time, it has become increasingly important to integrate the rapidly accumulating findings and insights. The need for integration is further enhanced by the multidisciplinary nature of emotion regulation research, which spans developmental, cognitive, social, personality, and clinical psychology, and, more recently, cognitive and affective neurosciences and psychophysiology.

The present article provides an integrative review of contemporary research on the psychology of emotion regulation. The relevant literature is too large to be covered exhaustively. Consequently, the present article gives priority to ideas and findings with broad implications for the psychology of emotion regulation. Because the development and disorders of emotion regulation have been reviewed elsewhere (Kring & Werner, 2004; Skinner & Zimmer-Gembeck, 2007; Southam-Gerow & Kendall, 2002; Taylor & Liberzon, 2007), the present article concentrates on emotion regulation among healthy adults. In the following paragraphs, I first consider more closely what emotion regulation is and how it relates to other forms of emotion processing. Next, I discuss several approaches to classifying strategies of emotion regulation and review empirical research on emotion-regulation strategies. Finally, I summarise the main conclusions of the present article and suggest avenues for future research on emotion regulation.

## WHAT IS EMOTION REGULATION?

In everyday life, people are continually exposed to potentially emotion-arousing stimuli, ranging from internal sensations like an upset stomach to external events such as juicy gossip about a colleague or music played in supermarkets. From the fact that these kinds of stimuli only occasionally trigger full-blown emotions, one could infer that people engage in some form of emotion regulation almost all of the time (Davidson, 1998). But emotion regulation may also become manifested in more overt ways. For instance, there are reliable observations that people may rapidly shift their attention away from threatening stimuli (Langens & Mörth, 2003), that people may overcome traumatic experiences by writing about them (Pennebaker & Chung, 2007), and that people may choose to hit a pillow instead of lashing out at the true cause of their anger (Bushman, Baumeister, & Phillips, 2001).

In each of the aforementioned cases, people resist being carried away or "hijacked" (Goleman, 1995) by the immediate emotional impact of the situation. Emotion regulation can thus be defined as the set of processes whereby people seek to redirect the spontaneous flow of their emotions. Some approaches have also considered emotion regulation by the external environment. For instance, developmental research indicates that caregivers may play a key role in regulating children's emotional states (Southam-Gerow & Kandell, 2002) and environmental research has shown that natural settings can promote more rapid recovery from stress than urban settings (Van den Berg, Hartig, & Staats, 2007). Emotion regulation by forces outside the self is clearly important. Nevertheless, following the predominant focus of the literature (Gross, 2007), the present article concentrates on the self-regulation of emotion.

The prototype of emotion regulation is a deliberate, effortful process that seeks to override people's spontaneous emotional responses. Some forms of emotion regulation indeed fit this prototype, by drawing upon the same psychological and neurobiological systems that are involved in the effortful control of action and attention (Ochsner & Gross, 2005, 2008; Tice &

Bratslavsky, 2000). However, other forms of emotion regulation are relatively automatic and effortless (Bargh & Williams, 2007; Koole & Kuhl, 2007; Mauss, Bunge, & Gross, 2007). Furthermore, emotion regulation does not always consist of an overriding process, in as far as this implies an antagonistic stance towards one's emotions. Indeed, some sophisticated forms of emotion regulation unfold in close collaboration with other types of emotion processing (Brown, Ryan, & Creswell, 2007; Pennebaker & Chung, 2007; Porges, 2007).

During emotion regulation, people may increase, maintain, or decrease positive and negative emotions. Accordingly, emotion regulation often involves changes in emotional responding. These changes may occur in the kinds of emotions that people have, when they have their emotions, and how they experience and express their emotions (Gross, 1999). Notably, the emotional changes that are produced by emotion regulation may or may not bring people closer to the emotional state that they desired. Indeed, some forms of emotion regulation ironically bring about the very emotional outcomes that people hope to avoid (e.g., Wegner, Erber, & Zanakos, 1993). Emotion regulation may also fail in other ways, such that people may still display unwanted emotions despite their best efforts to avoid them. When people are chronically unable to regulate their emotions, this may seriously disrupt psychological functioning. Indeed, chronic deficits in emotion regulation contribute to all major forms of psychopathology (Bradley, 2000; Kring & Werner, 2004).

## The scope of emotion regulation

Emotions have multiple components, consisting of a more or less coherent cluster of valenced (i.e., positive or negative) behavioural and physiological responses that are accompanied by specific thoughts and feelings (Cacioppo, Berntson, & Klein, 1992; Frijda, 2006; Mauss, Levenson, McCarter, Wilhelm, & Gross, 2005). Because emotion regulation operates on people's emotions, it follows that the effects of emotion regulation can be observed across all modalities of emotional responding, including behaviour, physiology, thoughts, and feelings.

According to some classic theories of emotion, each emotion triggers a discrete pattern of behaviour, physiology, thoughts, and feelings. However, the available evidence does not support the existence of discrete emotional states (Mauss & Robinson, 2009; Russell, 2003). Instead, emotional responding appears to be organised in terms of a few fundamental dimensions, including valence, arousal, and approach–avoidance. The influence of emotion regulation on people's emotional states is therefore likely to be similarly dimensional. In other words, emotion regulation may not be so much concerned with getting people in or out of discrete emotional states like anger, sadness, or joy. Rather, emotion regulation may change people's emotional states along dimensions such as valence, arousal, and approach–avoidance.

Closely related to emotion regulation are constructs such as mood regulation, coping with stress, and affect regulation. Although it is possible to distinguish semantically between these constructs, their substantive overlap is considerable. At the heart of all emotional states is *core affect* (Russell, 2003), basic states of feeling good or bad, energised or enervated. The regulation of specific emotions, moods, stress, and diffuse affect is therefore always aimed at changing core affect. Moreover, the empirical borders between these different emotion constructs are very fuzzy (Russell, 2003). In view of these considerations, it seems most productive to conceive of emotion regulation broadly, as relating to the management of all emotionally charged states, including discrete emotions, mood, stress, and affect. Ultimately, it may be possible to derive more fine-grained distinctions between different types of emotional states that are being regulated. At present, however, a broad conception of emotion regulation offers the best promise of uncovering the basic principles that underlie various emotion-regulatory activities.

## Emotion regulation versus emotional sensitivity

A longstanding issue is the distinction between emotion regulation and other forms of emotion processing. One seemingly straightforward approach would be to observe the differences between regulated and unregulated emotions. Unfortunately, this comparison is often difficult to make. People can regulate their emotions very rapidly (Jostmann, Koole, Van der Wulp, & Fockenberg, 2005; Rothermund et al., 2008). It is therefore often unclear "where an emotion ends and regulation begins" (Davidson, 1998, p. 308).

A conceptual solution to this problem lies in the temporal unfolding of an emotional response (Baumann, Kaschel, & Kuhl, 2007; Davidson, Jackson, & Kalin, 2000; Skinner & Zimmer-Gembeck, 2007). As it turns out, people's primary emotional response to the situation can be qualitatively different from their secondary emotional response—see also Lazarus' (1991) distinction between primary versus secondary appraisals. People's primary emotional response presumably reflects their emotional sensitivity, whereas their secondary emotional response presumably reflects emotion regulation. This distinction is grounded in the conceptualisation of emotion regulation as a control process. Control processes, as they are commonly understood, consist of the monitoring and adjusting of a lower-level process with respect to a given standard (Carver & Scheier, 1998). Applied to emotion regulation, this implies that an unwanted emotional response must occur initially before any emotion regulation can take place. Although people's primary emotional response is not yet regulated, it serves as vital input for the subsequent monitoring and control processes that constitute emotion regulation.

To illustrate the distinction between emotional sensitivity and emotion regulation, Figure 5.1 displays the development of an emotional response over time (after Kuhl, 2008). To simplify matters, the figure only shows a single emotional response with a single maximum strength. Emotional sensitivity is represented by the entry gradient, or the steepness with which the emotional response reaches its full force. Emotional sensitivity is determined by any variable that influences people's initial emotional response to the situation, including the nature of the stimuli that people encounter, personal characteristics, and the broader situation. The offset of the emotional response is depicted in Figure 5.1 as the exit gradient, or the steepness with which the emotional response returns to a neutral baseline. Variables that influence the exit gradient belong to the process of emotion regulation. Similar to emotional sensitivity, emotion regulation is determined by the characteristics of the person, the stimuli that the person encounters, and the broader situation.

Down-regulation processes aim to achieve a steeper exit gradient, resulting in a speedier return to the baseline (e.g., Gross, 1998a). By contrast, maintenance processes aim to achieve a flatter exit gradient, such that the emotional response is maintained over a longer period of time (e.g., Nolen-Hoeksema, 2000). Up-regulation processes may even increase the magnitude of the emotion response, for instance, when people engage in response exaggeration (Schmeichel, Demaree, Robinson, & Pu, 2006). Emotion regulation may also influence aspects of emotion processing besides the exit gradient, such as the coherence, intensity, awareness, and goal-directedness of emotional responses. Nevertheless, it is the impact on the exit gradient of an emotional response that sets emotion regulation apart from other types of emotion processing.

Distinguishing between emotional sensitivity and emotion regulation is relatively straightforward when people are engaged in the on-line regulation of their emotions. However, some forms of emotion regulation occur

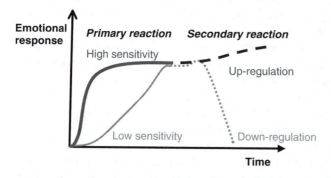

*Figure 5.1* Model of emotional sensitivity versus emotion regulation.

proactively, for instance, when people avoid an upcoming situation that is expected to elicit an undesired emotion (Aspinwall & Taylor, 1997; Zeelenberg & Pieters, 2007). In such cases, emotion regulation subjectively precedes the onset of emotion. Indeed, to the extent that proactive coping is successful, people may never experience any unwanted emotion at all. However, studies have shown that anticipating an emotional experience leads to a partial simulation of that experience, in which emotional responses of the brain and body become activated (Niedenthal, 2007; Niedenthal, Barsalou, Winkielman, Krauth-Gruber, & Ric, 2005). Therefore emotional sensitivity already comes into play during the anticipation of unwanted emotions. The distinction between emotional sensitivity and emotion regulation is therefore meaningful regardless of whether people regulate their emotions on line, in the heat of the moment, or proactively, before an emotion-arousing situation has actually occurred.

Separate contributions of emotional sensitivity and emotion regulation have been observed throughout the lifespan. Infants and young children display inborn physiological differences that relate to emotional sensitivity, whereas other physiological differences relate to children's ability to regulate their emotional responses (Derryberry, Reed, & Pilkenton-Taylor, 2003; Eisenberg, Fabes, & Guthrie, 1997; Rothbart, Derryberry, & Posner, 1994). Emotion sensitivity follows an intrinsic path of development that is largely independent of environmental influences and changes less as people grow older (McCrae et al., 2000; Terracciano, Costa, & McCrae, 2005). By contrast, competencies at emotion regulation are strongly influenced by the quality of children's social interactions with their caregivers (Mikulincer, Shaver, & Pereg, 2003; Southam-Gerow & Kendall, 2002) and continue to improve even into old age (Carstensen, Fung, & Charles, 2003; Gröpel, Kuhl, & Kazén, 2004; John & Gross, 2004). Across the lifespan, traits related to emotion regulation and traits related to emotional reactivity interact in predicting psychological functioning (Baumann et al., 2007; Davidson, 1998; Skinner & Zimmer-Gembeck, 2007).

## Summary

Emotion regulation consists of people's active attempts to manage their emotional states. In its broadest sense, emotion regulation subsumes the regulation of all states that are emotionally charged, including moods, stress, and positive or negative affect. Emotion regulation determines the offset of an emotional response, and can thus be distinguished from emotional sensitivity, which determines the onset of an emotional response. Emotional sensitivity and emotion regulation follow different developmental paths and are functionally distinct throughout the lifespan.

## CLASSIFYING EMOTION-REGULATION STRATEGIES

Emotion-regulation strategies refer to the concrete approach that people take in managing their emotions. For instance, after a romantic break-up, people may focus their attention on a neutral activity (Van Dillen & Koole, 2007), cognitively reframe the situation (Tugade & Frederickson, 2004), write about their feelings (Pennebaker & Chung, 2007), or eat away at tasty but fattening foods (Tice, Bratslavsky, & Baumeister, 2001). Although the notion of "strategies" seems to imply conscious deliberation, the term as it is used in the present article is agnostic about the underlying process. The strategic aspect of a given emotion-regulation process refers to its specification of how a given act of emotion regulation is implemented. This specification requires making decisions about the implementation of emotion regulation, but people may not be always fully aware of these decisions.

### The ordering problem

The potential variety of emotion-regulation strategies is enormous, given that any activity that impacts people's emotions may (at least, in principle) be recruited in the service of emotion regulation. Finding an underlying order in people's emotion-regulation strategies therefore represents a formidable scientific challenge. One empirical method used to classify emotion-regulation strategies is exploratory factor analysis (e.g., Thayer, Newman, & McCain, 1994). However, this approach suffers from problems of interpretability and difficulties in ensuring the comprehensiveness of the categories that are derived (see Skinner, Edge, Altman, & Sherwood, 2003). For instance, in the coping domain, multiple factor analyses, even on the same set of items, have not produced a replicable structure in coping strategies (Skinner et al., 2003). Another empirical method is rational sorting, which involves grouping items that share common features and separating items that differ (e.g., Parkinson & Totterdell, 1999). Rational sorting is similarly associated with problems of comprehensiveness, and has not converged on a common set of categories in the coping domain (Skinner et al., 2003).

The most rigorous approach to the ordering problem combines top-down (theoretical) and bottom-up (empirical) approaches. In this combined approach, one first defines the higher-order categories of emotion-regulation strategies, after which an empirical approach (such as confirmatory factor analysis) is used to test the fit of specific emotion-regulation strategies into the higher-order categories. To date, a combined top-down/bottom-up approach has not been applied to the classification of emotion-regulation strategies (though see Skinner et al., 2003, for illustrations in the coping domain). Nevertheless, researchers have proposed several concepts that seem potentially useful in fleshing out the higher-order categories of emotion-regulation strategies.

One potentially useful category distinguishes between automatic versus controlled emotion-regulation processes. An attractive aspect of this distinction is that it cuts across the complete range of emotion-regulation strategies (Mauss et al., 2007). However, automaticity is a heterogeneous construct. Indeed, a recent conceptual analysis identified as many as eight concepts associated with automaticity that may vary more or less independently: intentionality; goal dependence; controllability; autonomy; the extent to which a process is stimulus driven; consciousness; efficiency; and speed (Moors & De Houwer, 2006). For constructing a taxonomy, it is desirable to have categories that are functionally homogeneous (see Skinner et al., 2003, on criteria for a scientific taxonomy). The concept of automaticity is therefore less suitable in classifying emotion-regulation strategies.

Another influential approach, the so-called "process model" of emotion regulation, has proposed that emotion-regulation strategies may be classified by the time at which they intervene in the emotion-generation process (Gross, 1998a,b, 2001). The process model assumes that emotion responses are generated in a fixed cycle, such that attention to emotionally relevant information precedes cognitive appraisals, which in turn precede emotionally expressive behaviour. However, research indicates that the order in which emotion responses are generated is in fact variable. Attention, cognitive appraisals, or behaviour may each occur early or late in the emotion-generation process. For instance, bodily movements may directly activate emotional experiences (Niedenthal et al., 2005; Strack, Martin, & Stepper, 1988), and merely attending to emotional stimuli may directly trigger emotional behaviour without any intervening cognitive appraisals (e.g., Neumann, Förster, & Strack, 2003). The temporal order of the emotion-generation process therefore offers no basis for systematically relating emotion-regulation strategies to different classes of emotion responses.

## Targets of emotion regulation

Regardless of considerations about the timing of emotion-generation processes, the process model (Gross, 1998a,b, 2001) calls attention to the targets of emotion regulation. Emotion regulation is always directed at manipulating some emotional response. It is plausible that the type of emotional response that is targeted for regulation will at least partly determine how people go about the emotion-regulation process. The emotion-generation system that is targeted for regulation may thus serve as a higher-order category to classify different emotion-regulation strategies. Among the three most widely studied emotion-generating systems are attention, knowledge, and bodily expressions of emotion. Emotion regulation may thus target one or more of these three broad emotion-generating systems (Gross, 1998a,b, 2001; Parkinson & Totterdell, 1999; Philippot, Baeyens, Douilliez, & Francart, 2004).

The first of the emotion-generating systems, attention, consists of a set of neurological networks that allow people to select incoming information from sensory input (Fan, McCandliss, Fossella, Flombaum, & Posner, 2005). Attention has been extensively researched within cognitive psychology and cognitive neuroscience (see Posner & Rothbart, 2007, for a review). The resulting insights and methods are increasingly finding their way to the study of emotion regulation (Derakshan, Eysenck, & Myers, 2007; Ochsner & Gross, 2005; Van Dillen & Koole, 2007, 2009). For instance, emotion regulation has been examined in well-established attentional paradigms such as the emotional Stroop task (e.g., Newman & McKinney, 2002), and the dot-probe task (e.g., Fox, 1993). Attentional processing in emotion regulation has also been manipulated, for instance by providing people with an attention-demanding task (Van Dillen & Koole, 2007) or training exercises (Brown et al., 2007).

Emotion-relevant knowledge constitutes a second broad, emotion-generating system. Among the most widely studied types of emotion knowledge are cognitive appraisals, which consist of people's subjective evaluations during their encounter with emotionally significant events (Lazarus, 1991; Scherer, Schorr, & Johnstone, 2001). Particularly important is the appraisal whether or not an event is relevant to the satisfaction or frustration of important goals and motives (Lazarus, 1991; Moors, 2007). Other important appraisals include attributions of an event to self versus others, controllability of the event, accountability, expectations (Ortony, Clore, & Collins, 1988; Smith & Lazarus, 1993), and implicit theories of emotion (Tamir, John, Srivastava, & Gross, 2007b). Emotionally significant knowledge may also be retrieved from memory (e.g., Joormann & Siemer, 2004), and may differ in terms of structure and processing aspects, including their differentiation (Tugade, Frederickson, & Barrett, 2004), complexity (Kang & Shaver, 2004), and awareness (Ruys & Stapel, 2008).

The third of the emotion-generating systems includes the many embodied ways in which emotions unfold, including facial expressions, bodily postures, voluntary and involuntary motor movements, and psychophysiological responses (see Mauss & Robinson, 2009, for a review). In as far as attention and appraisals influence the body (e.g., Dandeneau, Baldwin, Baccus, Sakellaropoulo, & Pruessner, 2007; Sapolsky, 2007), one might question whether the body represents a separate emotion-generating system. Nevertheless, bodily emotion responses often follow different patterns than cognitive emotion responses (Mauss & Robinson, 2009). Moreover, bodily emotion responses shape the course of people's emotions in ways that cannot be reduced to attention or appraisal processes (Niedenthal et al., 2005; Zajonc, 1998). A separate status for the body is further warranted because several important emotion-regulation strategies, such as expressive suppression (Gross, 1998a) and progressive muscle relaxation (Esch, Fricchione, & Stefano, 2003), primarily target bodily manifestations of emotion.

When emotion-regulation strategies are merely classified by their targeted emotion-generation system, this results in rather heterogeneous groupings. For instance, repressive coping (Langens & Mörth, 2003) and mindfulness training (Brown et al., 2007) may both target attention, even though the latter involves purposefully paying attention to negative emotion, whereas the former avoids negative emotion altogether. In this regard, mindfulness training seems more similar to expressive writing about one's emotional experiences (Pennebaker & Chung, 2007). However, expressive writing also involves acquiring more insight into one's emotions, and hence targets knowledge systems. Although these are just a few examples, it appears that some important element is still missing from the classification of emotion-regulation strategies.

## Functions of emotion regulation

The missing element may be the functions of emotion regulation. By regulating their emotions, people seek to achieve certain psychological outcomes or functions. The functions of emotion regulation cut across all emotion-regulation strategies, and apply regardless of whether these strategies are directed at attention, knowledge, or the body. As such, the functions of emotion regulation represent a basic category for characterising different emotion strategies, a category that is independent of which emotion-generating system is targeted.

Traditionally, psychologists have assumed that people's emotion-regulation efforts serve hedonic needs that are aimed at promoting pleasure and preventing pain (e.g., Larsen, 2000; Westen, 1994). Negative emotional states are costly, because they mobilise a wide array of mental and physical resources within the individual (Sapolsky, 2007). Need-oriented emotion regulation may thus be adaptive, by allowing individuals to conserve these resources by promoting a rapid return to hedonically agreeable states. Because hedonic needs presumably operate on subcognitive levels of information processing (Panksepp, 1998), need-oriented emotion regulation may operate even in the absence of any conscious emotion-regulation goal. Indeed, hedonic needs may be immediately activated upon encountering emotional stimuli (Berridge & Winkielman, 2003; Neumann et al., 2003). Because the need-oriented functions of emotion regulation are directed towards immediate gratification, this type of emotion regulation often has an impulsive quality (Tice et al., 2001).

Although hedonic needs are important, they cannot account for the full range of emotion-regulation processes (Erber, 1996; Erber & Erber, 2000). For instance, social interactions often require people to remain "cool and collected", and hence may lead people to down-regulate both negative *and* positive moods (Erber, Wegner, & Therriault, 1996). Other types of goals may similarly increase the utility of hedonically aversive states (Achtzinger, Gollwitzer, & Sheeran, 2008; Tamir, Chiu, & Gross, 2007a), and thereby motivate emotion regulation efforts to attain or maintain those states. For instance, because many people believe that fear and worry promote the attainment of avoidance goals, people who adopt avoidance goals may be motivated to maintain these negative emotions (Tamir et al., 2007a). In a related vein, changes in task demands may decrease the relevance of emotionally charged information, leading people to devote fewer processing resources to emotion-eliciting information (Van Dillen & Koole, 2009). Rather than being hedonically oriented, the latter forms of emotion regulation are oriented towards the priorities that are set by specific norms, goals, or tasks. Emotion regulation may thus serve important goal-oriented functions.

Some of the functions of emotion regulation may extend even beyond single goals. In particular, emotion regulation may allow people to balance multiple goal pursuits (Koole & Kuhl, 2007; Rothermund et al., 2008) and promote integration among personality processes (Baumann, Kaschel, & Kuhl, 2005; Kuhl, 2000). Human personality consists of many interacting processes, the joint functioning of which has emergent, system-level properties that cannot be reduced to the behaviour of its individual elements (Nowak, Vallacher, Tesser, & Borkowski, 2000). As such, emotion-regulation processes at the level of the whole person serve distinct psychological functions. The person-oriented functions of emotion regulation have been elaborated by personality systems interactions theory (PSI) (Kuhl, 2000). According to PSI theory, emotion regulation may facilitate personality functioning in two major ways. First, by preventing people becoming locked up in specific motivational-emotional states, emotion regulation may promote flexibility in personality functioning (see Rothermund et al., 2008). Second, by stimulating the dynamic exchange between personality processes, emotion regulation may promote coherence and long-term stability within the overall personality system (Baumann et al., 2005).

Emotion regulation may thus serve multiple functions, including the satisfaction of hedonic needs, facilitation of specific goals and tasks, and optimisation of personality functioning. In many cases, people may combine these functions. For instance, when people experience emotional distress, boosting positive emotions may simultaneously satisfy hedonic needs, facilitate compliance with social norms for emotional neutrality, and increase the overall flexibility of the personality system. The functions may also conflict. Both goal- and person-oriented emotion regulation may require people to tolerate negative emotional states, and may thus conflict with need-oriented emotion regulation. Moreover, goal-oriented emotion regulation may conflict with person-oriented emotion regulation because the former has a narrower focus. For instance, extended activation of goal-oriented emotion regulation may cause over-activation of the sympathetic nervous system (Thayer & Lane, 2007). When the latter occurs, person-oriented emotion regulation will aim to restore autonomic balance and thus conflict with goal-oriented emotion regulation.

How people resolve conflicts between need-, goal-, or person-oriented functions is largely unknown. Conceivably, people alternate between functions. Need-oriented functions may become more important when people are experiencing acute emotional distress; goal-oriented functions when there are strong situational norms for appropriate emotional responding; and person-oriented functions when people are oriented towards their long-term well-being. It is also plausible that there exist individual differences in the preferential use of each function. For instance, need-oriented functions may be more important among repressive copers (Derakshan et al., 2007), and person-oriented functions may be more important among individuals with a secure attachment style (Mikulincer et al., 2003) or action-oriented individuals (Kuhl & Beckmann, 1994).

## Summary

Emotion-regulation strategies specify how people go about managing a particular unwanted emotion. A consensual, empirically validated taxonomy that spans all known emotion-regulation strategies has yet to be developed. Nevertheless, the literature has yielded several higher-order categories that seem useful in classifying emotion-regulation strategies. The most viable higher-order categories to this end are the emotion-generating system that is targeted and the psychological functions that are served by emotion regulation. Among the major emotion-generating systems that are targeted in emotion regulation are attention, knowledge, and the body. The main functions of emotion regulation are promoting the satisfaction of hedonic needs, facilitating goal achievement, and optimising global personality functioning.

## EMPIRICAL RESEARCH ON EMOTION-REGULATION STRATEGIES

The classification of emotion-regulation strategies by their targets and functions offers a preliminary basis for reviewing the extant literature. An overview of the target by function classification is provided in Table 5.1. Notably, this classification scheme does not propose a new theoretical explanation of emotion-regulation strategies. Rather, it provides a descriptive framework for organising the known universe of emotion-regulation strategies. The classification will hopefully stimulate the development of more sophisticated models that can provide a mechanistic explanation for the observed differences between emotion-regulation strategies.

*Table 5.1* Target by function classification of emotion-regulation strategies

| | Psychological function | | |
| --- | --- | --- | --- |
| Emotion-generating system | *Need-oriented* | *Goal-oriented* | *Person-oriented* |
| Attention | Thinking pleasurable or relaxing thoughts (Langens & Mörth, 2003); Attentional avoidance (Derakshan et al., 2007) | Effortful distraction (Van Dillen & Koole, 2007); Thought suppression (Wenzlaff & Wegner, 2000) | Attentional counter-regulation (Rothermund et al., 2008); Meditation (Cahn & Polich, 2006); Mindfulness training (Brown et al., 2007) |
| Knowledge | Cognitive dissonance reduction (Harmon-Jones & Mills, 1999); Motivated reasoning (Kunda, 1990); Self-defence (Tesser, 2000) | Cognitive reappraisal (Gross, 1998b; Ochsner & Gross, 2008) | Expressive writing (Pennebaker, 1997); Specification of emotional experience (Neumann & Philippot, 2007); Activating stored networks of emotion knowledge (Barrett et al., 2001) |
| Body | Stress-induced eating (Greeno & Wing, 1994); Stress-induced affiliation (Taylor et al., 2000) | Expressive suppression (Gross, 1998a); Response exaggeration (Schmeichel et al., 2006) Venting (Bushman et al., 2001) | Controlled breathing (Philippot et al., 2002); Progressive muscle relaxation (Esch et al., 2003) |

*Note*: Cited articles refer to relevant empirical demonstrations or literature reviews.

The remainder of this section will use the target by function classification to organise the literature on emotion-regulation strategies. For each psychological function of emotion regulation, I first discuss the criteria for deciding whether emotion-regulation strategies fit with this function. I then review the empirical evidence for emotion-regulation strategies that are oriented towards each function, which may respectively target attention, knowledge representations, or bodily manifestations of emotion. Some work has suggested that emotion-regulation strategies that target attention or knowledge are more effective than strategies that target bodily expressions of emotion (Gross, 1998a,b, 2001). Accordingly, I also consider the relative effectiveness of cognitive versus bodily emotion-regulation strategies for each psychological function of emotion regulation.

The present review is necessarily selective, and focuses on well-controlled, process-oriented research. The main emphasis is on emotion-regulation strategies that are widely used among psychologically healthy individuals. When relevant, however, the present review considers individual differences in emotion regulation. For instance, if an emotion-regulation strategy is used particularly often by certain individuals, highlighting this group can bring into sharper focus those processes that are involved in this particular emotion-regulation strategy. Moreover, in as far as individual differences in emotion regulation are stable over time, their study can shed more light on the potential long-term consequences of using specific emotion-regulation strategies.

## Need-oriented emotion regulation

Need-oriented emotion regulation is driven by people's needs to experience hedonically rewarding states, which consist of low levels of negative and high levels of positive emotion. Because needs can operate on a subcognitive level (Panksepp, 1998), need-oriented strategies can emerge in the absence of explicit goals or instructions to strive for a favourable hedonic state. The strongest evidence for need-oriented emotion regulation is provided by emotion-regulation behaviour that maximises short-term emotional benefits at the expense of long-term well-being (cf. Tice et al., 2001). Nevertheless, need-oriented emotion regulation does not inevitably lead to poor long-term outcomes. Theoretically, need-oriented emotion regulation should mainly undermine long-term well-being in cases where there exists a conflict between short-term hedonic benefits and long-term outcomes. In the absence of such conflicts, need-oriented emotion regulation may be adaptive. Consequently, discriminate use of need-oriented emotion regulation could be beneficial, whereas chronic use of need-oriented emotion regulation is likely to have adverse consequences.

### Attention

Some of the most robust evidence for need-oriented regulation of attention is based on research on individual differences in repressive coping style (Derakshan et al., 2007; Weinberger, Schwarz, & Davidson, 1979). In this research, individuals who score high on a measure of social desirability (indicative of a self-aggrandising response style) and low on a measure of trait anxiety are identified as repressors. Over many studies, repressors have been found to avoid negative emotional stimuli to a greater degree than non-repressors (see Derakshan et al., 2007, for a review). For instance, relative to non-repressors, repressors avert their gaze more often from unpleasant emotional stimuli (Haley, 1974; Olson & Zanna, 1979), and spend less time reading negative personality feedback (Baumeister & Cairns, 1992).

Attentional avoidance of negative stimuli among repressors has further emerged in well-established cognitive tasks, including the emotional Stroop task (Myers & McKenna, 1996; Newman & McKinney, 2002), the dot-probe task (Fox, 1993), and the lexical decision task (Langens & Mörth, 2003). A sophisticated model of repressive coping is vigilance-avoidance theory, which proposes that repressors respond to threatening stimuli in two stages (Derakshan et al., 2007). The first stage, which is presumably automatic and non-conscious, consists of a vigilance response of elevated behavioural and physiological anxiety. The second stage, which presumably involves more strategic and controlled processes, consists of attentional avoidance and cognitive denial of anxiety.

When faced with threatening information, repressors may also increase their attention to positive information (Boden & Baumeister, 1997; Langens & Mörth, 2003). The level of threat may determine whether repressors cope with threats by avoiding negative information or seeking out positive information (Langens & Mörth, 2003). When threat levels are low, repressors may avoid emotionally threatening information by shifting their attention away from the threat. When threat levels are high, repressors may be forced to pay a certain amount of attention to the threat and thus resort to more effortful distraction strategies such as generating positive imagery.

Repressive coping is associated with short-term relief from emotional distress (e.g., Boden & Baumeister, 1997). Many long-term outcomes that are linked to repressive coping are negative. Relative to non-repressors, repressors possess less insight into their own emotional states (Lane, Sechrest, Riedel, Shapiro, & Kaszniak, 2000), and display intrusive thoughts, even after initial success at thought suppression (Geraerts, Merckelbach, Jelicic, & Smeets, 2006 ). Repressive coping is also associated with adverse health outcomes[1] (see Myers, 2000; Myers et al., 2008, for reviews), such as heightened susceptibility to infectious disease (Jamner,

---

1 The literature on repressive coping has reported some positive effects on health (e.g., Coifman, Bonanno, Ray, & Gross, 2007). However, this research used affective–autonomic response discrepancy (AARD) as an index of repressive coping. With the AARD measure, repressors are those who report low levels of negative affect following threat while simultaneously displaying high levels of physiological activity, such as elevated heart rate or skin conductance. An important problem of this index is that the underlying physiological measures are not informative about emotional valence. Thus, high AARD scores could be due to unreported negative emotion or unreported positive emotion. To the extent that AARD scores are driven by unreported positive emotion, this measure may index counter-regulation processes (Rothermund et al., 2008) rather than repressive coping. Because of this ambiguity, the present review only considers the results for the more conventional self-report measure of repressive coping.

Schwarz, & Leigh, 1988), inhibited immune function (Barger, Bachen, Marsland, & Manuck, 2000), and increased risk for coronary heart disease, cancer, and asthma (Weinberger, 1990).

*Knowledge*

Ever since Freud (1915/1961) introduced the notion of psychological defence mechanisms, generations of researchers have been intrigued by the idea that people may distort their perceptions of reality to ward off anxiety and other types of negative emotion. In social psychology, Festinger's (1957) pioneering work on cognitive dissonance reduction (see Harmon-Jones & Mills, 1999, for a recent overview) has spawned a large and sophisticated body of research on interpretive biases (Baumeister & Newman, 1994; Pyszczynski & Greenberg, 1987; Tesser, 2000). Among other things, people may engage in selective criticism of threatening information (Liberman & Chaiken, 1992), trivialise the information (Simon, Greenberg, & Brehm, 1995), selectively forget the information (Sedikides & Green, 2004), make self-serving attributions (Campbell & Sedikides, 1999), inflate their self-conceptions in a non-threatened domain (McGregor, 2006), engage in downward social comparison (Taylor & Lobel, 1989), and derogate others (Fein & Spencer, 1997). From this list of defences, which is far from complete, it appears that people may recruit virtually any type of judgement for defensive purposes (Roese & Olson, 2007).

Defensive processes are mutually substitutable (Tesser, 2000), consistent with the notion that they serve the common purpose of emotion regulation. The emotion regulation function of defensive bias is further supported by findings that affirming positive views of the self down-regulates negative emotion, especially when emotion is assessed by physiological or implicit measures (Creswell et al., 2005; Koole, Smeets, van Knippenberg, & Dijksterhuis, 1999; Roese & Olson, 2007). In addition, defensive bias is associated with neural activity in regions that are implicated in emotion regulation, such as the ventromedial prefrontal cortex (Westen, Kilts, Blagov, Harenski, & Hamann, 2006). Notably, defensive bias is not associated with activation in brain regions that support effortful self-regulation, even though such regions are implicated in goal-oriented emotion-regulation strategies (Ochsner & Gross, 2008).

The potential adaptiveness of defensive bias has been subject to considerable debate. Extreme and rigid forms of defensive bias appear to undermine psychological adjustment (Colvin & Block, 1994). Moreover, defensive bias has been linked to the repressive coping style (Derakshan et al., 2007), which in turn is associated with poor health outcomes (Myers, 2000; Myers et al., 2008). However, more moderate and flexible forms of defensive bias are positively associated with mental health (Baumeister, 1989; Kunda, 1990; Taylor, Kemeny, Reed, Bower, & Gruenewald, 2000).

*Body*

Bodily activities that provide immediate gratification represent a major target for need-oriented emotion regulation. One such activity is eating. Eating palatable food provides pleasant sensations to the mouth and stomach, and thus can be used for need-oriented emotion regulation. Stress-induced eating is a common emotion-regulation strategy, especially among restrained eaters (Greeno & Wing, 1994). Chronic use of eating as an emotion-regulation strategy may result in unhealthy behaviour patterns such as overeating or binge eating (Heatherton & Baumeister, 1991). There are also psychological disadvantages associated with this strategy, given that chronic overeaters have greater difficulty identifying and making sense of their emotional states (Whiteside et al., 2007). Notably, the emotional profile of overeaters resembles that of repressors, suggesting that stress-induced eating may be linked to repressive coping (cf. Derakshan et al., 2007).

The emotion regulation effects of eating may be partly explained by attentional processes. For instance, binge eating may down-regulate emotional distress by focusing people's attention on their immediate physical sensations (Heatherton & Baumeister, 1991). However, eating also has neuro-endocrine effects that may reduce emotional distress. For instance, eating palatable food can stimulate the endogenous release of opioids (Adam & Epel, 2007; Morley & Levine, 1980). Because opioids relieve stress, this mechanism may explain why individuals engage in stress-induced eating. Animal research has offered some support for this model: When rats are treated with opioid antagonists, they display a marked reduction in stress-induced eating (Hawkins, Cubic, Baumeister, & Barton, 1992).

Physical activities other than eating may also be recruited in need-oriented emotion regulation. Potential candidates are stress-induced consumption behaviours such as alcohol intake (Mohr, Brennan, Mohr, Armeli, & Tennen, 2008; Sher & Grekin, 2007; Zack, Poulos, Fragopoulos, Woodford, & MacLeod, 2006) and smoking (Gilbert et al., 2007). Other bodily emotion-regulation strategies that may be at least partly need-oriented are regular physical exercise, particularly when people have developed exercise habits (Thayer, 1987), and stress-induced proximity seeking, particularly among women (Taylor et al., 2000). These bodily emotion-regulation strategies may provide immediate hedonic benefits, in as far as they involve behaviours that can be easily and spontaneously executed.

## Summary

Need-oriented strategies regulate emotional responses to promote the satisfaction of hedonic needs. Overall, the literature has emphasised the need to minimise negative emotion over the need to maximise positive emotion. On an attentional level, need-oriented emotion regulation may occur through avoidance of threatening information or distraction by positive information, tendencies that are especially prevalent among repressive copers. On a representational level, need-oriented emotion regulation may take the form of various interpretive biases, which may serve anxiety-reducing functions. Finally, on a physical level, need-oriented emotion regulation may occur through activities such as eating, physical exercise, or proximity seeking. Regardless of whether they target attention, knowledge representations, or the body, need-oriented strategies of emotion regulation are associated with immediate emotional relief that often comes at the expense of long-term well-being (Tice et al., 2001).

## Goal-oriented emotion regulation

Goal-oriented emotion regulation is directed by a single verbally reportable goal, norm, or task. There are two major ways in which goal-oriented emotion regulation may operate. First, goal-oriented emotion regulation may be driven by people's beliefs about the utility of particular emotional states. These beliefs may be influenced by verbal instructions about the desirability of certain emotional states (e.g., Achtzinger et al., 2008; Gross, 1998a), by implicit or explicit beliefs about the utility of particular emotional states (Tamir et al., 2007a), or by more abstract theories that people have about emotion regulation (Tamir et al., 2007b). Second, an ongoing goal, task, or norm may change the relevance of emotionally charged information. Emotionally charged information that is (potentially) relevant to the ongoing task is likely to be maintained, whereas emotionally charged information that is irrelevant is likely to be ignored or down-regulated (Van Dillen & Koole, 2009). Because goals, norms, or tasks may favour various types of emotional outcomes, goal-oriented emotion regulation may either promote or inhibit emotional states that are hedonically rewarding.

### Attention

Goals can control attention in a top-down manner (Posner & Rothbart, 2007). Accordingly, attention forms a prime target for goal-oriented emotion-regulation strategies. Erber et al. (1996) found that people who anticipated interacting with an unknown other attended more to materials of the opposite emotional valence to their current mood state. Presumably, people engaged in this form of attention regulation because it is counter-normative to behave highly emotionally in dealing with strangers. Importantly, social-interaction goals fostered attention to negative stimuli when people's initial moods were positive. As such, these studies demonstrate that goal-oriented emotion regulation can be dissociated from people's hedonic needs (see Erber & Erber, 2000).

A critical factor in goal-oriented regulation of attention appears to be the availability of distracting stimuli. Indeed, simply instructing individuals "not to think about" an unwanted emotion may ironically serve to heighten the activation of this emotion (Wegner et al., 1993; Wegner & Gold, 1995). Research on mental control (Wegner, 1994) has found that providing people with a focused distracter (such as, "Think about a red Volkswagen") greatly increases the efficiency of thought suppression attempts. Depressed individuals seem to have particular difficulties in finding suitable distracters (Wenzlaff, Wegner, & Roper, 1988). As such, the breakdown of self-generation of distracters may play a key role in the persistence of depression (Joormann & Siemer, 2004).

Given that any demanding task can divert attention, even neutral tasks may have emotion-regulatory implications (Erber & Tesser, 1992). Indeed, studies have shown that distraction with neutral materials can reduce depression (Morrow & Nolen-Hoeksema, 1990; Nolen-Hoeksema & Morrow, 1993), and anger (Gerin, Davidson, Goyal, Christenfeld, & Schwartz, 2006; Rusting & Nolen-Hoeksema, 1998). For instance, in one study (Nolen-Hoeksema & Morrow, 1993), focusing attention on descriptions of geographic locations and objects led depressed participants to experience reductions in depressed mood, whereas focusing on current feeling states and personal characteristics led depressed participants to experience increases in depressed mood.

The effects of performing a neutral task on emotion regulation may be understood in terms of underlying working-memory processes (Van Dillen & Koole, 2007). Emotional states spontaneously and unintentionally activate emotion-congruent cognitions in working memory (Bower & Mayer, 1989; Siemer, 2005). This congruent processing stream may be interrupted when working memory is loaded with an alternative task. Consistent with this model, tasks that draw upon working memory have been found to be particularly effective in reducing the emotional impact of vivid emotion-laden stimuli (Erber & Tesser, 1992; Van Dillen & Koole, 2007, 2009). Moreover, performing a working-memory task attenuates the neural response to negative emotional stimuli (Van Dillen, Heslenfeld, & Koole, 2008). Working-memory load can even eliminate attentional interference of negative stimuli (Van Dillen & Koole, 2009), an effect that has previously been regarded as automatic (Pratto & John, 1991).

## Knowledge

The explicit goals and norms that guide goal-oriented emotion regulation are encoded in a linguistic format (Ochsner & Gross, 2005, 2008). Goal-oriented emotion regulation is therefore highly compatible with linguistic appraisal processes. During *cognitive reappraisal*, people reduce the emotional impact of an event by changing their subjective evaluations of this event (Gross, 1998a,b, 2001). Cognitive reappraisal may take the form of: (a) reinterpreting situational or contextual aspects of stimuli (e.g., imagining a potentially upsetting image is fake); or (b) distancing oneself from stimuli by adopting a detached, third-person perspective (Ochsner & Gross, 2008). Cognitive reappraisal can inhibit the experience of unwanted emotions, although it does not consistently decrease psycho-physiological arousal (Gross, 1998a; Steptoe & Vogele, 1986). The strategy draws upon working-memory resources (Schmeichel, Volokhov, & Demaree, 2008), but is relatively efficient in that it does not impair people's memory for ongoing social interactions (Richards & Gross, 2000).

Reappraisal processes have been intensely researched in neuroimaging studies (e.g., Beauregard, Levesque, & Bourgouin, 2001; Ochsner, Bunge, Gross, & Gabrieli, 2002; see Ochsner & Gross, 2005, 2008, for reviews). These studies have shown consistently that cognitive reappraisal inhibits activation in emotional regions, including the amygdalae and insula, and increases activation in dorsal anterior cingulate cortex and prefrontal cortex, regions that support working memory, language, and long-term memory. During reappraisal, emotional regions of the brain may become inversely coupled to the activation of specific regions in the prefrontal cortex (Urry et al., 2006). These findings are consistent with the idea that reappraisal triggers top-down control of emotion-generating systems. Notably, reappraisal activates some of the same brain regions as tasks involving top-down attention control (Ochsner et al., 2002), and the effects of reappraisal are partly explained by shifts in visual attention away from emotion-eliciting stimuli (Van Reekum et al., 2007). Some reappraisal processes may thus be driven by attentional mechanisms rather than changes in knowledge representations.

## Body

The verbal processes that mediate goal-oriented emotion regulation have limited access to embodied emotion processes (Loewenstein, 1996; Nordgren, van der Pligt, & van Harreveld, 2006). Accordingly, goal-oriented emotion regulation may resort to more indirect ways of regulating the body. Goal-oriented control of the body is typically focused on outward bodily manifestations of emotion, such as facial expressions or overt movements and bodily postures, because these are under the control of explicit norms and goals.

One goal-oriented strategy of emotion regulation that targets the body is *expressive suppression* (Gross, 1998a,b, 2001). In this strategy, people actively inhibit their emotional expressions. For example, an individual might try to keep a straight face while telling a lie. Expressive suppression has been found to draw upon working-memory resources (Schmeichel et al., 2008), to interfere with people's memory of ongoing social interactions (Richards & Gross, 2000), and increase sympathetic control of the heart (Demaree et al., 2006). Despite its effortful nature, expressive suppression does little to prevent the experience of unwanted emotions, even when it effectively inhibits bodily expressions of emotion (Gross, 1998a; Schmeichel et al., 2008).

The foregoing suggests that expressive suppression may often create a discrepancy between inner experience and outer expression, a condition that may arouse "expressive dissonance" (Robinson & Demaree, 2007). Indeed, individuals who chronically use expressive suppression report a sense of being inauthentic or "fake" in their social relationships (Gross & John, 2003). These alienating effects may be part of the reason why chronic expressive suppression is linked to low emotional well-being (Gross & John, 2003). Notably, the negative effects of expression suppression may be specific to members of Western cultures (Butler, Lee, & Gross, 2007). Whereas Western cultures traditionally value open emotion expression, Asian cultures traditionally value emotional restraint (Frijda & Sundararajan, 2007). Consequently, expressive suppression may be perceived as less negative by individuals with Asian cultural values. Consistent with this, recent work has shown that, among individuals with Asian cultural values, expressive suppression is associated with neither increased negative emotion nor reduced social responsiveness (Butler et al., 2007).

Given the difficulties of expressive suppression (at least, among members of Western cultures), goal-oriented regulation processes may try to redirect bodily emotion responses rather than eliminating them altogether. For instance, people may engage in *response exaggeration*, by deliberately exaggerating their responses to an emotional stimulus (Schmeichel et al., 2006). Another redirection strategy is *venting*, an emotion-regulation process in which people intentionally give free reign to their emotional impulses (Breuer & Freud, 1893–1895/1955; see Bushman et al., 2001). Venting is a popular strategy in controlling anger and aggression (Bushman et al., 2001). On the surface, venting seems to be the opposite of expressive suppression. Nevertheless, venting is a goal-driven strategy to regulate bodily expressions of emotion, just as expressive suppression (Bushman et al., 2001). Although venting is widely advertised, research indicates that venting anger actually increases anger and aggression (Geen & Quanty, 1977). Presumably, venting adds fuel to the flame by heightening the activation of angry thoughts and action tendencies (Bushman, 2002), which in turn promote angry emotion and behaviour.

## Summary

Goal-oriented strategies of emotion regulation are driven by a single explicit goal, task, or norm. Some of the most effective goal-oriented strategies direct attention away from stimuli that could trigger unwanted emotions. Effortful tasks that draw upon working memory resources have been found to be particularly potent distracters. Other relatively effective goal-oriented strategies use cognitive reappraisal, a process that modifies the emotional impact of events by changing people's assessments of these events. Some of the least effective goal-oriented strategies target bodily expressions of emotion, through processes such as expressive suppression, response exaggeration, or venting. Overall, in the domain of goal-oriented emotion regulation, cognitive strategies appear to be more effective than bodily strategies.

## Person-oriented emotion regulation

Person-oriented emotion regulation maintains the integrity of the overall personality system, which consists of the entirety of a person's needs, goals, motives, and other self-aspects. A first signature of person-oriented emotion regulation is its holistic focus. Whereas need-oriented and goal-oriented emotion regulation focus on aspects of emotional or task-related functioning, person-oriented emotion regulation is geared to the functioning of the whole person. A second signature of person-oriented emotion regulation is contextual sensitivity, which is expressed in the ability to alternate between different motivational, cognitive, or affective subsystems in a context-appropriate manner (Rothermund et al., 2008). A third signature of person-oriented emotion regulation is integration, which is manifested in the co-ordinated functioning of personality systems that are traditionally regarded as antagonistic, such as positive versus negative emotions, body versus mind, passion versus reason, and top-down versus bottom-up processing.

### Attention

An important pattern in the person-oriented regulation of attention is the *counter-regulation principle* (Rothermund et al., 2008). According to this principle, people are equipped with attentional biases that prevent the perseveration of current motivational or emotional states. Attentional counter-regulation presumably helps to restore a balanced receptiveness to positive and negative information despite currently active affective-motivational states. Counter-regulation thus fosters contextual sensitivity, an important signature of person-oriented emotion regulation.

Counter-regulation processes are indirectly supported by many studies showing that positive and negative events tend to have only short-term consequences for people's emotional states (e.g., Gilbert, Lieberman, Morewedge, & Wilson, 2004). In addition, controlled experimental studies have confirmed the existence of attentional biases in the opposite direction as people's current emotional-motivational states (Derryberry, 1993; Rothermund et al., 2008; Tugade & Frederickson, 2004). Depending on the context, attentional counter-regulation may inhibit either positive or negative emotion (Rothermund et al., 2008). Accordingly, counter-regulation is distinct from need-oriented emotion regulation. Consistent with its global adaptive functions, attentional counter-regulation is most pronounced among individuals disposed towards flexible action control (Jostmann et al., 2005; Koole & Coenen, 2007; Koole & Jostmann, 2004), and largely absent among individuals suffering from chronic anxiety, phobia, or dysphoria (Mathews & MacLeod, 2005).

Person-oriented regulation of attention may be stimulated by activities such as meditation (Cahn & Polich, 2006) and mindfulness training (Brown et al., 2007). Meditation refers to practices that "self-regulate the body and mind, thereby affecting mental events by engaging in a specific attentional set" (Cahn & Polich, 2006, p. 180). Mindfulness training evolved out of certain meditative practices, and encourages people to engage in a mere noticing of their internal and external experiences in an objective manner, without the biasing influence of pre-existing cognitive schemas (Brown et al., 2007). Meditation and mindfulness training both foster emotion-regulation abilities (see Brown et al., 2007; Cahn & Polich, 2006, for reviews). The mechanisms that underlie meditation and mindfulness training are incompletely understood. Nevertheless, both practices promote personality integration, as indicated by greater neurological synchronisation (Cahn & Polich, 2006) and increased congruence between implicit and explicit self-aspects (Brown & Ryan, 2003; Koole, Govorun, & Cheng, 2008). The latter findings fit with the involvement of person-oriented emotion regulation.

*Knowledge*

Common sense has long held that people may overcome traumatic experiences by "putting their feelings in perspective" or "working through" their emotions. These metaphors appear to describe cognitive integration processes, in which emotionally charged information becomes incorporated into larger networks of the person's experiences. Though initially painful, cognitive integration processes may eventually down-regulate unwanted emotions and create the conditions for personal growth (Baumann & Kuhl, 2002; Kuhl, 2000). Integration of aversive emotional experiences thus represents an important form of person-oriented emotion regulation.

Expressive writing is one activity that may foster integration of emotional experiences. Studies have shown that expressive writing down-regulates emotional distress and improves both physical and psychological health (Pennebaker, 1997; Pennebaker & Chung, 2007). These beneficial effects may arise because expressive writing helps to turn initially disturbing emotional experiences into coherent narratives (Smyth, True, & Souto, 2001), which down-regulates emotional distress and promotes insight into the self and one's emotions (Klein & Boals, 2001; Pennebaker, Mayne, & Francis, 1997).

Once emotion-relevant knowledge has been acquired, this knowledge may assist in subsequent emotion-regulation efforts. Specifically, as people's emotion knowledge becomes broader and more differentiated, new emotional experiences may be incorporated more easily into their existing cognitive schema (Kuhl, 2000). Individuals who possess relatively differentiated knowledge of self and emotion indeed display more efficient emotion regulation, both in childhood (Diamond & Aspinwall, 2003) and adulthood (Barrett, Gross, Conner, & Benvenuto, 2001; Linville, 1985, 1987; Rafaeli-Mor & Steinberg, 2002). Autobiographical knowledge about the self and emotion may thus form an extended memory system that allows people to down-regulate unwanted emotions (Kuhl, 2000; Philippot et al., 2004).

People may access the emotion-regulatory functions of the autobiographical memory system whenever they process the specific details of an emotional experience. Indeed, imagining the distinctive details of emotional memories, rather than their general aspects, reduces the emotional intensity of these memories (Neumann & Philippot, 2007). Furthermore, deficits in emotion regulation, such as chronic depression and ruminative thinking, are associated with reduced specificity of autobiographical memory (Williams et al., 2007). Experimental studies have shown that concrete, experiential thoughts (e.g., "How did you feel moment by moment?"), relative to abstract, attributional thoughts (e.g., "Why did you feel this way?"), lead to faster recovery from a negative emotion (Moberly & Watkins, 2006; Watkins, 2004). Concrete rather than abstract processing of emotional experience also leads to global improvements in cognitive flexibility (Watkins & Moulds, 2005), consistent with the person-oriented functions of this type of emotion regulation.

## Body

In regulating bodily expressions of emotion, person-oriented emotion regulation seeks to forge a mutual exchange between higher mental processes and peripherally mediated emotion responses. Throughout this exchange, mind and body are equally important, and each system is allowed to express its natural tendencies. It is noteworthy that meditation (Cahn & Polich, 2006) and mindfulness training (Brown et al., 2007), which are often regarded as attentional strategies of emotion regulation, typically include bodily activities such as breathing and relaxation exercises. This dual focus on mind and body fits with the holistic orientation of systematic emotion regulation.

One bodily activity that may foster person-oriented emotion regulation relies on the voluntary control of breath. Some forms of controlled breathing may facilitate emotion regulation, in that specific breathing patterns are associated with general mood and distinct emotions (Boiten, Frijda, & Wientjes, 1994). Indeed, voluntarily engaging in specific breathing patterns can selectively activate specific emotional states (Philippot, Chapelle, & Blairy, 2002) and reduce emotional distress (Franck, Schäfer, Stiels, Wasserman, & Hermann, 1994; Meuret, Wilhelm, & Roth, 2001). The effects of controlled breathing involve both bottom-up processes, such as respiratory feedback (Philippot et al., 2002), and top-down processes, given that attention to one's own respiratory rhythms enhances the emotion-regulation effects of controlled breathing (Arch & Craske, 2006; Clark & Hirschman, 1990; Zeier, 1984). This co-ordinated interplay of top-down and bottom-up functions fits with the integrative aspects of person-oriented emotion regulation.

Another bodily activity that may foster person-oriented emotion regulation relies on muscle relaxation (Esch et al., 2003). Much research has used Jacobson's (1928) classic technique of *progressive muscle relaxation*. In this technique, people successively tense and relax their muscle groups in different parts of the body. Experimental studies have shown that progressive muscle relaxation down-regulates state anxiety and perceived stress (Pawlow & Jones, 2002; Rankin, Gilner, Gfeller, & Katz, 1993; Rausch, Gramling, & Auerbach, 2006). Progressive muscle relaxation further reduces heart rate and salivary cortisol (Pawlow & Jones, 2002) and stress-related disease (Carlson & Hoyle, 1993; Esch et al., 2003). Consistent with the involvement of high-level processes in progressive muscle relaxation, the technique is most effective when it is combined with attention to muscle sensations (Borkovec & Hennings, 1978) or biofeedback (Lehrer, 1982).

## Summary

Person-oriented strategies of emotion regulation promote the overall functioning of the personality system. Some person-oriented emotion-regulation strategies rely on counter-regulation, a process that directs attention to information that is of opposite valence to people's current emotional state. Alternatively, person-oriented emotion regulation may foster cognitive integration of unwanted emotional experiences, through activities such as expressive writing. Over time, integration of emotional experiences may give rise to an extensive autobiographical knowledge base, and accessing this knowledge base may further stimulate person-oriented emotion regulation. Bodily forms of person-oriented emotion regulation involve such activities as controlled breathing and progressive muscle relaxation. Person-oriented emotion regulation is associated with long-term benefits, regardless of whether it targets attention, knowledge, or the body.

## SUMMARY, CONCLUSIONS, AND FUTURE DIRECTIONS

The present article has reviewed contemporary insights and findings on the psychology of emotion regulation. Emotion regulation was defined as the set of processes whereby people seek to redirect the spontaneous flow of their emotions. In a broad sense, emotion regulation refers to the set of processes whereby people manage all of their emotionally charged states, including specific emotions, affect, mood, and stress. Emotion regulation determines how easily people can leave a given emotional state. It can thus be distinguished from emotional sensitivity, which determines how easily people can enter an emotional state.

Presently, there exists no consensual and empirically validated taxonomy of emotion-regulation strategies. Nevertheless, researchers have identified several higher-order categories that could lay the foundation for such a taxonomy. The most viable higher-order categories for classifying emotion-regulation strategies are currently the emotion-generating systems that are targeted in emotion regulation (Gross, 1998a,b, 2001) and the psychological functions of emotion regulation. Among the chief targets of emotion regulation are attention, cognitive emotion-relevant knowledge, and bodily manifestations of emotion. Among the major psychological functions of emotion regulation are the satisfaction of hedonic needs, supporting goal pursuits, and maintenance of the global personality system.

A dual classification in terms of targets and functions was found to be helpful in organising the literature on emotion-regulation strategies. Need-oriented emotion regulation includes strategies of: (a) turning attention away from negative information or towards positive information; (b) interpretative biases; and (c) bodily activities such as binge eating or smoking. Goal-oriented emotion regulation includes strategies of: (a) distraction through cognitive load; (b) cognitive reappraisal; and (c) bodily activities such as expressive suppression, response exaggeration, and venting. Finally, person-oriented emotion regulation includes strategies of: (a) attentional counter-regulation; (b) cognitive activities such as expressive writing or accessing autobiographical memories; and (c) bodily activities such as controlled breathing and progressive muscle relaxation. There is consistent empirical support for each of these strategies, though more work remains necessary to fully understand their underlying processes.

The hypothesis that cognitive strategies are more effective than bodily strategies of emotion regulation (Gross, 1998a,b, 2001) was only partly supported. With respect to goal-oriented emotion regulation, attentional and reappraisal strategies indeed appear to have an edge over bodily strategies such as expressive suppression or venting. However, the picture is different with respect to need- and person-oriented emotion regulation. In the domain of need-oriented emotion regulation, cognitive strategies appear to be relatively ineffective, especially in the long run. For instance, attentional avoidance of threatening information among repressors is associated with intrusive thoughts and poor health outcomes (Geraerts et al., 2006; Myers, 2000). Conversely, in the domain of person-oriented emotion regulation, bodily strategies appear to be relatively effective. For instance, progressive muscle relaxation effectively down-regulates stress and stress-related disease (Pawlow & Jones, 2002; Esch et al., 2003). Taken together, the advantage of cognitive over bodily strategies of emotion regulation appears to be specific to goal-oriented emotion regulation and does not apply across all known emotion-regulation strategies.

Because emotions are fundamentally embodied (Niedenthal, 2007), all emotion-regulation processes must ultimately interface with bodily functions. Nevertheless, only few studies to date have systematically addressed the physiology of emotion regulation. One intriguing line of work suggests an important role for *cardiac vagal tone* in emotion regulation (Appelhans & Luecken, 2006; Porges, 2007; Thayer & Lane, 2000, 2007). The vagal nerve may function as an active brake on heart rate that puts the individual into a calm emotional state. In emotion regulation, vagal tone may be dynamically controlled in a top-down manner by cortical systems (Porges, Doussard-Roosevelt, & Maita, 1994; Thayer & Lane, 2000, 2007). Identifying mechanisms such as vagal tone will be of key significance in relating the physiology of emotion regulation to its cognitive and neurological manifestations.

At a general level, the present article attests to the considerable growth and vitality of modern research on emotion regulation. There is good reason to believe that emotion regulation research will continue to flourish, given the growing recognition that emotion regulation plays a major role in physical and psychological well-being, combined with the development of ever more powerful methods of investigation. One particularly exciting set of recent discoveries has been that emotion-regulatory competencies are susceptible to social learning experiences (see also Butler et al., 2007). Indeed, emotion-regulatory competencies may be improved through directed exercises (Brown et al., 2007; Dandeneau et al., 2007; Serrano, Latorre, Gatz, & Montañés, 2004) and may continue to develop even into old age (Carstensen et al., 2003). Studying the social-cognitive processes that allow people to improve their competencies in emotion regulation is likely to generate important new insights into the nature of emotion regulation. Moreover, such investigations may eventually lead to better interventions for improving emotion-regulatory competencies.

Some might fear that boosting people's capacity for emotion regulation will inevitably narrow emotional experience. In fact, research suggests just the opposite. Drawing from Chinese poetics and Confucian philosophy, Frijda and Sundararajan (2007) described how emotional restraint contributes to a deeper and more differentiated appreciation of one's emotions. In line with this, empirical evidence indicates that individuals with high emotion-regulation competencies are characterised by greater self-reflexivity and a more profound awareness of their emotions (Barrett et al., 2001; Brown et al., 2007). People's emotional lives are thus likely to become enriched as people learn new and more powerful ways of regulating their emotions.

## REFERENCES

Achtzinger, A., Gollwitzer, P. M., & Sheeran, P. (2008). Implementation intentions and shielding goal striving from unwanted thoughts and feelings. *Personality and Social Psychology Bulletin, 34*, 381–393.

Adam, T. C., & Epel, E. S. (2007). Stress, eating, and the reward system. *Physiology and Behavior, 91*, 449–458.

Appelhans, B. M., & Luecken, L. J. (2006). Heart rate variability as an index of regulated emotional responding. *Review of General Psychology, 10*, 229–240.

Arch, J., & Craske, M. (2006). Mechanisms of mindfulness: Emotion regulation following a focused breathing induction. *Behaviour Research and Therapy, 44*, 1849–1858.

Aspinwall, L. G., & Taylor, S. E. (1997). A stitch in time: Self-regulation and proactive coping. *Psychological Bulletin, 121*, 417–436.

Barger, S. D., Bachen, E. A., Marsland, A. L., & Manuck, S. B. (2000). Repressive coping and blood measures of disease risk: Lipids and endocrine and immunological responses to a laboratory stressor. *Journal of Applied Social Psychology, 30*, 1619–1638.

Bargh, J. A., & Williams, L. E. (2007). The case for nonconscious emotion regulation. In J. J. Gross (Ed.), *Handbook of emotion regulation* (pp. 429–445). New York: Guilford Press.

Barrett, L. F., Gross, J. J., Conner, T., & Benvenuto, M. (2001). Knowing what you're feeling and knowing what to do about it: Mapping the relation between emotion differentiation and emotion regulation. *Cognition and Emotion, 15*, 713–724.

Baumann, N., Kaschel, R., & Kuhl, J. (2005). Striving for unwanted goals: Stress-dependent discrepancies between explicit and implicit achievement motives reduce subjective well-being and increase psychosomatic symptoms. *Journal of Personality and Social Psychology, 89*, 781–799.

Baumann, N., Kaschel, R., & Kuhl, J. (2007). Affect sensitivity and affect regulation in dealing with positive and negative affect. *Journal of Research in Personality, 41*, 239–248.

Baumann, N., & Kuhl, J. (2002). Intuition, affect, and personality: Unconscious coherence judgments and self-regulation of negative affect. *Journal of Personality and Social Psychology, 83*, 1213–1223.

Baumeister, R. F. (1989). The optimal margin of illusion. *Journal of Social and Clinical Psychology, 8*, 176–189.

Baumeister, R. F., & Cairns, K. J. (1992). Repression and self-presentation: When audiences interfere with self-deceptive strategies. *Journal of Personality and Social Psychology, 62*, 851–862.

Baumeister, R. F., & Newman, L. S. (1994). Self-regulation of cognitive inference and decision processes. *Personality and Social Psychology Bulletin, 20*, 3–19.

Beauregard, M., Levesque, J., & Bourgouin, P. (2001). Neural correlates of conscious self-regulation of emotion. *Journal of Neuroscience, 21*, 1–6.

Berridge, K. C., & Winkielman, P. (2003). What is an unconscious emotion: The case for unconscious "liking". *Cognition and Emotion, 17,* 181–211.

Boden, J. M., & Baumeister, R. F. (1997). Repressive coping: Distraction using pleasant thoughts and memories. *Journal of Personality and Social Psychology, 73,* 45–62.

Boiten, F. A., Frijda, N. H., & Wientjes, C. J. E. (1994). Emotions and respiratory patterns: Review and critical analysis. *International Journal of Psychophysiology, 17,* 103–128.

Borkovec, T. D., & Hennings, B. L. (1978). The role of physiological attention-focusing in the relaxation treatment of sleep disturbance general tension and specific stress reaction. *Behavior Research and Therapy, 16,* 7–19.

Bower, G. H., & Mayer, J. D. (1989). In search of mood-dependent retrieval. *Journal of Social Behavior and Personality, 4,* 121–156.

Bradley, S. J. (2000). *Affect regulation and the development of psychopathology.* New York: Guilford Press.

Breuer, J. & Freud, S. (1955). *Studies on hysteria* (Standard ed., Vol. II). London: Hogarth Press. (Original work published 1893–1895)

Brown, K. W., & Ryan, R. M. (2003). The benefits of being present: The role of mindfulness in psychological well-being. *Journal of Personality and Social Psychology, 84,* 822–848.

Brown, K. W., Ryan, R. M., & Creswell, J. D. (2007). Mindfulness: Theoretical foundations and evidence for its salutary effects. *Psychological Inquiry, 18,* 211–237.

Bushman, B. J. (2002). Does venting anger feed or extinguish the flame? Catharsis, rumination, distraction, anger, and aggressive responding. *Personality and Social Psychology Bulletin, 28,* 724–731.

Bushman, B. J., Baumeister, R. F., & Phillips, C. M. (2001). Do people aggress to improve their mood? Catharsis beliefs, affect regulation opportunity, and aggressive responding. *Journal of Personality and Social Psychology, 81,* 17–32.

Butler, E. A., Lee, T. L., & Gross, J. J. (2007). Emotion regulation and culture: Are the social consequences of emotion suppression culture-specific? *Emotion, 7,* 30–48.

Cacioppo, J. T., Berntson, G. G., & Klein, D. J. (1992). What is an emotion? The role of somatovisceral afference, with special emphasis on somatovisceral "illusions". *Review of Personality and Social Psychology, 14,* 63–98.

Cahn, B. R., & Polich, J. (2006). Meditation states and traits: EEG, ERP, and neuroimaging studies. *Psychological Bulletin, 132,* 180–211.

Campbell, W. K., & Sedikides, C. (1999). Self-threat magnifies the self-serving bias: A meta-analytic integration. *Review of General Psychology, 3,* 23–43.

Carlson, C. R., & Hoyle, R. H. (1993). Efficacy of abbreviated progressive muscle relaxation training: A quantitative review of behavioral medicine research. *Journal of Consulting and Clinical Psychology, 61,* 1059–1067.

Carstensen, L. L., Fung, H., & Charles, S. (2003). Socioemotional selectivity theory and the regulation of emotion in the second half of life. *Motivation and Emotion, 27,* 103–123.

Carver, C. S., & Scheier, M. F. (1998). *On the self-regulation of behavior.* New York: Cambridge University Press.

Clark, M., & Hirschman, R. (1990). Effects of paced respiration on anxiety reduction in a clinical population. *Applied Psychophysiology and Biofeedback*, *15*, 273–284.

Coifman, K. G., Bonanno, G. A., Ray, R. D., & Gross, J. J. (2007). Does repressive coping promote resilience? Affective-autonomic response discrepancy during bereavement. *Journal of Personality and Social Psychology*, *92*, 745–758.

Colvin, C. R., & Block, J. (1994). Do positive illusions foster mental health? An examination of the Taylor and Brown formulation. *Psychological Bulletin*, *116*, 3–20.

Creswell, J. D., Welch, W. T., Taylor, S. E., Sherman, D. K., Gruenewald, T. L., & Mann, T. (2005). Affirmation of personal values buffers neuroendocrine and psychological stress responses. *Psychological Science*, *16*, 846–851.

Dandeneau, S. D., Baldwin, M. W., Baccus, J. R., Sakellaropoulo, M., & Pruessner, J. C. (2007). Cutting stress off at the pass: Reducing stress and hypervigilance to social threat by manipulating attention. *Journal of Personality and Social Psychology*, *93*, 651–666.

Davidson, R. J. (1998). Affective style and affective disorders: Perspectives from affective neuroscience. *Cognition and Emotion*, *12*, 307–330.

Davidson, R. J., Jackson, D. C., & Kalin, N. H. (2000). Emotion, plasticity, context and regulation: Perspectives from affective neuroscience. *Psychological Bulletin*, *126*, 890–906.

Demaree, H. A., Schmeichel, B. J., Robinson, J. L., Pu, J., Everhart, D. E., & Berntson, G. G. (2006). Up- and down-regulating facial disgust: Affective, vagal, sympathetic, and respiratory consequences. *Biological Psychology*, *71*, 90–99.

Derakshan, N., Eysenck, M. W., & Myers, L. B. (2007). Emotional information processing in repressors: The vigilance–avoidance theory. *Cognition and Emotion*, *21*, 1585–1614.

Derryberry, D. (1993). Attentional consequences of outcome-related motivational states: Congruent, incongruent, and focusing effects. *Motivation and Emotion*, *17*, 65–89.

Derryberry, D., Reed, M. A., & Pilkenton-Taylor, C. (2003). Temperament and coping: Advantages of an individual differences perspective. *Development and Psychopathology*, *15*, 1049–1066.

Diamond, L. M., & Aspinwall, L. G. (2003). Emotion regulation across the lifespan: An integrative approach emphasizing self-regulation, positive affect, and dyadic processes. *Motivation and Emotion*, *27*, 125–156.

Diefendorff, J. M., Hall, R. J., Lord, R. G., & Strean, M. L. (2000). Action-state orientation: Construct validity of a revised measure and its relationship to work-related variables. *Journal of Applied Psychology*, *85*, 250–263.

Eisenberg, N., Fabes, R. A., & Guthrie, I. K. (1997). Coping with stress: The roles of regulation and development. In S. A. Wolchik & I. N. Sandler (Eds.), *Handbook of children's coping: Linking theory and intervention* (pp. 41–70). New York: Plenum Press.

Erber, R. (1996). The self-regulation of moods. In L. L. Martin & A. Tesser (Eds.), *Striving and feeling: Interactions between goals and affect* (pp. 251–275). Hillsdale, NJ: Lawrence Erlbaum Associates, Inc.

Erber, R., & Erber, M. W. (2000). The self-regulation of moods: Second thoughts on the importance of happiness in everyday life. *Psychological Inquiry*, *11*, 142–148.

Erber, R., & Tesser, A. (1992). Task effort and the regulation of mood: The absorption hypothesis. *Journal of Experimental Social Psychology, 28,* 339–359.

Erber, R., Wegner, D. M., & Therriault, N. (1996). On being cool and collected: Mood regulation in anticipation of social interaction. *Journal of Personality and Social Psychology, 70,* 757–766.

Esch, T., Fricchione, G. L., & Stefano, G. B. (2003). The therapeutic use of the relaxation response in stress-related diseases. *Medical Science Monitor, 9,* 23–34.

Fan, J., McCandliss, B. D., Fossella, J., Flombaum, J. I., & Posner, M. I. (2005). The activation of attentional networks. *NeuroImage, 26,* 471–479.

Fein, S., & Spencer, S. J. (1997). Prejudice as self-image maintenance: Affirming the self through derogating others. *Journal of Personality and Social Psychology, 73,* 31–44.

Festinger, L. (1957). *A theory of cognitive dissonance.* Stanford, CA: Stanford University Press.

Fox, E. (1993). Allocation of visual attention and anxiety. *Cognition and Emotion, 2,* 207–215.

Franck, M., Schäfer, H., Stiels, W., Wasserman, R., & Hermann, J. M. (1994). Relaxation therapy with respiratory feedback in patients with essential hypertension. Psychotherapie, Psychosomatik. *Medizinische Psychologie, 44,* 316–322.

Freud, S. (1961). Repression. In J. Strachy (Ed.). (Ed. & Trans.), *The standard edition of the complete works of Sigmund Freud* (Vol. 14, pp. 143–160). London: Hogarth Press. (Originally published 1915)

Frijda, N. (2006). *The laws of emotion.* New York: Lawrence Erlbaum Associates, Inc.

Frijda, N. H., & Sundararajan, L. (2007). Emotion refinement: A theory inspired by Chinese poetics. *Perspectives on Psychological Science, 2,* 227–241.

Geen, R. G., & Quanty, M. B. (1977). The catharsis of aggression: An evaluation of a hypothesis. In L. Berkowitz (Ed.), *Advances in experimental social psychology* (Vol. 10, pp. 1–37). New York: Academic Press.

Geraerts, E., Merckelbach, H., Jelicic, M., & Smeets, E. (2006). Long term consequences of suppression of intrusive thoughts and repressive coping. *Behaviour Research and Therapy, 44,* 1451–1460.

Gerin, W., Davidson, K. W., Goyal, T., Christenfeld, N., & Schwartz, J. E. (2006). The role of rumination and distraction in blood pressure recovery from anger. *Psychosomatic Medicine, 68,* 64–72.

Gilbert, D. G., Sugai, C., Zuo, Y., Rabinovich, N. E., McClernon, F. J., & Froeliger, B. E. (2007). Brain indices of nicotine's effects on attentional bias to smoking and emotional pictures and to task-relevant targets. *Nicotine and Tobacco Research, 9,* 351–363.

Gilbert, D. T., Lieberman, M. D., Morewedge, C. K., & Wilson, T. D. (2004). The peculiar longevity of things not so bad. *Psychological Science, 15,* 14–19.

Goleman, D. (1995). *Emotional intelligence: Why it can matter more than IQ.* London: Bloomsbury.

Greeno, C. G., & Wing, R. R. (1994). Stress-induced eating. *Psychological Bulletin, 115,* 444–464.

Gröpel, P. Kuhl, J. & Kazén, M. (2004). Toward an integrated self: Age differences and the role of action orientation. *Conference proceedings of the Third*

*International SELF Research Conference* [CD-Rom]. Sydney, Australia: SELF Research Centre.

Gross, J. J. (1998a). Antecedent- and response-focused emotion regulation: Divergent consequences for experience, expression, and physiology. *Journal of Personality and Social Psychology, 74,* 224–237.

Gross, J. J. (1998b). The emerging field of emotion regulation: An integrative review. *Review of General Psychology, 2,* 271–299.

Gross, J. J. (1999). Emotion regulation: Past, present, future. *Cognition and Emotion, 13,* 551–573.

Gross, J. J. (2001). Emotion regulation in adulthood: Timing is everything. *Current Directions in Psychological Science, 10,* 214–219.

Gross, J. J. (Ed.). (2007). *Handbook of emotion regulation.* New York: Guilford Press.

Gross, J. J., & John, O. (2003). Individual differences in two emotion-regulation processes: Implications for affect, relationships, and well-being. *Journal of Personality and Social Psychology, 85,* 348–362.

Gross, J. J., & Muñoz, R. F. (1995). Emotion regulation and mental health. *Clinical Psychology: Science and Practice, 2,* 151–164.

Haley, G. A. (1974). Eye movement responses of repressors and sensitizers to a stressful film. *Journal of Research in Personality, 8,* 88–94.

Harmon-Jones, E., & Mills, J. (1999). *Cognitive dissonance: Progress on a pivotal theory in social psychology.* Washington, DC: American Psychological Association.

Hawkins, M. F., Cubic, B., Baumeister, A. A., & Barton, C. (1992). Microinjection of opioid antagonists into the substantia nigra reduces stress-induced eating in rats. *Brain Research, 584,* 261–265.

Heatherton, T. F., & Baumeister, R. F. (1991). Binge eating as escape from self-awareness. *Psychological Bulletin, 110,* 86–108.

Jacobson, E. (1928). *Progressive relaxation.* Chicago: University of Chicago Press.

Jamner, L. D., Schwartz, G. E., & Leigh, H. (1988). The relationship between repressive and defensive coping styles and monocyte, eosinophile and serum glucose levels: Support for the opioid-peptide hypothesis of repression. *Psychosomatic Medicine, 50,* 567–575.

John, O. P., & Gross, J. J. (2004). Healthy and unhealthy emotion regulation: Personality processes, individual differences, and lifespan development. *Journal of Personality, 72,* 1301–1334.

Joormann, J., & Siemer, M. (2004). Memory accessibility, mood regulation, and dysphoria: Difficulties in repairing sad mood with happy memories? *Journal of Abnormal Psychology, 113,* 179–188.

Jostmann, N., Koole, S. L., Van der Wulp, N., & Fockenberg, D. (2005). Subliminal affect regulation: The moderating role of action versus state orientation. *European Psychologist, 10,* 209–217.

Kang, S., & Shaver, P. R. (2004). Individual differences in emotional complexity: Their psychological implications. *Journal of Personality, 72,* 687–726.

Klein, K., & Boals, A. (2001). Expressive writing can increase working memory capacity. *Journal of Experimental Psychology: General, 130,* 520–533.

Koole, S. L., & Coenen, L. H. M. (2007). Implicit self and affect regulation: Effects of action orientation and subliminal self-priming in an affective priming task. *Self and Identity, 6,* 118–136.

Koole, S. L., Govorun, O., & Cheng, C. (2008). *Pulling your self together: Meditation promotes the congruence between implicit and explicit self-esteem.* Manuscript submitted for publication: VU Amsterdam.

Koole, S. L., & Jostmann, N. B. (2004). Getting a grip on your feelings: Effects of action orientation and external demands on intuitive affect regulation. *Journal of Personality and Social Psychology, 87,* 974–990.

Koole, S. L., & Kuhl, J. (2007). Dealing with unwanted feelings: The role of affect regulation in volitional action control. In J. Shah & W. Gardner (Eds.), *Handbook of motivation science.* New York: Guilford Press.

Koole, S. L., Smeets, K., Van Knippenberg, A., & Dijksterhuis, A. (1999). The cessation of rumination through self-affirmation. *Journal of Personality and Social Psychology, 11,* 111–125.

Kring, A. M., & Werner, K. H. (2004). Emotion regulation in psychopathology. In P. Philippot & R. S. Feldman (Eds.), *The regulation of emotion* (pp. 359–385). Mahwah, NJ: Lawrence Erlbaum Associates, Inc.

Kuhl, J. (2000). A functional-design approach to motivation and self-regulation: The dynamics of personality systems interactions. In M. Boekaerts, P. R. Pintrich, & M. Zeidner (Eds.), *Handbook of self-regulation* (pp. 111–169). San Diego, CA: Academic Press.

Kuhl, J. (2008, January). *Einführung in die Persönlichkeitspsychologie: 4. Coping* [Introduction to personality psychology: 4. Coping.]. Lecture at the University of Osnabrück, Germany.

Kuhl, J., & Beckmann, J. (1994). *Volition and personality: Action versus state orientation.* Göttingen, Germany: Hogrefe & Huber.

Kunda, Z. (1990). The case for motivated reasoning. *Psychological Bulletin, 108,* 480–498.

Lane, R. D., Sechrest, L., Riedel, R., Shapiro, D. E., & Kaszniak, A. W. (2000). Pervasive emotion recognition deficit common to alexithymia and the repressive coping style. *Psychosomatic Medicine, 62,* 492–501.

Langens, T. A., & Mörth, S. (2003). Repressive coping and the use of passive and active coping strategies. *Personality and Individual Differences, 35,* 461–473.

Larsen, R. J. (2000). Toward a science of mood regulation. *Psychological Inquiry, 11,* 129–141.

Lazarus, R. S. (1991). Progress on a cognitive-motivational-relational theory of emotion. *American Psychologist, 46,* 819–834.

Lehrer, P. M. (1982). How to relax and how not to relax: A re-evaluation of the work of Edmund Jacobson. *Behaviour Research and Therapy, 20,* 417–428.

Liberman, A., & Chaiken, S. (1992). Defensive processing of personally relevant health messages. *Personality and Social Psychology Bulletin, 18,* 669–679.

Linville, P. W. (1985). Self-complexity and affective extremity: Don't put all of your eggs in one cognitive basket. *Social Cognition, 3,* 94–120.

Linville, P. W. (1987). Self-complexity as a cognitive buffer against stress-related illness and depression. *Journal of Personality and Social Psychology, 52,* 663–676.

Loewenstein, G. (1996). Out of control: Visceral influences on behavior. *Organizational Behavior and Human Decision Processes, 65,* 272–92.

Mathews, A., & MacLeod, C. (2005). Cognitive vulnerability to emotional disorders. *Annual Review of Clinical Psychology, 1,* 167–195.

Mauss, I. B., Bunge, S. A., & Gross, J. J. (2007). Automatic emotion regulation. *Social and Personality Psychology Compass, 1*, 146–167.

Mauss, I. B., Levenson, R. W., McCarter, L., Wilhelm, F., & Gross, J. J. (2005). The tie that binds? Coherence among emotion experience, behavior, and physiology. *Emotion, 5*, 175–190.

Mauss, I. B. & Robinson, M. D. (2009). Measures of emotion: A review. *Cognition and Emotion, 23*, 209–237.

McCrae, R. R. Costa, P. T., Jr. , Ostendorf, F. Angleitner, A. Hrebrikova, M. Avia, M. D. et al. (2000). Nature over nurture: Temperament, personality, and lifespan development. *Journal of Personality and Social Psychology, 78*, 173–186.

McGregor, I. (2006). Offensive defensiveness: Toward an integrative neuroscience of compensatory zeal after mortality salience, personal uncertainty, and other poignant self-threats. *Psychological Inquiry, 17*, 299–308.

Meuret, A. E., Wilhelm, F. H., & Roth, W. T. (2001). Respiratory biofeedback-assisted therapy in panic disorder. *Behavior Modification, 25*, 584–605.

Mikulincer, M., Shaver, P. R., & Pereg, D. (2003). Attachment theory and affect regulation: The dynamics, development, and cognitive consequences of attachment-related strategies. *Motivation and Emotion, 27*, 77–102.

Moberly, N. J., & Watkins, E. (2006). Processing mode influences the relationship between trait rumination and emotional vulnerability. *Behavior Therapy, 37*, 281–291.

Mohr, C. D., Brennan, D., Mohr, J., Armeli, S., & Tennen, H. (2008). Evidence for positive mood buffering among college student drinkers. *Personality and Social Psychology Bulletin, 34*, 1249–1259.

Moors, A. (2007). Can cognitive methods be used to study the unique aspect of emotion? An appraisal theorist's answer. *Cognition and Emotion, 21*, 1238–1269.

Moors, A., & De Houwer, J. (2006). Automaticity: A theoretical and conceptual analysis. *Psychological Bulletin, 132*, 297–326.

Morley, J. E., & Levine, A. S. (1980). Stress-induced eating is mediated through endogenous opiates. *Science, 209*, 1259–1261.

Morrow, J., & Nolen-Hoeksema, S. (1990). Effects of responses to depression on the remediation of depressive affect. *Journal of Personality and Social Psychology, 58*, 519–527.

Murray, S. L. (2005). Regulating the risks of closeness: A relationship-specific sense of felt security. *Current Directions in Psychological Science, 14*, 74–78.

Myers, L. B. (2000). Identifying repressors: A methodological issue for health psychology. *Psychology and Health, 15*, 205–214.

Myers, L. B., Burns, J. W., Derakshan, N., Elfant, E., Eysenck, M. W., & Phipps, S. (2008). Twenty five years on: Current issues in repressive coping and health. In A. Vingerhoets, I. Nyklicek, & L. Temoshok (Eds.), *Behavioural perspectives on health and disease prevention*. New York: Routledge.

Myers, L. B., & McKenna, F. P. (1996). The color naming of socially threatening words. *Journal of Personality and Individual Differences, 20*, 801–803.

Neumann, A., & Philippot, P. (2007). Specifying what makes a personal memory unique enhances emotion regulation. *Emotion, 7*, 566–578.

Neumann, R., Förster, J., & Strack, F. (2003). Motor compatibility: The bidirectional link between behavior and evaluation. In J. Musch & K. C. Klauer

(Eds.), *The psychology of evaluation: Affective processes in cognition and emotion* (pp. 7–49). Mahwah, NJ: Lawrence Erlbaum Associates, Inc.

Newman, L. S., & McKinney, L. C. (2002). Repressive coping and threat-avoidance: An idiographic Stroop study. *Personality and Social Psychology Bulletin, 28*, 409–422.

Niedenthal, P. M. (2007). Embodying emotion. *Science, 316*, 1002–1005.

Niedenthal, P. M., Barsalou, L. W., Winkielman, P., Krauth-Gruber, S., & Ric, F. (2005). Embodiment in attitudes, social perception, and emotion. *Personality and Social Psychology Review, 9*, 184–211.

Nolen-Hoeksema, S. (2000). The role of rumination in depressive disorders and mixed anxiety/depressive symptoms. *Journal of Abnormal Psychology, 109*, 504–511.

Nolen-Hoeksema, S., & Morrow, J. (1993). Effects of rumination and distraction on naturally occurring depressed mood. *Cognition and Emotion, 7*, 561–570.

Nordgren, L. F., van der Pligt, J., & van Harreveld, F. (2006). Visceral drives in retrospect: Making attributions about the inaccessible past. *Psychological Science, 17*, 635–640.

Nowak, A., Vallacher, R. R., Tesser, A., & Borkowski, W. (2000). Society of self: The emergence of collective properties in self-structure. *Psychological Review, 107*, 39–61.

Ochsner, K. N., Bunge, S. A., Gross, J. J., & Gabrieli, J. D. E. (2002). Rethinking feelings: An fMRI study of the cognitive regulation of emotion. *Journal of Cognitive Neuroscience, 14*, 1215–1299.

Ochsner, K. N., & Gross, J. J. (2005). The cognitive control of emotion. *Trends in Cognitive Sciences, 9*, 242–249.

Ochsner, K. N., & Gross, J. J. (2008). Cognitive emotion regulation: Insights from social cognitive and affective neuroscience. *Current Directions in Psychological Science, 17*, 153–158.

Olson, J. M., & Zanna, M. P. (1979). A new look at selective exposure. *Journal of Experimental Social Psychology, 15*, 1–15.

Ortony, A., Clore, G. L., & Collins, A. (1988). *The cognitive structure of emotions.* Cambridge, UK: Cambridge University Press.

Panksepp, J. (1998). *Affective neuroscience: The foundations of human and animal emotions.* New York: Oxford University Press.

Parkinson, B., & Totterdell, P. (1999). Classifying affect-regulation strategies. *Cognition and Emotion, 13*, 277–303.

Pawlow, L. A., & Jones, G. E. (2002). The impact of abbreviated progressive muscle relaxation on salivary cortisol. *Biological Psychology, 60*, 1–16.

Pennebaker, J. W. (1997). Writing about emotional experiences as a therapeutic process. *Psychological Science, 8*, 162–166.

Pennebaker, J. W., & Chung, C. K. (2007). Expressive writing, emotional upheavals, and health. In H. Friedman & R. Silver (Eds.), *Handbook of health psychology* (pp. 263–284). New York: Oxford University Press.

Pennebaker, J. W., Mayne, T. J., & Francis, M. E. (1997). Linguistic predictors of adaptive bereavement. *Journal of Personality and Social Psychology, 72*, 166–183.

Philippot, P., Baeyens, C., Douilliez, C., & Francart, B. (2004). Cognitive regulation of emotion. In P. Philippot & R. S. Feldman (Eds.), *The regulation of emotion.* New York: Lawrence Erlbaum Associates, Inc.

Philippot, P., Chapelle, C., & Blairy, S. (2002). Respiratory feedback in the generation of emotion. *Cognition and Emotion, 16*, 605–627.

Porges, S. W. (2007). The polyvagal perspective. *Biological Psychology, 74*, 116–143.

Porges, S. W., Doussard-Roosevelt, J. A., & Maita, A. K. (1994). Vagal tone and the physiological regulation of emotion. *Monographs of the Society for Research in Child Development, 59*, 167–186.

Posner, M. I., & Rothbart, M. K. (2007). Research on attention networks as a model for the integration of psychological sciences. *Annual Review of Psychology, 58*, 1–23.

Pratto, F., & John, O. P. (1991). Automatic vigilance—The attention-grabbing power of negative social information. *Journal of Personality and Social Psychology, 61*, 380–391.

Pyszczynski, T., & Greenberg, J. (1987). Toward an integration of cognitive and motivational perspectives on social inference: A biased hypothesis-testing model. In L. Berkowitz (Ed.), *Advances in experimental social psychology* (Vol. 20, pp. 297–340). Hillsdale, NJ: Lawrence Erlbaum Associates, Inc.

Rafaeli-Mor, E., & Steinberg, J. (2002). Self-complexity and well-being: A review and research synthesis. *Personality and Social Psychology Review, 6*, 31–58.

Rankin, E. J., Gilner, F. H., Gfeller, J. D., & Katz, B. M. (1993). Efficacy of progressive muscle relaxation for reducing state anxiety among elderly adults on memory tasks. *Perceptual and Motor Skills, 77*, 1395–1402.

Rausch, S. M., Gramling, S. E., & Auerbach, S. M. (2006). Effects of a single session of large-group meditation and progressive muscle relaxation training on stress reduction, reactivity, and recovery. *International Journal of Stress Management, 13*, 273–290.

Richards, J. M., & Gross, J. J. (2000). Emotion regulation and memory: The cognitive costs of keeping one's cool. *Journal of Personality and Social Psychology, 79*, 410–424.

Robinson, J. L., & Demaree, H. (2007). Physiological and cognitive effects of expressive dissonance. *Brain and Cognition, 63*, 70–78.

Roese, N. J., & Olson, J. M. (2007). Better, stronger, faster: Self-serving judgment, affect regulation, and the optimal vigilance hypothesis. *Perspectives on Psychological Science, 2*, 124–141.

Rothbart, M. K., Derryberry, D., & Posner, M. I. (1994). A psychobiological approach to the development of temperament. In J. E. Bates & T. D. Wachs (Eds.), *Temperament: Individual differences at the interface of biology and behavior* (pp. 83–116). Washington, DC: American Psychological Association.

Rothermund, K., Voss, A., & Wentura, D. (2008). Counter-regulation in affective attentional bias: A basic mechanism that warrants flexibility in motivation and emotion. *Emotion, 8*, 34–46.

Russell, J. A. (2003). Core affect and the psychological construction of emotion. *Psychological Review, 110*, 145–172.

Rusting, C. L., & Nolen-Hoeksema, S. (1998). Regulating responses to anger: Effects of rumination and distraction on angry mood. *Journal of Personality and Social Psychology, 74*, 790–803.

Ruys, K. I., & Stapel, D. A. (2008). The secret life of emotions. *Psychological Science, 19*, 385–391.

Sapolsky, R. M. (2007). Stress, stress-related disease, and emotional regulation. In J. J. Gross (Ed.), *Handbook of emotion regulation*. New York: Guilford Press.

Scherer, K. R., Schorr, A., & Johnstone, T. (2001). *Appraisal processes in emotion: Theory, methods, research*. New York: Oxford University Press.

Schmeichel, B. J., Demaree, H. A., Robinson, J. L., & Pu, J. (2006). Ego depletion by response exaggeration. *Journal of Experimental Social Psychology*, 42, 95–102.

Schmeichel, B. J. Volokhov, R. N. & Demaree, H. A. (2008). Working memory capacity and the self-regulation of emotional expression and experience. *Journal of Personality and Social Psychology*, 95, 1526–1540.

Sedikides, C., & Green, J. D. (2004). What I don't recall can't hurt me: Information negativity versus information inconsistency as determinants of memorial self-defense. *Social Cognition*, 22, 4–29.

Serrano, J. P., Latorre, J. M., Gatz, M., & Montañés, J. (2004). Life review therapy using autobiographical retrieval practice for older adults with depressive symptomatology. *Psychology and Aging*, 19, 272–277.

Sher, K. J., & Grekin, E. R. (2007). Alcohol and affect regulation. In J. J. Gross (Ed.), *Handbook of emotion regulation* (pp. 560–580). New York: Guilford Press.

Siemer, M. (2005). Mood-congruent cognitions constitute mood experience. *Emotion*, 5, 296–308.

Simon, L., Greenberg, J., & Brehm, J. (1995). Trivialization: The forgotten mode of dissonance reduction. *Journal of Personality & Social Psychology*, 68, 247–260.

Skinner, E. A., Edge, K., Altman, J., & Sherwood, H. (2003). Searching for the structure of coping: A review and critique of category systems for classifying ways of coping. *Psychological Bulletin*, 129, 216–269.

Skinner, E. A., & Zimmer-Gembeck, M. J. (2007). The development of coping. *Annual Review of Psychology*, 58, 119–144.

Smith, C. A., & Lazarus, R. S. (1993). Appraisal components, core relational themes, and the emotions. *Cognition and Emotion*, 7, 233–269.

Smyth, J. M., True, N., & Souto, J. (2001). Effects of writing about traumatic experiences: The necessity for narrative structuring. *Journal of Social and Clinical Psychology*, 20, 161–172.

Southam-Gerow, M. A., & Kendall, P. C. (2002). Emotion regulation and understanding: Implications for child psychopathology and therapy. *Clinical Psychology Review*, 22, 189–222.

Steptoe, A., & Vogele, C. (1986). Are stress responses influenced by cognitive appraisal? *British Journal of Psychology*, 77, 243–255.

Strack, F., Martin, L., & Stepper, S. (1988). Inhibiting and facilitating conditions of the human smile: A nonobtrusive test of the facial feedback hypothesis. *Journal of Personality and Social Psychology*, 54, 768–777.

Tamir, M., Chiu, C., & Gross, J. J. (2007a). Business or pleasure? Utilitarian versus hedonic considerations in emotion regulation. *Emotion*, 7, 546–554.

Tamir, M., John, O. P., Srivastava, S., & Gross, J. J. (2007b). Implicit theories of emotion: Affective and social outcomes across a major life transition. *Journal of Personality and Social Psychology*, 92, 731–744.

Taylor, S., & Liberzon, I. (2007). Neural correlates of emotion regulation in psychopathology. *Trends in Cognitive Sciences*, 11, 413–418.

Taylor, S. E., Kemeny, M. E., Reed, G. M., Bower, J. E., & Gruenewald, T. L. (2000). Psychological resources, positive illusions, and health. *American Psychologist, 55*, 99–109.

Taylor, S. E., & Lobel, M. (1989). Social comparison activity under threat: Downward evaluation and upward contacts. *Psychological Review, 96*, 569–575.

Terracciano, A. Costa, P. T., Jr. , & McCrae, R. R. (2005). Personality plasticity after age 30. *Personality and Social Psychology Bulletin, 32*, 999–1009.

Tesser, A. (2000). On the confluence of self-esteem maintenance mechanisms. *Personality and Social Psychology Review, 4*, 290–299.

Thayer, J. F., & Lane, R. D. (2000). A model of neurovisceral integration in emotion regulation and dysregulation. *Journal of Affective Disorders, 61*, 201–216.

Thayer, J. F., & Lane, R. D. (2007). The role of vagal function in the risk for cardiovascular disease and mortality. *Biological Psychology, 74*, 224–242.

Thayer, R. E. (1987). Energy, tiredness and tension effects of a sugar snack vs. moderate exercise. *Journal of Personality and Social Psychology, 52*, 119–125.

Thayer, R. E., Newman, J. R., & McClain, T. M. (1994). Self-regulation of mood: Strategies for changing a bad mood, raising energy, and reducing tension. *Journal of Personality and Social Psychology, 67*, 910–925.

Tice, D. M., & Bratslavsky, E. (2000). Giving in to feel good: The place of emotion regulation in the context of general self-control. *Psychological Inquiry, 11*, 149–159.

Tice, D. M., Bratslavsky, E., & Baumeister, R. F. (2001). Emotional distress regulation takes precedence over impulse control: If you feel bad, do it! *Journal of Personality and Social Psychology, 80*, 53–67.

Tugade, M. M., & Frederickson, B. L. (2004). Resilient individuals use positive emotions to bounce back from negative emotional experiences. *Journal of Personality and Social Psychology, 86*, 320–333.

Tugade, M. M., Fredrickson, B. L., & Barrett, L. F. (2004). Psychological resilience and positive emotional granularity: Examining the benefits of positive emotions on coping and health. *Journal of Personality, 72*, 1161–1190.

Urry, H. L., van Reekum, C. M., Johnstone, T., Kalin, N. H., Thurow, M. E., Schaefer, H. S., et al. (2006). Amygdala and ventromedial prefrontal cortex are inversely coupled during regulation of negative affect and predict the diurnal pattern of cortisol secretion among older adults. *Journal of Neuroscience, 26*, 4415–4425.

Van den Berg, A. E., Hartig, T., & Staats, H. (2007). Preference for nature in urbanized societies: Stress, restoration, and the pursuit of sustainability. *Journal of Social Issues, 63*, 79–96.

Van Dillen, L. F., Heslenfeld, D., & Koole, S. L. (2008). *Working memory modulates the emotional brain. Manuscript submitted for publication.* VU Amsterdam.

Van Dillen, L. F., & Koole, S. L. (2007). Clearing the mind: A working memory model of distraction from negative emotion. *Emotion, 7*, 715–723.

Van Dillen, L. F. & Koole, S. L. (2009). How automatic is "automatic vigilance"? The role of working memory in attentional interference of negative information. *Cognition and Emotion, 23*, 1106–1117.

van Reekum, C. M., Johnstone, T., Urry, H. L., Thurow, M. T., Schaefer, H. S., Alexander, A. L., et al. (2007). Gaze fixations predict brain activation during the voluntary regulation of picture-induced negative affect. *NeuroImage, 36,* 1041–1055.

Watkins, E. (2004). Adaptive and maladaptive ruminative self-focus during emotional processing. *Behaviour Research and Therapy, 42,* 1037–1052.

Watkins, E., & Moulds, M. (2005). Distinct modes of ruminative self-focus: Impact of abstract versus concrete rumination on problem solving in depression. *Emotion, 5,* 319–328.

Wegner, D. M. (1994). Ironic processes of mental control. *Psychological Review, 101,* 34–52.

Wegner, D. M., Erber, R., & Zanakos, S. (1993). Ironic processes in the mental control of mood and mood-related thought. *Journal of Personality and Social Psychology, 65,* 1093–1104.

Wegner, D. M., & Gold, D. B. (1995). Fanning old flames: Emotional and cognitive effects of suppressing thoughts of a past relationship. *Journal of Personality and Social Psychology, 68,* 782–792.

Weinberger, D. A. (1990). The construct validity of repressive coping style. In J. L. Singer (Ed.), *Repression and dissociation: Implications for personality theory, psychopathology, and health* (pp. 337–386). Chicago: The University of Chicago Press.

Weinberger, D. A., Schwartz, G. E., & Davidson, R. J. (1979). Low-anxious, high-anxious and repressive coping styles: Psychometric patterns and behavioral and physiological responses to stress. *Journal of Abnormal Psychology, 88,* 369–380.

Wenzlaff, R. M., & Wegner, D. M. (2000). Thought suppression. In S. T. Fiske (Ed.), *Annual review of psychology* (Vol. 51, pp. 59–91). Palo Alto, CA: Annual Reviews.

Wenzlaff, R. M., Wegner, D. M., & Roper, D. (1988). Depression and mental control: The resurgence of unwanted negative thoughts. *Journal of Personality and Social Psychology, 55,* 882–892.

Westen, D. (1994). Toward an integrative model of affect regulation: Applications to social-psychological research. *Journal of Personality, 62,* 641–647.

Westen, D., Kilts, C., Blagov, P., Harenski, K., & Hamann, S. (2006). The neural basis of motivated reasoning: An fMRI study of emotional constraints on political judgment during the U. S. Presidential election of 2004. *Journal of Cognitive Neuroscience, 18,* 1947–1958.

Whiteside, U., Chen, E., Neighbors, C., Hunter, D., Lo, T., & Larimer, M. E. (2007). Difficulties regulating emotions: Do binge eaters have fewer strategies to modulate and tolerate negative affect? *Eating Behaviors, 8,* 162–169.

Williams, J. M. G., Barnhofer, T., Crane, C., Hermans, D., Raes, F., Watkins, E., et al. (2007). Autobiographical memory specificity and emotional disorder. *Psychological Bulletin, 133,* 122–148.

Zack, M., Poulos, C. X., Fragopoulos, F., Woodford, T. M., & MacLeod, C. M. (2006). Negative affect words prime beer consumption in young drinkers. *Addictive Behaviors, 31,* 169–173.

Zajonc, R. B. (1998). Emotions. In D. Gilbert, S. T. Fiske, & G. Lindzey (Eds.), *Handbook of social psychology* (4th ed., Vol. 1, pp. 591–632). New York: McGraw-Hill.

Zeelenberg, M., & Pieters, R. (2007). A theory of regret regulation 1.0. *Journal of Consumer Psychology, 17*, 3–18.

Zeier, H. (1984). Arousal reduction with biofeedback-supported respiratory meditation. *Applied Psychophysiology and Biofeedback, 9*, 497–508.

Correspondence should be addressed to: Sander Koole, Department of Social Psychology, Vrije Universiteit Amsterdam, van der Boechorststraat 1, NL-1081 BT, Amsterdam, the Netherlands. E-mail: SL.koole@psy.vu.nl

The author would like to thank Jan De Houwer, Daniel Fockenberg, Miguel Kazén, Julius Kuhl, Klaus Rothermund, Hester Ruigendijk, Markus Quirin, Lotte van Dillen, and two anonymous reviewers for their insightful feedback on a previous version of this paper.

# 6 Emotion and memory narrowing: A review and goal-relevance approach

Linda J. Levine
*University of California, Irvine, CA, USA*

Robin S. Edelstein
*University of Michigan, Ann Arbor, MI, USA*

A wedding, a dispute, a grim diagnosis, a natural disaster ... our most vivid and lasting memories are typically emotional ones. These memories are selective, however. Like a spotlight that illuminates the centre of a scene, throwing the periphery into shadow, emotion enhances memory for central features of emotional events but impairs memory for peripheral details. Memory narrowing as a result of emotion has been demonstrated in numerous studies but several sources of controversy remain. Defining "central" is one. What constitutes the core of an emotional event? Does central refer to whatever people happen to be paying attention to at the time they are emotionally aroused? Does it refer only to information that forms an integral part of an emotional event? Or does it refer to information that bodes well or ill for a person's well-being? What constitutes peripheral information, destined to be forgotten? Another source of controversy concerns the mechanisms by which emotion fortifies some memories while allowing others to fade. Extending the scope of these questions, investigators recently have begun to ask whether all emotions, or only particular negative emotions, bring about a trade-off between memory for central and peripheral information. This paper reviews current research and theory on these issues.

We begin by reviewing evidence that emotion promotes memory narrowing. Not all studies show memory narrowing, however. In some cases, people show excellent memory for details of emotional events that might be considered peripheral; in other cases, people show poor memory for information that might be considered central. To make sense both of the general pattern of findings that emotion leads to memory narrowing, and of findings that appear to violate this pattern, we review mechanisms that underlie good memory for central information and poor memory for peripheral details. We also review different approaches to defining information as central versus peripheral. Contrasting these approaches helps clarify when and how emotion enhances memory and provides important directions for future research. We propose that memory narrowing as a result of emotion can be explained by the view that emotion enhances memory for information relevant to currently active goals. Defining central information in terms of goal relevance helps clarify when emotion leads to memory narrowing and when it does not. This approach also leads to specific predictions about the types of information that should be central, and hence well-remembered, in discrete emotional states.

## EMOTION AND MEMORY FOR CENTRAL VERSUS PERIPHERAL INFORMATION

Memory narrowing (e.g., Reisberg & Heuer, 2004), tunnel memory (Safer, Christianson, Autry, & Osterlund, 1998), and the memory trade-off effect (e.g., Kensinger, Garoff-Eaton, & Schacter, 2007a) all refer to the finding that memory is enhanced for central or core features of emotional events but memory for peripheral or background features is not enhanced and may even be impaired. This phenomenon has been demonstrated in real-world contexts where emotional intensity runs high as well as in controlled laboratory settings involving low levels of emotional intensity. In real-world contexts, people often show lasting and accurate memory for central features of traumatic experiences such as natural disasters (Bahrick, Parker, Fivush, & Levitt, 1998; Sotgiu & Galati, 2007), child sexual abuse (e.g., Alexander et al., 2005), and physical injuries (Peterson & Bell, 1996). For instance, in an examination of children's memory for stressful injuries and resulting emergency-room visits, Peterson and Whalen (2001) found that children were more accurate about central components of their injury experience than about peripheral details concerning their hospital visit. Robbery witnesses similarly showed more accurate memory for central than for peripheral details of the crime (Christianson & Hübinette, 1993; see Kihlstrom, 2006; Reisberg & Heuer, 2007, for reviews).

In the laboratory, enhanced memory has been found for central features of emotional stories, pictures, and word lists. In one early study, Christianson and Loftus (1987) showed people a slide sequence depicting either an emotional event (a boy hit by a car) or a neutral event (a boy passing beside a car), and asked them to write down the essential feature in each slide. Later, people who had viewed the emotional slide sequence were better able to recall these essential features than those who had viewed the neutral sequence; they were less able, though, to recognise the particular slides they had seen. Details that would have allowed them to distinguish between similar emotional slides were not well preserved in memory. Similar effects have been shown in studies of memory for unrelated emotional images. Kensinger et al. (2007a) had people view pictures of an emotionally aversive object against a neutral background (e.g., a snake by a river) and pictures of a neutral object against a neutral background (e.g., a chipmunk in a forest). People were better at remembering emotional than neutral objects. They showed worse memory, though, for neutral backgrounds of emotional objects than for neutral backgrounds of neutral objects.

Studies of very simple emotional stimuli have shown enhanced memory for information that constitutes a spatially integral part of the stimulus, such as the colour of the font in which an emotional versus neutral word was presented (MacKay & Ahmetzanov, 2005), or the location of an emotional word on a computer screen (Mather, 2007; Mather & Nesmith, 2008). Moving from spatial to temporal proximity, there may be a memory advantage for information encountered during rather than before or after an emotional event, though the length of this temporal window has yet to be determined (e.g., Burke, Heuer, & Reisberg, 1992; Schmidt, 2002). Strange, Hurleman, and Dolan (2003) presented people with lists of neutral words, each of which included an embedded emotional word (e.g., murder). People were better at remembering emotional than neutral words, but memory was worst for the neutral word that immediately preceded an emotional word. Impaired memory for the word preceding an emotional word did not appear to be due to distinctiveness since words in distinctive colours or fonts did not impair memory for preceding words. Taken together these findings suggest that, both in the real world and in the laboratory, information that is central to an emotional stimulus, conceptually, spatially, or temporally, is likely to be remembered whereas information that is removed may not.

Evidence that emotion leads to a trade-off between memory for central and peripheral information is not as uniform as it may appear from the findings reviewed above, however. In some cases, emotion enhances memory for details that may be considered peripheral. For example, people presented with slides and narratives that evoked an empathic emotional response to the plight of the protagonist showed good memory for details as well as central events (Laney, Campbell, Heuer, & Reisberg, 2004). In other cases, emotion or stress impairs memory for information that could be considered central. Soldiers who endured an extremely stressful interrogation as part of military survival training, including food and sleep deprivation and physical confrontation, were less likely to recognise their interrogator than soldiers who underwent a less stressful interrogation (Morgan et al., 2004; also see Deffenbacher, Bornstein, Penrod, & McGorty, 2004). To make sense of emotion-induced memory narrowing, and of results that violate this pattern of findings, it is necessary to be more explicit about the mechanisms that underlie accurate and lasting memory for emotional material and poor memory for peripheral detail. It is also necessary to be more explicit about how to characterise the types of information that are integral, as opposed to peripheral, to an emotional event or stimulus. Below we address these issues in turn, beginning with mechanisms that underlie enhanced memory for emotional information.

## HOW EMOTION ENHANCES MEMORY

Unlike memories of neutral events, which fade quickly over time, memories of emotional events are often well preserved after delays as brief as minutes and as long as years. This is because emotion enhances information processing at multiple stages and in multiple memory systems. Research indicates that emotional and non-emotional information differ with respect to how quickly they are detected, how long they remain the focus of attention, how long they are retained, and how likely they are to be retrieved.

### Capturing attention

It is well-documented that people mull over and talk about emotional events after they have occurred, and that rehearsal aids memory (e.g., Finkenauer et al., 1998; Rimé, Mesquita, Philippot, & Boca, 1991). This raises the question of whether ordinary memory mechanisms such as rehearsal fully account for enhanced memory for emotional events (e.g., McCloskey, Wible, & Cohen, 1988). To find out, Hulse, Allan, Memon, and Read (2007) showed people an emotional video about a woman being attacked and a neutral video. About 10 minutes later, memory for the videos was assessed. An intervening task before memory assessment prevented people from rehearsing the videos. Eliminating the opportunity for rehearsal, however, did not eliminate the memory advantage for the emotional video after this brief delay (also see Harris & Pashler, 2005). Thus, early information processing, prior to rehearsal, likely contributes to enhanced memory for emotional information.

Studies measuring event-related potentials (ERPs) bear this out. Measurements of electrical changes over the scalp immediately after a stimulus is presented indicate that emotion impacts even the earliest stages of information processing. When presented with emotional versus neutral stimuli, people react to the emotional stimuli faster—within the first 100 to 300 milliseconds after exposure (e.g., Kissler, Herbert, Peyk, & Junghofer, 2007; Koster, Crombez, Verschuere, Vanvolsem, & De Houwer, 2007). Indeed, even before people are aware that they have perceived a stimulus, its emotional value can produce an autonomic response and influence evaluative judgements. For example, Öhman and Soares (1998) found that fear-conditioned visual stimuli evoked an autonomic response even though stimuli were backward masked and presented so briefly that people were unable to identify what they had seen. Thus registration of emotional significance occurs very rapidly.

Emotional information is also more likely to reach conscious awareness than neutral information. It can be difficult to detect a visual stimulus if it follows too closely after the presentation of a preceding visual stimulus—a finding referred to as the "attentional blink". If subsequent information is emotional, though, people are more likely to detect it (e.g., Anderson & Phelps, 2001). People are also faster at shifting attention to the spatial locations of emotional words than neutral words (Stormark, Nordby, & Hugdahl, 1995). Greater attention to emotional than neutral pictures has been shown to account in part (though not entirely) for the greater memorability of emotional pictures after brief delays (e.g., Talmi, Anderson, Riggs, Caplan, & Moscovitch, 2008). Relative to neutral stimuli, then, emotional stimuli benefit from faster, more efficient, and more extensive early processing (see Compton, 2003; LaBar & Cabeza, 2006; Mather, 2007, for reviews).

## Working memory

Given emotion's effects on preattentive processes and on attention, it is reasonable to hypothesize that emotion should similarly enhance working memory, providing another pathway to accurate and lasting memory. Working memory refers to the processes involved in the short-term maintenance, manipulation, and rehearsal of information. It serves as the gateway for long-term retention and retrieval (Baddeley & Logie, 1999). Few studies have examined working memory for information with emotional content, however, and the evidence generated by these studies is mixed.

Edelstein (2006) examined individual differences in working memory for information varying in emotional valence and relevance to close relationships. People were asked to remember several series of words (which were matched for semantic relatedness) while solving simple math problems. The number of to-be-remembered words became progressively longer throughout the task, placing an ever-greater demand on working memory. The results showed that working memory capacity was higher for positive and negative emotional words than for neutral words. Interestingly, one group of participants proved an exception to the general tendency to hold more emotional words in working memory. People with an avoidant attachment style, who are motivated to avoid relationships (e.g., Edelstein et al., 2005), showed impaired working memory capacity for those emotional words that had relationship-related themes. Overall, then, people were able to hold more emotional than neutral words in working memory but individual differences in goals moderated this effect.

Other findings, however, show no advantage or a disadvantage for emotional stimuli in working memory. Kensinger and Corkin (2003) compared working-memory performance for negative, positive, and neutral information. Several working-memory tasks were used across five studies including backward and alphabetical word-span tasks (in which people must repeat a series of presented words in reverse or alphabetical order, respectively), and *n*-back tasks (in which people must indicate whether a stimulus was presented *n* trials previously). The information to be remembered varied across studies and included both emotional words and pictures. With the exception of one task, an *n*-back task employing emotional faces, in which emotion hindered working memory, task performance was unrelated to the emotional content of the stimuli. When long-term memory for the same stimuli was assessed, however, the typical enhancement of memory for emotional versus neutral information was obtained. It should be noted, though, that unlike the working-memory tasks, assessments of long-term memory required people to retain only the emotional items themselves and not contextual information such as the order in which the items appeared.

Together, these studies paint a mixed picture of the effects of emotion on working memory. Further research is clearly needed to elucidate the conditions under which emotion enhances and impairs working memory. Kensinger and Corkin (2003) argued that the differing effects of emotion on working versus long-term memory may reflect the different processes that benefit these two memory systems. For instance, elaborating on emotional stimuli may promote long-term retention but may lessen the amount of emotional information that can be maintained in working memory. Another possibility is that working-memory tasks that require people to remember only emotional items themselves show enhancement (e.g., Edelstein, 2006) whereas working-memory tasks that require maintaining information that is not integral to the emotional items, such as the order in which they were presented or their locations relative to each other, do not (Kensinger & Corkin, 2003). Thus, a challenge for future research will be to vary, not just whether or not the items to be remembered are emotional, but also whether the working-memory task requires maintenance of central or peripheral information about those items. Edelstein's (2006) findings also suggest that assessments of people's goals in emotional situations (e.g., goals to approach or avoid relationships) may provide important information about the conditions under which emotion facilitates or hinders working memory (also see Rusting & Larsen, 1998; Yuille & Daylen, 1998).

Investigators have also examined the amount of time that information remains in working memory and the depth with which information is processed. Results show that emotional stimuli benefit from increased rehearsal in working memory. Indeed, the more relevant information is to people's goals, the more time they spend thinking about it. For example, extroverts, who tend to set goals to attain positive outcomes, dwell longer than introverts on stimuli associated with reward. Introverts and anxious people, who tend to set goals to avoid negative outcomes, dwell longer on, and have greater difficulty disengaging their attention from, stimuli associated with threat (Derryberry & Reed, 1994; Fox, Russo, Bowles, & Dutton, 2001; Mineka, Rafaeli, & Yovel, 2003). Once a stimulus has attracted attention, then, emotional information is more likely than neutral information to hold attention and be rehearsed in working memory, increasing the likelihood that it will be stored in long-term memory.

## Long-term memory

We have seen that emotional stimuli are more likely than neutral stimuli both to attract attention and to remain the focus of attention. These influences promote the encoding of emotional material, resulting in memory enhancements that are evident at brief delays (Ochsner, 2000; Sharot & Phelps, 2004). Over time, memory advantages for emotional material are further augmented while memory for neutral material tends to fade. For example, after controlling for differences in attention, Sharot and Phelps (2004) found no differences between memory for emotional and neutral words on an immediate recognition test but better memory for emotional than neutral words after a 24-hour delay. Other studies have also shown that the retention advantage for emotionally arousing words relative to neutral words is greater when memory is tested after delay periods ranging from an hour to a day than after delays of minutes (Kleinsmith & Kaplan, 1963; LaBar & Cabeza, 2006; LaBar & Phelps, 1998).

Distinctiveness and rehearsal contribute to (e.g., Finkenauer et al., 1998), but are not sufficient to explain, enhanced memory for emotional stimuli after long delays. With respect to distinctiveness, different neural processes are associated with accurate memory for emotional stimuli versus stimuli that are affectively neutral but distinctive. Specifically, accurate memory for emotional stimuli is predicted by correlated activity in the amygdala, hippocampus, and orbitofrontal cortex during encoding; accurate memory for distinctive stimuli is primarily associated with activity in the hippocampus (e.g., Hamann, Ely, Grafton, & Kilts, 1999). With respect to rehearsal, Guy and Cahill (1999) had people watch a series of emotional and neutral film clips and recall the topics of the films a week later. Regardless of whether people were told to talk about the films during that week, or were told not to talk about them, they recalled more emotional than neutral films. Thus, just as rehearsal does not fully account for enhanced memory for emotional events after brief retention intervals (Harris & Pashler, 2005; Hulse et al., 2007), it does not fully account for enhanced memory for emotional events after a delay.

Retention of emotional events also benefits from greater consolidation of information in long-term memory. For a period of time following encoding, memories are particularly subject to loss. Consolidation refers to a biochemical process, involving activation of hormonal and brain systems, that strengthens memories and renders them more likely to endure. When events evoke emotions, the sympathetic nervous system releases hormones such as epinephrine. These hormones in turn activate noradrenergic systems in the basolateral amygdala, which mediate consolidation of long-term memory in other brain regions (Cahill, Prins, Weber, & McGaugh, 1994;

see McGaugh, 2004, for a review). The amygdala plays a critical role in this strengthening of emotional memories. For example, infusing norepinephrine directly into the basolateral amygdala enhances long-term memory for emotional events. Inactivating this region, using lesions or drugs, attenuates the enhancing effects of such hormones on memory (McGaugh, 2004). Thus, distinctiveness, rehearsal, and consolidation all contribute to long-term retention of emotional events.

## Retrieval

In contrast to the large body of research on attention and encoding processes, relatively little research has addressed the effects of emotion on memory retrieval in humans. This research indicates that emotional information is more reliably retrieved than neutral information, and suggests overlap in brain regions, such as the amygdala, involved in the encoding and retrieval of emotional information (e.g., Buchanan, 2007; Dolan, Lane, Chua, & Fletcher, 2000; Dolcos, LaBar, & Cabeza, 2005; Maratos, Dolan, Morris, Henson, & Rugg, 2001). In one study, emotional pictures were more accurately recognised than neutral pictures, even after a one-year delay. Greater activity in the amygdala and hippocampus at retrieval was associated with the more accurate recollection of emotional pictures (Dolcos et al., 2005). Similarly, when retrieving autobiographical memories, greater emotional intensity and personal significance were associated with greater retrieval accuracy and with activation in several brain regions including the amygdala (Daselaar et al., 2008; Sharot, Martorella, Delgado, & Phelps, 2007).

It can be difficult, though, to disentangle effects of emotion on encoding versus retrieval. Insofar as emotional information initially captures attention and promotes encoding, more accurate retrieval of emotional than neutral information could simply be due to these initial processing differences (Maratos et al., 2001). Moreover, most recognition memory tasks present emotional stimuli such as pictures both at study and at test. Thus, activation of particular brain regions at test could be due to re-exposure to emotional stimuli as part of the recognition test rather than to processes involved in the retrieval of emotional stimuli. To begin to address this issue, Smith, Stephan, Rugg, and Dolan (2006) examined recognition memory for neutral pictures (e.g., tools, clothing) that had been superimposed at encoding on emotional or neutral backgrounds. At retrieval, memory was tested only for the neutral pictures and not for the backgrounds with which they had been encoded. In this way, retrieval of information studied in emotional versus neutral contexts could be assessed, without presenting the emotional stimuli again at retrieval. Smith et al. found greater recognition accuracy for pictures that had been studied in emotional compared to neutral contexts. Brain activity during retrieval, assessed using fMRI, also differed depending on the context in which items were studied. Activation in the hippocampus and amygdala was more highly correlated when items studied in emotional contexts were retrieved; a finding similar to those obtained during the encoding of emotional images (e.g., Dolan, 2002; Hamann, Ely, Hoffman, & Kilts, 2002).

Buchanan (2007) suggested that reminders of an emotional event during retrieval elicit affective states comparable to those experienced when the event was initially experienced and encoded. Thus, similarities in brain activity during emotional encoding and retrieval may reflect the common emotional experience occurring at these two stages of information processing. Although the evidence so far suggests considerable overlap in the processes supporting encoding and retrieval of emotional information, most studies consider the various stages of information processing in isolation rather than manipulating processes occurring at different stages in the same study. Thus, further work is needed to gauge the relative contributions of encoding and retrieval processes to enhanced memory for emotional information. Changes in the goals that experimenters set for participants (e.g., increasing or decreasing the incentive value of stimuli) can render information that was emotional at the time of encoding insignificant at the time of retrieval; such changes can also imbue information that was emotionally neutral at the time of encoding with emotional significance at the time of retrieval. In future research, by systematically varying the emotional significance of stimuli at encoding and retrieval, it may be possible to further tease apart the effects of emotion on these two memory processes.

How, then, is memory enhanced for central features of emotional events? Further research is needed to clarify the effects of emotion on working-memory capacity and to disentangle effects of emotion on retrieval from those on encoding. It is well established, though, that events with emotional significance receive privileged processing in several memory systems. Preferential access to early information-processing resources, more rehearsal, greater consolidation, and the presence of retrieval cues all contribute to enhanced memory for emotional information relative to neutral information.

## HOW EMOTION IMPAIRS MEMORY

The other piece of the memory-narrowing puzzle is that neutral information can be especially poorly remembered when it appears in proximity to an emotional stimulus or event (e.g., Burke et al., 1992; Kensinger et al., 2007a; Touryan, Marian, & Shimamura, 2007). The negative effect of emotion on memory for peripheral details can be attributed, at least in part, to neglect. If attention is directed toward emotional stimuli, information that is not emotional does not receive as much attention and is less likely to be encoded (e.g., Compton, 2003; Öhman, Flykt, & Esteves, 2001). If encoded neutral information may not be rehearsed or processed deeply, making storage in long-term memory less likely (e.g., Finkenauer et al., 1998). In long-term memory, neutral information does not benefit from amygdala activation that promotes consolidation (e.g., Cahill et al., 1994; LaBar & Phelps, 1998). Indeed, the same adrenergic mechanisms that subserve consolidation of memory for central emotional information contribute to the neglect of peripheral details (e.g., Kensinger, Garoff-Eaton, & Schacter, 2007b; Strange et al., 2003). At retrieval, people tend to dwell on information they consider important and relevant to their well-being, providing retrieval cues for emotional information. Fewer retrieval cues are available for neutral information (e.g., Lyubomirsky, Caldwell, & Nolen-Hoeksema, 1998). To the extent that attention and memory processes are limited in capacity, then, emotional information dominates processing, leaving fewer resources for peripheral details.

Memory impairment can also result from stress (e.g., Deffenbacher et al., 2004; Morgan et al., 2004). Stressful events are those that not only elicit arousal (leading to the release of norepinephrine in the basolateral amygdala), but also activate the hypothalamus pituitary adrenal axis, leading to the release of glucocorticoid stress hormones. Norepinephrine release has been shown to enhance memory (McGaugh, 2004), but over an extended period of time, glucocorticoids can damage brain structures, including the hippocampus, necessary for encoding coherent episodic memories with contextual details (e.g., Belanoff, Gross, Yager, & Schatzberg, 2001; McEwen & Sapolsky, 1995).

With respect to acute stress, a range of elicitors (e.g., trauma, glucocorticoid administration, public speaking, and, in rats, footshock) has been shown to impair working memory (e.g., Klein & Boals, 2001; Morgan, Doran, Steffian, & Southwick, 2006; Oei, Everaerd, Elzinga, Van Well, & Bermond, 2006) and retrieval (e.g., Het, Ramlow, & Wolf, 2005; Roozendaal, 2002), though this work has not assessed memory for information related to the source of stress. Findings concerning the effects of acute stress on encoding and memory consolidation have been mixed. Some research shows that acute stress can either hinder or improve memory for material such as word lists and pictures, depending on moderating variables such as natural variations in cortisol levels in the morning versus afternoon (Het et al., 2005). Other research shows that acute stress accompanied by arousal enhances encoding and consolidation (Roozendaal, 2002; Roozendaal, Okuda, Van der Zee, & McGaugh, 2006), particularly when the information being encoded is emotional (Buchanan & Lovallo, 2001; Cahill, Gorski, & Le, 2003; Payne et al., 2006; but see Kuhlmann, Piel, & Wolf, 2005). Thus, the effects of acute stress on memory are complex and appear to vary depending on the memory processes involved (working memory and retrieval versus encoding and consolidation), the level of stress hormones, and the type of information being remembered. Long-term, chronic stress, however, reliably impairs memory.

Finally, emotion can impair memory by launching efforts directed at regulating distress. Several forms of emotion regulation, including distraction and expressive suppression, impair memory for emotional events (Edelstein, 2006; Raes, Hermans, Williams, & Eelen, 2006; Richards & Gross, 2000, 2006). For example, people who suppress behavioural displays of emotion, either habitually or following experimental instructions, have worse memory for emotion-eliciting events than people who do not use this regulatory strategy (Bonanno, Papa, Lalande, Westphal, & Coifman, 2004; Richards & Gross, 2000, 2006). Thus, emotion regulation strategies that focus attention away from emotional events impair memory for these events.

In summary, emotion can enhance and impair memory via a range of mechanisms. Preferential access to early information-processing resources, rehearsal, consolidation, and the presence of retrieval cues all contribute to enhanced memory for emotional information relative to neutral information. Because the capacities of attention and working memory are limited, emotional information can dominate processing leaving fewer resources for peripheral details. Thus, the source of emotional arousal benefits from privileged processing, resulting in the typical pattern of enhanced memory for core features of emotional events and poorer memory for peripheral features (e.g., Adolphs, Denburg, & Tranel, 2001; Burke et al., 1992; Cahill et al., 1994; Christianson, 1992; Kensinger et al., 2007a; Safer et al., 1998).

Complicating the picture, though, emotion sometimes enhances memory generally, including both central and peripheral information (Hulse et al., 2007; Laney et al., 2004), and sometimes impairs memory generally (Deffenbacher et al., 2004; Morgan et al., 2004). One way to account for these varying effects of emotion focuses on the intensity of emotional arousal (e.g., Yerkes & Dodson, 1908). At low to moderate levels of arousal, emotion may enhance memory across the board. As the intensity of arousal increases, the range of stimuli to which an organism can attend may decrease (Easterbrook, 1959) resulting in poor memory for peripheral information. At extremely high levels of arousal, the range of attention may be so narrow as to impair memory generally. Several findings lead us to question this explanation, however. Memory narrowing has been demonstrated repeatedly in the laboratory with stimuli such as emotional words and pictures that elicit low or moderate levels of arousal (Mather, 2007). Memory narrowing has also been demonstrated with traumatic events, such as injuries leading to emergency-room visits that likely elicited a high level of arousal (e.g., Peterson & Whalen, 2001; see Reisberg & Heuer, 2004, for a review). Thus the intensity of emotional arousal alone is not sufficient to explain when emotion enhances, and when it impairs, memory.

Taking another approach, Christianson (1992) argued that studies showing memory enhancement as a result of emotion have focused on the accuracy of memory for the central or core features of emotional events whereas studies showing memory impairment have focused on errors in memory for peripheral details. This leads directly to a critical question: What are the core features of emotional events? What types of information are central versus peripheral to a person experiencing emotion? To understand emotional memory narrowing, it is essential to address not only "how" the emotional spotlight works (mechanisms through which emotion enhances and impairs memory), but also "what" the emotional spotlight illuminates and what it excludes.

## DEFINING CENTRAL AND PERIPHERAL INFORMATION

Investigators differ about the best way to characterise the types of information that are "central" and preserved in memory as a result of emotion, and the types that are "peripheral" and unlikely to be encoded or retained. Table 6.1 summarises some important approaches. Central information has been characterised as: (a) information that captures an emotionally aroused person's attention; (b) information that constitutes an integral part of an emotional stimulus, either spatially, temporally, or conceptually; and (c) information that is relevant to currently active goals. These three perspectives, which are described in detail below, are not mutually exclusive and many investigators identify information as central using combinations of these definitions. Moreover, as can be seen in Table 6.1, certain features of emotional events (such as a gruesome injury) are considered central under a variety of definitions. Different predictions follow from each approach, however. By laying out these predictions and examining the extent to which current data support them, we hope both to sharpen understanding of emotional memory narrowing and to encourage further research on this issue.

### Attention magnets

According to Laney, Heuer, and Reisberg (2003), the general effect of emotion on memory is to make it better. Emotion enhances memory for whatever information a person is attending to at the time they are emotionally aroused. This attentional focus may be narrow but is not necessarily so. Impaired memory for peripheral detail is most likely to occur in the presence of a shocking visual stimulus that dominates attention. Laney et al. point out that most situations in which memory narrowing has been observed include a specific gruesome or shocking stimulus (e.g., a child whose legs have been severed, a bloody face, or a weapon). Thus memory narrowing may not be due to emotion per se but rather to the presence of stimuli that are visually unusual or striking and serve as what Laney et al. called "attention magnets", becoming the focus of subsequent recall. If so, emotional events that lack attention magnets should not produce memory narrowing (see Reisberg & Heuer, 2007, for a review).

*Table 6.1* Common definitions of central features of emotional events and examples of research or reviews using each definition

| Central features | Definition | Examples | Research |
|---|---|---|---|
| Attention magnets | Features of an emotional event that capture a person's attention | A car accident; a bloody face; a weapon; erotic images | Laney et al., 2003, 2004; Reisberg & Heuer, 2004 |
| Spatially integral features | Features that are perceptually or spatially part of, rather than distant from, an emotional event | Colour of an injured person's clothing; location of an emotional picture on a computer screen | Christianson & Loftus, 1991; Mather & Nesmith, 2008; Safer et al., 1998 |
| Temporally integral features | Features that occur during, rather than before or after, an emotional event | Pictures of a car accident or nude model rather than preceding or subsequent pictures | Burke et al., 1992; Schmidt, 2002; Strange et al., 2003 |
| Conceptually integral features | Gist or features that cannot be changed without changing the basic nature of the emotional event | A child's experience of being injured; a picture of a surgeon operating on an accident victim | Adolphs et al., 2001; Heuer & Reisberg, 1990; Peterson & Whalen, 2001 |
| Goal-relevant features | Features of an emotional event that increase or decrease the likelihood of goal attainment or change the salience of a goal | Person who caused a valued project to fail; consequences of failure; images signalling loss or threat, or eliciting desire | Compton, 2003; Gable & Harmon-Jones, 2008; Levine & Burgess, 1997; Levine & Pizarro, 2004 |

To test this hypothesis, Laney et al. (2004) showed people a slide sequence with an accompanying narrative that elicited emotion by virtue of empathy with the characters rather than through the use of shocking or gory images. People in neutral and emotional narrative groups viewed slides that were identical except for one slide late in the sequence. The neutral narrative group heard about a woman who felt relaxed and happy about going on a date, had a pleasant time, and later called her friend to tell her about the date. The emotional group also heard about a woman going on a date but early warning signals aroused the woman's apprehension about the man. He later attacked her and she called her friend to discuss her distress. Significant differences in heart rate suggested that the emotional group was more aroused by the narrative than the control group. Memory was tested for the slides and narratives. No evidence of memory narrowing was found for the emotional narrative group. Instead, people remembered the slides accompanied by emotional stories better than those accompanied by the neutral stories, including both central and peripheral details. In a second experiment, the emotional and neutral narrative groups viewed identical slides that were presented for a fixed length of time. The emotional narrative described a college student's problems and suicidal thoughts; the neutral narrative described her doing well in school and having a birthday. Again, people remembered more central and peripheral information from the emotional story than from the neutral story.

The authors concluded that memory narrowing is not an inevitable outcome of emotional arousal and does not occur when emotion is elicited by involvement with unfolding events rather than by a visually salient target. To find out whether naturally occurring emotional events typically include attention magnets, Laney et al. (2003) asked people to provide detailed descriptions of autobiographical events that elicited intense emotion. They coded the descriptions with respect to whether or not they included a clear visual focus or attention magnet (e.g., blood, gore, a weapon). Memories without a clear visual focus were classified as "thematic" (e.g., a phone call in which a participant learned that her father had died; a marriage proposal). The vast majority of the memories collected lacked shocking visual images and instead focused on human concerns such as love, death, beauty, and sex. They conclude that, to the extent that naturally occurring emotional events typically lack attention magnets, memory narrowing may be the exception rather than the rule—an artefact of the way in which emotion and memory experiments are often conducted in the laboratory.

This is an important claim that invites further research. Memory narrowing has been found for emotional events outside of the laboratory (e.g., Bahrick et al., 1998; Peterson & Bell, 1996; Peterson & Whalen, 2001; Sotgiu & Galati, 2007). It is not known though whether these events included images that served as attention magnets. Thus, research is needed to assess the extent to which real-world emotional events include attention magnets, and to assess the extent to which emotional events without vivid sensory experiences produce memory narrowing. The views outlined by Laney et al. (2003) also raise the question of why certain stimuli and not others serve as attention magnets. What is it about gory images, for example, that make them so riveting? Does emotion enhance memory for any information to which a person is attending at the time they are emotionally aroused or only for specific types of information? Two other approaches to defining central information take up these questions.

## Integral features of emotional events

Investigators have also defined central information as features that are integral to an emotional event. Integral features can be spatially part of, rather than distant from, an emotional event; temporally integral, occurring during, rather than before or after, an emotional event; or conceptually integral, consisting of the gist or elements that cannot be omitted or altered without changing the basic nature of the event (e.g., Adolphs et al., 2001; Adolphs, Tranel, & Buchanan, 2005; Burke et al., 1992; Christianson & Loftus, 1991; Heuer & Reisberg, 1990; Kensinger & Schacter, 2006a). Drawing on Easterbrook's (1959) cue-utilisation hypothesis, Christianson (1992) argued that attention to information that elicits an emotional response, and elaboration on that information, enhances memory. Because emotion-eliciting information dominates processing, memory for other information suffers.

Extending this view, investigators have recently posited that the effects of arousal on encoding depend on the type of association being encoded. In an excellent review of laboratory research on memory for emotional images and words, Mather (2007) noted that forming a representation of a single stimulus and its integral features (e.g., the colour of an emotional image) involves different processes than forming a representation of the associations between different stimuli or between a stimulus and its context. She argued that attention to the source of emotional arousal is likely to promote the binding of intrinsic features of an emotional stimulus into a coherent representation during initial encoding and in working memory. This would enhance long-term retention of emotional events. Maintaining contextual associations among different stimuli is taxing, though, and requires focusing on the big picture. So, attention allocated to intrinsic features of an emotional stimulus is likely to interfere with the formation of other associations in working memory, making it more difficult for these associations to be encoded (also see Kensinger & Schacter, 2006a; Mather et al., 2006).

In support of this view, laboratory research on memory for emotional words and images shows that, in general, information that can be considered an intrinsic part of an emotional stimulus, such as the colour and location of emotional objects, is preserved in memory (e.g., MacKay & Ahmetzanov, 2005; Mather & Nesmith, 2008; see Mather, 2007, for a review). In contrast, the presence of an emotional stimulus either impairs or has no effect on memory for separate but associated stimuli and contextual information. For example, Kensinger and Schacter (2006a) examined people's memory for emotional and neutral words and for source judgements about those words. As each word was presented, people were asked whether the word referred to something animate, or they were asked whether the word referred to something commonly encountered. People later remembered the emotional words better than the neutral words but emotion did not enhance memory for the judgements they had made about the words. Moreover, greater amygdala activity was associated with successful encoding of emotion words but not with successful encoding of source judgements.

In another study, Touryan et al. (2007) showed people negative pictures (e.g., a robbery on a subway) and neutral pictures, each of which included an unrelated neutral object that had been added in the corner of the picture (e.g., mitten, feather). Memory was tested for the pictures and for whether people could match pictures to the correct neutral objects. People remembered emotional pictures better than neutral pictures. They displayed equivalent memory for the neutral objects displayed in the corner of emotional and neutral pictures. But people's memory for which neutral object appeared with which picture was worse for emotional than for neutral pictures. These findings suggest that associations among items are harder to remember than the items themselves. When information is not an integral part of an emotional stimulus, memory for its association with the emotional stimulus is impaired.

But what constitutes an integral part of an emotional stimulus? Mather (2007) suggested that perceptual principles such as continuity, similarity, and closure may help to make that determination when the emotional stimuli in question are simple images or words. As one moves to even slightly more complex stimuli such as emotional words embedded in sentences, however, the issue of identifying the constituent features of the emotional stimulus becomes far from trivial. It becomes more difficult still as one considers real-world emotional experiences. Taking sentences as an example, Brierley, Medford, Shaw, and David (2007) had people read statements such as, "the sailor was responsible for the rape", which contained an emotional target word (rape) and a neutral word (sailor). Another group read neutral statements containing the same neutral word such as, "the sailor was responsible for the dock". Surprise memory tests showed that people remembered emotional words better than neutral words. But memory for neutral words (e.g., sailor) was enhanced when the neutral words had been presented in a sentence that contained an emotional word. The investigators suggested that neutral words that are embedded in sentences with emotional words become semantically associated with the emotion words; the whole sentence thus picks up an "emotional flavour", resulting in enhanced memory. This study thus highlighted the need to better understand the types of information that are an integral part of an emotional stimulus and the types that are truly peripheral.

Moving to stimuli that more closely approximate emotional events, several investigators have suggested that the features that will be bound together in memory as constituent parts of an emotional stimulus may depend on a person's goals (e.g., Compton, 2003; Levine & Pizarro, 2004; Mather, 2007; Ochsner, 2000; Reisberg & Heuer, 2004). This is a promising approach that may prove to explain violations of the pattern of results showing memory narrowing. For example, Wessel, van der Kooy, and Merckelbach (2000) presented people with a series of slides about a student on the way to the university to take an exam. Groups viewed one of three versions of the slide sequence, which were identical except for a critical slide that depicted a girl on a pedestrian crossing. The girl was either lying down and bleeding from a head injury (emotional), in a gymnastic position (unusual), or walking (neutral). In this critical slide, features of the girl were considered to be central information; a pink bicycle at the margin of the slide served as the peripheral detail. In a cued recall task, the crossing slide was presented without the girl or the bicycle. People were asked to recall the missing items in as much detail as possible including their colour, shape, size, and position. In contrast to previous findings (Christianson & Loftus, 1991), people who viewed the emotional slide did not show enhanced memory for central information, nor did they display impaired memory for peripheral information. The information defined as central in this study (e.g., the colour of the injured girl's shirt; the location of the injured girl on the crossing) were spatially integral parts of the emotional image. But, as the investigators pointed out, this information may not have been well remembered because it had no significance for the theme or goal activated by the image, which likely concerned the girl's well-being.

In summary, Mather's (2007) review showed that intrinsic features of emotional stimuli are most likely to be bound together and retained in memory. In light of this finding, it becomes essential, as we move from considering simple stimuli such as emotional words and images to more complex emotional sentences and events, to determine what features constitute an integral part of an emotional stimulus. Turning to the suggestion that goal relevance may be important, we consider evidence for this next.

## Goal relevance

According to functional theories of emotion, goals are at the heart of what it means for an event to be emotional. Goals are states that people want to attain or avoid. They can be universal (e.g., survival, nurturing offspring, maintaining social relationships, avoiding injury), situation specific (e.g., catching a flight), or person specific (e.g., avoiding heights). People are attuned to the relevance of incoming information for their goals. They experience emotions when they perceive that a goal has been attained or obstructed and it becomes necessary for them to revise prior beliefs or construct new plans. Once evoked, emotions are thought to direct subsequent cognition in a manner that is likely to be useful for preventing, altering, or adjusting to the change in the status of their goals (Arnold, 1960; Frijda, 1987; Lazarus, 1991; Lerner & Keltner, 2000; Oatley & Johnson-Laird, 1987; Scherer, 1998; Stein & Levine, 1987). Given limitations on attention and working memory, it is adaptive to prioritise processing of those features of emotional events that facilitate or obstruct goals (see Compton, 2003; Levine & Pizarro, 2004, for reviews). So, "central" information may be information that is relevant to currently active goals.

What determines whether information is goal relevant and hence likely to be remembered? Relevant information has been defined as that which furthers or impedes the likelihood of accomplishing a goal (Gorayska & Lindsay, 1993; Hjørland & Sejer Christensen, 2002) or changes the salience or importance of a goal (Evans & Over, 1996). Rather than being "all or none", goal relevance is a matter of degree and depends on context. At any given time, people are assailed by information from multiple sources that could have at least some relevance to one of their goals, but they cannot attend to it all. Sperber and Wilson (1995, p. 252) argued that, "what makes an input worth picking out from the mass of competing stimuli is not just that it is relevant, but that it is *more* relevant than any alternative input available to us at that time". In a laboratory study, then, a picture of a skull embedded in a series of neutral pictures is likely to be noticed and remembered. In this context—impoverished of goal-relevant information other than the participant's goal of earning partial course credit—the skull at least increases the salience of the universal goal of survival. The same picture, encountered flipping through a magazine while waiting for a late plane is unlikely to be noticed, and, if noticed, unlikely to be remembered later. In that context, other information such as the implications of missing a connecting flight, announcements from airline personnel, and whether passengers are lining up to board, is more relevant. Because information processing capacity is limited, the information most relevant to a person's goals in a given context is likely to be noticed and remembered, whereas less-relevant information is likely to be ignored or quickly forgotten (Sperber & Wilson, 1995).

Several investigators have argued that goal relevance plays a role in emotional memory narrowing (e.g., Compton, 2003; Conway & Pleydell-Pearce, 2000; Davis, Quas, & Levine, 2008; Lang, Bradley, & Cuthbert, 1997; Levine & Pizarro, 2004; Mather, 2007; Ochsner, 2000; Öhman et al., 2001; Reisberg & Heuer, 2004). It is well documented that people's goals influence the salience of information in memory and the information-processing strategies they use. Moreover, certain findings concerning the effects of goals on memory map remarkably well onto the emotional memory narrowing effect. For example, not only does goal-relevant information capture attention and remain highly accessible in memory, the accessibility of information relevant to fulfilled and competing goals may actually be suppressed. We review these findings below and then discuss how they lead to specific predictions about emotional memory narrowing.

Emotional information may capture attention because it is relevant to people's goals. People are often functionally blind to irrelevant stimuli they encounter if they are performing an attention-demanding task at the same time; a phenomenon known as "inattentional blindness". Stimuli related to a person's current goals or interests, though, tend to escape inattentional blindness (Koivisto & Revonsuo, 2007). Thus, preattentive processing of goal-relevant information may allow people to notice the kinds of things in which they are currently interested, including emotional stimuli. The tendency for emotional information to activate the amygdala is also modulated by the extent to which that information is relevant to a person's goals. During functional magnetic resonance imaging (fMRI), Cunningham, Van Bavel, and Johnsen (2008) had participants rate their reactions to famous people (e.g., Adolph Hitler, Paris Hilton, Mother Teresa, George Clooney). Participants were given one of three different goals: to rate how positively they reacted to each person (ignoring anything negative), to rate how negatively they reacted to each person (ignoring anything positive), or to rate each person on a bivalent scale ranging from negative to positive. Amygdala activation was greatest when people evaluated positive stimuli in the positive condition; negative stimuli in the negative condition; and both positive and negative stimuli in the condition in which they used a bivalent scale. These findings suggest that the amygdala's role in processing emotional information is a flexible one that is responsive to people's current goals (also see Smith et al., 2006).

In addition to capturing attention and being associated with amygdala activation, goal-relevant information benefits from increased accessibility in memory. For example, information processed in terms of universal goals such as survival is exceptionally well remembered (Nairne, Pandeirada, & Thompson, 2008). Once goals have been fulfilled, however, information that was previously relevant becomes less accessible (e.g., Förster, Liberman, & Higgins, 2005). In early work on this phenomenon, Zeigarnik (1967) found that people tend to remember uncompleted or interrupted tasks better than completed tasks. In a recent extension of this work, Förster, Liberman, and Higgins (2005) had people search a series of pictures with a specific goal in mind (e.g., finding a picture of eyeglasses followed by scissors). One group found the target picture sequence; a second group did not; a control group looked at the same stimuli, for the same amount of time, with no goal in mind. Later, lexical decision and Stroop tasks were administered to assess the accessibility of words related to the target picture sequence and the accessibility of unrelated words. The results showed that, relative to the control group (no goal), people who had not achieved their goal (target not found) showed greater accessibility of goal-related words. Moreover, relative to the control group, people who had achieved their goal (target found) showed reduced accessibility of goal-relevant words. Thus, having a currently active goal enhanced the accessibility of goal-related information but goal fulfilment reduced this accessibility (also see Förster, Liberman, & Friedman, 2007).

When people are committed to a goal, not only is goal-relevant information more accessible, information relevant to competing goals may be inhibited. Shah, Friedman, and Kruglanski (2002, Study 3) asked people to list three goals, that is, activities they planned to accomplish in the coming week (e.g., studying, reading, running). They also had people list non-goals; desirable activities that they did not plan to pursue (e.g., skiing). Later, people were primed with a goal or non-goal and engaged in a lexical decision task. When primed with a goal, people were slower to recognise competing goals (activities they intended to pursue that had not been primed) than when primed with a non-goal. Moreover, the more committed people were to a goal, the greater the inhibition of information related to competing goals.

In summary, goal-relevant information benefits from preattentive processing and increased accessibility in memory. Emotional stimuli that are goal relevant benefit from increased activation of the amygdala. In contrast, decreased memory accessibility is found for information related to fulfilled goals and competing goals. How might these findings inform our understanding of the effects of emotion on memory? Given that emotions are evoked when situations impact people's goals, a promising definition of "central" information might be goal-relevant information. A promising definition of "peripheral" information might be information that is irrelevant to the current goal or relevant to a competing goal. To fulfil this promise, though, findings concerning the accessibility of goal-relevant information must help to explain when emotion leads to memory narrowing and when it does not. So, we turn next to considering the predictions that follow from a goal-relevance model of emotional memory narrowing.

## GOAL RELEVANCE AND EMOTIONAL MEMORY NARROWING

Defining central information in terms of goal relevance leads to three predictions about when emotion should lead to memory narrowing and when it should not. First, the more relevant information is to currently active goals, the better it should be remembered. Examining the relevance of information to current goals helps to explain why people sometimes have excellent memory for details of emotional events that might be considered peripheral (e.g., Hulse et al., 2007; Laney et al., 2004), and sometimes forget information that might be considered central (e.g., Morgan et al., 2004; Talarico & Rubin, 2003; Wessel et al., 2000). Second, emotions should not produce memory narrowing under all conditions. Having an active goal enhances the accessibility of relevant information only so long as that goal has not been attained (e.g., Förster et al., 2005). Thus, negative emotion, elicited by threats to goals, should produce memory narrowing but positive emotion, elicited by goal attainment, should not. Third, when a specific goal is activated, information relevant to competing goals may be suppressed (e.g., Shah et al., 2002). Discrete emotions such as fear, anger, and sadness increase the salience of different goals such as avoiding, altering, or adjusting to negative outcomes, respectively. Feeling fear, anger, or sadness, then, should enhance memory for information relevant to the salient goal in that discrete emotional state but should impair memory for irrelevant information, including information that would be relevant in alternative emotional states. Evidence supporting these three predictions is described below.

## Emotion enhances memory for information relevant to goals

The greater the relevance of emotional information to currently active goals, the better it is typically remembered. In studies of emotional narratives, for example, details that are closely tied to the plot or goals of protagonists are remembered best (Burke et al.,1992; see Reisberg & Heuer, 2004, for a review). Even seemingly neutral details, that are not part of an emotional stimulus, are nevertheless well remembered if those details are causally connected to the goal made salient by the stimulus. For example, in the study discussed above of memory for emotional and neutral words in sentences (e.g., "the sailor was responsible for the rape"; Brierley et al., 2007), memory was enhanced not only for emotional words but for neutral words that were causally related to emotional words. In contrast, information that is irrelevant to people's goals is less likely to be remembered (e.g., MacLeod & Mathews, 2004).

Some studies, though, have shown general enhancement, rather than memory narrowing, when people recall emotional as opposed to neutral events (e.g., Hulse et al., 2007; Laney et al., 2004). Defining central information in terms of goal relevance helps account for these findings. In comprehending sequences of events in daily life and in narratives and films, people try to impose meaning and coherence on their experiences by drawing on their knowledge of the causal links among events. Research on text comprehension shows that events can be linked locally (i.e., sequentially) to their immediate causes or consequences, but extended sequences of events are best understood and remembered if they are organised globally in terms of goals, plans to attain those goals, and their outcomes (Goldman & Varnhagen, 1986; Graesser, Singer, & Trabasso, 1994). Because emotions are evoked when events impact people's goals, narratives that depict or evoke emotion, particularly negative emotion, tend to be more cohesive than neutral narratives (e.g., Fivush, McDermott Sales, & Bohanek, 2008). Even when emotionally evocative and neutral narratives are carefully matched, the greater cohesiveness of emotional event sequences would be likely to enhance memory.

As an example, Hulse et al. (2007) compared memory for a neutral video and an emotional video that contained no gory sensory details that would be likely to capture attention. To prevent rumination, people engaged in a challenging cognitive task after watching a critical scene in the videos. The emotional and neutral videos were carefully matched. The first and final scenes, as well as several events in the critical middle scene, were identical across conditions. Nonetheless, people showed better memory for the emotional than the neutral video, including both central information and peripheral details. The findings were taken as support for the claim that, in the absence of attention magnets, emotion enhances memory generally—both for central information and peripheral details.

Greater cohesiveness among the emotional than neutral events, however, may have endowed details that were peripheral in the neutral video with significance in the emotional video. Specifically, although both the neutral and emotional video showed a woman taking a ride in a taxi, the links among events in the neutral video were primarily sequential. During the ride, the taxi driver prolonged the journey by taking a wrong turn and then by stopping to take a cell phone call; the woman was mildly annoyed. In the emotional video, each event was causally linked to a central threatening event. During the ride, the taxi driver took a wrong turn so he could stop the taxi in a deserted area and assault the woman; she reacted with distress. Even the final scene—identical in the emotional and neutral videos—had greater significance in the emotional video. The woman's daughter decided not to call to check on her mother. In the neutral video, her decision was unrelated to the events that occurred during the taxi ride. People watching the emotional video would be hard-pressed not to relate the daughter's decision to the events that had just occurred. Thus, more details from the emotional video than the neutral video were causally related to a salient goal—a characteristic that would be expected to enhance memory for the emotional video.

Even when events in emotional and neutral narratives are matched in terms of language complexity, familiarity, phrasing, and structure (e.g., Laney et al., 2004, Experiment 2), empathising with the emotions of others may lead people to adopt protagonists' goals and draw more connections among story details. Bourg, Risden, Thompson, and Davis (1993) presented two groups of sixth graders with the same story. One group was instructed to read the story aloud; the other, to read the story aloud and empathise with the story characters. Relative to children who merely read the story aloud, children encouraged to empathise with the characters performed better on cued recall questions that required integrating the information presented in the story. Bourg (1996) argued that empathising with characters in a narrative provides a motive for attending carefully to the goals and outcomes important to the character and for actively trying to determine the relations among events. Moreover, people come to understand characters' emotions by imagining how they themselves would feel if they had similar experiences (Ames, Jenkins, Banaji, & Mitchell, 2008). Using personal experiences as a foundation for forming expectations about events enhances memory. Thus, when presented with an emotional narrative in which a critical goal is at stake (e.g., the risk of suicide; Laney et al., 2004) people are likely to draw causal relations connecting details to the emotional core of the story. To the extent that people draw more causal inferences when comprehending emotional events, fewer details may be peripheral in emotional than in neutral event sequences.

Why, then, do investigators sometimes find general memory enhancement as a result of emotion? We have argued that event sequences that evoke emotion are typically more cohesive than event sequences that do not. Moreover, empathising with emotions leads people to draw more causal links among events, further enhancing comprehension and memory. Thus, the links between emotions and goals, and failure to limit the details assessed to those that are truly irrelevant, may explain why investigators sometimes find general memory enhancement for emotional events rather than memory narrowing. To test this view, it will be necessary to compare events with and without shocking sensory stimuli. It will also be necessary to parse details based on whether or not they are relevant to the goals made salient by emotional events. This will clarify whether, in the absence of shocking sensory stimuli, emotion improves memory across the board or, as we would expect, specifically for goal-relevant information.

## Emotional valence and memory narrowing

The vast majority of research on the effects of emotion on memory treats emotion as "arousal"; a state ranging from relaxation to excitement. Positive and negative emotions, of equivalent intensity, sometimes affect memory differently, however. Defining central information in terms of goal relevance clarifies when positive and negative emotions have similar effects on memory and when they do not. Irrespective of whether the valence of the stimuli is positive or negative, goal-relevant stimuli capture attention (e.g., Brosch, Sander, Pourtois, & Scherer, 2008). Relative to neutral stimuli, both positive and negative stimuli activate the amygdala (Cunningham et al., 2008; Hamann et al., 2002), and are likely to be remembered after short and long delays (Hamann et al., 1999). Moreover, like negative stimuli, positive stimuli can lead to memory narrowing. In one study, investigators assessed people's memory for central and peripheral information in positive, negative, and neutral anime film clips. Relative to memory for the neutral film, people showed enhanced memory for erotic and comical events, and poor memory for peripheral details, in the positive film (Moyer, 2002, unpublished study cited in Reisberg & Heuer, 2004).

Sometimes positive and negative emotions differ in their effects, though, with negative emotion promoting narrowing, and positive emotion promoting broadening, of attention and memory. Examining the relation between emotional valence and goals helps explain why. People feel negative emotion when goals are threatened; they feel positive emotion when goal attainment is anticipated or has been achieved. Research on goals indicates that information relevant to uncompleted goals tends to be well remembered whereas information relevant to completed goals tends to be forgotten (e.g., Förster et al., 2005). In the service of future goal attainment, then, both negative emotion elicited by threatened goals, and positive emotion elicited by anticipated goals, should promote accurate and detailed memory for goal-relevant information. However, positive emotion following goal attainment should not.

Consistent with this view, Berridge and colleagues argued that positive emotion (or reward) has two separable components: a motivational component ("desire") and the affective consequence of attaining the desired state or goal ("pleasure"). These two components have different neural substrates, are dissociable, and serve unique functions. Desiring a stimulus or outcome depends on dopaminergic systems and is associated with activation in the basolateral amygdala and nucleus accumbens core—brain systems that overlap those activated by aversive events. Manipulation of dopamine increases or decreases the desire to attain rewards and consumption behaviours. In contrast, opioid stimulation in other brain regions (including the nucleus accumbens shell, ventral pallidum, and brainstem) has a causal role in increasing or decreasing the pleasure experienced when a goal is attained (Berridge & Kringelbach, 2008; Berridge & Robinson, 2003; also see Panksepp, 1998).

Recent research suggests that it is the motivational component of positive emotion (an active goal state) that, like negative emotion, leads to narrowing of attention and memory. In contrast, pleasure following goal attainment leads to broadening of attention. For example, to induce desire, Gable and Harmon-Jones (2008) had people watch a film about delicious desserts. To induce pleasure, another group watched a humorous film about cats. The breadth of people's attention was then assessed with a global/local judgement task (i.e., asking people whether target shapes were most similar to other shapes that shared their global outline or their constituent details). The results showed that inducing desire narrowed attentional focus whereas inducing pleasure broadened attentional focus.

Gable and Harmon-Jones argued that desire, unlike pleasure, causes people to shut out irrelevant stimuli as they approach desired objects. Other studies have also shown that positive stimuli that elicit desire, e.g., pictures of babies, nudes, appetising foods, capture attention much more reliably than positive stimuli that elicit pleasure, e.g., pictures of happy faces, sunsets (Brosch et al., 2008; also see Tamir & Robinson, 2007). In contrast, positive emotion induced by giving people gifts, having them view funny films, or asking them to recall events that made them happy has been associated with a broadening of attention and with flexibility and creativity in problem solving (e.g., Fredrickson, 2001; Isen, Daubman, & Nowicki, 1987; Talarico, Berntsen, & Rubin, 2009). Thus the key feature that determines whether positive emotion promotes narrowing or broadening of attention appears to be whether positive emotion consists of the desire to attain a goal or pleasure experienced after a goal has been attained (Gable & Harmon-Jones, 2008).

Turning from attention and problem solving to memory, the information-processing strategies adopted by people feeling positive versus negative emotions have implications for memory accuracy. Many information-processing models make a fundamental distinction between bottom-up, item-specific, or verbatim processing, on one hand, and top-down, relational, or gist processing on the other (e.g., Anderson, 1972; Hunt & Einstein, 1981; Reyna & Brainerd, 1995). When making sense of an event, people using a bottom-up processing strategy focus on its specific features; people using a top-down processing strategy draw on general knowledge about how the event relates to other events. These two information-processing strategies have different implications for memory. Top-down processing promotes creativity by drawing connections among disparate events, but can lead to errors in which events are falsely remembered as more consistent with general knowledge than they actually were. Bottom-up processing is detail-oriented and associated with less creativity but greater memory accuracy (e.g., McCabe, Presmanes, Robertson, & Smith, 2004; Roediger, Balota, & Watson, 2001).

Because negative and positive emotions are evoked by different appraisals of the effects of events on people's goals, people might be expected to process information differently when they experience emotions of differing valence. Negative emotion signals the threat of goal failure and indicates that there is a problem to solve. Solving problems requires monitoring the details of incoming and remembered information. So, negative emotion should promote bottom-up processing, leading to detailed and accurate recall of goal-relevant information. In contrast, positive emotion following goal attainment should promote a top-down processing strategy, leading people to draw on relational knowledge. Perceiving broad relations among events may facilitate attaining future goals but also leads to reconstructive memory errors (Bless et al., 1996; Clore et al., 2001; Levine & Bluck, 2004; Levine & Pizarro, 2004).

A growing body of evidence supports the view that negative emotion and positive emotion following goal attainment are associated with differing information-processing strategies that influence memory accuracy (Bless et al., 1996; Forgas, Laham, & Vargas, 2005; Gasper & Clore, 2002; Johnson & Fredrickson, 2005; Levine & Bluck, 2004; Ochsner, 2000; Park & Banaji, 2000; Storbeck & Clore, 2005). For instance, Bless et al. (1996) induced a happy or sad mood in people, and then presented them with information about common activities (e.g., eating at a restaurant). Some of the information presented was consistent with general knowledge (e.g., "The hostess placed the menus on the table") and some was not (e.g., "He put away his tennis racket"). The results of a subsequent surprise recognition test showed that happy people were more likely than sad people to "recognise" information consistent with general knowledge—independent of whether that information had actually been presented. In contrast, sad people were more accurate in their recognition judgements.

Storbeck and Clore (2005) examined memory for lists of closely associated words. They found that sad people were less likely than people in a happy or neutral state to falsely remember closely associated words that had not been presented. Thus, laboratory studies suggest that positive emotion leads to greater reliance on general knowledge, and to intrusion errors in memory, whereas negative emotion makes people resistant to such errors.

Levine and Bluck (2004) demonstrated that these findings extend beyond brief laboratory studies to memory for real-world events and over prolonged retention intervals. People's emotions and memories were assessed concerning the televised announcement of the verdict in the murder trial of O. J. Simpson. In the memory assessment, half of the events presented had occurred; half were plausible but had not occurred. The results showed that, after more than a year, people who were happy about the verdict recognised more events than people whose reaction was negative, independent of whether the events had actually occurred. Replicating and extending these findings, Kensinger and Schacter (2006b) had Red Sox and Yankees fans describe their memories of the final game of the 2004 playoff series that resulted in victory for the Red Sox. The valence of the fans' response to the game did not affect the quantity of information they remembered but did influence the likelihood of memory distortions. Red Sox fans, who were happy about the outcome, showed more memory inconsistencies than did Yankees fans. These findings again suggest that, compared to positive emotion, negative emotion may lead to a focus on specific details, reducing the likelihood of reconstructive memory errors. Because the intensity of positive and negative emotion was equivalent in both Levine and Bluck's and in Kensinger and Schacter's studies, these findings are difficult to explain in terms of a simple model based only on emotional arousal. Instead they suggest that people experiencing positive and negative emotions have different motivations, process information differently as a result, and these differences affect memory.

Further research is needed before definitive conclusions can be drawn about the differing effects of negative and positive emotion on memory narrowing and memory accuracy. Findings suggest the following pattern, however. When experiencing negative emotion or desire (signalling that a goal is threatened or anticipated), people tend to adopt a detail-oriented, bottom-up strategy when encoding and retrieving events. When experiencing positive emotion (signalling that goals have been attained), people tend to draw on relational knowledge, sometimes confusing plausible and actual events. These different information-processing strategies affect memory narrowing, with negative emotion and desire leading to detailed and accurate memory for goal-relevant central information, and positive emotion following goal attainment leading to a broader focus and less accuracy.

## Discrete emotions and memory narrowing

Moving beyond emotional valence, researchers have recently begun to examine the effects of discrete emotions on memory. Enhanced memory for goal-relevant information would be expected regardless of the discrete emotion experienced. But people have different goals when they are experiencing discrete emotions; for instance, avoiding danger for fear, adjusting to irrevocable loss for sadness, removing obstacles to goal attainment for anger. Because people's goals differ, the content of their memories (i.e., the types of information that are central and hence well-remembered) would also be expected to differ when they are experiencing discrete emotions (Davis et al., 2008; Lench & Levine, 2005; Levine & Bluck, 2004; Levine & Burgess, 1997; Levine & Pizarro, 2004). In contrast to mood-congruent memory, which is thought to result from spreading activation among information that is semantically related to a particular emotional state (e.g., Eich & Forgas, 2003), enhanced memory would be expected for information relevant to people's goals in specific emotional states. For example, for a person who is angry that his wallet has been stolen, references on the evening news to "thieves" and "credit cards" (not mood congruent but goal relevant) should be more memorable than references to "road rage" (mood congruent but not goal relevant). Förster et al. (2007) provided a detailed review of how goal relevance differs from non-goal constructs such as semantic relatedness.

Integrating these findings with work on the effects of emotional valence on memory leads to a model of the effects of discrete emotions on memory. According to the goal-relevance model (Levine & Pizarro, 2004), happiness following goal attainment promotes top-down processing, leading to memory intrusion errors consistent with general knowledge. Negative emotion promotes bottom-up processing; a focus on details in the service of responding to goal failure. However, people should be most likely to engage in bottom-up processing of information that is of central importance in their discrete emotional state. Thus, bottom-up processing (and hence accurate memory for details and few intrusion errors) should be found when fearful people remember information about risks, when sad people remember information about losses, and when angry people remember information about the agents or causes of goal obstruction. Poorer memory should be found for information peripheral to people's goals in discrete emotional states. In short, people look for, notice, and remember information relevant to currently active goals. Since people's goals differ depending on their current emotion, the information that is most salient and memorable for them should also differ in systematic ways.

To test these predictions, it is necessary to directly contrast the types of information remembered in discrete emotional states. To date, few studies have done so, but work focusing on individual emotions suggests that this would be a fruitful direction for future research. For example, fearful people display enhanced memory for threat-related information and poorer memory for threat-irrelevant information (e.g., Lench & Levine 2005; MacLeod & Mathews, 2004; Mathews & Klug, 1993; Wessel & Merckelbach, 1998). In contrast, people in a sad mood who are asked to recall autobiographical events tend to focus, not on sources of threat, but on losses and defeats (e.g., Lyubomirsky et al., 1998). Moreover, although post-traumatic stress disorder (PTSD) and depression are both characterised by the presence of intrusive memories, the content of the intrusive information for these two disorders differs. Consistent with the goal of avoiding danger, PTSD is characterised by intrusive memories related to past threats to safety. Consistent with the goal of adjusting to loss, depression is characterised by rumination on past losses and their consequences for the self (e.g., Lyubomirsky et al., 1998; Reynolds & Brewin, 1999; Watkins & Teasdale, 2001).

Levine and Burgess (1997) examined the effects of discrete emotions on memory for a narrative. Emotions were evoked in undergraduates by randomly assigning grades of "A" or "D" on a surprise quiz. As part of a purportedly unrelated study, participants then heard and later recalled a narrative about a student's first term in college. Finally, participants rated how happy, sad, and angry they had felt when they received their quiz grade. Happy participants demonstrated good memory for the narrative as a whole, but those who reported feeling primarily sad or primarily angry tended to recall specific types of information. Consistent with the view that sad people focus on consequences of goal failure, sad participants recalled significantly more information concerning event outcomes such as losses than did angry participants (e.g., "They receive a bad grade on the speech"). Consistent with the view that angry people focus on goal reinstatement, angry participants showed a non-significant tendency to recall more information about protagonists' goals than did sad participants (e.g., "Mary wants her speech to be really good"). In addition, a significant correlation was found between the intensity of anger reported and the amount of information that participants recalled about goals.

Finally, priming a goal makes goal-relevant information more accessible than neutral information, but further suppresses the accessibility of information relevant to competing goals (e.g., Shah et al., 2002). These findings have implications for the salience and accessibility of different types of information in discrete emotional states. When a person is feeling a specific emotion, the accessibility of goal-relevant information should be enhanced relative to neutral information; the accessibility of information relevant in alternative emotional states should be suppressed relative to neutral information. For instance, for an angry person, information relevant to the blameworthiness of a perpetrator should be highly accessible in memory. However, memory for situational factors that constrained the perpetrators' actions (making the perpetrator less culpable and goal failure irrevocable) may actually be suppressed. Characterising central emotional information as goal relevant thus opens up exciting new avenues for research on the effects of discrete emotions on memory.

## SUMMARY AND CONCLUSIONS

Emotional memories are vivid, lasting, and selective. Whether people are remembering real-world events (a celebration, injury, or dispute) or laboratory stimuli (emotional words, images, or narratives), they typically show good memory for central features of emotional events and poorer memory for peripheral features. One goal of this review was to examine the mechanisms through which emotion spotlights central information at the expense of peripheral information. Research shows that emotional information is more likely than neutral information to capture and to remain the focus of attention (Compton, 2003; LaBar & Cabeza, 2006; Mather, 2007). Attention and rehearsal in turn promote encoding, resulting in enhanced memory for emotional information after brief delays (Hamann et al., 1999; Ochsner, 2000). Over time, consolidation and the presence of retrieval cues augment these memory advantages, resulting in lasting and accessible memories for central features of emotional events (Finkenauer et al., 1998; LaBar & Cabeza, 2006; Sharot & Phelps, 2004). Poor memory for peripheral features is due in part to the limited capacities of attention and working memory. To the extent that central features dominate processing, fewer resources are directed toward peripheral features (e.g., Compton, 2003; Öhman et al., 2001). When neutral or background information does receive attention, this information is less likely to be elaborated on and stored in long-term memory (e.g., Finkenauer et al., 1998) and less likely to be associated with amygdala activation that promotes memory consolidation and retrieval (Cahill et al., 1994; LaBar & Phelps, 1998). Thus emotional information benefits from privileged processing in several memory systems, but these benefits accrue at the expense of information less central to the source of emotional arousal.

The arousing nature of emotional experience is commonly viewed as the key mechanism underlying emotional memory narrowing. In support of this view, both positive and negative stimuli that elicit arousal serve to capture attention, dominate working memory, and activate the amygdala, promoting memory encoding and consolidation (Compton, 2003; McGaugh, 2004). Moreover, the more arousing people find stimuli at encoding, the greater the amygdala activation, and the more likely it is that the stimuli will later be remembered (e.g., Canli, Zhao, Brewer, Gabrieli, & Cahill, 2000; Hamann et al., 1999, 2002; Hurlemann et al., 2007). Because processing arousing information leaves fewer resources for encoding peripheral details, arousal (elicited by negative stimuli in most studies) is also associated with poorer memory for peripheral details (e.g., Adolphs et al., 2005; Cahill et al., 1994; Kensinger et al., 2007a; Mather et al., 2006;

also see Easterbrook, 1959). Thus, arousal clearly contributes to both enhanced memory for emotional information and poor memory for peripheral detail.

To understand how emotion affects memory, however, aspects of emotion other than arousal must also be considered. Arousal is commonly viewed as indicating the degree of urgency or importance of a situation to an individual (e.g., Compton, 2003; McGaugh, 2004). But emotions incorporate both a sense of urgency and a direction. That is, emotions consist of urges toward attaining desired states, avoiding aversive states, or adapting to changes in the status of goals that have already occurred (e.g., Brehm, 1999). Memory is affected not only by the strength of these urges but also by their direction. For example, Hurlemann et al. (2005) assessed people's memory for several series of neutral pictures with an arousing picture embedded in each series. Memory for the neutral pictures was affected by the valence of the emotional pictures. Retrograde amnesia was observed for neutral pictures that were followed by a negative picture, but retrograde hypermnesia was observed for neutral pictures that were followed by a positive picture. Importantly, increasing or decreasing participants' arousal through pretraining administration of drugs affected the magnitude of these retrograde effects but their quality (i.e., amnesia vs. hypermnesia) depended on valence. These findings are consistent with a growing body of evidence that positive and negative emotion of equivalent intensity can nonetheless have different effects on attention (e.g., Gable & Harmon-Jones, 2008, Study 1) and memory, with negative emotion leading to memory narrowing and positive emotion to broadening (e.g., Kensinger & Schacter, 2006b; Levine & Bluck, 2004; but see Corson & Verrier, 2007). Thus arousal plays a critical role in emotional memory narrowing but does not provide a complete explanation.

Further, memory narrowing as a result of emotion is not ubiquitous. Seemingly peripheral features of emotional events are sometimes preserved (e.g., Hulse et al., 2007; Laney et al., 2004) and critically important emotional information is sometimes forgotten (e.g., Deffenbacher et al., 2004; Morgan et al., 2004). Christianson (1992) suggested that studies showing general memory enhancement as a result of emotion may have focused on the accuracy of memory for central features of emotional events whereas studies showing general memory impairment may have focused on errors in memory for peripheral details. To understand emotional memory narrowing, then, it is important to address not only *how* the emotional spotlight works but also the types of information it illuminates and excludes. Thus, the second goal of this review was to address the critical question of what constitutes the central features of emotional events.

Investigators have variously defined central information as information that captures an emotionally aroused person's attention; information that constitutes an integral part of an emotional stimulus; and information relevant to goals. The first approach accounts for the fact that memory narrowing is reliably found when laboratory stimuli include shocking sensory images, such as a bloody face, weapon, or accident scene, which serve as magnets for an emotionally aroused person's attention (Laney et al., 2003, 2004; Reisberg & Heuer, 2004, 2007). An important question for future research is whether real-world emotional events that lack such stimuli also lead to memory narrowing. The second approach accounts for findings that even neutral features of simple emotional stimuli (e.g., the colour or location of an emotional word) are well remembered, as long as those features constitute an integral part of the emotional stimulus. This approach raises the question of what constitutes an integral feature as one moves from simple laboratory stimuli to real-world emotional events.

We have argued for the third approach: that memory narrowing as a result of emotion, and violations of the memory-narrowing pattern, can best be explained by the view that emotion enhances memory for information relevant to currently active goals. People experience emotions when they perceive changes in the status of their goals. Once evoked, emotions are thought to direct cognition in a manner that is likely to be useful for responding such changes (Arnold, 1960; Frijda, 1987; Lazarus, 1991; Lerner & Keltner, 2000; Oatley & Johnson-Laird, 1987; Scherer, 1998; Stein & Levine, 1987). The more relevant information is to the goals activated by an emotional event, then, the better it should be remembered. According to this view, emotional stimuli that serve as a magnet for attention and reliably lead to memory narrowing (e.g., a bloody face, weapon, or accident scene) may do so because they increase the salience of the universal goal of survival. This implies though that emotional stimuli that increase the salience of other important goals (e.g., a threat to a relationship, self-esteem, financial stability) should also lead to memory narrowing. Thus, the importance of the goal activated by an emotional event, and the relevance of information to that goal, rather than the presence of gruesome sensory details per se, should predict the features of emotional events that are remembered.

Examining the relevance of information to current goals helps to explain why people sometimes have excellent memory for details of emotional events that might be considered peripheral (e.g., Hulse et al., 2007; Laney et al., 2004), and sometimes forget information that might be considered central (e.g., Deffenbacher et al., 2004; Morgan et al., 2004). With respect to general memory enhancement, event sequences that evoke emotion tend to be more cohesive than event sequences that do not (Fivush et al., 2008; Goldman & Varnhagen, 1986; Graesser et al., 1994). Empathising with emotions leads people to draw additional causal links among events, further enhancing comprehension and memory (Bourg, 1996). The greater cohesiveness of emotional than neutral events can endow details that are peripheral in neutral event sequences with significance in the emotional event sequences. Thus, good memory for emotional event sequences may result because details that investigators have classified as peripheral have more relevance to people's goals in emotional than in neutral event sequences. In future research, it will be important to classify details a priori based on whether or not they are relevant to the goals made salient by emotional events, and to compare events with and without shocking sensory stimuli. This will clarify whether emotion improves memory generally when shocking sensory stimuli are not present or improves memory specifically for goal-relevant information.

Emotion can also impair memory for information that might be considered central. It is well documented that chronic stress impairs memory (e.g., Belanoff et al., 2001; McEwen & Sapolsky, 1995). In addition, efforts to regulate acute emotional reactions by suppressing emotion, or by engaging in distraction or avoidance strategies, are associated with poor memory for emotional events (e.g., Bonanno et al., 2004; Edelstein, 2006; Richards & Gross, 2000, 2006). Attempts to regulate emotion and "get through" the experience may have contributed to Morgan et al.'s (2004) finding that soldiers who underwent an extremely stressful interrogation were less likely to recognise their interrogator than soldiers who underwent a less-stressful interrogation. When people appraise emotional events as overwhelming and out of their control, their goals may shift from understanding the implications of those events to managing their emotional response (Deffenbacher et al., 2004). Emotion-regulation strategies that focus attention away from emotional events lead to generally poor memory for those events.

Defining central information in terms of goal relevance also elucidates the effects of emotional valence and discrete emotions on memory narrowing. Having an active goal enhances the accessibility of relevant information only so long as that goal has not been attained (e.g., Förster et al., 2005; Zeigarnik, 1967). Consistent with this effect of goals on memory, negative emotion and desire have been shown to promote narrowing of attention and memory (e.g., Brosch et al., 2008; Gable & Harmon-Jones, 2008; Storbeck & Clore, 2005). Positive emotion following goal attainment has been shown to promote broadening of attention and memory (e.g., Fredrickson, 2001; Gable & Harmon-Jones, 2008; Isen et al., 1987) and vulnerability to reconstructive memory errors (e.g., Kensinger & Schacter, 2006b; Levine & Bluck, 2004). Preliminary findings also suggest that the types of information that are central, and hence well remembered, differ depending on a person's discrete emotional state (Levine & Burgess, 1997; Levine & Pizarro, 2004). Fearful people show enhanced memory for information about risks (e.g., Lench & Levine 2005; MacLeod & Mathews, 2004; Mathews & Klug, 1993; Wessel & Merckelbach, 1998), sad people for information about losses (e.g., Lyubomirsky et al., 1998; Reynolds & Brewin, 1999; Watkins & Teasdale, 2001), and angry people for information about the agents or causes of goal obstruction (Lerner & Tiedens, 2006). In short, people look for, notice, and remember information relevant to currently active goals. Because people's goals differ depending on their discrete emotion, the kinds of information that are most salient and memorable should also differ in systematic ways.

Limitations of this approach should also be noted. The claim that emotion enhances memory for goal-relevant information at the expense of irrelevant details is circular if investigators decide whether or not a particular detail was goal relevant based on whether or not it was remembered. Thus, defining central information in terms of goal relevance raises the thorny issue of how to determine a priori the goals that will be salient for a particular individual in a particular situation. When emotions are evoked by events that impact universal goals (e.g., survival, access to food, sex, nurturance, avoiding injury), it is often possible to predict the features of events that are relevant and likely to be remembered. For example, when a person is angry, the agent responsible for obstructing his or her goal is central. In the context of a laboratory study, the word "murder" embedded in a list of neutral words such as "shop", "towel", and "mountain" is almost certain to be remembered. When emotions pertain to personal, idiosyncratic goals, however, the features of events that are of central importance may be hard to determine a priori. A person with the goal of avoiding heights may remember the word "mountain" whereas others may not. So, it will be necessary to test this model by assessing memory after varying the relevance of details to universal goals associated with emotions.

It must also be acknowledged that some findings are inconsistent with this goal-based perspective. Enhanced memory has been found for information that is neither part of an emotional stimulus, nor goal relevant, but simply spatially or temporally proximal to an emotional stimulus. For example, memory for neutral pictures was found to be enhanced if those pictures alternated with emotional pictures rather than with other neutral pictures (Anderson, Wais, & Gabrieli, 2006; also see McGaugh, 2006). Such findings suggest that the effects of emotion on memory may differ depending on the stage of information processing. When people are emotionally aroused, attentional and encoding processes should privilege goal-relevant information. Once information has been encoded, however, emotional or not, it may benefit from consolidation in long-term memory, ensuring rich and detailed memories for significant life events (Anderson et al., 2006).

We have reviewed three approaches to defining the features of emotional events that will be preserved in memory. Each of these approaches explains some findings in the emotion and memory literature and conflicts with others. We have laid them out side by side to facilitate research that directly contrasts the predictions made by different models. An important avenue for future research will be to assess memory accuracy for emotional events with and without shocking sensory details, for information that varies in terms of whether or not it is an integral part of the emotional event, and for information that varies with respect to whether or not it is relevant to the goal activated by the emotion. Further research is also needed to clarify the mechanisms underlying the differing effects of positive and negative emotions, and of discrete emotions, on memory.

The potential benefits of such work are profound. Emotion affects memory on a daily basis and in situations in which detailed and accurate memory really matters. The importance of understanding the effects of emotion on memory for evaluating the accuracy of eyewitness testimony concerning crimes is often noted. But people are also faced daily with the need to accurately remember information while experiencing a range of emotional states. An attorney angered by the acts of opposing counsel, a patient saddened by a diagnosis, a rescue worker frightened by a disaster, must nonetheless encode and retrieve detailed information accurately if they are to make good decisions. Further research on emotion-induced memory narrowing may help people guard against the tendency to forget information that appears unimportant under emotion's sway, and harness the capacity of emotion to enhance memory. The essential link between emotions and goals may provide the key to understanding the selective nature of memory for emotional events.

## REFERENCES

Adolphs, R., Denburg, N. L., & Tranel, D. (2001). The amygdala's role in long-term declarative memory for gist and detail. *Behavioral Neuroscience, 115,* 983–992.

Adolphs, R., Tranel, D., & Buchanan, T. W. (2005). Amygdala damage impairs emotional memory for gist but not details of complex stimuli. *Nature Neuroscience, 8,* 512–518.

Alexander, K. W., Quas, J. A., Goodman, G. S., Ghetti, S., Edelstein, R. S., Redlich, A. D., et al. (2005). Traumatic impact predicts long-term memory for documented child sexual abuse. *Psychological Science, 16,* 33–40.

Ames, D. L., Jenkins, A. C., Banaji, M. R., & Mitchell, J. P. (2008). Taking another person's perspective increases self-referential neural processing. *Psychological Science, 19,* 642–644.

Anderson, A. K., & Phelps, E. A. (2001). Lesions of the human amygdala impair enhanced perception of emotionally salient events. *Nature, 411,* 305–309.

Anderson, A. K., Wais, P. E., & Gabrieli, J. D. E. (2006). Emotion enhances remembrance of neutral events past. *Proceedings of the National Academy of Sciences, 103,* 1599–1604.

Anderson, R. C. (1972). Semantic organization and retrieval of information from sentences. *Journal of Verbal Learning and Verbal Behavior, 11,* 794–800.

Arnold, M. B. (1960). *Emotion and personality. Vol. I: Psychological aspects.* New York: Columbia University Press.

Baddeley, A. D., & Logie, R. H. (1999). Working memory: The multiple-component model. In A. Miyake & P. Shah (Eds.), *Models of working memory: Mechanisms of active maintenance and executive control* (pp. 28–61). New York: Cambridge University Press.

Bahrick, L. E., Parker, J. F., Fivush, R., & Levitt, M. (1998). The effects of stress on young children's memory for a natural disaster. *Journal of Experimental Psychology: Applied, 4,* 308–331.

Belanoff, J. K., Gross, K., Yager, A., & Schatzberg, A. F. (2001). Corticosteroids and cognition. *Journal of Psychiatric Research, 35,* 127–145.

Berridge, K. C., & Kringelbach, M. L. (2008). Affective neuroscience of pleasure: Reward in humans and animals. *Psychopharmacology, 199,* 457–480.

Berridge, K. C., & Robinson, T. E. (2003). Parsing reward. *Trends in Neurosciences, 26,* 507–513.

Bless, H., Clore, G. L., Schwarz, N., Golisano, V., Rabe, C., & Wolk, M. (1996). Emotion and the use of scripts: Does a happy emotion really lead to mindlessness? *Journal of Personality and Social Psychology, 71,* 665–679.

Bonanno, G. A., Papa, A., Lalande, K., Westphal, M., & Coifman, K. (2004). The importance of being flexible: The ability to both enhance and suppress emotional expression predicts long-term adjustment. *Psychological Science, 15,* 482–487.

Bourg, T. (1996). The role of emotion, empathy, and text structure in children's and adults' narrative text comprehension. In R. J. Kreuz and M. S. MacNealy (Eds.), *Empirical approaches to literature and aesthetics* (pp. 241–260). Westport, CT: Ablex Publishing.

Bourg, T., Risden, K., Thompson, S., & Davis, R. C. (1993). The effects of an empathy-building strategy on 6th graders' causal inferencing in narrative text comprehension. *Poetics, 22,* 117–133.

Brehm, J. W. (1999). The intensity of emotion. *Personality and Social Psychology Review, 3,* 2–22.

Brierley, B., Medford, N., Shaw, P., & David, A. (2007). Emotional memory for words: Separating content and context. *Cognition and Emotion, 21,* 495–521.

Brosch, T., Sander, D., Pourtois, G., & Scherer, K. R. (2008). Beyond fear: Rapid spatial orienting toward positive emotional stimuli. *Psychological Science, 19,* 362–370.

Buchanan, T. W. (2007). Retrieval of emotional memories. *Psychological Bulletin, 133,* 761–779.

Buchanan, T. W., & Lovallo, W. R. (2001). Enhanced memory for emotional material following stress-level cortisol treatment in humans. *Psychoneuroendocrinology, 26,* 307–317.

Burke, A., Heuer, F., & Reisberg, D. (1992). Remembering emotional events. *Memory and Cognition, 20,* 277–290.

Cahill, L., Gorski, L., & Le, K. (2003). Enhanced human memory consolidation with post-learning stress: Interaction with the degree of arousal at encoding. *Learning and Memory, 10,* 270–274.

Cahill, L., Prins, B., Weber, M., & McGaugh, J. L. (1994). Adrenergic activation and memory for emotional events. *Nature, 371,* 702–704.

Canli, T., Zhao, Z., Brewer, J., Gabrieli, J. D. E., & Cahill, L. (2000). Activation in the human amygdala associates event-related arousal with later memory for individual emotional experience. *The Journal of Neuroscience, 20,* 1–5.

Christianson, S.-Å. (1992). Emotional stress and eyewitness memory: A critical review. *Psychological Bulletin, 112,* 284–309.

Christianson, S.-Å., & Hübinette, B. (1993). Hands up: A study of witnesses' emotional reactions and memories associated with bank robberies. *Applied Cognitive Psychology, 7,* 365–379.

Christianson, S.-Å., & Loftus, E. (1987). Memory for traumatic events. *Applied Cognitive Psychology, 1,* 225–239.

Christianson, S.-Å., & Loftus, E. (1991). Remembering emotional events: The fate of detailed information. *Cognition and Emotion, 5,* 81–108.

Clore, G. L., Wyer, R. S., Dienes, B., Gasper, K., Gohm, C., & Isbell, L. (2001). Affective feelings as feedback: Some cognitive consequences. In L. L. Martin & G. L. Clore (Eds.), *Theories of mood and cognition: A user's guidebook* (pp. 27–62). Mahwah, NJ: Lawrence Erlbaum Associates, Inc.

Compton, R. J. (2003). The interface between emotion and attention: A review of evidence from psychology and neuroscience. *Behavioral and Cognitive Neuroscience Reviews, 2,* 115–129.

Conway, M. A., & Pleydell-Pearce, C. W. (2000). The construction of autobiographical memories in the self-memory system. *Psychological Review, 107,* 261–288.

Corson, Y., & Verrier, N. (2007). Emotions and false memories: Valence or arousal? *Psychological Science, 18,* 208–211.

Cunningham, W. A., Van Bavel, J. J., & Johnsen, I. R. (2008). Affective flexibility: Evaluative processing goals shape amygdala activity. *Psychological Science, 19,* 152–160.

Daselaar, S., Rice, H., Greenberg, D., Cabeza, R., LaBar, K., & Rubin, D. (2008). The spatiotemporal dynamics of autobiographical memory: Neural correlates of recall, emotional intensity, and reliving. *Cerebral Cortex, 18,* 217–229.

Davis, E., Quas, J. A., & Levine, L. J. (2008). Children's memory for stressful events: Exploring the role of discrete emotions. In M. Howe, D. Cicchetti, & G. Goodman (Eds.), *Stress, trauma, and children's memory development: Neurobiological, cognitive, clinical, and legal perspectives* (pp. 236–264). Oxford, UK: Oxford University Press.

Deffenbacher, K. A., Bornstein, B. H., Penrod, S. D., & McGorty, E. K. (2004). A meta-analytic review of the effects of high stress on eyewitness memory. *Law and Human Behavior, 28,* 687–706.

Derryberry, D., & Reed, M. A. (1994). Temperament and attention: Orienting toward and away from positive and negative signals. *Journal of Personality and Social Psychology, 66,* 1128–1139.

Dolan, R. J. (2002). Emotion, cognition, and behavior. *Science, 298,* 1191–1194.

Dolan, R. J., Lane, R., Chua, P., & Fletcher, P. (2000). Dissociable temporal lobe activations during emotional episodic memory retrieval. *NeuroImage, 11,* 203–209.

Dolcos, F., LaBar, K. S., & Cabeza, R. (2005). Remembering one year later: Role of the amygdala and the medial temporal lobe memory system in retrieving emotional memories. *Proceedings of the National Academy of Sciences, 102,* 2626–2631.

Easterbrook, J. A. (1959). The effect of emotion on cue utilization and the organization of behavior. *Psychological Review, 66,* 183–201.

Edelstein, R. S. (2006). Attachment and emotional memory: Investigating the source and extent of avoidant memory impairments. *Emotion, 6,* 340–345.

Edelstein, R. S., Ghetti, S., Quas, J. A., Goodman, G. S., Alexander, K. W., Redlich, A. D., et al. (2005). Individual differences in emotional memory: Adult attachment and long-term memory for child sexual abuse. *Personality and Social Psychology Bulletin, 31,* 1537–1548.

Eich, E., & Forgas, J. P. (2003). Mood, cognition, and memory. In A. F. Healy & R. W. Proctor (Eds.), *Handbook of psychology. Vol. 4: Experimental psychology* (pp. 61–83). New York: Wiley.

Evans, J. S., & Over, D. E. (1996). *Rationality and reasoning.* Hove, UK: Psychology Press.

Finkenauer, C., Luminet, O., Gisle, L., El-Ahmadi, A., Van der Linden, M., & Philippot, P. (1998). Flashbulb memories and the underlying mechanisms of their formation: Toward an emotional-integrative model. *Memory and Cognition, 26,* 516–531.

Fivush, R., McDermott Sales, J., & Bohanek, J. G. (2008). Meaning making in mothers' and children's narratives of emotional events. *Memory, 16,* 579–594.

Forgas, J. P., Laham, S. M., & Vargas, P. T. (2005). Mood effects on eyewitness testimony: Affective influences on susceptibility to misinformation. *Journal of Experimental Social Psychology, 41,* 574–588.

Förster, J., Liberman, N., & Friedman, R. S. (2007). Seven principles of goal activation: A systematic approach to distinguishing goal priming from priming of non-goal constructs. *Personality and Social Psychology Review, 11,* 211–233.

Förster, J., Liberman, N., & Higgins, E. T. (2005). Accessibility from active and fulfilled goals. *Journal of Experimental Social Psychology, 41,* 220–239.

Fox, E., Russo, R., Bowles, R., & Dutton, K. (2001). Do threatening stimuli draw and hold visual attention in subclinical anxiety? *Journal of Experimental Social Psychology, 130,* 681–700.

Fredrickson, B. L. (2001). The role of positive emotions in positive psychology: The broaden-and-build theory of positive emotions. *American Psychologist, 56,* 218–226.

Frijda, N. H. (1987). Emotion, cognitive structure, and action tendency. *Cognition and Emotion, 1,* 115–143.

Gable, P. A., & Harmon-Jones, E. (2008). Approach-motivated positive affect reduces breadth of attention. *Psychological Science, 19,* 476–482.

Gasper, K., & Clore, G. L. (2002). Emotion and global versus local processing. *Psychological Science, 13,* 34–40.

Goldman, S. R., & Varnhagen, C. K. (1986). Memory for embedded and sequential story structures. *Journal of Memory and Language, 25,* 401–418.

Gorayska, B., & Lindsay, R. O. (1993). The roots of relevance. *Journal of Pragmatics, 19,* 301–323.

Graesser, A. C., Singer, M., & Trabasso, T. (1994). Constructing inferences during narrative text comprehension. *Psychological Review, 101,* 371–395.

Guy, S. C., & Cahill, L. (1999). The role of overt rehearsal in enhanced conscious memory for emotional events. *Consciousness and Cognition, 8,* 114–122.

Hamann, S. B., Ely, T. D., Grafton, S. T., & Kilts, C. D. (1999). Amygdala activity related to enhanced memory for pleasant and aversive stimuli. *Nature Neuroscience, 2,* 289–293.

Hamann, S. B., Ely, T. D., Hoffman, J. M., & Kilts, C. D. (2002). Ecstasy and agony: Activation of the human amygdala in positive and negative emotion. *Psychological Science, 13,* 135–141.

Harris, C. R., & Pashler, H. (2005). Enhanced memory for negatively emotionally charges pictures without selective rumination. *Emotion, 5,* 191–199.

Het, S., Ramlow, G., & Wolf, O. T. (2005). A meta-analytic review of the effects of acute cortisol administration on human memory. *Psychoneuroendocrinology, 30*, 771–784.

Heuer, F., & Reisberg, D. (1990). Vivid memories of emotional events: The accuracy of remembered minutiae. *Memory and Cognition, 18*, 496–506.

Hjørland, B., & Sejer Christensen, F. (2002). Work tasks and socio-cognitive relevance: A specific example. *Journal of the American Society for Information Science and Technology, 53*, 960–965.

Hulse, L. M., Allan, K., Memon, A., & Read, J. D. (2007). Emotional arousal and memory: A test of the poststimulus processing hypothesis. *American Journal of Psychology, 120*, 73–90.

Hunt, R. R., & Einstein, G. O. (1981). Relational and item-specific information in memory. *Journal of Verbal Learning and Verbal Behavior, 20*, 497–514.

Hurlemann, R., Hawellek, B., Matusch, A., Kolsch, H., Wollersen, H., Madea, B., et al. (2005). Noradrenergic modulation of emotion-induced forgetting and remembering. *Journal of Neuroscience, 25*, 6343–6349.

Hurlemann, R., Matusch, A., Hawellek, B., Klingmuller, D., Kolsch, H., Maier, W., et al. (2007). Emotion-induced retrograde amnesia varies as a function of noradrenergic-glucocorticoid activity. *Psychopharmacology, 194*, 261–269.

Isen, A. M., Daubman, K. A., & Nowicki, G. P. (1987). Positive affect facilitates creative problem solving. *Journal of Personality and Social Psychology, 52*, 1122–1131.

Johnson, K. J., & Fredrickson, B. L. (2005). "We all look the same to me": Positive emotions eliminate the own-race bias in face recognition. *Psychological Science, 16*, 875–881.

Kensinger, E. A., & Corkin, S. (2003). Effect of negative emotional content on working memory and long-term memory. *Emotion, 3*, 378–393.

Kensinger, E. A., Garoff-Eaton, R. J., & Schacter, D. L. (2007a). Effects of emotion on memory specificity: Memory trade-offs elicited by negative visually arousing stimuli. *Journal of Memory and Language, 56*, 575–591.

Kensinger, E. A., Garoff-Eaton, R. J., & Schacter, D. L. (2007b). How negative emotion enhances the visual specificity of a memory. *Journal of Cognitive Neuroscience, 19*, 1872–1887.

Kensinger, E. A., & Schacter, D. L. (2006a). Amygdala activity is associated with the successful encoding of item, but not source, information for positive and negative stimuli. *Journal of Neuroscience, 26*, 2564–2570.

Kensinger, E. A., & Schacter, D. L. (2006b). When the Red Sox shocked the Yankees: Comparing negative and positive memories. *Psychonomic Bulletin and Review, 13*, 757–763.

Kihlstrom, J. F. (2006). Trauma and memory revisited. In B. Uttl, N. Ohta, & A. L. Siegenthaler (Eds.), *Memory and emotion: Interdisciplinary perspectives* (pp. 259–291). Malden, MA: Blackwell Publishing.

Kissler, J., Herbert, C., Peyk, P., & Junghofer, M. (2007). Buzzwords: Early cortical responses to emotional words during reading. *Psychological Science, 18*, 475–480.

Klein, K., & Boals, A. (2001). The relationship of life events stress and working memory capacity. *Applied Cognitive Psychology, 15*, 565–579.

Kleinsmith, L., & Kaplan, S. (1963). Paired-associate learning as a function of arousal and interpolated interval. *Journal of Experimental Psychology, 65*, 190–193.

Koivisto, M., & Revonsuo, A. (2007). How meaning shapes seeing. *Psychological Science, 18*, 845–849.

Koster, E. H. W., Crombez, G., Verschuere, B., Vanvolsem, P., & De Houwer, J. (2007). A time-course analysis of attentional cueing by threatening scenes. *Experimental Psychology, 54*, 161–171.

Kuhlmann, S., Piel, M., & Wolf, O. T. (2005). Impaired memory retrieval after psychosocial stress in healthy young men. *Journal of Neuroscience, 25*, 2977–2982.

LaBar, K. S., & Cabeza, R. (2006). Cognitive neuroscience of emotional memory. *Nature Reviews, 7*, 54–64.

LaBar, K. S., & Phelps, E. A. (1998). Arousal-mediated memory consolidation: Role of the medial temporal lobe in humans. *Psychological Science, 9*, 490–493.

Laney, C., Campbell, H. V., Heuer, F., & Reisberg, D. (2004). Memory for thematically arousing events. *Memory and Cognition, 32*, 1149–1159.

Laney, C., Heuer, F., & Reisberg, D. (2003). Thematically induced arousal in naturally occurring emotional memories. *Applied Cognitive Psychology, 17*, 995–1004.

Lang, P. J., Bradley, M. M., & Cuthbert, B. N. (1997). Motivated attention: Affect, activation, and action. In P. J. Lang, R. F. Simmons, & M. T. Balaban (Eds.), *Attention and orienting: Sensory and motivational processes* (pp. 97–135). Mahwah, NJ: Lawrence Erlbaum Associates, Inc.

Lazarus, R. S. (1991). *Emotion and adaptation*. New York: Oxford University Press.

Lench, H. C., & Levine, L. J. (2005). Effects of fear on risk and control judgments and memory: Implications for health promotion messages. *Cognition and Emotion, 19*, 1049–1069.

Lerner, J. S., & Keltner, D. (2000). Beyond valence: Toward a model of emotion-specific influences on judgment and choice. *Cognition and Emotion, 14*, 473–493.

Lerner, J. S., & Tiedens, L. Z. (2006). Portrait of the angry decision maker: How appraisal tendencies shape anger's influence on cognition. *Journal of Behavioral Decision Making, 19*, 115–137.

Levine, L. J., & Bluck, S. (2004). Painting with broad strokes: Happiness and the malleability of event memory. *Cognition and Emotion, 18*, 559–574.

Levine, L. J., & Burgess, S. L. (1997). Beyond general arousal: Effects of specific emotions on memory. *Social Cognition, 15*, 157–181.

Levine, L. J., & Pizarro, D. A. (2004). Emotion and memory research: A grumpy overview. *Social Cognition, 22*, 530–554.

Lyubomirsky, S., Caldwell, N. D., & Nolen-Hoeksema, S. (1998). Effects of ruminative and distracting responses to depressed mood on retrieval of autobiographical memories. *Journal of Personality and Social Psychology, 75*, 166–177.

MacKay, D. G., & Ahmetzanov, M. V. (2005). Emotion, memory, and attention in the taboo Stroop paradigm: An experimental analogue of flashbulb memories. *Psychological Science, 16*, 25–32.

MacLeod, C., & Mathews, A. (2004). Selective memory effects in anxiety disorders: An overview of research findings and their implications. In D. Reisberg & P. Hertel (Eds.), *Memory and emotion* (pp. 155–185). New York: Oxford University Press.

Maratos, E. J., Dolan, R. J., Morris, J. S., Henson, R. N., & Rugg, M. D. (2001). Neural activity associated with episodic memory for emotional context. *Neuropsychologia, 39,* 910–920.

Mather, M. (2007). Emotional arousal and memory binding: An object-based framework. *Perspectives on Psychological Science, 2,* 33–52.

Mather, M., Mitchell, K. J., Raye, C. L., Novak, D. L., Greene, E. J., & Johnson, M. K. (2006). Emotional arousal can impair feature binding in working memory. *Journal of Cognitive Neuroscience, 18,* 614–625.

Mather, M., & Nesmith, K. (2008). Arousal-enhanced location memory for pictures. *Journal of Memory and Language, 58,* 449–464.

Mathews, A. M., & Klug, F. (1993). Emotionality and interference with color-naming in anxiety. *Behavior Research and Therapy, 29,* 147–160.

McCabe, D. P., Presmanes, A. G., Robertson, C. L., & Smith, A. D. (2004). Item-specific processing reduces false memories. *Psychonomic Bulletin and Review, 11,* 1074–1079.

McCloskey, M., Wible, C. G., & Cohen, N. J. (1988). Is there a special flashbulb memory mechanism? *Journal of Experimental Psychology: General, 177,* 171–181.

McEwen, B. S., & Sapolsky, R. (1995). Stress and cognitive function. *Current Opinions in Neurobiology, 5,* 205.

McGaugh, J. L. (2004). The amygdala modulates the consolidation of memories of emotionally arousing experiences. *Annual Review of Neuroscience, 27,* 1–28.

McGaugh, J. L. (2006). Make mild moments memorable: Add a little arousal. *Trends in Cognitive Neuroscience, 10,* 345–347.

Mineka, S., Rafaeli, E., & Yovel, I. (2003). Cognitive biases in emotional disorders: Information processing and social-cognitive perspectives. In R. J. Davidson, K. R. Scherer, & H. H. Goldsmith (Eds.), *Handbook of affective sciences* (pp. 976–1009). New York: Oxford University Press.

Morgan, C. A., Doran, A., Steffian, G., Hazlett, G., & Southwick, S. M. (2006). Stress-induced deficits in working memory and visuo-constructive abilities in special operations soldiers. *Biological Psychiatry, 60,* 722–729.

Morgan, C. A., Hazlett, G., Doran, A., Garrett, S., Hoyt, G., Thomas, P., et al. (2004). Accuracy of eyewitness memory for persons encountered during exposure to highly intense stress. *International Journal of Law and Psychiatry, 27,* 265–279.

Nairne, J. S., Pandeirada, J. N. S., & Thompson, S. R. (2008). Adaptive memory: The comparative value of survival processing. *Psychological Science, 19,* 176–180.

Oatley, K., & Johnson-Laird, P. N. (1987). Toward a cognitive theory of emotions. *Cognition and Emotion, 1,* 29–50.

Ochsner, K. N. (2000). Are affective events richly recollected or simply familiar? The experience and process of recognizing feelings past. *Journal of Experimental Psychology: General, 129,* 242–261.

Oei, N. Y. L., Everaerd, W. T. A. M., Elzinga, B. M., Van Well, S., & Bermond, B. (2006). Psychosocial stress impairs working memory at high loads: An association with cortisol levels and memory retrieval. *Stress: The International Journal on the Biology of Stress, 9*, 133–141.

Öhman, A., Flykt, A., & Esteves, F. (2001). Emotion drives attention: Detecting the snake in the grass. *Journal of Experimental Psychology: General, 130*, 466–478.

Öhman, A., & Soares, J. J. F. (1998). Emotional conditioning to masked stimuli: Expectancies for aversive outcomes following nonrecognized fear-relevant stimuli. *Journal of Experimental Psychology: General, 127*, 69–82.

Panksepp, J. (1998). *Affective neuroscience: The foundations of human and animal emotions.* New York: Oxford University Press.

Park, J., & Banaji, M. R. (2000). Mood and heuristics: The influence of happy and sad states on sensitivity and bias in stereotyping. *Journal of Personality and Social Psychology, 78*, 1005–1023.

Payne, J. D., Jackson, E. D., Ryan, L., Hoscheidt, S., Jacobs, W. J., & Nadel, L. (2006). The impact of stress on neutral and emotional aspects of episodic memory. *Memory, 14*, 1–16.

Peterson, C., & Bell, M. (1996). Children's memory for traumatic injury. *Child Development, 67*, 3045–3070.

Peterson, C., & Whalen, N. (2001). Five years later: Children's memory for medical emergencies. *Applied Cognitive Psychology, 15*, 17–24.

Raes, F., Hermans, D., Williams, J. M. G., & Eelen, P. (2006). Reduced autobiographical memory specificity and affect regulation. *Cognition and Emotion, 20*, 402–429.

Reisberg, D., & Heuer, F. (2004). Memory for emotional events. In D. Reisberg & P. Hertel (Eds.), *Memory and emotion* (pp. 3–41). New York: Oxford University Press.

Reisberg, D., & Heuer, F. (2007). The influence of emotion on memory in forensic settings. In M. P. Toglia, D. J. Read, D. F. Ross, & R. C. L. Lindsay (Eds.), *The handbook of eyewitness psychology. Vol. I: Memory for events* (pp. 81–116). Mahwah, NJ: Lawrence Erlbaum Associates, Inc.

Reyna, V. F., & Brainerd, C. J. (1995). Fuzzy-trace theory: An interim synthesis. *Learning and Individual Differences, 7*, 1–75.

Reynolds, M., & Brewin, C. R. (1999). Intrusive memories in depression and posttraumatic stress disorder. *Behaviour Research and Therapy, 37*, 201–215.

Richards, J. M., & Gross, J. J. (2000). Emotion regulation and memory: The cognitive costs of keeping one's cool. *Journal of Personality and Social Psychology, 79*, 410–424.

Richards, J. M., & Gross, J. J. (2006). Personality and emotional memory: How regulating emotion impairs memory for emotional events. *Journal of Research in Personality, 40*, 631–651.

Rimé, B., Mesquita, B., Philippot, P., & Boca, S. (1991). Beyond the emotional event: Six studies on the social sharing of emotion. *Cognition and Emotion, 5*, 435–465.

Roediger, HL., III, Balota, D. A., & Watson, J. M. (2001). Spreading activation and arousal of false memories. In H. L. Roediger, III, J. S. Nairne, I. Neath, & A. M. Surprenant (Eds.), *The nature of remembering: Essays in honor of Robert G. Crowder* (pp. 95–115). Washington, DC: American Psychological Association.

Roozendaal, B. (2002). Stress and memory: Opposing effects of glucocorticoids on memory consolidation and memory retrieval. *Neurobiology of Learning and Memory, 78*, 578–595.

Roozendaal, B., Okuda, S., Van der Zee, E. A., & McGaugh, J. L. (2006). Glucocorticoid enhancement of memory requires arousal-induced noradrenergic activation in the basolateral amygdala. *Proceedings of the National Academy of Sciences, 103*, 6741–6746.

Rusting, C. L., & Larsen, R. J. (1998). Personality and cognitive processing of affective information. *Personality and Social Psychology Bulletin, 24*, 200–213.

Safer, M. A., Christianson, S. A., Autry, M. W., & Osterlund, K. (1998). Tunnel memory for traumatic events. *Applied Cognitive Psychology, 12*, 99–117.

Scherer, K. R. (1998). Appraisal theory. In T. Dalgleish & M. Power (Eds.), *Handbook of cognition and emotion* (pp. 637–664). Chichester, UK: Wiley.

Schmidt, S. R. (2002). Outstanding memories: The positive and negative effects of nudes on memory. *Journal of Experimental Psychology: Learning, Memory, and Cognition, 28*, 353–361.

Shah, J. Y., Friedman, R., & Kruglanski, A. W. (2002). Forgetting all else: On the antecedents and consequences of goal shielding. *Journal of Personality and Social Psychology, 83*, 1261–1280.

Sharot, T., Martorella, E., Delgado, M., & Phelps, E. (2007). How personal experience modulates the neural circuitry of memories of September 11. *Proceedings of the National Academy of Sciences, 104*, 389–394.

Sharot, T., & Phelps, E. (2004). How arousal modulates memory: Disentangling the effects of attention and retention. *Cognitive, Affective, and Behavioral Neuroscience, 4*, 294–306.

Smith, A. P. R., Stephan, K. E., Rugg, M. D., & Dolan, R. J. (2006). Task and content modulate amygdala–hippocampal connectivity in emotional retrieval. *Neuron, 49*, 631–638.

Sotgiu, I., & Galati, D. (2007). Long-term memory for traumatic events: Experiences and emotional reactions during the 2000 flood in Italy. *Journal of Psychology, 141*, 91–108.

Sperber, D., & Wilson, D. (1995). *Relevance: Communication and cognition* (2nd ed). Oxford, UK: Blackwell Publishers.

Stein, N. L., & Levine, L. J. (1987). Thinking about feelings: The development and organization of emotional knowledge. In R. E. Snow & M. Farr (Eds.), *Aptitude, learning, and instruction. Vol. 3: Cognition, conation and affect* (pp. 165–197). Hillsdale, NJ: Lawrence Erlbaum Associates, Inc.

Storbeck, J., & Clore, G. L. (2005). With sadness comes accuracy; with happiness, false memory: Mood and the false memory effect. *Psychological Science, 16*, 785–791.

Stormark, K. M., Nordby, H., & Hugdahl, K. (1995). Attentional shifts to emotionally charged cues: Behavioural and ERP data. *Cognition and Emotion, 9*, 507–523.

Strange, B. A., Hurlemann, R., & Dolan, R. J. (2003). An emotion-induced retrograde amnesia in humans is amygdala- and β-adrenergic-dependent. *Proceedings of the National Academy of Sciences, 100*, 13626–13631.

Talarico, J. M., Berntsen, D., & Rubin, D. C. (2009). Positive emotions enhance recall of peripheral details. *Cognition and Emotion, 23*, 380–398.

Talarico, J. M., & Rubin, D. C. (2003). Confidence, not consistency, characterizes flashbulb memories. *Psychological Science, 14*, 455–461.

Talmi, D., Anderson, A. K., Riggs, L., Caplan, J. B., & Moscovitch, M. (2008). Immediate memory consequences of the effect of emotion on attention to pictures. *Learning and Memory, 15,* 172–182.

Tamir, M., & Robinson, M. D. (2007). The happy spotlight: Positive mood and selective attention to rewarding information. *Personality and Social Psychology Bulletin, 33,* 1124–1136.

Touryan, S. R., Marian, D. E., & Shimamura, A. P. (2007). Effect of negative emotional pictures on associative memory for peripheral information. *Memory, 15,* 154–166.

Watkins, E., & Teasdale, J. D. (2001). Rumination and over general memory in depression. *Journal of Abnormal Psychology, 110,* 353–357.

Wessel, I., & Merckelbach, H. (1998). Memory for threat-relevant and threat-irrelevant cues in spider phobics. *Cognition and Emotion, 12,* 93–104.

Wessel, I., van der Kooy, P., & Merckelbach, H. (2000). Differential recall of central and peripheral details of emotional slides is not a stable phenomenon. *Memory, 8,* 95–109.

Yerkes, R. M., & Dodson, J. D. (1908). The relation of strength of stimulus to rapidity of habit formation. *Journal of Comparative Neurology and Psychology, 18,* 459–482.

Yuille, J., & Daylen, J. (1998). The impact of traumatic events on eyewitness memory. In *Eyewitness memory: Theoretical and applied perspectives* (pp. 155–178). Mahwah, NJ: Lawrence Erlbaum Associates, Inc.

Zeigarnik, B. (1967). On finished and unfinished tasks. In W. D. Ellis (Ed.), *A sourcebook of Gestalt psychology* (pp. 300–314). New York: Humanities Press.

Correspondence should be addressed to: Linda J. Levine, Department of Psychology and Social Behavior, University of California, Irvine, 3340 Social Ecology II, Irvine, CA 92697–7085, USA. E-mail: llevine@uci.edu

We are indebted to Dirk Hermans, Daniel Reisberg, Martin Safer, Susan Charles, Robin Kaplan, Elizabeth Davis and two anonymous reviewers for their helpful comments on drafts of this paper. We also thank Carly Magner for help with preparation of the reference section.

# 7    The effects of emotion on attention: A review of attentional processing of emotional information

Jenny Yiend
*University of Oxford, Oxford, UK*

## INTRODUCTION

What has emotion got to do with attention? Why does the interface between these two warrant additional empirical and theoretical consideration? The answer lies in the many interactions that can occur between emotion and attention and that would otherwise be overlooked by either field in isolation. These interactions are important to basic research. They must be reconciled with existing theories of emotion and attention and may also trigger new theoretical insights. Equally important, research at this interface can inform both the understanding and treatment of various psychopathologies. This, then, is the rationale for our topic. The body of accrued evidence at this interface confirms that the connection between attention and emotion is a robust, reliable and important one.

## Focus of the review

I will review the evidence from behavioural experimental studies on emotion and attention. Throughout the body of the review the primary focus will be the effect on attentional processing of varying the emotional tone of the information being processed. This contrasts with work that seeks to examine how manipulating selective attention might alter emotional responses (e.g., Koster, Fox, & MacLeod, 2009; Raymond, Fenske, & Tavassoli, 2003). When studying the effect of "emotion" on selective attention, the term "emotion" can refer to the emotional quality of the stimulus or to the emotional state of the individual. In the first case, the term "attention to emotion" is used. In the second case, specific reference is made to a mood state, personality predisposition (trait) or clinical disorder (DSM-IV; American Psychiatric Association, 1994). Investigations involving an individual attending to their own internal emotional state, trait or disorder are not the subject of this review.

The review considers research in the general population and how these findings are qualified by individual differences in psychopathology and vulnerability to psychopathology. When investigating psychopathologies researchers often make use of extreme variations in personality traits within the non-clinical population to provide a convenient window onto clinical performance, especially in the early stages of hypothesis testing. Similar biases are usually found, albeit less consistently, among those with high levels of trait anxiety, depression, or other dimensions. Indeed, a recent review found no significant difference between the biased attentional processing shown by high trait versus clinically anxious individuals (Bar-Haim et al., 2007). Concurrent state mood is thought to exacerbate the effects of any trait vulnerability in an interactive fashion (Broadbent & Broadbent, 1988; Farrin, Hull, Unwin, Wykes, & David, 2003; Rusting, 1999). There is therefore a tacit assumption that these "analogue" samples exhibit differences of degree rather than kind from clinical populations (see Rosen & Schulkin, 1998, for a biological account of the continuity of psychopathology). Consistent with this view, the empirical evidence reviewed will incorporate studies of both populations including natural and induced variations in transient mood states.

The main aims of the review are, first, to provide readers with an overview of this relatively complex field of research, which will serve as an introduction to it and, second, to identify emerging themes and under-exploited techniques to encourage those more experienced in the field to reflect on current research endeavours and future priorities. The review starts by describing and evaluating the main conceptual issues that have dominated the field, followed by a consideration of key theories used to account for the data. Theories range from mainstream approaches to selective attention to highly specific accounts of attentional function in individual psychopathologies. The empirical review that follows aims to give a concise overview of older work, describing the scientific consensus using selected key citations. As this has been well described previously (e.g., Mathews & MacLeod, 1994; Williams, Watts, MacLeod, & Mathews, 1988; Williams, Watts, MacLeod, & Mathews, 1997, to name but three good sources) I do not seek to provide an exhaustive revisitation of this literature, but instead to provide an accurate reflection of its most important content. In contrast, more recent work from the last decade will be considered in greater detail, to highlight challenges to the established patterns and areas of emergent or current interest.

Both the section on theories and the empirical review will consider attentional processing of emotional information in the general population and consider how this is qualified by work on individual differences in psychopathology (and vulnerability to it). These two approaches to investigating attentional processing of emotional information have grown up largely in parallel, with little cross talk between them. It is hoped that, by considering them together in this review, researchers working primarily within one domain will be encouraged to integrate their conceptualisation of the field. In studies of *attention to emotion in the general population* the main question of interest has been the extent to which emotional material (and more specifically negative or positive) may be processed differently to neutral material. Usually no specific consideration is given to the possible presence or impact of psychopathology or related vulnerabilities. In studies of *attention to emotion in psychopathology* the purpose is to characterise the attentional processing of emotional information in samples with either diagnosed clinical disorder or known vulnerability to it. Specifically, emotional material matching individuals' emotional characteristics (e.g., fear-relevant material for the generalised anxiety disorder patient; socially threatening information for the social phobia patient) is found to be attended differently (often given priority) from non-emotional (neutral) material. This effect is not apparent in matched controls.

These psychopathology-related effects are commonly called "*attentional biases*" and are referred to as "*emotion congruent*" reflecting the link between the emotional material, which elicits the attentional effects, and the disorder or vulnerability of the individual. Emotion-congruent attentional biases have been recognised as being of more than passing interest because of their possible role in maintaining and causally contributing to disordered affective states, such as anxiety and depression. For example, an enhanced tendency to select threatening items for processing, is likely to lead to an artificially increased perception of the extent of threat in the environment, thereby enhancing anxious mood (Mathews, 1990). Empirical evidence confirms that the attentional biases reviewed here represent cognitive vulnerabilities for both anxiety (Beevers & Carver, 2003; Joormann, Talbot, & Gotlib, 2007; MacLeod, Campbell, Rutherford, & Wilson, 2004; Yiend & Mackintosh, 2004) and depression (Phelps, Ling, & Carrasco, 2006).

## Exclusions

There are inevitably some areas that, while falling within the broad heading of emotion and attention, cannot be considered either for reasons of space and coherence, or because the methodology falls outside the present focus on behavioural work. These are described now in order to place the work to be discussed within an accurate context and are referenced to provide suitable points of entry to these literatures. Executive performance deficits in anxiety involving attention to all types of material are not covered in detail, but will be mentioned and referenced in passing (Eysenck, Derakshan, Santos, & Calvo, 2007; Williams et al., 1997). Biological approaches (data and theory) will not be considered in any detail. This most obviously includes a growing body of work using functional neuroimaging to investigate emotion-relevant information processing in both healthy (Armony et al., 2000; Compton et al., 2003; Davidson, 2000) and, to a lesser extent, clinical and subclinical populations (Davidson, 1998; Davidson, 2002; Davidson, Pizzagalli, Nitschke, & Putnam, 2002). Other notable neuroscientific approaches yielding interesting data on emotion and attention include psychophysiological and ERP studies (Eimer & Holmes, 2007; Palermo & Rhodes, 2007; Vuilleumier, 2002).

Neither is it possible to give comprehensive accounts pertaining to specific clinically disordered populations, although I may dip in and out of this literature by way of illustration. Detailed empirical and theoretical consideration has already been given to the role of attention in eating disorders (Faunce, 2002; Lee & Shafran, 2004; Williamson, Muller, Reas, & Thaw, 1999), panic and phobias, obsessive-compulsive disorder (Muller & Roberts, 2005), social anxiety (Bogels & Mansell, 2004; Ledley & Heimberg, 2006; Turk, Lerner, Heimberg, & Rapee, 2001; Weary & Edwards, 1994) and, most recently, effects in childhood and adolescent psychopathology (Field, Cartwright-Hatton, Reynolds, & Creswell, 2008; Puliafico & Kendall, 2006).

There are other areas of related specialised literature. These include attentional deficits associated with the disorders of ADHD (Soo & Bailey, 2006), the autistic spectrum (Bruinsma, Koegel, & Koegel, 2004) and schizophrenia (Bentall, 1994; Gold & Thaker, 2002; Langdon & Coltheart, 2000; Suslow, Schonauer, & Arolt, 2001), as well as investigations of attentional deterioration in ageing populations (Lawton, 2001), biases and other phenomena associated with addictions (Cox, Fadardi, & Pothos, 2006) and the influence of attention on the perception and experience of pain (Eccleston & Crombez, 1999; Pincus & Morley, 2001; Roelofs, Peters, Zeegers, & Vlaeyen, 2002).

## CONCEPTS

Given that phenomena in emotion and attention are linked in at least the ways outlined above, does it follow that the important conceptual issues therein are simply the sum of those from the parent disciplines? The answer to this question is no. Many of the concepts that are relevant for attention researchers have also dominated research into the relation between emotion and attention. Far fewer have transferred from mainstream research on emotion. I now introduce the most important of these.

### Selection

Perhaps the concept most central to attention/emotion interactions is that of selection. The idea is that from the multiplicity of inputs bombarding the cognitive system, certain items are singled out as being appropriate for processing, at any one time, while the rest are rejected. The key questions for research have thus been how and at what point this selection occurs and, in research on emotion and attention, defining the characteristics of emotional stimuli that may influence this. The current prevailing view is that of biased competition (Desimone & Duncan, 1995) whereby the allocation of attention towards competing representations is influenced and ultimately determined by a variable composite of bottom-up and top-down processes. Thus, the capture of perceptual resources by a given stimulus is influenced not only by the characteristics of the stimulus itself, but also by those of its competitors as well as by higher control systems acting upon the representations of stimuli. Attentional selection is therefore determined by the outcome of competition between these multiple and potentially "biased" representations.

## Orienting

Although similar to selection, orienting is more specific and could be considered one example of how selection may occur. Selection could be thought of as a result, whereas orienting is a mechanism that the cognitive system can use to achieve selection. Orienting is the process of moving attention to a location, whether that is a location in space (spatial orienting) or, less commonly, in time (temporal orienting). Attention also may be oriented to particular stimulus dimensions which co-occur in the same spatial location at the same time (e.g., to the colour or content of a word). Orienting implies that stimuli or signals at a given location become amplified (whether for internal, endogenous reasons, or due to external, exogenous effects) and this triggers the detection of and orienting towards a possibly significant event. A long-standing concept in attention, it has recently been of particular interest within emotion and attention, hence its separate consideration here.

The orienting of spatial attention has been divided into three key components: disengaging, shifting and engaging (e.g., Posner, Walker, Friedrich, & Rafal, 1984). "Engagement" is taken to mean evidence of selection and facilitated processing of a given stimulus or location. "Shifting" is taken to mean the spatial relocation of attention across the visual (or other modality) field. "Disengagement" is taken to mean the process by which selection and facilitated processing of a given stimulus or location is withdrawn or inhibited. There is evidence of distinct neural substrates for each of these mechanisms: the parietal lobe, the midbrain area, and the pulvinar nucleus, respectively (Posner & Peterson, 1990). Researchers applying these concepts to emotion tend to be somewhat looser in their use of terminology. For example "shifts of attention" can, on closer inspection of a method, relate more to the above notion of "engagement" with a particular stimulus or location than the idea of the movement of selective attention across space (which can be closer to the term "distract-ibility", also widely used by those interested in attention to emotion). Likewise "dwell time" and "holding" can be synonymous with the notion of disengagement. For clarity only the terms defined above will be used here, if necessary overriding authors' own terminology.

## Attending versus responding

A critical distinction in all studies of cognition is that between the cognitive process and the response output that is assumed to reflect the process. Here the key difference is between two systems, those involved in *attentional processing of* emotional stimuli and those involved in *outputting a response to* those stimuli, either of which might be affected by the particular task parameters. Cognitive researchers strive to keep their tasks "process pure", which in this case means avoiding, as much as possible, effects on response processes, so that differences can be attributed to attentional effects (cognitive processes) alone. Response biases arise in different ways and understanding their potential triggers allows their contaminating effects to be minimised. First, response biases are likely when the responses required of participants are themselves differentially valenced (for example pressing buttons labelled "positive" and "negative"). Thus, one way to reduce response bias is to use only neutral response options (for example press "*" for positive and "#" for negative). Second, response biases can be reduced by ensuring responses are elicited in the absence of any valenced material being present at the time of responding. This is used, for example, in cuing tasks where responses are the orientation of a line or the identity of a letter (thus addressing the first point) and this task is delivered *after* the emotional stimulus presentation has ceased. Thus two core requirements to achieve "process pure" measures of attentional effects involving emotion are: (i) neutral response options; and (ii) no valenced material present at the time of responding. However, a differential interference effect (interference which is larger on emotional than neutral trials, but not related to attentional effects measured by the task design) can still occur even when the above two conditions are met (see Yiend & Mathews, 2001, and Mogg, Holmes, Garner, & Bradley, 2008, for further discussion of this effect). This could, arguably, also be classed as a "response bias" although the term "emotion-related interference effect" would be a more accurate designation. It appears unpredictable and the most effective means of preventing it, if desired, remains a question for future work.

## Specificity

"Specificity" refers to the degree to which biased attentional processing of emotional information is moderated by additional factors, or specifiers. These specifiers further delineate the conditions under which biased attention is observed. There are two main categories of specifiers relevant to this review. These are: (i) the stimulus content of the emotional material (stimulus specificity); and (ii) in psychopathology populations, the diagnosis or vulnerability present (psychopathology specificity).

Stimulus specificity (also called content specificity) refers to the specific type of emotional information under investigation. Work has examined the importance of valence (positive versus negative emotional material, with some of the better studies controlling for the potentially confounding effects of arousal), intensity (whether the relative intensity of the emotional material depicted influences attentional selection) and biological relevance (comparing attentional selection of biologically prepared fear stimuli such as snakes and spiders with acquired fear stimuli such as weapons). Others aspects of stimulus content are also important to the field. For example, diversity of stimulus materials (faces, pictures, video clips) is crucial to allow generalisation of conclusions from early studies based almost exclusively on words or text.

Psychopathology specificity is of particular interest in studies of clinical or vulnerable populations, where the question arises to what extent attentional biases are specific to the disorder under investigation, or are common across various psychopathologies. This has led to studies of a wide range of specific psychopathologies with those covered here including depression, general anxiety and social anxiety. The specificity to a psychopathology usually interacts with the specificity of the material, which is reflected in the term "emotion congruence" (increasing the match with individuals' concerns increases attentional prioritisation). Emotion congruent specificity has amassed considerable evidence. Thus while generally emotion congruent material (e.g., negative) is often sufficient to elicit psychopathology-related effects, stronger effects are usually seen the greater the match of materials with the concerns relevant to the psychopathology (for example generally anxious participants tend to show stronger attentional biases towards social than physical threat stimuli). The question of psychopathology specificity and emotion congruence is important because of the aetiological arguments outlined above. The more specific the biases, the more likely they are to reflect causal maintaining mechanisms for the disorders themselves.

## Automaticity

Attention research on skill acquisition and practice effects shows that combinations of tasks that are initially hard to perform can, through repetition, become fast and apparently effortless. A classic example would be the complex co-ordination of behaviours and cognitions involved in driving a car. A key concept is that processing is located, and can shift, along a continuum between a "strategic" operation performed by a limited capacity system to an "automatic" one proceeding largely independently of such limits (Posner & Snyder, 1975; Schneider & Shiffrin, 1977; Shiffrin & Schneider, 1977). Exactly where effects of emotion on attention lie on this continuum has been the topic of much research activity. Furthermore, a distinction can be drawn between the "innate" automaticity of certain cognitive processes (e.g., the many computations handled by the perceptual system) and the "acquired" automaticity of the kind of processes described above involving extended practice. There is room for debate concerning whether patterns of automatic attentional selectivity involving threat stimuli result from more innate or more acquired forms of automaticity, or, indeed, from some combination of the two.

The meaning of the term "automatic" has itself been the subject of debate (see Moors & De Houwer, 2006, for the latest analysis; also Santangelo & Spence, 2008). Most agree that core features include speed, operation in parallel, minimal resource requirements, occurring below the threshold of conscious awareness (subliminal), being resistant to intentional control and being inevitable or obligatory. The different features of automaticity do not always co-occur and I will therefore always specify the sense in which the term is used. The feature of automaticity most often subject to empirical investigation within the field of attention to emotional information has been that of awareness, in particular whether biased attention to emotional material occurs subliminally. This has usually been inferred by using very brief (typically < 14 ms) backwardly masked presentations of stimuli. Finally the concept of automaticity is closely related to that of pre-attentive (in contrast to post-attentive) processing and features heavily in some theories (see below). Pre-attentive processing occurs early, prior to attentional selection and in parallel, and is therefore a specifier for the notion of automaticity within the field of attention. Two of the remaining concepts related to automaticity, control and capacity, warrant separate consideration due to their potential importance within work on attention to emotion.

## Control

The concept of control can be problematic, since some argue this merely postpones an explanation of the mechanisms underlying the executive "controller" (Allport, 1980; Posner & Snyder, 2004; Styles, 1997). However in recent years it has become an increasingly tenable concept in both empirical and theoretical work, thanks in part to the availability of biological measures that can provide more objective dependent measures. Control has been defined in various ways. Wegner and Bargh (1998) proposed that control happens when some occurrence is not random, but instead is influenced in a certain direction. Bargh (1994) proposed that "control" refers to an individual's ability to alter or stop a process once it has started and is closely related to but distinct from intentionality, which refers to the individual's ability to initiate a process. Moors and De Houwer (2006), in an impressive in-depth analysis, proposed that control involves an individual pursuing and achieving a proximal goal, that is, a goal about the process that is being studied. For instance, a process is controlled if the goal to stop the process actually leads to the termination of the process. Other proximal goals are the goal to start or alter the process. Their definition is thus a broader one than Bargh's and maps more closely to current usage of the term in ongoing empirical work (for example studies of "emotion regulation"; see Koole, 2009, for a review).

The view that control may or may not be conscious is consistent with Moors and De Houwer's (2006) analysis. Some researchers have investigated control using explicit instructions to vary attention to emotion (Gross, 2002; Ochsner & Gross, 2005), whereas others have used task manipulations or other implicit means of implementing control (Yiend et al., 2008). In psychopathology the breakdown of control has been suggested to underlie the shift from subclinical pathology to clinical disorder (Mathews, 1990), and correspondingly that previous constraints on extensive processing of emotional information are lost.

## Capacity

It is generally assumed that there is a central pool of resources, which is utilised flexibly during attentional operations according to processing priorities, but that these resources are limited so that under some conditions capacity will be exhausted and performance decrements will follow (Johnston & Heinz, 1978; Kahneman, 1973; Wickens, 1984). The similarity of two tasks has sometimes appeared to be a more important factor than resource demand, leading to suggestions of separate, multiple systems of resources applicable to specific types of operation (e.g., Allport, 1980; Hancock, Oron-Gilad, & Szalma, 2007; Humphreys & Revelle, 1984; Wickens, 1984). Thus, if two tasks tap into different resource systems, then there will be little competition for resources whereas if tasks are similar, interference occurs (see Allport, 1980, for a review).

For emotion and attention there are two important corollaries of the "capacity" concept. First, information-processing resources will be influenced according to the particular conditions and stimuli of the task. In particular, emotional information is thought to place heavier demands on resources than non-emotional information as evidenced by widespread, general interference effects. Second, capacity is characteristically depleted in psychopathology. Higher individual levels of emotion (e.g., anxious mood) are thought to consume resources in some generic way (e.g., rumination about current worries), which is likely to impact upon task performance as well as impacting on the ability to deploy top-down control. Deficits arising from capacity limitations and their impact on the control of emotion processing are therefore a key feature in some theories (Eysenck & Calvo, 1992; Eysenck et al., 2007; Mathews & Mackintosh, 1998) and, increasingly, in empirical work (Ansari, Derakshan, & Richards, 2008; Hayes, Hirsch, & Mathews, 2008; Mathews, Yiend, & Lawrence, 2004).

## THEORETICAL PERSPECTIVES

Theoretical understanding of how emotion influences attention can be divided into two broad domains: (1) those which seek to account for attentional effects toward salient material (whether due to its emotional nature, or some other characteristic); and (2) those accounting specifically for psychopathology-related individual differences in the processing of emotional, usually emotion congruent, material.

### Theories of attention to emotional material

Interest from mainstream cognitive researchers in attention to emotion although rapidly growing empirically, is still in its infancy theoretically. The processing of emotional material can be linked to theories of attention by taking emotional material as one example of highly salient information. However, new areas of research interest such as this start by borrowing existing theories and adapting them to explain the new phenomena. Here I specify in general terms how two important theories of attention can be related to attentional processing of emotional information.

Theories of selective attention can account for the general finding that high-intensity emotional information is often prioritised for attentional processing if one adds the simple assumption that emotional information is a specific case of a high-salience stimulus. One problem is that these theories do not articulate how and why this salience is attributed to the emotional material in the first place, but one may either invoke other accounts to do this, such as the biological preparedness of some stimuli (e.g., dangerous animals to signal fear; excrement to signify disgust) and the acquired meaning of others (e.g., weapons acquire an association with danger), or borrow a "valence evaluator" mechanism from theories of psychopathology.

#### Feature integration theory

This classic theory (Treisman & Gelade, 1980) of visual attention describes how certain perceptual characteristics (such as orientation or colour) are processed automatically (in all its senses) and prior to any attentional selection occurring. Attention is conceived as the process by which representations of more complex stimuli are formed through the combination of individual features ("conjunctions of features"). Searching the visual environment for complex targets (conjunction search) is therefore a slower process of serial search requiring repeated attentional selection, processing and rejection until the target is found. Other similar models include those of Wolfe (Wolfe, 1994; Woolfe, Cave, & Franzel, 1989).

In classic visual search experiments, cited in support of such theories, participants are presented with an array of stimuli and asked to locate or identify the discrepant one as quickly as possible (note the similarity with visual search for discrepant facial expressions, below). They are just as fast to detect a target distinguished by a unique feature (e.g., colour), no matter how many distracter items are present, whereas for more complex targets, the larger the array the slower the responses as attention is presumed to systematically search through items. Typically reaction times are plotted against increasing array size (number of distracters) and the "search slope" of the resulting graph is characteristically flat for targets that "pop out", or inclined for those requiring attentional selection (Treisman & Gelade, 1980). These slopes are taken to represent fast, parallel and slow serial-search processes, respectively and are used to quantify the extent of parallel processing. The question for emotion and attention is thus how emotional material is processed within this model of attention: as a highly salient conjunction of features that nevertheless "pops out" from the visual environment (as evolutionary views of emotion may suggest) or as a more complex piece of information requiring selection to ascertain its emotional significance? The data on emotional pop out reviewed later suggest something more towards the former of this continuum.

*Biased competition*

This is the currently preferred approach within the attentional literature accounting for attentional selection between competing items (Buehlmann & Deco, 2008; Desimone & Duncan, 1995; Duncan, 2006; Kastner & Ungerleider, 2000, 2001). Our limited-capacity processing system deals with an overload of information (which may be both internal and external) by competition for attention between representations of that information. Both bottom-up and top-down factors can influence the relative activation of any representation, thereby "biasing" the competition. This results in a selection of what is important and a rejection of the remainder. In the context of attention to emotion, inherent characteristics of emotional material, such as enhanced perceptual distinctiveness and biological preparedness can be thought of as acting to increase relative salience, leading to bottom-up attentional prioritisation. Similarly top-down factors such as environmental context, past experience or prior knowledge could exert similar competitive biasing influences. Several more-specific models of attention and emotion in psychopathology considered below use the notion of biased competition as an integral part of their framework.

One important implication of biased-competition models (including models using this concept, such as that of Mathews & Mackintosh, 1998, discussed below) is that evidence of selective attentional effects will only be seen when stimulus presentation conditions allow competition. Thus, presenting a single emotional stimulus and comparing a reaction-time response between this and a singly presented neutral stimulus, should not result in evidence of selective attention to either, whereas presenting the two stimuli simultaneously (and therefore in direct competition) should. This dissociation is both predicted by biased competition and related models, and supported by the empirical evidence. Specifically, it is usually only under conditions of competition between stimuli that one sees preferential attention to emotional over neutral information, both in the general population (Calvo, Nummenmaa, & Hyönä, 2008) and in relation to individual differences (MacLeod & Mathews, 1991; Mathews & Milroy, 1994). This pattern of results implies that emotion-related differences underlying attentional effects depend on variations in processing priority of exactly the sort that biased-competition theory predicts.

## Theories of attention to emotional material in psychopathology

The most specific theories of emotion and attention are those that seek to account for the pattern of biased attentional processing of emotionally congruent material in mood disordered or subclinical individuals. Emotion-congruent biases in attention typically comprise those with anxiety, depression, or other clinically-related states displaying enhanced attention to negative material (in particular that matching their particular mood state, see "specificity" sections) and/or reduced attention to positive material. Theories about these biases therefore need to take account of the emotional nature of the material being processed as well the emotional state of the disordered individuals themselves.

Two early theories used to explain the emerging empirical data were those of Beck (1976) and Bower (1981, 1987). Beck proposed the existence of negative dysfunctional schemata (sets of related beliefs and attitudes about the self, the world and the future), which bias information processing, while Bower used an associative-network model in which spreading activation from emotion nodes increases access to material of similar content. Although both remain influential today in other domains, they no longer suffice to explain the pattern of biased cognition associated with disorders, primarily because their common prediction, that all forms of information processing will be biased similarly across all disorders, has not been supported by the empirical evidence. Rather, a double dissociation became apparent, whereby trait anxiety was more closely related to biased attention than biased recall, with the reverse pattern found in depression (a pattern now further qualified by the duration of presentation of stimulus material, as described later). It was these findings that triggered the development of the first theory specifically designed to account for biased cognition in psychopathology, considered next.

### Williams et al.'s two-stage theory (1988, 1997)

The theory proposed by Williams and colleagues (Williams et al., 1988, 1997) distinguishes "priming" from "elaboration" (Graf & Mandler,

1984). Priming is conceived as an early automatic activation of the internal representation of a stimulus, which temporarily enhances its accessibility. Williams et al. claim that effects of individual trait anxiety are largely due to processes occurring at automatic (specifically involuntary and unconscious) stages. Elaboration is a later strategic process, which creates and strengthens interconnections between representations, thereby affecting processes such as retrieval. Biases at elaboration supposedly underlie emotion-congruent effects in depression. The specification of these two mechanisms means that any factors influencing processing (such as trait anxiety or depression) need not apply equally across all types of cognitive operation (for example memory or attention). This is a critical difference from the earlier models of Beck (1976) and Bower (1981, 1987), which predicted that individual differences should bias all types of cognition in an identical manner (see above). It gives the model explanatory power to account for findings implicating different cognitive-processing biases in different emotional disorders (for example depression associated more with biases in recall than attention, and the reverse for trait anxiety). In terms of attention, which is our focus here, the two-stage theory predicts that attentional tasks allowing only differential priming of emotional and non-emotional material (for example rapid presentations not allowing sufficient time for elaboration) should show biases in trait anxiety, but not depression, whereas attentional tasks allowing elaborative processing (for example those using longer presentation times, allowing more elaborative processing to occur) should reveal similar biases in depression but not trait anxiety. In fact these predictions have been largely supported by the data, most notably the variety of evidence suggestive of trait-anxiety-related (but not depression) attentional bias effects when stimulus presentation durations are very short and more recent work demonstrating attentional biases in depression when elaborative attentional processing is made possible by using longer presentation durations.

The theory is considerably more detailed than there is space to expound here, but there is one additional aspect important to note. Two structures are proposed within the model, the affective decision mechanism (ADM), which evaluates the valence of stimulus input, and the resource allocation mechanism (RAM), which determines how processing resources are deployed across incoming stimuli. Transient effects of *state* emotion are presumed to act on the ADM, leading for example to higher valence evaluations (i.e., more salient, highly activated stimulus representations) when in current anxious or depressed mood. In contrast, individual differences in emotional *trait* predisposition affect the RAM, leading to greater processing resources being directed towards the processing of emotion-congruent material (at priming in trait anxiety and at elaboration in depression). This means that the explanation for transient effects of *state* mood on attention rests on the evaluation of stimuli, whereas that for personality *trait* effects relies on the extent and direction of processing resources deployed. This unique theoretical distinction has set the theory apart from many others in its predictive and explanatory power, but also raised counterintuitive predictions (see "intensity" sections).

## Cognitive motivational analysis

This model (Mogg & Bradley, 1998) is primarily concerned with accounting for the effects of state and trait anxiety on the cognitive processing of threat, but it also speaks to other emotion-congruent effects, most notably in depression. The model specifies two cognitive structures. A "valence evaluation system" (VES) assesses stimulus threat value (much like the ADM above) and feeds into a second structure the "goal engagement system" (GES; analogous to, although theoretically distinct from, the RAM above). When a high-intensity evaluation is output from the VES, the GES interrupts current goals and orients resources towards that material; otherwise the GES operates in a default "safety mode", which prioritises positive stimuli and ignores negative stimuli (those which are insufficient to activate the VES). As well as being influenced by a range of factors in addition to basic stimulus input (e.g., situational context, biological preparedness), the reactivity of the VES varies according to *both* trait and state anxiety. The VES is more sensitive in high- than in low-anxious individuals, leading the former to make "higher threat" evaluations where the latter would not, resulting in differences in attention at low levels of threat. Thus, the cognitive-motivational view proposes that it is the evaluation of what constitutes a threat, rather than how the attentional system responds to a threat, that differs in high and low trait anxiety and it is primarily this which distinguishes it from previous theories.

Depression is characterised by disengagement from external goals, which allows the model to account for the absence of emotion-congruent phenomena that might otherwise be expected in depression (e.g., the absence of early attentional biases). An adjunct to the central model is the "vigilance avoidance hypothesis", which proposes a curvilinear relationship between threat value and attentional bias, such that all individuals show a pattern of initial (adaptive) avoidance of mild threat followed by increasingly strong vigilance (orienting towards) as threat intensity increases. Individual differences in trait anxiety are said to shift this curve such that attentional responses normally characteristic of higher intensity threat material are now elicited at relatively lower intensity levels. To date this hypothesis has received limited supporting evidence (relevant studies are few, but supportive) from attentional studies and remains theoretically consistent with evidence from cuing studies showing maintenance of attention (Weierich, Treat, & Hollingworth, 2008).

*Mathews and Mackintosh (1998)*

The model proposed by Mathews and Mackintosh (1998) suggests that stimulus information is represented in a competitive activation network. It could therefore be considered an emotion-specific example of the biased-competition approach described earlier, but with specific application to individual differences in the processing of emotional information. A "threat-evaluation system" (similar to the VES and ADM of previously discussed models) enhances the activation of any items "tagged" as potentially threatening thereby increasing automatic selective attention and processing resources devoted to such items. Attention will therefore be biased towards such items. Individual differences arise through the effect of trait anxiety on the threat-evaluation system, which is to raise its output. Higher anxiety, whether mood state or personality trait, will thus lead to greater activation of threatening representations of a given stimulus thereby producing enhanced competition with alternatives on, which may be sufficient to elicit attentional selection of a threatening stimulus. Anxiety is the only individual-difference dimension that the model explicitly addresses, and the usefulness and validity of its extension to other emotion-relevant dimensions has not yet been explored. A key strength of the model is an additional feature accounting for possible top-down effects on emotional processing (see Control above). The model does this explicitly via an effortful "task demand" unit that can enhance the activation of *any* item within the competitive network. Within this framework all stimuli, including emotional and non-emotional ones constitute separate representations upon which the task demand unit may operate according to task instructions or contextual conditions. This feature gives the model explanatory power for a range of results that other studies struggle to account for, such as the paradoxical elimination of biases in the presence of genuine threat (Amir et al., 1996; Mathews & Sebastian, 1993).

Both this and the preceding theoretical account converge on the assumption that individual differences in attention to emotional material are a result of differences in early stimulus appraisal or evaluation, rather than in the allocation of resources for the deployment of attention. This is a key theoretical difference from the "two-stage theory" (Williams et al., 1997), which places differences in the *direction* of attention based on differential resources at the heart of emotion-congruent biases in attention.

The current consensus favours either of the last two models discussed (Mogg & Bradley, 1998; Mathews & Mackintosh, 1998), without a clear preference between them. While the cognitive motivational analysis offers a wider explanatory framework (covering all affective disorders, rather than just anxiety) and accounting for most of the extant data, Mathews and Mackintosh (1998) utilise a currently favoured competition mechanism (which invites mathematical implementation) and allows for both bottom-up and top-down influences.

## EMPIRICAL REVIEW: ATTENTION TO EMOTION IN GENERAL AND PSYCHOPATHOLOGY POPULATIONS

Any empirical literature is to some extent driven by the availability of suitable methods to interrogate the phenomena of interest. In attention and emotion these methods can be divided into *Filtering*, *Search*, *Cuing*, and *Multiple task* paradigms (Cowan, 2005; Yiend, Mathews, & Cowan, 2005). This is more than just a convenient way of dividing the empirical literature. Each technique allows different inferences to be made about the mechanisms by which attention is operating, some offering greater precision than others. Together they allow us to build up a convergent picture of what exactly is going on when people "attend to emotion". There are, of course, issues that cut across the particular method used to interrogate attention. Some of these have already been highlighted under the "concepts" section; others will be picked up en route.

*Filtering* tasks involve presenting targets and distracters together, testing participants' ability to suppress or ignore the latter. The emotional Stroop task is perhaps the most obvious although controversial (see below) example of this. In *Search* tasks, participants must find and report on a particular target in an array of distracters. One example is considered in this review, namely visual search. When face stimuli are used this is also known as "the face-in-the-crowd" method. *Cuing* tasks include methods in which a stimulus or event attracts attention to a particular location(s) and is followed by a target to be detected, with attention usually measured by the speed or accuracy of participants' response. In *Multiple* tasks, participants must allocate their limited processing capacity to meet more than one demand, as when having to report two sequential targets. The example considered in this review is the attentional-blink method. Attending to one target takes time, meaning that another arriving too soon afterward is often missed.

Each type of task is discussed in turn, starting with a description of the specific technique used, highlighting the logic behind it and the inferences made from it about attention to emotional material (*Method*). Any effects found in the general population are summarised with reference to seminal and recent literature (*The general population*), followed by a similar summary for results in populations selected to have relevance to psychopathology (*Psychopathology populations*). The significant conceptual issues addressed from this particular domain of empirical study are highlighted (*Conceptual inferences*). For some tasks these are very few, whereas for others a large body of literature has addressed many issues. In the latter case further subheadings are used to distinguish these in line with the distinctions made in Concepts. The discussion of each task finishes with an evaluation of the literature to date and identification of potential future contributions (*Evaluation*).

# Filtering

## *Dichotic listening*

### *Method*

Perhaps the earliest example of an attentional filtering task used to probe attention to emotion would be the dichotic-listening technique (Cherry, 1953; Conway, Cowan, & Bunting, 2001; Harris, Pashler, & Coburn, 2004; Moray, 1959; Wood & Cowan, 1995a). Two simultaneous auditory messages are presented. Participants are usually asked to "shadow" (repeat out loud) one of them and ignore the other, ensuring attention is focused on only one channel. The ignored channel is assumed to receive very little attention and experimenters can compare the degree to which different types of stimuli presented on this unattended channel intrude. Some measure is made of interference produced by the unattended stimuli, such as shadowing errors.

### *The general population*

Early findings indicated that especially salient messages such as one's own name (Moray, 1959) or taboo words (Nielsen & Sarason, 1981) produced errors during shadowing. Later studies used the method described above to show this can be attributed to attentional interference, specifically shifts of attention and capacity limitations (Conway et al., 2001; Wood & Cowan, 1995a,b). Although still widely used to investigate attention to non-emotional material in the general population, few if any of these studies include emotional material.

### *Psychopathology populations*

Dichotic listening was popular in early investigations of psychopathology and attention to emotional material. For example, Burgess, Jones, Robertson, Radcliffe, and Emerson (1981) and Foa and McNally (1986) found that anxious patients were better at detecting unattended anxiety-relevant stimuli compared to neutral ones, implying that these stimuli were particularly effective at commanding attentional resources. An influential study by Mathews and MacLeod (1986) sidestepped the response-bias problems (see Concepts section) of dichotic listening tasks by comparing the effects of emotional and neutral stimuli on performance of an independent task, in which all responses are neutral. They compared GAD patients and normal controls by requiring them to make a speeded response whenever they saw a "press" command appear on a screen in front of them while shadowing. They compared the effect of threat and non-threat words occurring in the unattended auditory channel on reaction-time performance to the visual task. GAD patients, but not normal controls, were slower to respond when the task coincided with a threat (compared to a non-threat) word on the unattended channel.

## Conceptual inferences

Dichotic listening studies allow assessment of the extent to which emotional information intrudes and disrupts the processing of neutral information. Initially results were attributed to the processing of salient semantic information outside awareness. However, later researchers have argued that awareness may momentarily switch between channels and now adopt stricter criteria for making inferences about participants' awareness of distracters, often involving other experimental paradigms (Holender, 1986). For example in the Mathews and Macleod study described above, subsequent recognition memory tests and unexpected probing of momentary awareness was used to strengthen the inference that effects were due to interference from semantic content that the participants were unaware of, rather than voluntary switching of attention between channels.

## Evaluation

It is surprising that so few studies have continued to use this technique, perhaps because of the interpretative problems highlighted. It is notable that few could be found specifically examining attention to emotional information in the general population. However, there remain several ways in which dichotic listening techniques, and auditory attention in general, could contribute new insights into the attentional processing of emotional information. One might explore other aspects of automaticity beyond awareness (e.g., temporal characteristics of intrusion effects or the effects of mental load). This and other paradigms could provide evidence from the auditory modality that could either converge with or challenge the evidence accruing in the visual domain (see Spence & Santangelo, 2008, for a review). Finally, dichotic listening is being increasingly used to explore cross-modal phenomena (Santangelo, Ho, & Spence, 2008), which are of interest in their own right and could yield added insights for the mechanisms underlying emotion effects on attention.

## Emotional Stroop

### Method

A large body of relevant evidence has built up around the use of the emotional Stroop task. In this task participants have to name as quickly as possible the colour of ink in which words are printed. It is found that the meaning of the word itself (which must be ignored to name the ink colour) tends to interfere, to varying degrees, with the speed of colour naming. In the original version subjects are particularly slow when the words are the names of colours, for example the word "red" printed in blue ink (Stroop, 1935). In the emotional Stroop the premise is that if greater attention is selectively paid to the content of particular *emotional* words, then greater impairment of colour-naming performance should be observed on these words. Consistent with this, the speed of colour naming emotion-relevant words (e.g., "disease", "failure") is typically slowed relative to the colour naming of matched neutral words.

*The general population*

There are few studies that specifically report emotional Stroop data in the general population. Pratto and John (1991) used unselected student volunteers and found longer colour-naming latencies for undesirable than desirable traits, replicated by Wentura, Rothermund, and Bak (2000). However, much of the Stroop literature addresses specific hypotheses that are only tangentially related to selective attention to emotional material. Questions have included identifying neural substrates (Compton et al., 2003; Engels et al., 2007; van Hooff, Dietz, Sharma, & Bowman, 2008); bilingual effects (Sutton, Altarriba, Gianico, & Basnight-Brown, 2007); effects of anxious mood (Salters-Pedneault, Gentes, & Roemer, 2007; Yovel & Mineka, 2005); attention to positive information (Strauss & Allen, 2006) and links between memory and attention (MacKay & Ahmetzanov, 2005). This does not necessarily mean that emotional Stroop interference is restricted to selected populations, but probably that other techniques have been chosen to investigate attention to emotion in the wider population. For example, a related phenomenon is that of the taboo Stroop (Siegrist, 1995), in which colour naming times are longer for taboo than for neutral words. The taboo Stroop appears to be a fairly robust phenomenon, the attentional effects of which transfer to later memory tasks (MacKay et al., 2004).

A recent meta-analysis provides further information about emotional Stroop effects from clinical controls and non-clinical low-vulnerable groups (Bar-Haim, Lamy, Pergamin, Bakermans-Kranenburg, & van IJzendoorn, 2007). Bar-Haim and colleagues found evidence of emotional-Stroop interference, but only in blocked designs, in which trials of a particular valence are grouped together. This qualification, which has been reported elsewhere in unselected samples (McKenna & Sharma, 2004), may be due to the cumulative exposure to valenced stimuli that occurs throughout blocks, leading to an enhanced perception of threat (consistent with the issues relating to intensity, discussed elsewhere). A particularly good review of the *non-emotional* Stroop literature and its methodology is given by MacLeod (1991) and Macleod (2005), respectively. That there are no specific reviews of the emotional Stroop in the general population under-lines the absence of data.

## Psychopathology populations

In contrast, the speed of colour naming pathology-relevant words (e.g., "disease", "failure") has been used to reveal exacerbated selective, emotion-congruent interference effects in emotional disorders across a wide range of studies including clinical anxiety (e.g., Martin, Williams, & Clark, 1991; Mathews & MacLeod, 1985; Mathews, Mogg, Kentish, & Eysenck, 1995; Mogg, Mathews, & Weinman, 1989; Owens, Asmundson, Hadjistavropoulos, & Owens, 2004) and high trait anxiety (e.g., Fox, 1993a; Mogg, Mathews, Bird, & MacGregor-Morris, 1990; Richards & French, 1990; Richards & Millwood, 1989). A particularly good review of the earlier literature is given in Williams, Mathews, and MacLeod (1996) and two recent meta-analyses provide more recent information (Bar-Haim et al., 2007; Phaf & Kan, 2007). This body of work has addressed the issues of specificity, awareness and the role of competition.

## Conceptual inferences

Thanks to the large body of work using the emotional Stroop in psychopathology, many conceptual issues have been addressed using this technique.

### SPECIFICITY: STIMULI

Earlier studies have shown that biases are greatest when the emotional stimuli match the specific concerns of subjects. Mogg et al. (1989) reported more interference from physical threat words for GAD patients who reported worries of a primarily physical nature (such as illness). Similarly, social threat words (e.g., criticism) produced strongest effects in those with social worries. Likewise, panic disorder appears to be associated with particularly strong interference for words related to physical symptoms (Ehlers, Margraf, Davies, & Roth, 1988; McNally, Riemann, Louro, Lukach, & Kim, 1992), as does social phobia for words related to social threat (Hope, Rapee, Heimberg, & Dombeck, 1990). One study suggested that Stroop interference was just as great for emotionally positive as negative words (Martin et al., 1991), however subsequent work indicated that positive stimuli that are related to the negative concerns of the individual (for example "health" and "disease") may elicit similar attentional effects by virtue of their semantic association with participants' primary concerns (e.g., Mathews & Klug, 1993). Thus it may be that any stimuli that are sufficiently related to the individuals' current concerns will produce attentional-bias effects. More recently, Rutherford and colleagues

(Rutherford, MacLeod, & Campbell, 2004) asked whether attentional biases in trait anxiety were specific for negative material, or extended to all emotional information, positive and negative. As hypothesised they found that elevated state anxiety produced interference on both positive and negative information, whereas high trait anxiety produced a more specific bias for negative over positive information. Consistent with emotion-congruent specificity Strauss and Allen (2006) reported a bias for high-intensity positive (but not low-intensity or negative) words in those reporting high levels of positive affect.

### SPECIFICITY: PSYCHOPATHOLOGY

The high comorbidity between anxiety and depressive disorders (and corresponding subclinical traits) has provided a continual challenge for researchers when attempting to attribute biases in attention to one or the other domain of psychopathology. This is usually resolved in one of two ways, either statistically by comparing the amount of variance in bias attributable to each psychopathology, or by stringent selection of participants to minimise the comorbidity itself. Early findings suggested that trait anxiety, but not depression, was associated with biased attention toward congruently valenced information (Mathews & MacLeod, 1994). Yovel and Mineka (2005) used both anxiety- and depression-relevant words and correlated indices of emotional interference with both dimensions of personality. Consistent with the pattern described they reported no relationship on depression indices, but a significant partial correlation between general anxious distress and interference for anxiety-relevant words.

### AUTOMATICITY: AWARENESS

Although no paradigms can fully rule out transient awareness, attempts have been made to test for automaticity using the emotional Stroop by restricting the potential for conscious processing as much as possible. An example is the presentation of stimuli for very brief durations (usually around 14–16 ms) using backward masking. This is usually referred to as "subliminal presentation", in contrast to standard "supraliminal presentations", in which awareness of the critical stimuli is possible. Interestingly, the attentional bias found by Yovel and Mineka was only exhibited under subliminal conditions, which the authors suggested was characteristic of the subclinical level of the psychopathology. A similar result was reported by Wikstrom, Lundh, and Westerlund (2003) when they examined stringently determined subliminal interference from threat words and its relationship with trait anxiety, depression and anger. Only trait anxiety was related to subliminal effects. Due to the detailed attention paid to determining awareness thresholds the authors could confidently conclude that anxiety-related Stroop interference operates below the level of conscious awareness and prior to attentional selection. This is consistent with previous studies reporting subliminal emotional-Stroop interference (Bradley, Mogg, Millar, & White, 1995; MacLeod & Hagan, 1992; MacLeod & Rutherford, 1992; Mogg, Bradley, Williams, & Mathews, 1993a; Mogg, Kentish, & Bradley, 1993b). Phaf and Kan (2007) specifically addressed the automaticity of emotional-Stroop effects and concluded less positively than the reading of individual studies might suggest. Their meta-analysis found no evidence of subliminal emotional-Stroop effects, a conclusion based in part on effects being limited to blocked (and not randomised) designs. In contrast Bar-Haim et al. (2007), in a broader meta-analysis, did find evidence supportive of both subliminal and supraliminal emotional-Stroop effects, although the latter had significantly larger effect sizes.

*Evaluation*

Where the primary aim is to make inferences about attention, other methods are increasingly preferred to the Stroop, despite its previous widespread use. This is due to the inherent ambiguity of the inferences that can be made from Stroop interference. The phenomenon could reflect emotional material being less readily suppressed or filtered, with negative consequences for primary-task performance. Other interpretations are also possible. Emotional stimuli may be more frequently used than neutral ones (e.g., Klein, 1964), or form a more coherent category in common language. Good studies, however, will match stimuli sets on familiarity and category coherence using norms for word frequency and category-association strength. Although participants are not responding directly to emotional stimuli, a response-bias interpretation remains possible, because responding occurs while emotional information is present. Another possibility is that emotional stimuli affect cognition in some other non-attentional manner, causing general disruption. This is because the fundamental nature of the cognitive processes giving rise to the emotional Stroop effect continues to be debated (see MacLeod, 2005, for an excellent insight). Kindt, Bierman, and Brosschot (1996), for example, reported evidence suggesting that the emotional Stroop effect may measure different underlying mechanisms according to the particular format of the task used.

   In the most recent example of this debate Algom, Chajut, and Lev (2004) have argued on the basis of six experiments that "the processes sustaining the classic and the emotional effects differ in a qualitative fashion" (p. 335). This remains a strong and contested claim (Algom et al., 2004; Chajut, Lev, & Algom, 2005; Dalgleish, 2005). However, it underlines what has been known for a long time, namely the conclusions that can be drawn about emotion and attention, per se, from studies involving this task are limited at best. Despite this, emotional-Stroop data are valuable because of the extent of existing data, confidence in their reliability and ability to make comparisons across populations relevant to psychopathology, stimulus materials and other independent factors of interest. Where a robust emotional Stroop effect is required, the blocked design will most reliably deliver this effect (Bar-Haim et al., 2007; Mckenna & Sharma, 2004).

## Visual search

### Method

The visual search method arises from a simple emotional adaptation of the standard attentional visual search task. In the typical procedure an array of stimuli, often faces, is presented, and the participant is required to pick out the one with a discrepant emotional expression as quickly as possible. Many combinations of target and distracter expressions are possible, the most obvious being differently valenced targets within neutral-distracter arrays. This allows clean conclusions about the speed of detection of the expression concerned and the presumed underlying mechanism of attentional capture. In contrast, a neutral target embedded in a valenced array provides a good way of considering distraction effects alone. Valenced arrays combined with valenced targets (for example so-called search-asymmetry designs; see Horstmann, 2009) produce search that will be a combination of distraction and detection, thus usually yielding data that is harder to interpret (see Frischen, Eastwood & Smilek, 2008, for more detail). As a result only studies including emotional targets in neutral arrays in one or more conditions are considered here for simplicity and to assist in the clarity of conclusions drawn.

### The general population

Of all the methods considered here, the largest literature on attention to emotion in the general population comes from visual search tasks. Generally speaking the current consensus suggests that negative (especially angry and fear-relevant, but also happy and sad—see Frischen et al., 2008; Williams, Moss, Bradshaw, & Mattingley, 2005) information is both detected faster and is more distracting than neutral (Eastwood, Smilek, & Merikle, 2001; Fox et al., 2000; Juth, Karlsson, Lundqvist, & Ohman, 2000; Öhman, Flykt, & Esteves, 2001a; Öhman, Lundqvist, & Esteves, 2001b; but see Tipples, Young, Quinlan, Broks, & Ellis, 2002). Many studies have used photographic images of real faces. An often-cited early example is that of Hansen and Hansen (1988), which was later criticised because the speeded-detection effect was found to be attributable to a confound, namely a small dark patch on the chin of the discrepant face (Purcell, Stewart, & Skov, 1996). Better control over arbitrary perceptual differences has been gained by using schematic faces, simple line drawings consisting of a circle, mouth, eyes and sometimes eyebrows, and by using neutral stimuli associated with fear through conditioning (e.g., Batty, Cave, & Pauli, 2005). A very useful review of the literature on visual search to emotional information in the general population (and touching on individual differences in state) is that of Frischen et al. (2008). Focusing specifically on facial expressions, they too conclude that pre-attentive visual search processes are sensitive to, and facilitated by, emotional information.

## Psychopathology populations

As an example of what we can infer from visual search in psychopathology let us consider the study by Byrne and Eysenck (1995). They required high and low trait anxious normals to detect a single happy or angry target face among an array of neutral faces. The groups performed equally for happy targets, but the high anxious were faster at detecting angry targets. This result suggests that the *speed* of threat detection was faster for high-anxious subjects, implicating an initial attentional capture process similar to the "engage" mechanism inferred from single-cuing studies (although probably contaminated by response-bias effects).

Additional studies looking at individual differences have mostly reported clear between-participant differences in specific phobias (Öhman et al., 2001a) and social anxiety (Gilboa-Schechtman, Foa, & Amir, 1999). An exception is Juth, Lundqvist, Karlsson, and Ohman (2005), who found no consistent effects of social anxiety, but speeded detection of angry compared to happy faces, especially during a social challenge. Eastwood et al. (2005) also looked at social phobia, as well as panic and OCD. They compared detection of positive and negative faces among neutral arrays of varying sizes and found shallower search slopes for negative than positive targets in both social anxiety and panic, but not OCD or controls. It is possible that clinical levels of psychopathology more reliably reveal evidence of biased attention using visual search and subclinical studies have remained unpublished. Alternatively subclinical populations may simply have been investigated less often. It is also worth noting that, consistent with the absence of depression-related effects on attention for emotion mentioned previously, Karparova, Kersting, and Suslow (2005) reported no differences on visual search for emotional information between major depression and controls.

## Conceptual inferences

Visual search studies can speak to the issues of both specificity and automaticity, primarily from data in the general population.

### SPECIFICITY: STIMULI

Research using increasingly ecologically valid stimuli continues to replicate the so called "threat superiority effect" (albeit losing tight control over perceptual matching of stimuli). Fox, Griggs, and Mouchlianitis (2007a) asked whether phylogenetically (stimuli "biologically prepared" to be associated with fear such as snakes and spiders) and ontogenetically (stimuli whose relevance to fear must be acquired, e.g., weapons) fear-relevant stimuli differed in their propensity to capture attention. Neither class of threat stimuli showed an advantage over the other, although all were more efficiently detected than neutral control pictures (e.g., mushrooms, flowers). In a further test of phylogenetic effects Lipp and Waters (2007) compared visual search for spiders and snakes (regarded as phylogenetically fear relevant) with search for similarly unpleasant animals that are not considered phylogenetically fear relevant (cockroaches and lizards). Enhanced attentional capture for the former was demonstrated. These data suggest stimuli of biological fear relevance are indeed prioritised for attentional selection.

AUTOMATICITY: PARALLEL PROCESSING

One issue much addressed using this paradigm has been the extent to which negatively valenced information is detected "automatically" (here meaning "in parallel" or "pre-attentive" as determined by near zero additional cost from increasing numbers of distracters). For example, Ohman and colleagues (Öhman, Flykt, & Esteves, 2001a) used threatening and neutral pictures (snakes, spiders, mushrooms and flowers) presented in arrays of either $2 \times 2$ or $3 \times 3$, and participants had to search for the discrepant picture, which was either neutral in an array of threat or threat in an array of neutral pictures. They compared detection times for threat and neutral targets and found, as predicted, that threatening pictures were located more quickly than non-threatening ones. They claimed that search for these threat stimuli occurred in parallel because no slowing was found on the $3 \times 3$ array compared to $2 \times 2$ one. Another more comprehensive test of this hypothesis was that of Eastwood et al. (2001). They used arrays of 7, 11, 15 and 19 schematic faces and either positive or negative targets among neutral distracters. Search slopes were not flat, but for negative targets they were shallower than those for positive, suggesting a serial search that was faster for negative targets. Fox et al. (2000) obtained similar results for angry compared to happy targets and concluded that although "pop out" did not occur, search for anger was particularly fast and efficient. Consistent with this Horstmann (Horstmann & Bauland, 2006) reported an advantage for facial threat but search slopes not suggestive of pre-attentive detection (well above 10 ms per stimulus). Calvo, Avero, and Lundqvist (2006) found similar advantages for angry faces, but using visual arrays presented parafoveally and at short display durations (150 ms).

Finally, in a rare study using visual search with varying set sizes to specifically examine individual differences in attention to threat, Batty et al. (2005) conditioned abstract shapes to carry neutral or negative valence, as a way of ruling out perceptual confounds of the sort described earlier. The conditioning procedure was validated on the basis of explicit ratings and an implicit association test. Although there was limited evidence of generally speeded detection of threat (Experiment 2 only), there was no evidence that this was modulated either by anxiety level or set size. It would seem important to replicate these findings in a clinical population.

*Evaluation*

It appears that there remains scope to exploit this paradigm further, especially within psychopathology populations, for example to examine issues of specificity (e.g., effects in biologically relevant emotional information) and automaticity (e.g., the extent of parallel processing) similar to those observed in the general population. In addition, visual search for emotional targets among neutral arrays offers a potential source of convergent data on the role of the "engage" mechanism of spatial attention. The method allows the increased speed of detecting emotional information to be measured directly without any predefined time window imposed by the experimenter. In this respect, and providing non-emotional distracters are used, it may be a better way of assessing attentional engagement than cuing studies (see below), although it loses some of the ecological validity of the complex visual arrays of visual-search tasks. However, it may be that the lack of studies using visual search in psychopathology result from the paradigm being less sensitive than others to individual differences present at subclinical levels.

# Cuing

One of the best-known methods of investigating selective attention to emotional information, although most often used to explore effects in psychopathology, is attentional cuing. Cuing tasks can be divided into "double" and "single" methods, reflecting, as the names suggest, the number of cues used per trial. A great advantage of cuing tasks includes that participants usually respond to a neutral target detection task and in the absence of any other emotional information being present at the time of response. This avoids response-bias explanations (see Concepts, above) and allows the underlying attentional mechanism to be more clearly inferred: usually effects can be attributed to the spatial allocation of attention rather than some general (perhaps non-attentional) interference.

*Double cuing*

*Method*

Also called the "attentional probe" or "dot probe" task, the visual form has been most widely used and was introduced in a seminal study by MacLeod,

Mathews, and Tata (1986), although Eysenck (1992) refers to an earlier auditory version of the task, with similar results. It involves displaying two stimuli, of different valence, simultaneously either side of a fixation point for a brief interval (traditionally 500 ms, although later studies explore variations of this). An emotionally neutral task (such as detection or identification of a dot, letter or arrow) follows in one or other location. By design the target stimulus occurs in the previous location of either the valenced or non-valenced stimulus (usually 50% each). The logic is that if attention is biased to one type of stimulus then participants should be relatively faster to perform the task when it is located in the same spatial position as that stimulus, because reaction times will benefit from attention already being fixated at the appropriate location. This is called attentional vigilance, with the opposite pattern indicative of attentional avoidance. The results of MacLeod et al. showed that anxious patients were consistently faster to detect (and in later studies, to identify) probes when they replaced threat stimuli than when they replaced non-threat stimuli, suggesting that they had attended to the threat words in preference to non-threat. Controls displayed a trend in the opposite direction, suggesting avoidance of threat. A detailed description of the task's subsequent methodological variations is given in Yiend and Mathews (2005).

*The general population*

Double cuing is largely the preserve of the field of emotion and attention in psychopathology. Studies in the general population are few, probably due to their relative recency, and have specifically focused on conceptual issues such as biological relevance, the intensity of stimuli, and stimulus duration. They are, therefore, discussed under conceptual issues below. In general their findings suggest that when specific stimulus material (biologically relevant and/or severely threatening) and short presentations ( < 500 ms) are used, attentional biases are indeed found in the general population.

*Psychopathology populations*

Since the early attentional probe studies described above there have been very many replications and variations. Research over the subsequent decade confirmed the presence of a spatial attentional bias favouring threat in both anxious patients (e.g., Horenstein & Segui, 1997; Mogg, Bradley, & Williams, 1995; Mogg, Mathews, & Eysenck, 1992) and high trait anxious normals (e.g., Bradley et al., 1997; Broadbent & Broadbent, 1988; Fox, 1993b; MacLeod & Mathews, 1988), with effects proving somewhat less reliable in subclinical groups (Mogg et al., 1990). Anxiety it seems, in most of its forms, is associated with preferential attentional bias for negativity. Much subsequent work has been done using double cuing to refine precisely the nature and characteristics of this bias, as discussed next.

*Conceptual inferences*

SPECIFICITY: STIMULI

*(a) Intensity.* Double cuing is increasingly being used to examine one aspect of the stimulus material, intensity, which appears to be critical to whether attention is biased. In the original MacLeod study, described above, control participants displayed a trend suggesting attentional avoidance of mild threat. Subsequent work using different types of stimulus material has occasionally suggested the same (e.g., Yiend & Mathews, 2001, Experiment 1, showing avoidance of mild threat pictures in low trait anxiety). Moreover the meta-analysis of Bar-Haim et al. (2007) reveals further evidence of threat avoidance in low-vulnerable and clinical-control groups. Not only does the avoidance of threat have an obvious adaptive function, but it is consistent with the vigilance-avoidance hypothesis of Mogg and Bradley (1998; see above). Indeed, this theorising prompted two specific studies investigating the pattern of orienting to threat in low trait anxiety (Mogg et al., 2000a; Wilson & MacLeod, 2003) both of which reported findings consistent with avoidance of minor threat and vigilance for high threat. Subsequently, Koster, Crombez, Verschuere, and De Houwer (2006) have reported a similar pattern of selective attention towards high threat in all participants (with trait-anxiety-related differences at mild levels of threat). Thus, a sensible working hypothesis, which has received initial empirical support, is that the general population show adaptive avoidance of milder threat and vigilance for more severe threat.

*(b) Biological relevance.* The biological relevance of threat stimuli has been a particular focus of interest in studies of normal volunteers, presumably because of the clear prediction that these stimuli should be particularly effective in the competition for attentional selection. Lipp and Derakshan (2005) found an attentional bias toward snakes and spiders compared to neutral stimuli in healthy volunteers and concluded that animal fear-relevant stimuli drew attention in healthy samples. Although consistent with the notion of an attentional advantage for biologically prepared threat as found with visual-search studies, this study did not include a non-biologically relevant threat control which would be necessary to draw this conclusion. Beaver, Mogg, and Bradley (2005) explored whether prior pairing of biologically relevant fear stimuli with an aversive event facilitates preferential attentional bias for those fear stimuli. They manipulated the occurrence of aversive conditioning to spider and snake stimuli and compared orienting patterns between these and biologically irrelevant images (flowers, mushrooms) on a probe task. As predicted, successful aversive conditioning increased selective attention to the biologically relevant material.

Using a different class of stimuli to capture the notion of biological relevance, Brosch, Sander, and Scherer (2007) used a 100 ms double-cue display to compare attention to adult and infant stimuli for several species (cats, dogs and humans), all with neutral expressions. Rating data indicated all infant stimuli were more pleasant and more arousing than adult ones, and probe reaction times showed an attentional bias for infant over adult faces specific to the human stimuli. The authors argue that biologically relevant positive stimuli can also capture attention. These data remain to be replicated, however, and it will be important to report direct comparisons separating out critical factors such as valence, arousal and biological relevance. For example would a similar pattern obtain with other supposedly biologically relevant positive stimuli; would the infant faces show equivalent patterns of orienting if valence (facial expressions) was manipulated? It is likely that "approach" or positive stimuli have evolved alongside negative ones to selectively attract attention (e.g., Mogg, Bradley, Hyare, & Lee, 1998).

SPECIFICITY: PSYCHOPATHOLOGY

*(a) Depression.* Early reviewers concluded that attentional biases associated with depression were largely absent (Mathews & Macleod, 1994). Indeed many studies of anxious populations failed to reveal equivalent attentional biases in corresponding depressed groups (MacLeod et al., 1986; Mogg, Millar, & Bradley, 2000b). A few reported a relative lack of bias towards positive stimuli in depressed subjects compared to normals using attentional probe tasks (e.g., Mogg et al., 1991) and a temporal order judgement task ("deployment of attention task" or DOAT; Gotlib, McLachlan, & Katz, 1988). However, this picture has shifted somewhat over recent years with several influential reports of attentional bias in depression (Bradley, Mogg, & Lee, 1997; Gotlib et al., 2004a; Gotlib, Krasnoperova, Yue, & Joormann, 2004b; Mathews, Ridgeway, & Williamson, 1996; Mogg et al., 1995). What appears to be common across such studies is the careful selection of participants to avoid comorbidity with trait anxiety and the use of methods allowing greater time for elaboration and encoding of stimulus material, which usually means lengthening presentation times. Some studies report findings carried mainly by effects on positive information (lack of a "normal" positive bias). For example in a study by Joorman and Gotlib (2007) unlike controls, depressed and recovered-depressed patients selectively attended to sad faces and lacked control participants' bias toward happy facial expressions. Importantly, cue exposure duration was 1 second, thus allowing elaborative attentional processes to occur. Shane and Peterson (2007) found attentional biases both away from positive and towards negative pictures in dysphoria and the two effects appeared to be uncorrelated. Other studies have reported a distinct attentional selectivity for negative information alone. In a carefully controlled hypothesis-driven test of the role elaboration plays in depression-related attentional effects Donaldson, Lam, and Mathews (2007)

found attentional bias towards negative words in major depression (which was stronger in ruminators) at 1000 but not 500 ms presentation duration. Although further studies are likely to emerge in this active area of interest, the current patterns are strongly indicative of depression-congruent attentional selection coupled with an absence of selectivity for mood-incongruent (positive) material that may normally be protective.

*(b) Social anxiety.* Attentional-probe tasks have yielded some potentially contradictory sets of findings within the specific domain of social anxiety or phobia. Some studies have suggested that the pattern of orienting in this disorder may be a reverse of the usual anxiety-related attention towards threat. Specifically, socially anxious have been found to selectively attend away from emotional faces of any valence (Mansell, Ehlers, Clark, & Chen, 2002) and sometimes away from faces per se whether emotional or not (Chen, Ehlers, Clark, & Mansell, 2002). However, other studies seem to contradict these findings, such as another by Mansell and colleagues (Mansell, Clark, Ehlers, & Chen, 1999) who found no evidence of selective attention in any direction using words in social anxiety, despite finding effects in trait anxiety on the same task. Similarly Sposari and Rapee (2007) showed attentional selection favouring faces over objects, regardless of expression and this was replicated in a second study. Pishyar, Harris, and Menzies (2004) found a classic emotion-congruent pattern of bias to negative faces in subclincially high social anxiety and toward positive faces in a low group. No bias to "external" threat (face stimuli) was reported by Pineles and Mineka (2005) but they did find a bias favouring "internal" threat (waveform pictures of participants' own heart rate).

Thus, many questions remain about attention to emotional information in this specific form of psychopathology. These include the presence of attentional biases at all, the direction of them when found and their level of content specificity (faces, emotional faces or negative emotional faces). These mixed data also raise the question of whether other specific pathologies would present similar patterns of inconsistency were they to be investigated to a similar degree. Alternatively, social anxiety may be a special and anomalous case, possibly due to a complex interaction between the facial stimuli used and the unique socially focused pathology of this disorder. Investigations across a wider range of socially relevant and irrelevant stimuli (beyond faces) would be one sensible way to move this area forward.

## AUTOMATICITY: AWARENESS

Subliminal masked stimulus presentations have been widely used in psychopathology populations, with data converging on the conclusion that attentional biases in anxiety operate at early automatic stages of processing (Mogg, Bradley, & Hallowell, 1994; Mogg et al., 1995) even when the more stringent "objective threshold" (see Cheeseman & Merikle,

1985) is used to determine levels of awareness. In a recent study of this issue Hunt, Keogh, and French (2006) found that high levels of physical anxiety sensitivity were associated with attentional vigilance for related masked and unmasked words. Overall the data provide convincing support for the idea that trait-anxiety-related attentional bias proceeds below the level of awareness. This conclusion has been confirmed by the meta-analysis of Bar-Haim et al. (2007), who reported significantly larger effects for subliminal than supraliminal attentional biases in single cuing tasks.

## AUTOMATICITY: TIME COURSE OF EFFECTS

The duration for which cues are presented prior to target appearance (stimulus onset asynchrony; SOA) has proven a critical parameter because this determines the instant at which inferences are made about the allocation of attention. Systematically varying SOA allows a more complete picture of attention allocation across time.

In a normal sample Cooper and Langton (2006) contrasted 100 ms and 500 ms cue durations, arguing that selective attention to threat may be faster in this population than in those with psychopathology and, indeed, results showed vigilance for threat faces compared to neutral (and neutral compared to happy) at the shorter duration. Short cue duration was also critical to demonstrating selective attention towards threat in Holmes, Green, and Vuillemier's study (2005). They found attentional biases toward fearful compared to neutral faces but only at 30 ms and 100 ms, not (in a later experiment) at 500 ms or 1000 ms. Thus, although not yet extensive in number, studies to date mostly converge on the conclusion that normal individuals display a selective visuospatial bias favouring threat, providing attention is probed early enough.

In contrast, several studies have found evidence of persisting attentional vigilance to threat throughout the first second or so in high-anxious samples. Studies have reported vigilance for threat in anxiety anywhere between 100 and 1500 ms SOA (Bradley, Mogg, Falla, & Hamilton, 1998; Mogg, Bradley, De Bono, & Painter, 1997; see also Derryberry & Reed, 2002, under single cuing below). Often vigilance seems to wane somewhat as SOA lengthens (Lee & Shafran, 2008). Few studies have found evidence for the hypothesised trait-anxiety-related vigilance followed by strategic avoidance pattern of attentional orienting[1] (although some eye-movement studies do: for example Pflugshaupt et al., 2005; Rohner, 2004; as do two double-cuing studies: Mogg, Bradley, Miles, & Dixon, 2004; Koster,

---

1 Note that this is a chronological pattern of vigilance and avoidance proposed in the literature to account for the apparent absence of anxiety-related biases in more strategic cognitive processes such as explicit memory (Mathews & MacLeod, 1994). It is distinct from the vigilance-avoidance hypothesis related to threat intensity discussed earlier.

Verschuere, Crombez, & Van Damme, 2005). As mentioned above, time course appears particularly important in depression-related attentional biases, where only long cue-exposure durations (around 1 second) elicit selective attention toward negative information.

There are important differences between attention and psychopathology researchers in the interpretation of these time-course effects. In mainstream attention endogenous or controlled attention is considered to take effect after around 50 ms, whereas 100 ms is still considered relatively early and indicative of automaticity (although not absence of awareness) within the field of emotion and attention. Similarly, while in the field of emotion and attention, durations of around 1000 ms are thought necessary for controlled processes to become active, in studies from mainstream attention endogenous effects seem to have dissipated by this point. These discrepant assumptions may in part be due to the temporal delay inherent in the processing of perceptually and semantically rich emotional material, but this remains subject to empirical verification.

*Evaluation*

Double cuing is probably the most widely used technique to investigate attention to emotion. This is probably because: (i) it allows the specific inference that selective attention to threat in preference to non-threat occurred; and (ii) it is not susceptible to many alternative interpretations that dog other tasks, such as response bias (a neutral response to a neutral stimulus is required) or general performance inefficiencies (detection is *speeded* by threat).

There are, of course, limits to the information we can glean from attentional probe research. For example, it only provides us with an isolated picture, or several discrete "snapshots" of the deployment of attention at the time of probe presentation. Although attentional resources may be devoted to processing emotional stimuli at the probed point in time, we cannot generalise beyond this, and cannot know the patterns of orienting before or after probing. For example the often used 500 ms is ample time to make several shifts in the direction of attention. As SOA lengthens further the degree of experimental control of attention deployment inevitably wanes.

Finally, although probe studies do suggest enhanced attentional processing of emotional material, they provide little information about the likely mechanisms behind this. For example, are these stimuli more effective at capturing anxious participants' attention, or is it their ability to maintain attention, or perhaps both, which produces the reaction-time effects on neutral probes? Such questions have prompted the development of the single cuing paradigm, to be discussed in the next section.

## Single cuing

### Method

The move from double to single cuing methods was triggered by the intellectual desire for greater specificity about the mechanisms underlying attentional effects of emotional material. This shift mirrors the conceptual distinction made earlier between selection and orienting. "Selection" refers to the attention system singling out stimuli for further processing, whereas "orienting" implicates the putative spatial mechanisms by which selection occurs. Double cuing traditionally uses the logic that if task performance is facilitated at one location, attention must have already been located there. However, it usually remains unclear whether effects are due to the ability of the emotional stimulus to capture attention or to hold attention once it has been captured, or both. This distinction corresponds to that already described between engaging attention to a location and disengaging attention from a location (see Concepts) and from now on I will use these more precise terms in preference to "capture" and "hold". The shift component could be thought to correspond to the concept of attentional "scanning" of the environment (Eysenck, 1992; Eysenck et al., 2007) and has yet to be explored within cuing methods.

#### PERIPHERAL CUING

The single cuing method uses two critical comparisons to determine engagement and disengagement respectively. On valid[2] trials a neutral probe task appears in the location of the preceding cue and we can infer that, at least for short cue durations, the speed of performing this task reflects the speed of engagement to the cued location. Thus, differences between valid emotional and neutral cued trials are taken to reflect differences in the engagement of attention to the emotional content of the cue. Conversely, on invalid trials the task appears in the opposite location to the cue, requiring disengagement of attention and re-orienting toward the task location. Thus, differences between different types of cue on invalid trials should reflect the relative ease of disengaging attention from the cues' respective content.

The first studies presented peripheral cues for 500 ms on the assumption that this would be the optimally sensitive time to examine anxiety-related differences, given the previous literature. However, some reports of generally speeded reaction times to invalid compared to valid trials (e.g.,

---

2 I use the terms "valid" (or "invalid") throughout to denote trials on which targets appear at cued (or opposite cued) locations, irrespective of predictive validity (i.e., the overall ratio within the task of valid to invalid trials). This usage is debated among attention researchers.

Waters, Nitz, Craske, & Johnson, 2007) have suggested that attention may have already disengaged the cued location by the time of probing at 500 ms (depending on the type of stimulus material used), and that inhibition of return[3] may be already taking effect (see below). Shorter cue durations have therefore been preferred in later studies so that effects can more unambiguously be attributed to early attentional cuing phenomena.

Although attentional search tasks have also been taken to reflect attentional capture (i.e., engagement), this inference is not as clean as with the single cuing method (but see also related problems with single cuing to be discussed later). This is due to the presence of multiple (sometimes emotional) distracters, such that speed of target detection in visual search could be a combination of engagement to target and disengagement from distracters.

CENTRAL CUEING

Some authors have argued that both single and double cueing are, for a priori reasons, unlikely to be sensitive to differences in engagement when those differences rely on content or meaning of cues. Sudden visual onsets are likely to attract attention irrespective of content, which may render the meaning contained in the cue powerless to influence probe reaction times. Disengagement from a cue is, on the other hand, far more likely to be influenced by content especially where cue duration allows discrimination (supra- or subliminally) of differences in cue content.

To provide a potentially more sensitive test of engagement differences, central cuing using eye gaze has been adapted to test for differences in psychopathology. Mathews, Fox, Yiend, and Calder (2003) used face cues varying in both emotional expression, and direction of eye gaze (rightward/ leftward). These were followed by letter targets on the left or right. Subclinically anxious participants were faster to detect a target if it followed a valid fearful face cue (i.e., when the gaze direction had indicated the location of the target). This clearly implies differential engagement at the location of a potential (but not actual) threat, since the target always appears at a location signalled by, but not the same as, the eye-gaze threat cue. The same group have replicated this result showing that high-trait-anxious participants showed an enhanced orienting to the gaze-cued location of faces with fearful expressions relative to all other expressions (Fox, Mathews, Calder, & Yiend, 2007b). Similar effects have

---

3 The phenomenon identified by Posner (1980) such that cued locations lose their attentional advantage after a certain time has elapsed, becoming inhibited relative to uncued locations. The effect is thought to represent an adaptive attentional mechanism whereby novel locations are prioritised for attentional processing over recently attended ones.

been found comparing high and low state anxiety (Holmes, Richards, & Green, 2006).

One innovative variation on the double cuing technique (above) adds a neutral–neutral baseline to allow inferences to be made about engagement and disengagement of attention to emotion. Trials involving critical threat/neutral stimulus pairs can be compared to baseline neutral/neutral pairs (not traditionally included in double-cuing attentional probe studies). Detection speed of probes replacing threat on the critical trials compared to baseline is taken to reflect relative speed of engagement to threat, whereas the same comparison when probes replace non-threat on critical trials reflects disengagement. This variation on double cuing has provided some important convergent evidence implicating impaired disengaging of attention from emotional information.

Koster and colleagues (Koster, Crombez, Verschuere, & De Houwer, 2004b) were the first to describe this variation, finding attentional bias for mild and severe threat pictures in the general population. Further work using this design has led to similar conclusions. Salemink, van den Hout, and Kindt (2007) found that trait anxiety was associated with disengagement, but not engagement, of attention and Koster and colleagues (2006) repeated their earlier study with a selected high- and low-anxious population. They reported that for severe threat shown at cue durations of 100 ms, high-anxious groups showed both speeded engagement and slowed disengagement relative to low.

A second variation, which can be used with single or double cuing, is that of gaze-contingent masking (Duchowski, Cournia, & Murphy, 2004; Loschky & McConkie, 2002; Reingold, Loschky, McConkie, & Stampe, 2003). This represents an important recent advance in the field of attention and emotion, because it allows a definitive separation of covert and overt phenomena. Covert attention does not involve eye movements and is thought to precede and direct overt attention, which comprises purely saccades and fixations (Hoffman, 1998; Wu & Remington, 2003). The single cuing methods described above derive from those within mainstream attention research, which placed great importance on the role of covert attention in driving the effects reported. Gaze-contingent masking involves masking a stimulus when a saccade towards it is initiated, so that overt attending to the item is impossible. Inferences about covert attentional effects can therefore be more confidently made. This provides a more sophisticated alternative to recording eye movements on a trial-by-trial basis and subsequently excluding those involving saccades and has been used to investigate attention to emotion by Calvo and colleagues (e.g., Calvo & Eysenck, 2008; Calvo & Nummenmaa, 2007).

*The general population*

Limited evidence from healthy samples to date suggests that both mechanisms are influenced by emotional salience. The studies of Stormark and colleagues were among the first to use single cuing in the general population (e.g., Stormark, Morten, & Hugdahl, 1996; Stormark, Nordby, & Hugdahl, 1995). They used classical conditioning to impart emotional salience to location cues and found faster reaction times (RTs) to validly cued targets, but only with emotion words as cues. Koster and colleagues (Koster, Crombez, Van Damme, Verschuere, & De Houwer, 2004a) used aversively conditioned neutral stimuli and reported straightforward evidence for facilitated engagement and impaired disengagement from threat compared to neutral information. Koster, Verschuere, Burssens, Custers, and Crombez (2007) replicated this using single cuing with emotional images, finding both facilitated engagement and impaired disengagement.

*Psychopathology populations*

Fox, Russo, Bowles, and Dutton (2001) and Yiend and Mathews (2001) were among the first to find support for the biased disengagement of attention using peripheral cuing (see also an earlier study by Derryberry & Reed, 1994). Single cues (faces or pictures) were presented briefly followed by a target in the same or different locations. There were no anxiety-related differences when targets followed in the same location as the cues, but only when threatening cues were followed by targets in a different location. This implies that there were no differences in engagement, but that anxious individuals were slower to disengage attention from the threatening stimuli in order to find the target elsewhere.

Since then several further studies have reported similar effects implicating impaired disengaging of attention as the major contributor to anxiety-related attentional bias for threat. Fox, Russo, and Dutton (2002) using angry, happy and neutral facial expressions as peripheral cues, found slowed disengagement for both emotions in high trait anxiety. Amir, Elias, Klumpp, and Przeworski (2003) reported similar effects in social phobia for social threat words, as did Waters et al. (2007) in a specific replication of Yiend and Mathews (2001).

*Conceptual inferences*

SPECIFICITY: STIMULI

*(a) Intensity.* Koster and colleagues (2004a) argued that the lack of evidence for threat-related attentional orienting effects in control groups and in healthy volunteers may be attributable to studies using stimuli of insufficient threat value. Koster and colleagues (2007) used exogenous cuing with

emotional images (neutral, severe and mild threat), finding both facilitated engagement and impaired disengagement. Consistent with double-cuing studies, selective attention to threat in their normal sample was limited to severe threat and short durations (100 ms, although not 28 ms, which was attributed to inherent processing limits on complex scenes). Both facilitated engagement and impaired disengagement were reported, and by cue durations of 200 ms there was some evidence of inhibition. This study is consistent with the overall pattern of vigilance and avoidance to threat being mediated by intensity and duration, as discussed above in relation to double cuing. It also underlines that it is essential to take into consideration both the intensity of threat and the time point at which attention is probed in future studies of patterns of selective attention to emotion.

AUTOMATICITY: TIME COURSE OF EFFECTS

As with double cuing, the duration of single-cue presentation is critical. Derryberry and Reed (2002) found the expected trait-anxiety-related effects at an SOA of 250 ms, which were relatively reduced at 500 ms. Lengthening presentation time has allowed the investigation of inhibitory effects of emotion on attention. Inhibition of return (IOR; Posner & Cohen, 1984) refers to the phenomenon whereby the reaction-time advantage produced by valid cuing reverses to become a disadvantage (relative to no cuing) at longer post-cue intervals (typically > 300 ms and up to 3000 ms; Posner & Cohen, 1984). This is thought to make attentional selection adaptive and efficient by biasing it away from recently selected locations, toward novel ones. Stoyanova, Pratt, and Anderson (2007) used fear and neutral face cues with durations ranging from 500 to 1500 ms. The cued location was always slowed compared to the uncued and never modulated by fearful expression, leading the authors to conclude that IOR is triggered by event onsets and not influenced by the affective meaning of those events. Fox et al. (2002) increased cue–target SOA to elicit inhibition of return. Angry faces eliminated the effect for all participants and, in a separate experiment, threat-related and ambiguous stimuli elicited less inhibition in high-trait-anxiety participants. However, not all results have found anxiety-related differences in inhibition of return (e.g., Yiend & Mathews, 2001, Experiment 3). Reduced IOR effects have also been found in depression. Leyman and colleagues (Leyman, De Raedt, Schacht, & Koster, 2007) compared depressed patients with healthy controls using angry and neutral peripheral cues presented for 1000 ms and reported reduced IOR for anger in patients, consistent with earlier conclusions concerning attention and depression.

*Evaluation*

The current research suggests that both engagement and disengagement differences are seen in attention to emotional material and that both mechanisms are implicated in biased attention in psychopathology. While many cuing studies have argued that disengagement of attention is the primary spatial attentional mechanism underlying previously reported emotion-congruent anxiety effects in attention, the evidence regarding engagement remains equivocal and few studies have used sufficiently short cue durations to allow maximum sensitivity to engagement differences. Furthermore, the data from visual search tasks (see above) appears to implicate processes more akin to speeded engagement, which should not be ignored. More studies specifically examining engagement differences are clearly warranted both in psychopathology and the general population.

The circumstances under which engagement and/or disengagement effects are seen may be complex. For example, both processes could involve orienting to content and, separately, to location. This has yet to be fully explored. Current data have found disengagement effects when content and location converge (as when a location of actual, recent threat must be disengaged). In contrast, engagement effects have been most obviously demonstrated when threat may not actually be present. Future work could explore this distinction more systematically.

The single cuing method to investigate mechanisms of attention to emotional material has generated much research interest since it was introduced. However, this has also highlighted an important weakness of the method. The critical effect can sometimes be confounded by a general interference effect, to which psychopathology groups are prone. Mogg and colleagues (Mogg, Holmes, Garner, & Bradley, 2008) have explored this problem in some detail. Specifically, processing is usually slower and more error prone in the presence of emotionally negative information (e.g., Pereira et al., 2006) and psychopathology groups tend to show similar interference effects but to a significantly greater degree than controls (e.g., Yiend & Mathews, 2001). Thus, if the psychopathology group is significantly slowed on all trials involving negative cues, then this generic slowdown may artificially enhance apparently slowed disengagement from (and reduce speeded engagement to) negativity in the same group.

There are currently at least two responses to this problem. The first is that not all studies find these generic interference group differences, thus bypassing the issue. The second is to treat the interference and spatial attentional effects as additive and to control for the former by subtraction (discussed in Mogg et al., 2008). A third, yet to be specified solution, is for researchers to devise a new experimental method that does not rely on selective impairments on negatively valenced trials. While the examination of error rates rather than reaction times may hold promise there appears to be an inherent limitation on the level of errors generated by cuing designs.

## Multiple task: Attentional blink

*Method*

In the attentional-blink task, participants have to report two sequential targets in a rapid stream of stimuli (called rapid serial visual presentation; RSVP). If the targets (T1 presented first followed by T2 presented second) are sufficiently close in presentation time to each other (typically a few hundred milliseconds apart) then the second (T2) is often missed. The "attentional blink" refers to the finding that the efficiency of detection of T2 is modulated by the time interval (lag) between T1 and T2, which is often defined in terms of the number of intervening stimuli in the presentation stream (Raymond, Shapiro, & Arnell, 1992). When T2 detection is plotted against lag a characteristic attenuation in T2 detection (or "blink" of attention) can be seen. This phenomenon is thought to stem from an overinvestment of attentional resources in stimulus processing (Olivers & Nieuwenhuis, 2006). Missing T2 is thought to occur because resources are still deployed in processing and therefore insufficient resources are still available at the time of T2 to allow it to be identified.

In emotional adaptations of this task it is crucial to be clear about the precise nature of the emotional manipulation. This is because predictions vary depending on when the emotional information is presented (e.g., at T1 or T2) and extant studies differ markedly. The most typical emotional adaptation of this task is to look at the effect of neutral targets identified at T1 on emotional versus neutral targets identified at T2. Under these conditions an attenuated attentional blink would be expected when T2 was emotional and therefore capable of commanding greater attentional resources. An alternative is to examine the differential effect of identifying emotional versus neutral targets at T1 on neutral T2 identification. If emotional information processing consumes additional capacity, as might be expected, the attentional blink should be enhanced when emotional information is processed at T1.

*The general population*

A few studies have examined affective modulation of the emotional attentional-blink phenomenon in the general population. For example, Keil and Ihssen (2004) looked at the effect of pleasant, unpleasant and neutral words presented at T2. Both emotional categories enhanced accuracy of T2 identification, especially at short lags, although not when emotional information rated low on arousal was used. Similarly, Anderson (2005) found the attentional blink was reduced when emotional words were presented at T2, even when other factors related to differential distinctiveness were controlled. He also reported that the enhanced attentional effects were attributable to the arousal rather than the valence of the emotional information.

In the emotional RSVP studies of Most and colleagues (also called "attentional rubbernecking"; Most, Smith, Cooter, Levy, & Zald, 2007) only one target has to be reported and the effects on detection accuracy when it is preceded by an emotional stimulus are compared to those of a preceding neutral stimulus (strictly speaking, then, this does not involve multiple tasks). These authors used series of pictures presented at 100 ms per item and asked participants to identify the orientation of one rotated image among a stream of upright ones. Accuracy dropped when targets appeared after emotional compared to non-emotional images (Most, Chun, Johnson, & Kiehl, 2006; Most, Chun, Widders, & Zald, 2005). Presumably this was as a result of the spontaneous attentional salience of the emotion, rather than as a result of purposeful attention to T1 (given that only T2 had to be identified). The same group has reported similar effects with arousing positive stimuli (Most et al., 2007) and stimuli made negative through aversive conditioning (Smith, Most, Newsome, & Zald, 2006). Others have reported similar, albeit smaller, effects using emotional and neutral words (Arnell, Killman, & Fijavz, 2007).

Most recently Most and Junge (2008) reported intriguing *retroactive* effects of unpleasant images on neutral target images. Specifically, they found that target detection accuracy was impaired even when the emotional distracter image appeared on the display *after* the target. A similar result was reported by de Jong and Martens (2007), in which anger at T2 interfered with happy identification at T1. These results are consistent with an iconic memory account of the attentional blink, whereby representations of sequential presentations can briefly co-exist and mutually interfere. Thus, biased competition of transient representations again could provide the basis of an explanation for these phenomena.

*Psychopathology populations*

Emotional variations of the attentional blink have now been used in several studies of psychopathology. In one of the first Rokke and colleagues (Rokke, Arnell, Koch, & Andrews, 2002) looked at low, mild and severe dysphoria in a carefully controlled experiment. There were no group differences when reporting single targets, but with two targets separated by less than 500 ms an attentional blink occurred as expected. This blink was significantly larger and longer for the severe dysphoric group. Although revealing mood-related attentional impairments, importantly these data are not able to speak to emotion-congruent effects, as emotional information was not examined. However Koster, De Raedt, Tibboel, De Jong, and Verschuere (2009) did use emotional words in selected high and low dysphoric groups. Within a 300 ms window T2 identification was impaired by negative words presented at T1 in the high dysphorics suggesting an enhanced attentional blink. This stands in contrast to work on depression and attention from other methods given the relatively short time period available for stimulus processing.

The attentional blink has been examined more widely in relation to anxiety. Fox, Russo, and Georgiou (2005) manipulated the valence of T2 and found that low trait and state anxious individuals showed a strong blink effect for fearful and happy faces, whereas in high trait anxiety for fearful expressions the blink was significantly reduced. This is consistent with the general pattern throughout this review of an anxiety-related attentional salience of fear and in this particular technique can be interpreted as an effect of reduced inhibition of threat. Barnard, Ramponi, Battye, and Mackintosh (2005) have reported similar findings whereby state-anxious participants showed a larger blink than non-anxious for threatening word distracters presented at T1. Contrasting with these data, de Jong and Martens (2007) failed to find any exacerbation of the attentional blink for happy and angry faces in selected high and low socially anxious participants. This is a further example of attentional effects in social anxiety not conforming to the wider anxiety literature. Finally Trippe and colleagues (Trippe, Hewig, Heydel, Hecht, & Miltner, 2007) examined the attentional blink in spider phobia but using neutral T1 targets and varying the content of T2. All participants showed a reduced attentional blink for emotional (positive and negative) T2 targets. Spider phobics, however, showed a particularly attenuated attentional blink for spider stimuli, detecting these at T2 more frequently than all other T2 targets.

*Evaluation*

The direction of the effect of emotional information on the attentional blink critically depends on the type of emotional manipulation carried out. Emotional information can act to either enhance or attenuate the blink dependent on whether it is identified (or in some studies merely presented) at the first or second target. Current research suggests that emotional information significantly modulates the attentional blink. It also suggests that emotional information recruits extra attentional resources during these tasks, consistent with the pattern of attentional biases seen in other paradigms. Such effects have been found both in general samples and exacerbated in psychopathology samples. Studies using this technique are relatively new to the field and replication and extension of their findings will be important. When participants perform more than one similar task at once limited processing capacities must be distributed across the tasks. Multiple tasks are therefore ideally placed to investigate the automaticity of emotion processing, specifically whether and to what extent resources are consumed.

## DISCUSSION

### Attention to emotion in the general population

In some paradigms, such as dichotic listening and emotional Stroop, there is very little extant data from the general population. Indeed the data from visual search methods in this group far outweighs that from any other paradigm. These data suggest that pre-attentive "pop out" of negative information (in its strictest sense) does not occur, but that search for negative information is significantly faster and more efficient than that for neutral. Findings have mostly been based on facial-expression stimuli, either schematic or pictorial, but other stimuli of biological relevance elicit similar patterns of speeded search. It will be important to gain convergent evidence for these conclusions and avoid relying entirely on a single technique.

Cuing studies are starting to provide converging evidence confirming the existence of attentional biases towards threat information in the general population. These studies have identified two critical conditions that appear necessary for their detection in these samples. One is stimulus threat level, which must be "sufficiently" high. Although this has yet to be quantified, biologically-relevant stimuli seem to fall above the threshold, as do high negative valence, high-arousal photographic images. There are also suggestions from the literature of adaptive avoidance of mild threat, but whether these characterise low vulnerability or are characteristic of the normal population as a whole awaits confirmation. A second factor is the chronological point at which attention is probed. Selective orienting in the general population occurs quickly, most current data suggesting around 100 ms.

Added to this there is strong evidence that facilitated engagement (assuming that visual search, as well as cuing, reflects a process of attentional engagement) and preliminary evidence that impaired disengagement contribute to the effects of negative material on orienting. As yet there is little evidence for emotion-related effects on inhibitory function, although this has rarely been explored in the general population. A cluster of multiple-task studies using RSVP, while still relatively young, have yielded important insights. These suggest that emotional material, both positive and negative, biases attentional resource deployment, producing an exacerbated attentional ("emotional") blink. Interestingly (according to current accounts of the attentional-blink phenomenon), this suggests that attentional resources are preferentially deployed towards emotional information and therefore that attention to emotion is not "automatic" in the sense of being capacity free.

Most other aspects of automaticity remain to be explored. While some data (mostly visual search) do suggest fast, efficient processing of negative emotion-relevant information this does not seem to occur in parallel in the strictest sense. There is no consistent body of work systematically addressing whether attention to negativity occurs without awareness (which has, though, been extensively explored in psychopathology) or whether attentional effects are amenable to intentional (or non-intentional) control. Similarly, we have yet to fully address stimulus specificity by identifying whether valence, arousal, discrete categories of emotion or some other dimension (e.g., biological relevance) best characterises the nature of the stimuli eliciting preferential attention. Other specificity effects, such as those across different modalities are only just beginning to be explored (Van Damme, Gallace, Spence, & Moseley, 2009).

## Attention to emotion in psychopathology populations

In psychopathology, the emotional Stroop and cuing techniques have together provided a considerable body of work. Both techniques have revealed emotion-congruent biases showing a high degree of stimulus content and psychopathology-related specificity. Biased attention is strongest towards material matching the concerns of the individual, an effect that seems to trump the valence of the material itself. In depression there is ambiguity over whether findings are driven by attenuation of attention to positivity or facilitation to negativity, with current evidence suggestive of both. Biases in anxiety-related disorders and related subclinical traits occur early, subliminally, and under circumstances of attentional competition. There is little evidence supporting strategic opposition of attentional bias in anxiety. Rather, the attentional salience of emotion-congruent material appears to persist across time, eventually waning in strength. Attentional biases in depression-related disorders and traits have now been reliably found, providing task parameters allow sufficient time (usually around 1 s or more) for elaborative stimulus processing. This relatively new empirical development remains consistent with recent theoretical models (Mathews & Mackintosh, 1998; Mogg & Bradley, 1998; Williams et al., 1997).

While cuing studies largely support these conclusions, they have also added significantly to understanding the putative mechanisms driving biases, by implicating impaired disengagement from and (sometimes) facilitated engagement to congruent material. While initial studies suggested that disengagement may be the primary mechanism, later work has confirmed that engagement is also involved. In particular this conclusion is supported by findings using central cuing and visual search, both of which could be exploited further in psychopathology populations. It is possible, however, given the pattern of current data, that visual search (specifically) is for some reason less sensitive to subclinical differences in attention to emotion, and that the dearth of psychopathology-related literature in fact masks a quantity of null findings. Peripheral-cuing studies need careful interpretation when there are general between-group differences in response speed to emotional information. However, these potential interpretative problems are not inevitable, nor insurmountable. One significant challenge for future work will be to address these and, in so doing, either validate or refute the current findings. There is no doubt that examination of spatial-orienting mechanisms represents one of the most significant areas of progress within this field in recent years.

There are several additional areas of potential future productive research. One is examination of attentional inhibition in depression using, for example, peripheral cuing or negative priming. Social anxiety continues to be an anomaly with quite contradictory accounts of the direction of attentional effects, necessitating further work to resolve. As with the general population, many aspects of automaticity remain to be systematically examined. Subliminal emotional Stroop and cuing studies suggest that anxiety-related attentional biases proceed in the absence of awareness, with the latter methodology revealing this most convincingly. In contrast, attentional-blink data suggest this bias involves differential deployment of resources. Whether attentional bias is amenable to intentional (or non-intentional) control has not been directly investigated although the proven ability to experimentally modify attentional biases would suggest this is likely to be the case (Koster, Fox, & MacLeod, 2009; Pury, 2002).

## Comparative conclusions

To sum up I will consider some broader conclusions in three main areas: the samples under study; the empirical findings; and theoretical implications. Starting with the samples, it will be clear from this review that there is a significantly stronger history of behavioural research on attention to emotion within psychopathology than within the general population. However, over recent years wider interest in emotion processing generally has led to a correspondingly increasing quantity of behavioural data. As a result these populations have been investigated largely in parallel, with little consideration given to the relationship between them. Let us consider for a moment what the nature of this relationship is (see Figure 7.1).

As shown in Figure 7.1, we can loosely identify three distinct populations, A, B and C. Area C represents "psychopathology". These individuals could comprise either non-clinical samples selected based on being above some threshold on a continuum of trait vulnerability, or clinical samples, selected by diagnosis, who would, by definition, fall within this upper-threshold range of the relevant trait (e.g., trait anxiety in the case of generalised anxiety disorder). Area A represents so called "healthy" control groups used as comparisons in studies of psychopathology. These individuals are selected in a similar fashion, but below a lower threshold on the given trait, or are likely to be so by virtue of rigorous screening for the absence of any diagnostic indicators. Areas A and C, therefore, reflect the samples being compared in most studies of psychopathology.

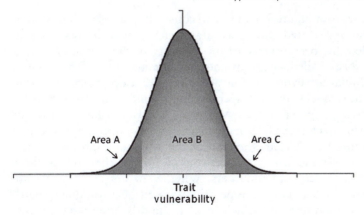

*Figure 7.1* The relationship between population trait vulnerabilities and study sampling and selection in attention to emotional information. The figure shows a histogram of a typical normally distributed personality trait measure, of the sort commonly administered or used for selection in studies of attention to emotional information. Area A represents low vulnerability, here illustrated as <1.5 standard deviations below the population mean. Area B represents the majority of the population (here termed the "general population"), illustrated as ±1.5 standard deviations from the population mean. Area C represents high vulnerability, illustrated as >1.5 standard deviations above the population mean.

In contrast, studies of the general population are represented in Figure 7.1 by area B. These studies can be more difficult to interpret, if the sample is not well characterised. For present purposes a "well-characterised" sample means obtaining participant scores on relevant measures of trait vulnerability at the time of testing. One such measure is neuroticism, a general scale indicative of levels of vulnerability to a wide range of psychopathology. Providing scores fall close to the population mean or within some predefined window around it (such as 2 standard deviations), a sample will reflect "average" or "typical" vulnerability and, correspondingly, "typical" performance on attentional processing of emotional information. Although often termed "unselected", this is not strictly true of these samples since some selection, in the form of screening out extreme scorers, has usually taken place. In practice, many studies do now routinely screen or incorporate relevant individual-difference measures of psychopathology-related traits (in particular many of those reviewed above) and it remains essential that researchers of attention to emotional information continue to do so, to allow clean inferences to be made. Conversely, those primarily interested in psychopathology should not overlook the potential importance of main-effect findings, which could reflect global differences in attention to emotional material. It is hoped that by considering both perspectives within this review that mutual benefit will result.

It is also clear from Figure 7.1 that low-vulnerable samples from studies of psychopathology-related differences (area A) cannot be assumed to accurately reflect the performance of the majority of the population (area B), since they form a distinct group and may (or may not) differ. Indeed there is accumulating evidence for attentional biases in the opposite direction to those associated with psychopathology including the avoidance of mild negativity (e.g., Yiend & Mathews, 2001) or the selection of positivity (Joormann et al., 2007). These may serve an important protective function and more detailed investigation of the attentional profile of low-vulnerability samples needs to be conducted to further characterise these potentially protective cognitive markers. Whether or not some biases are actively protective is becoming an especially relevant question due to work on cognitive-bias modification, which seeks to modify attentional processing in an attempt to improve psychopathology and reduce vulnerability. If low vulnerability is associated with its own set of protective biases, then modification work may wish to adopt a more ambitious set of targets for influencing cognition (see Koster et al., 2009, for the most recent discussion of the current status of bias-modification work).

Turning to the empirical data that have been reviewed, what key messages can be gleaned about attention to emotional material in general and psychopathology-related populations? In both there is sufficient evidence to draw the basic conclusion that emotional, and particularly negative, information elicits selective attentional priority over non-emotional and, in so doing, commands additional attentional resources. In both there is evidence that this bias proceeds automatically in some senses; in general samples the information is located faster (although not showing strict "pop out") and in psychopathology-related samples material presented below the level of conscious awareness can elicit biased attention. The inevitability of attention has occasionally been assessed in behavioural paradigms by measuring the extent of processing of unattended stimuli using negative priming (e.g., Grison, Tipper, & Hewitt, 2005; Joormann, 2004; Tipper, 1985, 2004; Tipper & Cranston, 1985). Other aspects of automaticity, require much further exploration in both populations, most notably control (e.g., Yiend et al., 2008) and capacity (e.g., Okon-Singer, Tzelgov, & Henik, 2008).

What features about biased attention toward emotion distinguish the two populations? Two points stand out at present, the intensity of emotional material involved and the time course over which attention is probed. First, psychopathology-related samples appear to show biased attention to negative emotional material at any level of intensity, whereas the general population seems to require somewhat higher intensity levels before selective attention is elicited. Second, while psychopathology-related samples show attentional biases across a range of stages of attentional processing, early and later, general samples seem to be subject to a narrower window of influence, falling early in the processing stream.

These differences suggest that what we observe in psychopathology is a more enduring and more easily activated form of a single common effect of valence on attentional processing, rather than some qualitative difference in the operation of attentional systems per se.

Finally, where does the field stand with respect to models of biased attentional processing? First, the above view suggests that recent models devised to explain psychopathology-related effects may be appropriate, with some modification, at a more general population level. Second, these models place differences in an "evaluative system" at the heart of attentional biases to emotional material (Mathews & Mackintosh, 1998; Mogg & Bradley, 1998). This stands in contrast to earlier models, which emphasised differential direction of resource allocation (Williams et al., 1997). It suggests that attentional response to emotional material is essentially similar across psychopathology and normal functioning (consistent with the empirical conclusions above) but that what differs is the degree to which that material is perceived as emotional prior to selective attention. Accounting for biased attention to emotion in this way, by reference to differences in "evaluation", remains consistent with currently favoured biased-competition approaches to explaining mainstream attentional selection. These evaluative differences may be one of many potential biasing factors operating in a "bottom-up" fashion. It is also the case that biases in attention to emotion shown by the general population warrant more explicit consideration within mainstream attentional theorising.

The next theoretical challenge is to define the proposed "evaluator". On the basis of the data reviewed here this evaluator must be acting at the very earliest stages of pre-attentive processing. The question is how and on what basis is the evaluation conducted? Must it necessarily rely on low-level perceptual characteristics associated with valence and if so what are these characteristics? To start to answer these questions requires applying and extending existing frameworks from within cognitive psychology. Primary visual perception is followed by pattern and object recognition. These specialties within cognitive psychology describe how the incoming information is parsed, grouped and ultimately identified as discrete objects and categories within the visual field. Humphreys and Bruce's (1989) influential framework proposed object recognition to comprise perceptual classification followed by semantic classification and naming; distinctions remaining widely accepted today. The "valence evaluator" black box in the models discussed above could therefore be conceived as performing a type of object recognition, which identifies information of valenced or hedonic tone. *Perceptual classification, semantic classification* or both could therefore be the source of biases at the valence-evaluation stage. Perceptual classification, according to current theories (e.g., Bruce & Young, 1986; Bruce & Green, 1990; Burton & Bruce, 1992), involves structural encoding, which uses structural descriptions (sets of verbal propositions) that specify individual structural elements and how they combine to make the whole. These perceptual-structural descriptions are compared to structural descriptions stored within memory, allowing perceptual classification of the object to occur. After this semantic information is accessed. Semantic classification involves accessing stored propositional knowledge about objects and their categories and associating it with incoming perceptual signals. Empirically separating perceptual from semantic classification to identify the locus of biased classification of valence will be key to future theoretical understanding of the process of valence evaluation.

Existing evidence already bears on this question. Many studies now suggest a perceptual basis to attentional biases toward emotion. Emotional stimulus content specifically enhances perceptual processing (Calvo & Nummenmaa, 2007, 2008; Calvo, Nummenmaa, & Hyönä, 2007; Zeelenberg, Wagenmakers, & Rotteveel, 2006), in particular contrast sensitivity (Phelps et al., 2006). Some studies point to the importance of individual perceptual features. For example, eye regions (Fox & Damjanovic, 2006) and eyebrows (Lundqvist & Ohman, 2005) isolated from their corresponding facial expressions have still been found to produce superior detection effects. However, perceptual classification comprises not only identifying individual features but also configural information: information about the arrangement of these features (a distinction widely used within the face-processing literature). Some work suggests that correct configuration is needed in order for perceptual classification of valence to occur. For example, presenting a mouth alone eliminates the speeded detection of "angry" faces in some studies (Fox et al., 2000; although see Experiment 4 in Öhman et al., 2001b, for contradictory results) and face inversion (known from face-processing studies to disrupt configural information, while retaining fundamental low-level perceptual features) has a similar effect (Fox et al., 2000; Lamy, Amunts, & Bar-Haim, 2008). Further evidence of the importance of perceptual classification comes from Calvo and colleagues, who have carried out considerable work on perceptual sensitivity using signal-detection analyses to quantify recognition accuracy for briefly presented foveal, parafoveal and peripheral emotional stimuli. Their findings suggest improved sensitivity for negative emotional information in faces (Calvo & Esteves, 2005), images (Calvo, 2006) and words (Calvo & Castillo, 2005; Calvo, Castillo, & Fuentes, 2006), which extends beyond the immediate foveal region. Finally, consistent with the involvement of semantic classification, subjective ratings of such features has been shown to reveal emotion-related differences (Horstmann & Bauland, 2006; Tipples, 2007).

The above view suggests that the central task facing researchers in attention and emotion is to define how the classification of valence occurs, in particular to what extent perceptual versus semantic classification processes are biased. This view also suggests that access to semantic information may not be a prerequisite for valence classification. It will be important for researchers to develop their ideas regarding exactly how valence evaluation occurs grounded on existing knowledge from cognitive psychology. Another challenge will be to integrate any proposed mechanism of valence evaluation across pictorial and verbal information. Latent semantic indexing (Landauer, 1998) offers one possible computational solution to describing how valenced information is extracted and has been applied to both verbal and pictorial information categorisation. At first sight, focusing on the basis for valence evaluation may seem a diversion from the issue of attention to emotional information, but it is not. Some discrete classification of visual input must be acquired in order for attentional selection of that grouping to occur. Attention to a visual grouping will improve classification, and improved classification will facilitate the directing of attention towards or away from objects. This is likely to operate in a cyclical fashion, of the sort originally invoked by Williams et al. (1997) and based on Neisser (1967).

Whatever the theoretical mechanisms operating within the "valence evaluator" of the current models, it seems that "desensitising" these over-reactive mechanisms would be the best approach to ameliorating the negative consequences of attentional biases in psychopathology. Research in the field is moving quickly in this direction, using top-down, strategic re-training of valence evaluation (e.g., Yiend et al., 2008) and bottom-up manipulations of attentional deployment (Hayes, Krebs, Mathews, & Hirsch, 2009; MacLeod et al., 2002; MacLeod et al., 2004) to normalise the cognitive processing of emotional material in psychopathology.

## REFERENCES

Algom, D., Chajut, E., & Lev, S. (2004). A rational look at the emotional Stroop phenomenon: A generic slowdown, not a Stroop effect. *Journal of Experimental Psychology: General, 133*(3), 323–338.

Allport, A. (1980). Attention and performance. In G. Claxton (Ed.), *Cognitive psychology: New directions*. London: Routledge.

American Psychiatric Association. (1994). *Diagnostic and statistical manual of mental disorders* (4th ed.). Washington, DC: American Psychiatric Association.

Amir, N., Elias, J., Klumpp, H., & Przeworski, A. (2003). Attentional bias to threat in social phobia: facilitated processing of threat or difficulty disengaging attention from threat? *Behaviour Research and Therapy, 41*(11), 1325–1335.

Amir, N., McNally, R. J., Riemann, B. C., Burns, J., Loenz, M., & Mullen, J. T. (1996). Suppression of the emotional Stroop effect by increased anxiety in patients with social phobia. *Behaviour Research and Therapy, 34*, 945–948.

Anderson, A. K. (2005). Affective influences on the attentional dynamics supporting awareness. *Journal of Experimental Psychology: General, 134*, 258–281.

Ansari, T. L., Derakshan, N., & Richards, A. (2008). Effects of anxiety on task switching: Evidence from the mixed antisaccade task. *Cognitive, Affective, & Behavioral Neuroscience, 8*(3), 229–238.

Armony, J. L., LeDoux, J. E., McGaugh, J. L., Roozendaal, B., Cahill, L., Ono, T., et al. (2000). Emotion. In M. S. Gazzaniga (Ed.), *The new cognitive neurosciences* (2nd ed., pp. 1067–1159). Cambridge, MA: MIT Press.

Arnell, K. M., Killman, K. V., & Fijavz, D. (2007). Blinded by emotion: Target misses follow attention capture by arousing distractors in RSVP. *Emotion, 7*(3), 465–477.

Bargh, J. A. (1994). The four horsemen of automaticity: Awareness, intention, efficiency, and control in social cognition. In R. S. Wyer & T. K. Srull (Eds.), *Handbook of social cognition* (pp. 1–40). Hillsdale, NJ: Lawrence Erlbaum Associates, Inc.

Bar-Haim, Y., Lamy, D., Pergamin, L., Bakermans-Kranenburg, M. J., & van IJzendoorn, M. H. (2007). Threat-related attentional bias in anxious and nonanxious individuals: A meta-analytic study. *Psychological Bulletin, 133*(1), 1–24.

Barnard, P. J., Ramponi, C., Battye, G., & Mackintosh, B. (2005). Anxiety and the deployment of visual attention over time. *Visual Cognition, 12*(1), 181–211.

Batty, M. J., Cave, K. R., & Pauli, P. (2005). Abstract stimuli associated with threat through conditioning cannot be detected preattentively. *Emotion, 5*, 418–430.

Beaver, J. D., Mogg, K., & Bradley, B. P. (2005). Emotional conditioning to masked stimuli and modulation of visuospatial attention. *Emotion, 5*(1), 67–79.

Beck, A. T. (1976). *Cognitive therapy and the emotional disorders*. New York: International Universities Press.

Beevers, C. G., & Carver, C. S. (2003). Attentional bias and mood persistence as prospective predictors of dysphoria. *Cognitive Therapy and Research, 27*(6), 619–637.

Bentall, R. P. (1994). Cognitive biases and abnormal beliefs: towards a model of persecutory delusions. In J. Cutting & A. S. David (Eds.), *The neuropsychology of schizophrenia* (pp. 337–360). Hove, UK: Lawrence Erlbaum Associates Ltd.

Bogels, S. M., & Mansell, W. (2004). Attention processes in the maintenance and treatment of social phobia: Hypervigilance, avoidance and self-focused attention. *Clinical Psychology Review, 24*(7), 827–856.

Bower, G. H. (1981). Mood and memory. *American Psychologist, 36*, 129–148.

Bower, G. H. (1987). Commentary on mood and memory. *Behaviour Research and Therapy, 25*, 443–455.

Bradley, B. P., Mogg, K., Falla, S. J., & Hamilton, L. R. (1998). Attentional bias for threatening facial expressions in anxiety: Manipulation of stimulus duration. *Cognition and Emotion, 12*(6), 737–753.

Bradley, B. P., Mogg, K., & Lee, S. C. (1997). Attentional biases for negative information in induced and naturally occurring dysphoria. *Behaviour Research and Therapy, 35*(10), 911–927.

Bradley, B. P., Mogg, K., Millar, N., & White, J. (1995). Selective processing of negative information: Effects of clinical anxiety, concurrent depression and awareness. *Journal of Abnormal Psychology, 104*, 532–536.

Broadbent, D., & Broadbent, M. (1988). Anxiety and attentional bias: State and trait. *Cognition and Emotion, 2*, 165–183.

Brosch, T., Sander, D., & Scherer, K. R. (2007). That baby caught my eye. Attention capture by infant faces. *Emotion, 7*(3), 685–689.

Bruce, V., & Green, P. (1990). *Visual perception: Physiology, psychology and ecology* (2nd ed.). Hove, UK: Lawrence Erlbaum Associates Ltd.

Bruce, V., & Young, A. W. (1986). Understanding face recognition. *British Journal of Psychology, 77*, 305–327.

Bruinsma, Y., Koegel, R. L., & Koegel, L. K. (2004). Joint attention and children with autism: A review of the literature. *Mental Retardation and Developmental Disabilities Research Reviews, 10*(3), 169–175.

Buehlmann, A., & Deco, G. (2008). The neuronal basis of attention: Rate versus synchronization modulation. *Journal of Neuroscience, 28*(30), 7679–7686.

Burgess, S., Jones, L. M., Robertson, S. A., Radcliffe, W. N., & Emerson, E. (1981). The degree of control exerted by phobic and non-phobic verbal stimuli over the recognition behaviour of phobic and non-phobic subjects. *Behaviour Research and Therapy, 19*, 223–243.

Burton, A. M., & Bruce, V. (1992). I recognize your face but I can't remember your name: A simple explanation? *British Journal of Psychology, 83*, 45–60.

Byrne, A., & Eysenck, M. W. (1995). Trait anxiety, anxious mood and threat detection. *Cognition and Emotion, 9*, 549–562.

Calvo, M. G. (2006). Processing of emotional visual scenes outside the focus of spatial attention: The role of eccentricity. *Visual Cognition, 13*(6), 666–676.

Calvo, M. G., Avero, P., & Lundqvist, D. (2006). Facilitated detection of angry faces: Initial orienting and processing efficiency. *Cognition and Emotion, 20*(6), 785–811.

Calvo, M. G., & Castillo, M. D. (2005). Foveal vs. parafoveal attention-grabbing power of threat-related information. *Experimental Psychology, 52*(2), 150–162.

Calvo, M. G., Castillo, M. D., & Fuentes, L. J. (2006). Processing of "unattended" threat-related information: Role of emotional content and context. *Cognition and Emotion, 20*(8), 1049–1074.

Calvo, M. G., & Esteves, F. (2005). Detection of emotional faces: low perceptual threshold and wide attentional span. *Visual Cognition, 12*(1), 13–27.

Calvo, M. G., & Eysenck, M. W. (2008). Affective significance enhances covert attention: Roles of anxiety and word familiarity. *The Quarterly Journal of Experimental Psychology, 61*(11), 1669–1686.

Calvo, M. G., & Nummenmaa, L. (2007). Processing of unattended emotional visual scenes. *Journal of Experimental Psychology: General, 136*(3), 347–369.

Calvo, M. G., & Nummenmaa, L. (2008). Detection of emotional faces: Salient physical features guide effective visual search. *Journal of Experimental Psychology: General, 137*(3), 471–494.

Calvo, M. G., Nummenmaa, L., & Hyönä, J. (2007). Emotional and neutral scenes in competition: Orienting, efficiency, and identification. *Quarterly Journal of Experimental Psychology, 60*(12), 1585–1593.

Calvo, M. G., Nummenmaa, L., & Hyönä, J. (2008). Emotional scenes in peripheral vision: Selective orienting and gist processing, but not content identification. *Emotion, 8*(1), 68–80.

Chajut, E., Lev, S., & Algom, D. (2005). Vicissitudes of a misnomer: Reply to Dalgleish (2005). *Journal of Experimental Psychology: General, 134*(4), 592–595.

Cheeseman, J., & Merikle, P. M. (1985). Word recognition and consciousness. In D. Besner, T. G. Waller, & G. E. MacKinnon (Eds.), *Reading research: Advances in theory and practice* (pp. 311–352). Orlando, FL: Academic Press.

Chen, Y. P., Ehlers, A., Clark, D. M., & Mansell, W. (2002). Patients with generalized social phobia direct their attention away from faces. *Behaviour Research and Therapy, 40*(6), 677–687.

Cherry, E. C. (1953). Some experiments on the recognition of speech with one and two ears. *Journal of the Acoustical Society of America, 25,* 975–979.

Compton, R. J., Banich, M. T., Mohanty, A., Milham, M. P., Herrington, J., Miller, G. A., et al. (2003). Paying attention to emotion: an fMRI investigation of cognitive and emotional Stroop tasks. *Cognitive, Affective & Behavioral Neuroscience, 3*(2), 81–96.

Conway, A. R. A., Cowan, N., & Bunting, M. F. (2001). The cocktail party phenomenon revisited: The importance of working memory capacity. *Psychonomic Bulletin & Review, 8*(2), 331–335.

Cooper, R. M., & Langton, S. R. (2006). Attentional bias to angry faces using the dot-probe task? It depends when you look for it. *Behaviour Research and Therapy, 44*(9), 1321–1329.

Cowan, N. (2005). Selective attention tasks in cognitive research. In A. Wenzel & D. C. Rubin (Eds.), *Cognitive methods in clinical research* (pp. 73–96). Washington, DC: American Psychological Association.

Cox, W., Fadardi, J. S., & Pothos, E. M. (2006). The addiction-Stroop test: Theoretical considerations and procedural recommendations. *Psychological Bulletin, 132*(3), 443–476.

Dalgleish, T. (2005). Putting some feeling into it—The conceptual and empirical relationships between the classic and emotional Stroop tasks: Comment on Algom, Chajut, and Lev (2004). *Journal of Experimental Psychology: General, 134*(4), 585–591.

Davidson, R. J. (1998). Affective style and affective disorders: Perspectives from affective neuroscience. *Cognition & Emotion, 12*(3), 307–330.

Davidson, R. J. (2000). Cognitive neuroscience needs affective neuroscience (and vice versa). *Brain and Cognition, 42*(1), 89–92.

Davidson, R. J. (2002). Anxiety and affective style: Role of prefrontal cortex and amygdala. *Biological Psychiatry, 51*(1), 68–80.

Davidson, R. J., Pizzagalli, D., Nitschke, J. B., & Putnam, K. (2002). Depression: Perspectives from affective neuroscience. *Annual Review of Psychology, 53*(1), 545–574.

de Jong, P. J., & Martens, S. (2007). Detection of emotional expressions in rapidly changing facial displays in high- and low-socially anxious women. *Behaviour Research and Therapy, 45*(6), 1285–1294.

Derryberry, D., & Reed, M. A. (1994). Temperament and attention: Orienting toward and away from positive and negative signals. *Journal of Personality and Social Psychology, 66,* 1128–1139.

Derryberry, D., & Reed, M. A. (2002). Anxiety-related attentional biases and their regulation by attentional control. *Journal of Abnormal Psychology, 111*(2), 225–236.

Desimone, R., & Duncan, J. (1995). Neural mechanisms of selective visual-attention. *Annual Review of Neuroscience, 18,* 193–222.

Donaldson, C., Lam, D., & Mathews, A. (2007). Rumination and attention in major depression. *Behaviour Research and Therapy, 45*(11), 2664–2678.

Duchowski, A. T., Cournia, N., & Murphy, H. (2004). Gaze-contingent displays: A review. *CyberPsychology & Behavior, 7*(6), 621–634.

Duncan, J. (2006). EPS Mid-Career Award 2004: Brain mechanisms of attention. *The Quarterly Journal of Experimental Psychology, 59*(1), 2–27.

Eastwood, J. D., Smilek, D., & Merikle, P. M. (2001). Differential attentional guidance by unattended faces expressing positive and negative emotion. *Perception & Psychophysics, 63*(6), 1004–1013.

Eastwood, J. D., Smilek, D., Oakman, J. M., Farvolden, P., van Ameringen, M., Mancini, C., et al. (2005). Individuals with social phobia are biased to become aware of negative faces. *Visual Cognition, 12*(1), 159–179.

Eccleston, C., & Crombez, G. (1999). Pain demands attention: A cognitive-affective model of the interruptive function of pain. *Psychological Bulletin, 125*(3), 356–366.

Ehlers, A., Margraf, J., Davies, S., & Roth, W. T. (1988). Selective processing of threat cues in subjects with panic attacks. *Cognition and Emotion, 2,* 201–219.

Eimer, M., & Holmes, A. (2007). Event-related brain potential correlates of emotional face processing. *Neuropsychologia, 45*(1), 15–31.

Engels, A. S., Heller, W., Mohanty, A., Herrington, J. D., Banich, M. T., Webb, A. G., et al. (2007). Specificity of regional brain activity in anxiety types during emotion processing. *Psychophysiology, 44*(3), 352–363.

Eysenck, M. W. (1992). *Anxiety: The cognitive perspective.* Hove, UK: Lawrence Erlbaum Associates, Inc.

Eysenck, M. W., & Calvo, M. G. (1992). Anxiety and peformance: The processing efficiency theory. *Cognition and Emotion, 6,* 409–434.

Eysenck, M. W., Derakshan, N., Santos, R., & Calvo, M. G. (2007). Anxiety and cognitive performance: Attentional control theory. *Emotion, 7*(2), 336–353.

Farrin, L., Hull, L., Unwin, C., Wykes, T., & David, A. (2003). Effects of depressed mood on objective and subjective measures of attention. *Journal of Neuropsychiatry & Clinical Neurosciences, 15*(1), 98–104.

Faunce, G. J. (2002). Eating disorders and attentional bias: A review. *Eating Disorders: The Journal of Treatment & Prevention, 10*(2), 125–139.

Field, A. P., Cartwright-Hatton, S., Reynolds, S., & Creswell, C. (2008). Future directions for child anxiety theory and treatment. *Cognition & Emotion, 22*(3), 385–394.

Foa, E. B., & McNally, R. J. (1986). Sensitivity to feared stimuli in obsessive-compulsives: A dichotic listening analysis. *Cognitive Therapy and Research, 10,* 477–486.

Fox, E. (1993a). Attentional bias in anxiety: Selective or not? *Behaviour Research and Therapy, 31,* 487–493.

Fox, E. (1993b). Allocation of visual attention and anxiety. *Cognition and Emotion, 7,* 207–215.

Fox, E., & Damjanovic, L. (2006). The eyes are sufficient to produce a threat superiority effect. *Emotion, 6*(3), 534–539.

Fox, E., Griggs, L., & Mouchlianitis, E. (2007a). The detection of fear-relevant stimuli: Are guns noticed as quickly as snakes. *Emotion, 7*(4), 691–696.

Fox, E., Lester, V., Russo, R., Bowles, R. J., Pichler, A., & Dutton, K. (2000). Facial expressions of emotion: Are angry faces detected more efficiently? *Cognition and Emotion, 14*(1), 61–92.

Fox, E., Mathews, A., Calder, A. J., & Yiend, J. (2007b). Anxiety and sensitivity to gaze direction in emotionally expressive faces. *Emotion, 7*(3), 478–486.

Fox, E., Russo, R., Bowles, R., & Dutton, K. (2001). Do threatening stimuli draw or hold visual attention in subclinical anxiety? *Journal of Experimental Psychology: General, 130*(4), 681–700.

Fox, E., Russo, R., & Dutton, K. (2002). Attentional bias for threat: Evidence for delayed disengagement from emotional faces. *Cognition and Emotion, 16*(3), 355–379.

Fox, E., Russo, R., & Georgiou, G. A. (2005). Anxiety modulates the degree of attentive resources required to process emotional faces. *Cognitive, Affective, & Behavioral Neuroscience, 5*(4), 396–404.

Frischen, A., Eastwood, J. D., & Smilek, D. (2008). Visual search for faces with emotional expressions. *Psychological Bulletin, 134*, 662–676.

Gilboa-Schechtman, E., Foa, E. B., & Amir, N. (1999). Attentional biases for facial expressions in social phobia: The face-in-the-crowd paradigm. *Cognition and Emotion, 13*(3), 305–318.

Gold, J. M., & Thaker, G. K. (2002). Current progress in schizophrenia research. Cognitive phenotypes of schizophrenia: Attention. *Journal of Nervous and Mental Disease, 190*(9), 638–639.

Gotlib, I. H., Kasch, K. L., Traill, S., Joormann, J., Arnow, B. A., & Johnson, S. L. (2004a). Coherence and specificity of information-processing biases in depression and social phobia. *Journal of Abnormal Psychology, 113*(3), 386–398.

Gotlib, I. H., Krasnoperova, E., Yue, D. N., & Joormann, J. (2004b). Attentional biases for negative interpersonal stimuli in clinical depression. *Journal of Abnormal Psychology, 113*(1), 127–135.

Gotlib, I. H., McLachlan, A. L., & Katz, A. N. (1988). Biases in visual attention in depressed and non-depressed individuals. *Cognition and Emotion, 2*, 185–200.

Graf, P., & Mandler, G. (1984). Activation makes words more accessible, but not necessarily more retrievable. *Journal of Verbal Learning and Verbal Behaviour, 23*, 553–568.

Grison, S., Tipper, S. P., & Hewitt, O. (2005). Long-term negative priming: Support for retrieval of prior attentional processes. *The Quarterly Journal of Experimental Psychology A: Human Experimental Psychology, 58A*(7), 1199–1224.

Gross, J. J. (2002). Emotion regulation: Affective, cognitive, and social consequences. *Psychophysiology, 39*(3), 281–291.

Hancock, P. A., Oron-Gilad, T., & Szalma, J. L. (2007). Elaborations of the multiple-resource theory of attention. In A. F. Kramer, D. A. Wiegmann, & A. Kirlik (Eds.), *Attention: From theory to practice* (pp. 45–56). Oxford, UK: Oxford University Press.

Hansen, C. H., & Hansen, R. D. (1988). Finding the face in the crowd—An anger superiority effect. *Journal of Personality and Social Psychology, 54*(6), 917–924.

Harris, C. R., Pashler, H. F., & Coburn, P. (2004). Moray revisited: High-priority affective stimuli and visual search. *Quarterly Journal of Experimental Psychology Section a: Human Experimental Psychology, 57*(1), 1–31.

Hayes, S., Hirsch, C., & Mathews, A. (2008). Restriction of working memory capacity during worry. *Journal of Abnormal Psychology, 117*(3), 712–717.

Hayes, S., Krebs, G., Mathews, A., & Hirsch, C. (2009). *Focusing on the positive: Facilitating a benign attentional bias reduces negative thought intrusions.* Manuscript submitted for publication.

Hoffman, J. E. (1998). Visual attention and eye movements. In H. Pashler (Ed.), *Attention* (pp. 119–153). Hove, UK: Psychology Press.

Holender, D. (1986). Semantic activation without conscious identification in dichotic listening, parafoveal vision, and visual masking: A survey and appraisal. *The Behavioural and Brain Sciences*, 9, 1–66.

Holmes, A., Green, S., & Vuilleumier, P. (2005). The involvement of distinct visual channels in rapid attention towards fearful facial expressions. *Cognition and Emotion*, 19(6), 899–922.

Holmes, A., Richards, A., & Green, S. (2006). Anxiety and sensitivity to eye gaze in emotional faces. *Brain and Cognition*, 60(3), 282–294.

Hope, D. A., Rapee, R. M., Heimberg, R. G., & Dombeck, M. J. (1990). Representations of the self in social phobia: vulnerability to social threat. *Cognitive Therapy and Research*, 14, 177–189.

Horenstein, M., & Segui, J. (1997). Chronometrics of attentional processes in anxiety disorders. *Psychopathology*, 30, 25–35.

Horstmann, G. (2009). Visual search for schematic affective faces: Stability and variability of search slopes with different instances. *Cognition and Emotion*, 23, 355–379.

Horstmann, G., & Bauland, A. (2006). Search asymmetries with real faces: Testing the anger-superiority effect. *Emotion*, 6(2), 193–207.

Humphreys, G. W., & Bruce, V. (1989). *Visual cognition: Computational, experimental and neuropsychological perspectives*. Hove, UK: Psychology Press.

Humphreys, M. S., & Revelle, W. (1984). Personality, motivation and performance: a theory of the relationship between individual differences and information processing. *Psychological Review*, 91, 153–184.

Hunt, C., Keogh, E., & French, C. C. (2006). Anxiety sensitivity: The role of conscious awareness and selective attentional bias to physical threat. *Emotion*, 6(3), 418–428.

Johnston, W. A., & Heinz, S. P. (1978). Flexibility and capacity demands of attention. *Journal of Experimental Psychology: General*, 107, 420–435.

Joormann, J. (2004). Attentional bias in dysphoria: The role of inhibitory processes. *Cognition & Emotion*, 18, 125–147.

Joormann, J., & Gotlib, I. H. (2007). Selective attention to emotional faces following recovery from depression. *Journal of Abnormal Psychology*, 116(1), 80–85.

Joormann, J., Talbot, L., & Gotlib, I. H. (2007). Biased processing of emotional information in girls at risk for depression. *Journal of Abnormal Psychology*, 116(1), 135–143.

Juth, P., Karlsson, A., Lundqvist, D., & Ohman, A. (2000). Finding a face in the crowd: effects of emotional expression, direction and social anxiety. *International Journal of Psychology*, 35(3–4), 434–443.

Juth, P., Lundqvist, D., Karlsson, A., & Ohman, A. (2005). Looking for foes and friends: Perceptual and emotional factors when finding a face in the crowd. *Emotion*, 5(4), 379–395.

Kahneman, D. (1973). *Attention and effort*. Englewood Cliffs, NJ: Prentice Hall.

Karparova, S. P., Kersting, A., & Suslow, T. (2005). Disengagement of attention from facial emotion in unipolar depression. *Psychiatry and Clinical Neurosciences*, 59(6), 723–729.

Kastner, S., & Ungerleider, L. G. (2000). Mechanisms of visual attention in the human cortex. *Annual Review of Neuroscience*, 23, 315–341.

Kastner, S., & Ungerleider, L. G. (2001). The neural basis of biased competition in human visual cortex. *Neuropsychologia, 39*(12), 1263–1276.

Keil, A., & Ihssen, N. (2004). Identification facilitation for emotionally arousing verbs during the attentional blink. *Emotion, 4,* 23–35.

Kindt, M., Bierman, D., & Brosschot, J. F. (1996). Stroop versus Stroop: Comparison of a card format and a single-trial format of the standard color-word Stroop task and the emotional Stroop task. *Personality and Individual Differences, 21*(5), 653–661.

Klein, G. S. (1964). Semantic power measured through the interference of words with color naming. *American Journal of Psychology, 77,* 576–588.

Koole, S. L. (2009). The psychology of emotion regulation: An integrative review. *Cognition & Emotion, 23,* 4–41.

Koster, E. H., Crombez, G., Verschuere, B., & De Houwer, J. (2006). Attention to threat in anxiety-prone individuals: Mechanisms underlying attentional bias. *Cognitive Therapy and Research, 30*(5), 635–643.

Koster, E. H., Verschuere, B., Crombez, G., & Van Damme, S. (2005). Time-course of attention for threatening pictures in high and low trait anxiety. *Behaviour Research and Therapy, 43,* 1087–1098.

Koster, E. H. W., Crombez, G., Van Damme, S., Verschuere, B., & De Houwer, J. (2004a). Does imminent threat capture and hold attention? *Emotion, 4*(3), 312–317.

Koster, E. H. W., Crombez, G., Verschuere, B., & De Houwer, J. (2004b). Selective attention to threat in the dot probe paradigm: differentiating vigilance and difficulty to disengage. *Behaviour Research and Therapy, 42*(10), 1183–1192.

Koster, E. H. W., De Raedt, R., Verschuere, B., Tibboel, H., & De Jong, P. J. (2009). Negative information enhances the attentional blink in dysphoria. *Depression and Anxiety, 26,* 16–22.

Koster, E. H. W., Fox, E., & MacLeod, C. (2009). Introduction. In the special section on cognitive bias modification in emotional disorders. *Journal of Abnormal Psychology, 118,* 1–4.

Koster, E. H. W., Verschuere, B., Burssens, B., Custers, R., & Crombez, G. (2007). Attention for emotional faces under restricted awareness revisited: Do emotional faces automatically attract attention? *Emotion, 7*(2), 285–295.

Lamy, D., Amunts, L., & Bar-Haim, Y. (2008). Emotional priming of pop-out in visual search. *Emotion, 8*(2), 151–161.

Landauer, T. K. (1998). Learning and representing verbal meaning: The latent semantic analysis theory. *Current Directions in Psychological Science, 7*(5), 161–164.

Langdon, R., & Coltheart, M. (2000). The cognitive neuropsychology of delusions. In M. Coltheart & M. Davies (Eds.), *Pathologies of belief* (pp. 183–216). Malden, MA: Blackwell Publishing.

Lawton, M. (2001). Emotion in later life. *Current Directions in Psychological Science, 10*(4), 120–123.

Ledley, D. R., & Heimberg, R. G. (2006). Cognitive vulnerability to social anxiety. *Journal of Social & Clinical Psychology, 25*(7), 755–778.

Lee, M., & Shafran, R. (2004). Information processing biases in eating disorders. *Clinical Psychology Review, 24*(2), 215–238.

Lee, M., & Shafran, R. (2008). Processing biases in eating disorders: The impact of temporal factors. *International Journal of Eating Disorders, 41*(4), 372–375.

Leyman, L., De Raedt, R., Schacht, R., & Koster, E. H. W. (2007). Attentional biases for angry faces in unipolar depression. *Psychological Medicine, 37*(3), 393–402.

Lipp, O. V., & Derakshan, N. (2005). Attentional bias to pictures of fear-relevant animals in a dot probe task. *Emotion, 5*(3), 365–369.

Lipp, O. V., & Waters, A. M. (2007). When danger lurks in the background: Attentional capture by animal fear-relevant distractors is specific and selectively enhanced by animal fear. *Emotion, 7*(1), 192–200.

Loschky, L. C., & McConkie, G. W. (2002). Investigating spatial vision and dynamic attentional selection using a gaze-contingent multiresolutional display. *Journal of Experimental Psychology: Applied, 8*(2), 99–117.

Lundqvist, D., & Ohman, A. (2005). Emotion regulates attention: The relation between facial configurations, facial emotion, and visual attention. *Visual Cognition, 12*(1), 51–84.

MacKay, D. G., & Ahmetzanov, M. V. (2005). Emotion, memory, and attention in the taboo Stroop paradigm: An experimental analogue of flashbulb memories. *Psychological Science, 16*(1), 25–32.

MacKay, D. G., Shafto, M., Taylor, J. K., Marian, D. E., Abrams, L., & Dyer, J. R. (2004). Relations between emotion, memory, and attention: Evidence from taboo Stroop, lexical decision, and immediate memory tasks. *Memory & Cognition, 32*, 474–488.

MacLeod, C. (2005). The Stroop task in clinical research. In A. Wenzel & D. C. Rubin (Eds.), *Cognitive methods and their application to clinical research* (pp. 41–62). Washington, DC: American Psychological Association.

MacLeod, C., Campbell, L., Rutherford, E., & Wilson, E. (2004). The causal status of anxiety-linked attentional and interpretive bias. In J. Yiend (Ed.), *Cognition, emotion and psychopathology* (pp. 172–189). Cambridge, UK: Cambridge University Press.

MacLeod, C., & Hagan, R. (1992). Individual differences in the selective processing of threatening information, and emotional responses to a stressful life event. *Behaviour Research and Therapy, 30*, 151–161.

MacLeod, C., & Mathews, A. (1988). Anxiety and the allocation of attention to threat. *Quarterly Journal of Experimental Psychology, 40A*, 653–670.

MacLeod, C., & Mathews, A. (1991). Biased cognitive operations in anxiety: Accessibility of information or assignment of processing priorities? *Behaviour Research and Therapy, 6*, 599–610.

MacLeod, C., Mathews, A., & Tata, P. (1986). Attentional bias in emotional disorders. *Journal of Abnormal Psychology, 95*(1), 15–20.

MacLeod, C., Rutherford, E., Campbell, L., Ebsworthy, G., & Holker, L. (2002). Selective attention and emotional vulnerability: Assessing the causal basis of their association through the experimental manipulation of attentional bias. *Journal of Abnormal Psychology, 111*(1), 107–123.

MacLeod, C., & Rutherford, E. M. (1992). Anxiety and the selective processing of emotional information: Mediating roles of awareness, trait and state variables, and personal relevance of stimulus materials. *Behaviour Research and Therapy, 30*, 479–491.

MacLeod, C. M. (1991). Half a century of research on the Stroop effect: An integrative review. *Psychological Bulletin, 109*(2), 163–203.

Mansell, W., Clark, D. M., Ehlers, A., & Chen, Y. P. (1999). Social anxiety and attention away from emotional faces. *Cognition and Emotion, 13*(6), 673–690.

Mansell, W., Ehlers, A., Clark, D. M., & Chen, Y. P. (2002). Attention to positive and negative social-evaluative words: Investigating the effects of social anxiety, trait anxiety and social threat. *Anxiety Stress and Coping, 15*(1), 19–29.

Martin, M., Williams, R. M., & Clark, D. M. (1991). Does anxiety lead to selective processing of threat related information? *Behaviour Research and Therapy, 29,* 147–160.

Mathews, A. (1990). Why worry? The cognitive function of anxiety. *Behaviour Research and Therapy, 28*(6), 455–468.

Mathews, A., Fox, E., Yiend, J., & Calder, A. (2003). The face of fear: Effects of eye gaze and emotion on visual attention. *Visual Cognition, 10*(7), 823–835.

Mathews, A., & Klug, F. (1993). Emotionality and interference with colour naming in anxiety. *Behaviour Research and Therapy, 31,* 57–62.

Mathews, A., & Mackintosh, B. (1998). A cognitive model of selective processing in anxiety. *Cognitive Therapy and Research, 22*(6), 539–560.

Mathews, A., & MacLeod, C. (1985). Selective processing of threat cues in anxiety states. *Behaviour Research and Therapy, 23,* 563–569.

Mathews, A., & MacLeod, C. (1986). Discrimination of threat cues without awareness in anxiety states. *Journal of Abnormal Psychology, 95,* 131–138.

Mathews, A., & MacLeod, C. (1994). Cognitive approaches to emotion and emotional disorders. *Annual Review of Psychology, 45,* 25–50.

Mathews, A., & MacLeod, C. (2002). Induced processing biases have causal effects on anxiety. *Cognition and Emotion, 16*(3), 331–354.

Mathews, A., & Milroy, R. (1994). Processing of emotional meaning in anxiety. *Cognition and Emotion, 8,* 535–553.

Mathews, A., Mogg, K., Kentish, J., & Eysenck, M. (1995). Effect of psychological treatment on cognitive bias in generalized anxiety disorder. *Behaviour Research and Therapy, 33,* 293–303.

Mathews, A., Ridgeway, V., & Williamson, D. A. (1996). Evidence for attention to threatening stimuli in depression. *Behaviour Research and Therapy, 34*(9), 695–705.

Mathews, A., & Sebastian, S. (1993). Suppression of emotional Stroop effects by fear arousal. *Cognition and Emotion, 7,* 517–530.

Mathews, A., Yiend, J., & Lawrence, A. D. (2004). Individual differences in the modulation of fear-related brain activation by attentional control. *Journal of Cognitive Neuroscience, 16*(10), 1683–1694.

McKenna, F. P., & Sharma, D. (2004). Reversing the emotional Stroop effect reveals that it is not what it seems: The role of fast and slow components. *Journal of Experimental Psychology: Learning, Memory and Cognition, 30,* 382–392.

McNally, R. J., Riemann, B. C., Louro, C. E., Lukach, B. M., & Kim, E. (1992). Cognitive processing of emotional information in panic disorder. *Behaviour Research and Therapy, 30,* 143–149.

Mogg, K., & Bradley, B. P. (1998). A cognitive-motivational analysis of anxiety. *Behaviour Research and Therapy, 36,* 809–848.

Mogg, K., Bradley, B. P., De Bono, J., & Painter, M. (1997). Time course of attentional bias for threat information in non-clinical anxiety. *Behaviour Research and Therapy, 35,* 297–303.

Mogg, K., Bradley, B. P., & Hallowell, N. (1994). Attentional bias to threat: Roles of trait anxiety, stressful events, and awareness. *Quarterly Journal of Experimental Psychology, 47A,* 841–864.

Mogg, K., Bradley, B. P., Hyare, H., & Lee, S. (1998). Selective attention to food-related stimuli in hunger: are attentional biases specific to emotional and psychopathological states, or are they also found in normal drive states? *Behaviour Research and Therapy, 36*(2), 227–237.

Mogg, K., Bradley, B. P., Miles, F., & Dixon, R. (2004). Time course of attentional bias for threat scenes: Testing the vigilance–avoidance hypothesis. *Cognition and Emotion, 18*(5), 689–700.

Mogg, K., Bradley, B. P., & Williams, R. (1995). Attentional bias in anxiety and depression: The role of awareness. *British Journal of Clinical Psychology, 34,* 17–36.

Mogg, K., Bradley, B. P., Williams, R., & Mathews, A. (1993a). Subliminal processing of emotional information in anxiety and depression. *Journal of Abnormal Psychology, 102,* 304–311.

Mogg, K., Holmes, A., Garner, M., & Bradley, B. P. (2008). Effects of threat cues on attentional shifting, disengagement and response slowing in anxious individuals. *Behaviour Research and Therapy, 46*(5), 656–667.

Mogg, K., Kentish, J., & Bradley, B. P. (1993b). Effects of anxiety and awareness on colour-identification latencies for emotional words. *Behaviour Research and Therapy, 31,* 559–567.

Mogg, K., Mathews, A., & Eysenck, M. (1992). Attentional bias to threat in clinical anxiety states. *Cognition and Emotion, 6*(2), 149–159.

Mogg, K., Mathews, A. M., Bird, C., & MacGregor-Morris, R. (1990). Effects of stress and anxiety on the processing of threat stimuli. *Journal of Personality and Social Psychology, 59,* 1230–1237.

Mogg, K., Mathews, A., May, J., Grove, M., Eysenck, M., & Weinman, J. (1991). Assessment of cognitive bias in anxiety and depression using a colour perception task. *Cognition and Emotion, 5,* 221–238.

Mogg, K., Mathews, A. M., & Weinman, J. (1989). Selective processing of threat cues in anxiety states: A replication. *Behaviour Research and Therapy, 27,* 317–323.

Mogg, K., McNamara, J., Powys, M., Rawlinson, H., Seiffer, A., & Bradley, B. P. (2000a). Selective attention to threat: A test of two cognitive models of anxiety. *Cognition and Emotion, 14*(3), 375–399.

Mogg, K., Millar, N., & Bradley, B. P. (2000b). Biases in eye movements to threatening facial expressions in generalized anxiety disorder and depressive disorder. *Journal of Abnormal Psychology, 109*(4), 695–704.

Moors, A., & De Houwer, J. (2006). Automaticity: A theoretical and conceptual analysis. *Psychological Bulletin, 132*(2), 297–326.

Moray, N. (1959). Attention in dichotic listening. *Quarterly Journal of Experimental Psychology, 11,* 56–60.

Most, S. B., Chun, M. M., Johnson, M. R., & Kiehl, K. A. (2006). Attentional modulation of the amygdala varies with personality. *NeuroImage, 31,* 934–944.

Most, S. B., Chun, M. M., Widders, D. M., & Zald, D. H. (2005). Attentional rubbernecking: Cognitive control and personality in emotion-induced blindness. *Psychonomic Bulletin & Review, 12,* 654–661.

Most, S. B., & Junge, J. A. (2008). Don't look back: Retroactive, dynamic costs and benefits of emotional capture. *Visual Cognition, 16*(2–3), 262–278.

Most, S. B., Smith, S. D., Cooter, A. B., Levy, B. N., & Zald, D. H. (2007). The naked truth: Positive, arousing distractors impair rapid target perception. *Cognition and Emotion, 21*(5), 964–981.

Muller, J., & Roberts, J. E. (2005). Memory and attention in obsessive-compulsive disorder: A review. *Journal of Anxiety Disorders, 19*(1), 1–28.

Neisser, U. (1967). *Cognitive psychology.* New York: Appleton-Century-Crofts.

Nielsen, S. L., & Sarason, I. G. (1981). Emotion, personality, and selective attention. *Journal of Personality and Social Psychology, 41*(5), 945–960.

Ochsner, K. N., & Gross, J. J. (2005). The cognitive control of emotion. *Trends in Cognitive Sciences, 9*(5), 242–249.

Öhman, A., Flykt, A., & Esteves, F. (2001a). Emotion drives attention: Detecting the snake in the grass. *Journal of Experimental Psychology: General, 130*(3), 466–478.

Öhman, A., Lundqvist, D., & Esteves, F. (2001b). The face in the crowd revisited: A threat advantage with schematic stimuli. *Journal of Personality and Social Psychology, 80*(3), 381–396.

Okon-Singer, H., Tzelgov, J., & Henik, A. (2008). Distinguishing between automaticity and attention in the processing of emotionally significant stimuli. *Emotion, 7*, 147–157.

Olivers, C. N. L., & Nieuwenhuis, S. (2006). The beneficial effects of additional task load, positive affect, and instruction on the attentional blink. *Journal of Experimental Psychology: Human Perception and Performance, 32*(2), 364–379.

Owens, K. M. B., Asmundson, G. J. G., Hadjistavropoulos, T., & Owens, T. J. (2004). Attentional bias toward illness threat in individuals with elevated health anxiety. *Cognitive Therapy and Research, 28*(1), 57–66.

Palermo, R., & Rhodes, G. (2007). Are you always on my mind? A review of how face perception and attention interact. *Neuropsychologia, 45*(1), 75–92.

Pereira, M. G., Volchan, E., de Souza, G. G. L., Oliveira, L., Campagnoli, R. R., Pinheiro, W. M., et al. (2006). Sustained and transient modulation of performance induced by emotional picture viewing. *Emotion, 6*(4), 622–634.

Pflugshaupt, T., Mosimann, U. P., von Wartburg, R., Schmitt, W., Nyffeler, T., & Müri, R. M. (2005). Hypervigilance–avoidance pattern in spider phobia. *Journal of Anxiety Disorders, 19*(1), 105–116.

Phaf, R. H., & Kan, K.-J. (2007). The automaticity of emotional Stroop: A meta-analysis. *Journal of Behavior Therapy and Experimental Psychiatry, 38*, 184–199.

Phelps, E. A., Ling, S., & Carrasco, M. (2006). Emotion facilitates perception and potentiates the perceptual benefits of attention. *Psychological Science, 17*(4), 292–299.

Pincus, T., & Morley, S. (2001). Cognitive-processing bias in chronic pain: A review and integration. *Psychological Bulletin, 127*(5), 599–617.

Pineles, S. L., & Mineka, S. (2005). Attentional biases to internal and external sources of potential threat in social anxiety. *Journal of Abnormal Psychology, 114*(2), 314–318.

Pishyar, R., Harris, L. M., & Menzies, R. G. (2004). Attentional bias for words and faces in social anxiety. *Anxiety, Stress & Coping: An International Journal, 17*(1), 23–36.

Posner, M. I. (1980). Orienting of attention. *Quarterly Journal of Experimental Psychology, 32*, 3–25.

Posner, M. I., & Cohen, Y. (1984). Components of visual orienting. In H. Bouma & D. Bouwhuis (Eds.), *Attention and performance* (Vol. X (pp. 531–556)). Hove, UK: Lawrence Erlbaum Associates, Inc.

Posner, M. I., & Peterson, S. E. (1990). The attention system of the human brain. *Annual Review of Neuroscience, 13*, 25–42.

Posner, M. I., & Snyder, C. R. R. (1975). Attention and cognitive control. In R. L. Solso (Ed.), *Information processing and cognition: The Loyola symposium.* Hillsdale, NJ: Lawrence Erlbaum Associates, Inc.

Posner, M. I., & Snyder, C. R. R. (2004). Attention and cognitive control. In D. A. Balota & E. J. Marsh (Eds.), *Cognitive psychology: Key readings* (pp. 205–223). New York: Psychology Press.

Posner, M. I., Walker, J. A., Friedrich, F. J., & Rafal, R. D. (1984). Effects of parietal lobe injury on covert orienting of visual attention. *Journal of Neuroscience, 4*, 1863–1874.

Pratto, F., & John, O. P. (1991). Automatic vigilance: The attention-grabbing power of negative social information. *Journal of Personality and Social Psychology, 61*, 380–391.

Puliafico, A. C., & Kendall, P. C. (2006). Threat-related attentional bias in anxious youth: A review. *Clinical Child and Family Psychology Review, 9*(3–4), 162–180.

Purcell, D. G., Stewart, A. L., & Skov, R. B. (1996). It takes a confounded face to pop out of a crowd. *Perception, 25*, 1091–1108.

Pury, C. L. S. (2002). Information-processing predictors of emotional response to stress. *Cognition and Emotion, 16*(5), 667–683.

Raymond, J. E., Fenske, M. J., & Tavassoli, N. T. (2003). Selective attention determines emotional responses to novel visual stimuli. *Psychological Science, 14*(6), 537–542.

Raymond, J. E., Shapiro, K. L., & Arnell, K. M. (1992). Temporary suppression of visual processing in an RSVP task: An attentional blink? *Journal of Experimental Psychology: Human Perception and Performance, 18*(3), 849–860.

Reingold, E. M., Loschky, L. C., McConkie, G. W., & Stampe, D. M. (2003). Gaze-contingent multiresolutional displays: An integrative review. *Human Factors, 45*(2), 307–328.

Richards, A., & French, C. C. (1990). Central versus peripheral presentation of stimuli in an emotional Stroop task. *Anxiety Research, 3*, 41–49.

Richards, A., & Millwood, B. (1989). Colour-identification of differentially valenced words in anxiety. *Cognition and Emotion, 3*, 171–176.

Roelofs, J., Peters, M. L., Zeegers, M. P., & Vlaeyen, J. W. (2002). The modified Stroop paradigm as a measure of selective attention towards pain-related stimuli among chronic pain patients: A meta-analysis. *European Journal of Pain, 6*(4), 273–281.

Rohner, J. C. (2004). Memory-based attentional biases: Anxiety is linked to threat avoidance. *Cognition and Emotion, 18*(8), 1027–1054.

Rokke, P. D., Arnell, K. M., Koch, M. D., & Andrews, J. T. (2002). Dual-task attention deficits in dysphoric mood. *Journal of Abnormal Psychology, 111*(2), 370–379.

Rosen, J. B., & Schulkin, J. (1998). From normal fear to pathological anxiety. *Psychological Review, 105*, 325–350.

Rusting, C. L. (1999). Interactive effects of personality and mood on emotion-congruent memory and judgment. *Journal of Personality and Social Psychology, 77*(5), 1073–1086.

Rutherford, E. M., MacLeod, C., & Campbell, L. W. (2004). Negative selectivity effects and emotional selectivity effects in anxiety: Differential attentional correlates of state and trait variables. *Cognition and Emotion, 18*(5), 711–720.

Salemink, E., van den Hout, M. A., & Kindt, M. (2007). Selective attention and threat: Quick orienting versus slow disengagement and two versions of the dot probe task. *Behaviour Research and Therapy, 45*(3), 607–615.

Salters-Pedneault, K., Gentes, E., & Roemer, L. (2007). The role of fear of emotion in distress, arousal, and cognitive interference following an emotional stimulus. *Cognitive Behaviour Therapy, 36*(1), 12–22.

Santangelo, V., Ho, C., & Spence, C. (2008). Capturing spatial attention with multisensory cues. *Psychonomic Bulletin & Review, 15*(2), 398–403.

Santangelo, V., & Spence, C. (2008). Is the exogenous orienting of spatial attention truly automatic? Evidence from unimodal and multisensory studies. *Consciousness and Cognition, 17*, 989–1015.

Schneider, W., & Shiffrin, R. M. (1977). Controlled and automatic human information processing: I Detection, search and attention. *Psychological Review, 84*, 1–66.

Shane, M. S., & Peterson, J. B. (2007). An evaluation of early and late stage attentional processing of positive and negative information in dysphoria. *Cognition and Emotion, 21*(4), 789–815.

Shiffrin, R. M., & Schneider, W. (1977). Controlled and automatic human information processing: II Perceptual learning, automatic attending and a general theory. *Psychological Review, 84*, 127–190.

Siegrist, M. (1995). Effects of taboo words on color-naming performance on a Stroop test. *Perceptual and Motor Skills, 81*, 1119–1122.

Smith, S. D., Most, S. B., Newsome, L. A., & Zald, D. H. (2006). An emotion-induced attentional blink elicited by aversively conditioned stimuli. *Emotion, 6*(3), 523–527.

Soo, C. A., & Bailey, J. G. (2006). A review of functioning of attentional components in children with attention-deficit/hyperactivity disorder and learning disabilities. *Brain Impairment, 7*(2), 133–147.

Spence, C., & Santangelo, V. (2008). Auditory attention. In C. Plack (Ed.), *Auditory perception (Oxford University Press handbook of auditory science)*. Oxford, UK: Oxford University Press.

Sposari, J. A., & Rapee, R. M. (2007). Attentional bias toward facial stimuli under conditions of social threat in socially phobic and nonclinical participants. *Cognitive Therapy and Research, 31*(1), 23–37.

Stormark, K., Morten., & Hugdahl, K. (1996). Peripheral cuing of covert spatial attention before and after emotional conditioning of the cue. *International Journal of Neuroscience, 86*, 225–240.

Stormark, K. M., Nordby, H., & Hugdahl, K. (1995). Attentional shifts to emotionally charged cues: Behavioural and ERP data. *Cognition and Emotion, 9*, 507–523.

Stoyanova, R. S., Pratt, J., & Anderson, A. K. (2007). Inhibition of return to social signals of fear. *Emotion, 7*(1), 49–56.

Strauss, G. P., & Allen, D. N. (2006). The experience of positive emotion is associated with the automatic processing of positive emotional words. *The Journal of Positive Psychology, 1*(3), 150–159.

Stroop, J. R. (1935). Studies of interference in serial verbal reactions. *Journal of Experimental Psychology, 18*, 643–662.

Styles, E. A. (1997). *The psychology of attention.* Hove, UK: Psychology Press.

Suslow, T., Schonauer, K., & Arolt, V. (2001). Attention training in the cognitive rehabilitation of schizophrenic patients: A review of efficacy studies. *Acta Psychiatrica Scandinavica, 103*(1), 15–23.

Sutton, T. M., Altarriba, J., Gianico, J. L., & Basnight-Brown, D. M. (2007). The automatic access of emotion: Emotional Stroop effects in Spanish–English bilingual speakers. *Cognition and Emotion, 21*(5), 1077–1090.

Tipper, S. P. (1985). The negative priming effect: Inhibitory effects of ignored primes. *Quarterly Journal of Experimental Psychology, 37A*, 571–590.

Tipper, S. P. (2004). Selection for action: The role of inhibitory mechanisms. In D. A. Balota & E. J. Marsh (Eds.), *Cognitive psychology: Key readings* (pp. 224–229). New York: Psychology Press.

Tipper, S. P., & Cranston, M. (1985). Selective attention and priming: Inhibitory and facilitatory effects of ignored primes. *The Quarterly Journal of Experimental Psychology, 37A*, 591–611.

Tipples, J. (2007). Wide eyes and an open mouth enhance facial threat. *Cognition and Emotion, 21*(3), 535–557.

Tipples, J., Young, A. W., Quinlan, P., Broks, P., & Ellis, A. W. (2002). Searching for threat. *Quarterly Journal of Experimental Psychology Section a: Human Experimental Psychology, 55*(3), 1007–1026.

Treisman, A. M., & Gelade, G. (1980). A feature-integration theory of attention. *Cognitive Psychology, 12*, 97–136.

Trippe, R. H., Hewig, J., Heydel, C., Hecht, H., & Miltner, W. H. (2007). Attentional blink to emotional and threatening pictures in spider phobics: Electrophysiology and behavior. *Brain Research, 1148*, 149–160.

Turk, C. L., Lerner, J., Heimberg, R. G., & Rapee, R. M. (2001). An integrated cognitive-behavioral model of social anxiety. In S. G. Hofmann & P. M. DiBartolo (Eds.), *From social anxiety to social phobia: Multiple perspectives* (pp. 281–303). Needham Heights, MA: Allyn & Bacon.

Van Damme, S., Gallace, A., Spence, C., & Moseley, G. L. (2009). Does the sight of physical threat induce a tactile processing bias? Modality-specific attentional facilitation induced by viewing threatening pictures. *Brain Research, 1253*, 100–106.

van Hooff, J. C., Dietz, K. C., Sharma, D., & Bowman, H. (2008). Neural correlates of intrusion of emotion words in a modified Stroop task. *International Journal of Psychophysiology, 67*(1), 23–34.

Vuilleumier, P. (2002). Facial expression and selective attention. *Current Opinion in Psychiatry, 15*(3), 291–300.

Waters, A. M., Nitz, A. B., Craske, M. G., & Johnson, C. (2007). The effects of anxiety upon attention allocation to affective stimuli. *Behaviour Research and Therapy, 45*(4), 763–774.

Weary, G., & Edwards, J. A. (1994). Social cognition and clinical psychology: Anxiety, depression, and the processing of social information. In R. S. Wyer Jr. & T. K. Srull (Eds.), *Handbook of social cognition* (2nd edn) (pp. 289–338). Hillsdale, NJ: Lawrence Erlbaum Associates, Inc.

Wegner, D. M., & Bargh, J. A. (1998). Control and automaticity in social life. In D. Gilbert, S. T. Fiske, & G. Lindzey (Eds.), *Handbook of social psychology* (Vol. 1 (4th ed) (pp. 446–496)). New York: McGraw-Hill.

Weierich, M. R., Treat, T. A., & Hollingworth, A. (2008). Theories and measurement of visual attentional processing in anxiety. *Cognition and Emotion, 22*, 985–1018.

Wentura, D., Rothermund, K., & Bak, P. (2000). Automatic vigilance: The attention-grabbing power of approach- and avoidance-related social information. *Journal of Personality and Social Psychology, 78*, 1024–1037.

Wickens, C. D. (1984). Processing resources in attention. In R. Parasuraman & D. R. Davies (Eds.), *Varieties of attention*. New York: Academic Press.

Wikstrom, J., Lundh, L. G., & Westerlund, J. (2003). Stroop effects for masked threat words: Pre-attentive bias or selective awareness? *Cognition and Emotion, 17*(6), 827–842.

Williams, J. M. G., Mathews, A., & MacLeod, C. (1996). The emotional Stroop task and psychopathology. *Psychological Bulletin, 120*, 3–24.

Williams, J. M. G., Watts, F. N., MacLeod, C., & Mathews, A. (1988). *Cognitive psychology and emotional disorders*. Chichester, UK: Wiley.

Williams, J. M. G., Watts, F. N., MacLeod, C., & Mathews, A. (1997). *Cognitive psychology and emotional disorders* (2nd ed). Chichester, UK: Wiley.

Williams, M. A., Moss, S. A., Bradshaw, J. L., & Mattingley, J. B. (2005). Look at me, I'm smiling: Visual search for threatening and nonthreatening facial expressions. *Visual Cognition, 12*(1), 29–50.

Williamson, D. A., Muller, S. L., Reas, D. L., & Thaw, J. M. (1999). Cognitive bias in eating disorders: Implications for theory and treatment. *Behavior Modification, 23*(4), 556–577.

Wilson, E., & MacLeod, C. (2003). Contrasting two accounts of anxiety-linked attentional bias: Selective attention to varying levels of stimulus threat intensity. *Journal of Abnormal Psychology, 112*(2), 212–218.

Wolfe, J. M. (1994). Guided Search 2.0: A revised model of visual search. *Psychonomic Bulletin & Review, 2*, 202–238.

Wolfe, J. M., Cave, K. R., & Franzel, S. L. (1989). Guided search: An alternative to the feature integration model of visual search. *Journal of Experimental Psychology: Human Perception and Performance, 15*, 419–433.

Wood, N., & Cowan, N. (1995a). The cocktail party phenomenon revisited: Attention and memory in the classic selective listening procedure of Cherry (1953). *Journal of Experimental Psychology: General, 124*(3), 243–262.

Wood, N., & Cowan, N. (1995b). The cocktail party phenomenon revisited: How frequent are attention shifts to one's name in an irrelevant auditory channel? *Journal of Experimental Psychology: Learning, Memory and Cognition, 21*(1), 255–260.

Wu, S. C., & Remington, R. (2003). Characteristics of covert and overt visual orienting: Evidence from attentional and oculomotor capture. *Journal of Experimental Psychology: Human Perception and Performance, 29*, 1050–1067.

Yiend, J., & Mackintosh, B. (2004). The experimental modification of processing biases. In J. Yiend (Ed.), *Cognition, emotion and psychopathology* (pp. 190–210). Cambridge, UK: Cambridge University Press.

Yiend, J., & Mathews, A. (2001). Anxiety and attention to threatening pictures. *Quarterly Journal of Experimental Psychology Section a: Human Experimental Psychology, 54*(3), 665–681.

Yiend, J., & Mathews, A. (2005). Selective attention tasks in cognitive research. Biases in attention: Methods, mechanisms and meaning. In A. Wenzel & D. C. Rubin (Eds.), *Cognitive methods in clinical research* (pp. 97–117). Washington, DC: American Psychological Association.

Yiend, J., Mathews, A., & Cowan, N. (2005). Selective attention in clinical and cognitive research. In A. Wenzel & D. C. Rubin (Eds.), *Cognitive methods in clinical research* (pp. 65–71). Washington, DC: American Psychological Association.

Yiend, J., Mathews, A., Weston, B., Dunn, B. D., Cusack, R., & Mackintosh, B. (2008). An investigation of the implicit control of the processing of negative pictures. *Emotion, 8*(6), 828–837.

Yovel, I., & Mineka, S. (2005). Emotion-congruent attentional biases: the perspective of hierarchical models of emotional disorders. *Personality and Individual Differences, 38*(4), 785–795.

Zeelenberg, R., Wagenmakers, E. J., & Rotteveel, M. (2006). The impact of emotion on perception: bias or enhanced processing? *Psychological Science, 17*(4), 288–291.

Correspondence should be addressed to: Jenny Yiend, PO63, Department of Psychiatry and Psychological Medicine, Institute of Psychiatry, King's College London, De Crespigny Park, London, SE5 8AF, UK. E-mail: jenny.yiend@kcl.ac.uk

I am most grateful to Brendan Bradley, Colin MacLeod, Andrew Mathews, Karin Mogg, Charles Spence, Nick Yeung, reviewers Manuel Calvo, Ernst Koster, Jan De Houwer and one anonymous reviewer for their valuable comments on previous drafts.

# 8 The influence of affect on higher level cognition: A review of research on interpretation, judgement, decision making and reasoning

Isabelle Blanchette*
*Université du Québec à Trois-Rivières, Trois-Rivières, Québec, Canada*
Anne Richards*
*Birkbeck College, University of London, London, UK*

Higher level cognitive processes are characteristically human. Until recently, these processes were studied in a vacuum, separately from the affective system, as if they were immune from such influence. This partition may have stemmed from early conceptual distinctions between reason and passion, with its implicit hierarchical distinction. More recent approaches propose a dynamic interaction between basic and complex processes, between cognitive and affective variables, and between subcortical and cortical regions of the brain. In this paper, we review behavioural research that has empirically examined these interactions, specifically focusing on the impact of affective variables on higher level cognitive processes. Our review attempts to answer two main questions: First, is there an effect of emotion on higher level cognitive functions? We examine four key processes: interpretation, judgement, decision making, and reasoning. Second, we ask what mechanisms underlie this effect. In each section, we examine whether the effect is general to all emotions or whether it is different for specific emotions.

Our review is not meant to be exhaustive, as the field is already too large to be reviewed comprehensively in a single paper. Rather, we hope to provide a relatively representative overview of some of the research on these four key processes, emphasising selected questions concerning underlying mechanisms and our own view of potential directions for future research.

Interpretation, judgement, reasoning, and decision making are four important processes that help us navigate a complex world. Collectively,

* Both authors should be considered joint first authors of this paper

they are the cognitive tools we use to form a coherent representation of the world, anticipate upon what may be coming next, and make choices about courses of action. Interpretation is the process through which one meaning is extracted from ambiguous information in order to construct a mental representation. Judgement is the process by which individuals consider and evaluate evidence and estimate the likelihood of occurrence of different outcomes. Decision-making research examines how people chose one out of several options, with a particular focus on how individuals select or avoid options that carry different levels of risk. Reasoning is the process by which participants use the information available to them to draw inferences. This process contributes to constructing an understanding of the world that surrounds them.

Obviously, all of these processes are complex, in the sense that they all rely on a number of constituent processes such as object recognition, attention, spreading activation in semantic memory, etc. Our primary goal is to review empirical evidence on the influence of affect on each process. Our second goal is to start to locate the mechanisms through which the impact of emotion operates. We propose that understanding how emotions influence the constituent processes that contribute to each of these higher level cognitive functions may help unify and integrate the diverse research findings in this disjointed field. We examine some core constituent mechanisms in the conclusions.

In this paper, we use the term emotion in its general sense, to refer to affective contents or states. We make a distinction between integral and incidental affect. Incidental affect may be induced affective states (moods) that are transient in nature or more stable personality differences in affective traits (e.g., anxiety) that are not evoked by the target materials. In those cases, the affective feeling state is orthogonal to the contents of the cognitive task. These are instances where affect is free floating, not evoked directly by the contents that participants are processing. For instance, a mood manipulation using a video on the death of a little boy, or sad music, followed by a task asking participants to judge the likelihood of different neutral events is looking at incidental affect. The affective state is not related to the stimuli that are the focus of the cognitive task. Much research using mood-induction procedures and their effects on different cognitive tasks falls within this category. By contrast, we call emotion situations integral where the affective feeling state is induced by the target materials that participants are processing in the task. For instance when comparing conditions where participants reason about emotional contents (e.g., estimate how many people die of leukaemia each year) the affective state is induced by the target contents and this is compared to a situation where the target contents do not evoke much emotion (e.g., estimate how many people consult a financial adviser each year). In those cases of integral emotion, there is an emotional state that results from the contents presented in the cognitive task. Analogous distinctions highlighting the source of the affective feeling have recently been proposed in other fields (Laney, Heuer, & Reisberg, 2003; Pham, 2007). We believe this distinction may be useful in trying to compare the findings across tasks examining the impact of affect on higher level cognitive functions.

## INTERPRETATION

The resolution of ambiguity is an integral part of our everyday interactions with the world, with ambiguous information being presented to all our sensory modalities. A slight touch on the skin could signal a gnat bite or an innocuous strand of hair falling on the skin. A sentence could be interpreted at face value or as having sarcastic intent. Of particular interest in emotion research is how emotional states influence these interpretations. Some research has examined the processing of ambiguous emotional information, and what processes are involved in resolution in all individuals, whereas other research has focused on individual differences in these interpretations. Ambiguity, both emotional and non-emotional, may be resolved with or without awareness, and some already established interpretation may be reappraised with volitional control. In general, the ability to correctly interpret ambiguous signs that could predict harm is obviously crucial for adaptive functioning. This is reflected in the fact that much of the research on interpretation has focused on threat and anxiety.

## Empirical effects

A whole range of behavioural measures have been used to examine how interpretation is influenced by emotion, particularly anxiety. Many forms of verbal and non-verbal ambiguity have been exploited to study interpretation in different tasks. In word recognition, lexical ambiguity may be evident at the word level in the form of homophones (e.g., *brews/ bruise*) or semantic ambiguity in the form of homographs (e.g., *stroke* can refer to a brain haemorrhage or to a caress). Studies have also examined ambiguity present in sentences or scenarios, and other research has employed ambiguous facial expressions. These investigations have used a range of dependent measures, including self-reports, ratings of alternative meanings, spellings, recognition, lexical decisions, reading times, naming and comprehension.

### *Anxiety-congruent interpretation*

Seminal research by Butler and Mathews (1983, 1987) used self-report methodology, and demonstrated clear differences in interpretation between anxious and non-anxious individuals. Anxious individuals made more negative interpretations of threat/neutral ambiguous scenarios, saw themselves as being at greater risk than other people, and perceived the cost to them personally of the negative event occurring as being higher than that for another person. Similar effects have been found in a socially anxious group using ambiguous sentences and scenarios (Amir, Foa, & Coles, 1998; Foa, Franklin, Perry, & Herbert, 1996; Huppert, Pasupuleti, Foa, & Mathews, 2007; Stopa & Clark, 2000). Socially anxious individuals generated more negative interpretations of ambiguous social scenarios in comparison with control and other anxiety-disordered individuals. Stopa and Clark went on to show that this bias was eliminated in recovered socially anxious individuals. These studies demonstrated that the interpretation of ambiguous stimuli is constrained by the person's affective state.

Robust findings have been obtained using a homophone-spelling task where a series of threat/neutral homophones together with filler words are presented auditorally ostensibly as a standard spelling test. Typically, high-trait anxious (Byrne & Eysenck, 1993; Eysenck, MacLeod, & Mathews, 1987; Hadwin, Frost, French, & Richards, 1997; Halberstadt, Niedenthal, & Kushner, 1995; Mogg, Bradley, & Hallowell, 1994; Richards, Reynolds, & French, 1993) and clinically anxious (Mathews, Richards, & Eysenck, 1989) participants produce more threat-related spellings than the controls—but see Russo and colleagues (Russo, Patterson, Roberson, Stevenson, & Upward, 1996) who found a bias for the *emotional* spelling rather than just mood-congruent interpretations.

Other studies have used methodologies where participants are not asked to produce one interpretation or another, but simply to recognise one or the other interpretation of the ambiguous stimulus. The facility with which this is done provides a clue as to which interpretation was adopted spontaneously. Eysenck, Mogg, May, Richards, and Mathews (1991) used a recognition paradigm and demonstrated mood-congruent interpretive bias for ambiguous sentences that had both threatening and neutral interpretations. Other researchers have used lexical decision to targets as their dependent measures following homographs (Richards & French, 1992; Richards, French, Johnson, Naparstek, & Williams, 1992), homophones (Blanchette & Richards, 2003) or ambiguous sentences (Calvo, Eysenck, & Estevez, 1994; Hirsch & Mathews, 1997). Reading times for different interpretations has also been used as a dependent measure (Calvo, Eysenck, & Castillo, 1997; MacLeod & Cohen, 1993). Finally, studies have examined how quickly participants name targets related to the threat or neutral interpretation of ambiguous stimuli (Calvo & Castillo, 2001a,b; Calvo et al., 1997). The typical finding, using all of these different methods, is that anxious individuals resolve the ambiguity in line with the more threatening interpretation in comparison with control participants.

Comparable effects have been observed using non-verbal stimuli such as facial expressions. A facial expression portrays dynamic displays of emotion, changing from, for example, surprise to fear. This quality of faces allows the generation of emotionally ambiguous expressions that can be used to detect interpretive biases. Ambiguous facial expressions can be created by morphing two emotions together in varying proportions along a continuum (e.g., 10% anger–90% happiness, 30% anger–70% happiness, and so on; Young, Rowland, Calder, & Etcoff, 1997). Sprengelmeyer and colleagues (1997) used such faces and found enhanced identification of fear and anger, and a borderline advantage for sadness in clinically anxious participants compared to a control group. In a non-clinical sample, Richards and colleagues (2002) presented ambiguous facial expressions to high and low socially anxious participants, and found that the high anxious participants were more sensitive to fear than the low anxious. When state anxiety was raised, there was enhanced sensitivity to anger.

Overall, research conducted over recent years has shown robust effects of anxiety on interpretation. This research has focused on incidental affect, with experimentally induced anxious states as well as stable individual differences in trait anxiety. By definition, because the stimuli are ambiguous and cannot clearly evoke one particular emotion, research on this topic has not examined integral affect. The effect of anxiety on interpretation has been shown using different tasks and different stimuli. The effect has also been investigated in real-life situations, for instance using elevated anxiety in patients waiting for a potentially painful dental operation (Atkinson & Caldwell, 1997; Richards, Blanchette, & Munjiza, 2007a; Weis & Lovejoy, 2002). The findings of these investigations are consistent with those obtained in the laboratory, thus confirming the robust effects of anxiety on interpretation.

## Use of context in ambiguity resolution

Most studies have examined how emotion modulates ambiguity resolution in a contextual vacuum, yet it is clear that context is highly influential in gearing interpretations in complex environments that provide multiple sources of information (Gaskell & Marslen Wilson, 2001). In the text-comprehension literature, modular (Onifer & Swinney, 1981) and inter-active (McClelland, 1987) models make different proposals about the specific way in which context affects interpretation. Yet it is clear in all models that context-congruent meanings should be preferred over incon-gruent meanings (Lucas, 1999).

In studies on emotion and interpretation, context can be an integral part of the task. For example, some studies have presented ambiguous words embedded within a sentence, and the meaning of the ambiguous word was constrained by the sentence. In this case, the task could not be performed without making reference to the contextual sentence (MacLeod & Cohen, 1993). In this section, we refer to context in the wider sense, where external information that is presented simultaneously with the ambiguous informa-tion but is additional to the main task and *may* influence the interpretation of that stimulus (e.g., classifying a facial expression without necessarily referring to the other expressions in the scene). In this instance, the context is not an inherent part of the task. Recent studies have integrated this aspect and shown that participants resolve emotionally ambiguous information using contextual information. For instance, Nygaard and Lunders (2002) found that threat/neutral homophones are interpreted in line with the tone of voice (sad, happy, neutral), showing that a non-linguistic property (i.e., voice tone) constrains the linguistic process of lexical ambiguity resolution. The classification of emotional expressions is influenced by context in individuals irrespective of their levels of anxiety (e.g., Aviezer et al., 2008; Barrett, Lindquist, & Gendron, 2007; de Gelder et al., 2006; Fernandez-Dols & Carroll, 1997; Halberstadt et al., 1995). For example, Aviezer and colleagues (2008) embedded facial expressions in affective contexts, and found that these contexts influenced the interpretation of the expressions. Using an adaptation paradigm, in which an emotional expression is repeatedly presented prior to a target ambiguous expression, context influences the classification of the target expression relative to when the target expression is presented without a context (e.g., Furl, van Rijsbergen, Treves, & Dolan, 2007; Pell & Richards, 2009). Halberstadt et al. (1995) proposed that emotional states direct the resolution of lexical ambiguity in the same way as semantic context. There is also some recent evidence showing that olfactory contextual information, specifically fear-related chemosignals (sweat collected from donors while watching a stressful video) can bias the interpretation of ambiguous facial expressions in the direction consistent with the chemosignal (Zhou & Chen, 2009).

Other research has examined how anxiety modulates the use of contextual information in ambiguity resolution, for verbal and non-verbal stimuli (Blanchette & Richards, 2003; Blanchette, Richards, & Cross, 2007a; Richards et al., 2007a). Blanchette and Richards (2003) used a homophone lexical decision task. There was simultaneous presentation of the homophone auditorally (e.g., *berry/bury*) and a biasing context, visually (e.g., *fruit*). This was followed by the threatening spelling of the homophone (i.e., *bury*), the neutral spelling (i.e., *berry*) or a non-word in a lexical decision task. All participants were faster to make context-congruent lexical decisions, whether the context was neutral or emotional. However, this effect was enhanced in anxious participants. Thus, anxious participants were in some cases quicker to make mood-*incongruent* decisions (e.g., they were faster to decide that *berry* was a word following the neutral context than were the control group). The effect of context appeared even when presented subliminally, albeit to a lesser extent. These findings are consistent with the view that negative affect is associated with an increase in bottom-up processing in which a wider range of information is sought in making a decision, even a basic decision that involves opting between two different interpretations (Fiedler, 2000).

To recap, research shows that when presented with emotionally ambiguous information, participants will use disambiguating contextual information. Furthermore while participants typically resolve ambiguity in a way consistent with their mood when ambiguous stimuli are presented in isolation, anxiety-congruent biases may be overridden when anxiety leads to greater reliance on contextual information.

## Mechanisms

Research has recently started to investigate mechanisms underlying the effect of anxiety on interpretation. Among the important questions that have been posed are:

1. At what stage in the information-processing sequence is anxiety influencing interpretation: the initial generation or the later selection of meaning?
2. What is the causal direction in the link between anxiety and interpretive biases?

### Information processing stage

An important question in understanding how anxiety affects interpretation is when exactly emotion influences ambiguity resolution. Part of this question is whether anxiety is really affecting interpretive processes, or simply affecting the response that participants choose to report. If anxiety is genuinely affecting interpretation, another question is whether it impacts on the initial generation of interpretations or on the selection of one meaning over another.

Initial work on interpretation relied on self-report and recall measures. Using these measures, both threat-related and neutral meanings may be available to the participant but one of these may be preferentially selected for response. Thus, all participants may produce both neutral and threatening interpretations but anxious participants may differ in that they selectively opt to report the threatening response.

In an attempt to investigate this possibility, Mathews et al. (1989) recorded skin conductance responses (SCRs) while clinically anxious, recovered anxious, and control participants completed the homophone-spelling test. The consistency between the SCR data and the written spelling was examined. If, for example, participants wrote down the neutral spelling but had an SCR that was similar to that observed when they spelled a threat word, then this would indicate a response bias. There was no evidence for a response bias. However, SCR is an indirect measure here. In 1992, Richards and French directly controlled for a response bias effect. In a lexical decision task, high- and low-anxious individuals saw threat/neutral homograph primes followed by targets that were related or unrelated, and threatening or neutral associates of the targets. Across participants, a threat-related associate for one participant was a threat-unrelated associate for another. Therefore, any observed priming effect must have been due to the facilitatory effect of the prime rather than any response bias, which would facilitate processing of unrelated threat associates. The researchers found evidence for a threat-related priming effect in anxiety and this could not be accounted for by a response-bias explanation. Thus, it seems that anxiety is genuinely affecting interpretation, not simply response selection.

Even if anxiety-congruent interpretation is a genuine interpretive bias, the question of the specific stage at which anxiety is having an effect remains. Different models make specific propositions about the time course of activation of alternative meanings. For instance exhaustive-access models propose that initially all meanings of the ambiguous stimulus are retrieved followed by the selection of the context-appropriate meaning with the non-selected meanings being actively suppressed (Gadsby, Arnott, & Copland, 2008; Gernsbacher & Faust, 1991) or dissipating over time (Simpson & Burgess, 1985). Alternatively, the selective-access models argue that only the contextually appropriate meaning is activated and selected. The context-sensitive model (Simpson, 1984) proposes that more than one meaning is activated initially, but the degree of activation is dependent on dominance of the meanings and the context in which it is presented. Based on these models, anxiety could be associated with the differential generation of meaning to an ambiguous stimulus or with differential selection of the mood-congruent meaning. Richards and French (1992) found that initially both threat-related and neutral meanings are activated for all participants, followed by context-appropriate or affect-congruent selection later on. Other studies also suggest that multiple interpretations are generated and that the affective state constrains later adoption of one possible meaning in socially anxious participants (Huppert et al., 2007).

These studies are limited in that they examine the results of selection at a conscious level, other studies have examined this in more detail and provided robust evidence that the threat-related resolution of ambiguous information observed in anxiety operates at the stage of postlexical processes. For instance, studies have presented ambiguous target information with primes and manipulated Stimulus Onset Asynchrony (SOA) between the prime and the target. Richards and French (1992) presented threat-related, neutral or unrelated targets 500 ms, 750 ms or 1250 ms after the presentation of a threat/neutral homograph in a lexical-decision semantic-priming paradigm. At the shortest SOA, both high- and low-anxiety participants showed semantic priming for both threat-related and neutral associates of the homographs. However, at the later intervals the high-anxious showed priming for the threatening meaning and the low-anxious group showed priming only for the neutral meanings. This suggests that the anxious group "locks onto" the threatening meaning of the homograph at a later stage of processing. Calvo and Castillo (1997) confirmed these findings in a Rapid Serial Visual Presentation (RSVP), in which ambiguous prime sentences were presented word by word. In this experiment, there was differential threat-related target naming at 1250 ms but not at 500 ms. This research suggests that anxiety is more likely affecting selection of one meaning rather than initial generation of possible interpretations.

These findings do not preclude the possibility that anxiety has an automatic impact on the selection process (Calvo & Castillo, 2001a,b; MacLeod, 1999). There is evidence that the resolution is performed on-line rather than being the consequence of later reconstructive processes that involve retrieval. Calvo, Castillo, and Estevez (1999) presented sentences followed by a target related to either the threat-related or neutral meaning of the sentence, and observed that a gap of around 1 second is required between the prime and the target in order for an inference to be drawn. Calvo and Castillo (2001a) extended this by examining the possibility that anxiety may increase the speed at which emotion congruent (i.e., threat-related) inferences are drawn compared to neutral inferences and to a control group. In a series of six experiments, high- and low-anxious individuals were presented with a Rapid Serial Visual Presentation (RSVP) task in which context sentences were presented at different speeds. The time interval between the end of the sentence and the presentation of the target was also varied. They found that additional time to read the context had no effect on the time needed between the end of the sentence and the presentation of the target. Thus, it appears that anxiety does not speed up the time needed to draw inferences, but affects the probability that a negative inference will be drawn.

It has been proposed that the same cognitive mechanisms underlie attentional and interpretive biases in anxiety (Mathews & Mackintosh, 1998; Mathews & MacLeod, 2002). Selective attention to threat and an interpretive bias for threat are said to arise as the result of competition between preattentive threat evaluation mechanisms and top-down attentional control mechanisms. Anxiety is proposed to increase the output of the former mechanism, resulting in an increased signal and a bias for threat. There is general agreement that the amygdala plays a central role in the processing of arousing and emotionally salient stimuli. The anterior insula is also implicated in threat-related processing, with insula activity correlating with subjective perception of emotional states (Craig, 2002, 2003) and with the aversive nature of stimuli (Anders, Lotze, Erb, Grodd, & Birbaumer, 2004). Bishop and colleagues (Bishop, Cohen, Fossella, Caswey, & Farah, 2006; Bishop, Duncan, & Lawrence, 2004) found that all participants showed an increase in amygdala activity in response to fearful expression when attention was directed to the expressions, but only the high-anxious individuals showed this amygdala activity when the fearful expressions were unattended. This is consistent with the idea that the balance between preattentive threat-detection mechanisms and top-down control processes is modulated by anxiety.

Bishop (2007) reviewed the animal and human research, and cites neurobiological evidence for this idea, concluding that there is common circuitry underlying both attention to threat and the interpretation of emotionally ambiguous stimuli, as well as the acquisition and extinction of conditioned fear. Processing of threat-related stimuli involves amygdala–prefrontal circuitry, with increased activation of the amygdala coupled with decreased recruitment of prefrontal control mechanisms. There are reciprocal connection between the amygdala and prefrontal cortical areas (Kim, Somerville, Johnstone, Alexander, & Whalen, 2003), with the medial prefrontal cortex (mPFC), lateral prefrontal cortex and the anterior cingulate cortex implicated in the downregulation of the amygdala.

Research examining the processes involved in the active reinterpretation of a situation lend support to the proposal of prefrontal downregulation of the amygdala and the insula (Ochsner & Gross, 2008; Phan et al., 2005; Ray et al., 2005). Goldin and colleagues (Goldin, McRae, Ramel, & Gross, 2008) found that reappraisal recruited the cognitive control regions of the prefrontal cortex (PFC), including enhanced signals in the dorsolateral, ventrolateral and medial areas, with activity in the amygdala and insula reduced. The PFC appears to be activated early on in the sequence (0 to 4.5 s) followed by a reduction in amygdala and insula activity at a later period (10.5 to 15 s). Another strategy, suppression, was related to later activity in PFC regions (10.5 to 15 s) but increased amygdala and insula activity. Thus it appears that the same circuitry may be involved in the interpretation of ambiguity and the reinterpretation of a selected meaning.

Bishop (2007) proposed that anxiety modulates the output from both the amygdala and the prefrontal regions, with anxiety being associated with amygdala hyper-responsivity and prefrontal hyporesponsivity. There is evidence from neuroimaging studies to support this amygdaloid–prefrontal circuitry. Amygdala activity when viewing neutral faces seen as mildly threatening is correlated with anxiety (Somerville, Kim, Johnstone, Alexander, & Whalen, 2004) as well as when surprise expressions are perceived to be negative (Kim et al., 2004).

In sum, anxiety appears to be associated with an interpretive bias that cannot be accounted for by a response bias for negativity. Anxiety appears to increase the likelihood that a threat-related inference will be drawn, rather than to increase the speed with which a threat-related inference is drawn. Although the effect of anxiety on ambiguity resolution occurs at a later more elaborative stage, the resolution occurs "on-line" rather than being the result of later reconstructive processes that involve retrieval. A growing body of neurobiological evidence suggests that a common circuitry underlies attention to, interpretation of, and reinterpretation of threat. The effect of anxiety on these processes may be related to increased amygdala activity coupled with a decrease in the recruitment of prefrontal control mechanisms.

*Causality*

Because a lot of the literature on anxiety and interpretation has used quasi-experimental designs where individuals with varying levels of trait anxiety are compared, the question of the direction of the causal link is particularly important. Anxiety may lead to more negative interpretations, but more threatening interpretations may also induce anxious states. There is actually a growing literature, using a training paradigm, that suggests a causal relationship between interpretive biases and anxiety (MacLeod, Campbell, Rutherford, & Wilson, 2004; Mathews & Mackintosh, 2000; Yiend & Mackintosh, 2004). In this paradigm, participants are trained to interpret threat/neutral ambiguous stimulus in either the threatening or neutral manner. The effects of this differential training on mood and subsequent interpretations are examined. Training methods have typically used emotional homographs (Grey & Mathews, 2000; Hertel, Mathews, Peterson, & Kintner, 2003; Wilson, MacLeod, Mathews, & Rutherford, 2006) or ambiguous text (Mathews & Mackintosh, 2000). The ambiguous stimulus (e.g., a threat/neutral homograph "batter") is followed by a fragment where the correct completion is threat-related (assault) or benign (pancake), depending on the condition. Following training, a series of new ambiguous homographs are presented to see if the novel interpretation is congruent with the training mode.

The typical finding is for the training to transfer to new materials, producing training-congruent interpretive bias. Effects of training can be apparent 24 hours after the training period, but further research is necessary to determine longer-term resilience and the effects of mood-incongruent intervening activities (Yiend & Mackintosh, 2004). The transfer of training to new material appears to occur irrespective of whether or not the training involved the individual having to actively generate the biased meaning or whether they simply were given the meaning. The evidence on whether the transfer of interpretive bias extends to different types of paradigms is, however, still equivocal (Hertel et al., 2003; Hirsch, Mathews, & Clark, 2007; Salemink, van den Hout, & Kindt, 2007).

In addition to the effect on later interpretation, researchers have examined the effect of induced interpretation bias on mood. It appears that for mood to be effected, active generation of meaning is necessary but not sufficient. Yiend, Mackintosh, and Mathews (2005) found mood change only following active generation in a text task but not a homograph task. However, latent mood effects have been observed by Wilson and colleagues (2006) following a homograph training task. Individuals trained to interpret benignly were less vulnerable to a stressful situation (watching stressful video clips) than negatively trained individuals. It therefore seems that interpretation training may offer some later protection from anxiety.

Overall, there are some very interesting effects emerging from the training studies, showing generalisation of interpretive biases as a result of induced interpretation biases as well as some effects on mood. The long-term efficacy of these effects, however, needs further investigation. The data suggest that interpretive biases may, at least to a certain extent, cause anxiety. Another way to examine the direction of the causal link between interpretive biases and anxious states is to examine the two variables over the course of development.

Different models make different predictions about whether interpretive biases found in anxious adults should be present in anxious children. Jones (1984, 1987) put forward the hypothesis that emotional biases develop over a period of time. The integral bias hypothesis (L. Martin, Harlow, & Strack, 1992; M. Martin, Horder, & Jones, 1992; Martin & Jones, 1995) proposes that cognitive processes are an inherent component of emotion and therefore biases that are present in anxious adults should also be evident in anxious children. The typical finding in empirical studies is that clinically anxious children make more threat-related interpretations of ambiguous stories than non-anxious children (Muris & van der Heiden, 2006; Taghavi, Moradi, Neshat-Doost, Yule, & Dalgleish, 2000; Waters, Craske, Bergman, & Treanor, 2008). This is also true of non-clinical high anxious children (Higa & Daleiden, 2008). Similar effects have also been reported using pictorial stimuli (In-Albon, Klein, Rinck, Becker, & Schneider, 2008), and when homophones/homographs are presented auditorally followed by disambiguating pictures (Gifford, Reynolds, Bell, & Wilson, 2008; Hadwin et al., 1997). Thus, findings generally show that even young children show interpretive biases consistent with those evidenced by adults, although there are some inconsistent findings (Richards, French, Nash, Hadwin, & Donnelly, 2007b). While these studies provide valuable information, further studies using methods other than self-reports and using some of the methodologies used with adults to investigate the underlying mechanisms will improve our understanding further.

## Specificity

There is robust evidence for an interpretive bias in both clinical and subclinical anxiety, but the evidence for other emotions and disorders is still equivocal. Early research using self-report methods (Butler & Mathews, 1983; Cane & Gotlib, 1985; Forgas, Bower, & Krantz, 1984; Nunn, Mathews, & Trower, 1997) showed negative interpretive biases in depressed individuals comparable to those observed in generalised anxiety. However, when more tightly controlled tasks have been employed, in attempts to control for response bias, there have been failures to find an interpretive bias in depression. In a sentence priming study in which participants were required to pronounce a target word following a sentence, Lawson and MacLeod (1999) failed to find evidence of an interpretive bias in their dysphoric group. There was also no support for a negative interpretive bias in a series of four studies by Bisson and Sears (2007). They used a cross-modal semantic priming paradigm in which participants had to make a lexical decision to a target that followed (at 0 ms, 1000 ms or 2000 ms SOA) an ambiguous prime sentence. There was significant semantic priming for all of the related targets, but this did not differ between the dysphoric and non-dysphoric groups. Even when a mood manipulation was employed in order to activate a negative schema, there was still no evidence of an interpretive bias associated with depression. These studies suggest that there is no interpretive bias in dysphoric individuals. There may be a negative response bias, a tendency to report the more negative interpretation, but no actual interpretive bias. This conclusion is also supported by the findings obtained by Mogg and colleagues, who presented a clinically depressed group and a control group with the homophone task, a text-comprehension task, and a memory task (Mogg, Bradbury, & Bradley, 2006). When there was minimal opportunity for a response bias to be observed (i.e., the text-comprehension task), there was no depression-related interpretive bias. However, there were depression-related negative biases observed for both the homophone task and the memory task, which provide greater opportunity for a response bias to be observed.

The case for disgust may be different from that for depression, as participants induced to feel disgusted may show the same interpretive biases as anxious participants. In an experiment that manipulated mood and examined the resolution of ambiguity using threat/neutral homophones, those in the disgust manipulation condition showed comparable negative biases for threat-related interpretation to those observed in anxiety (Davey, Bickerstaffe, & MacDonald, 2006).

Various subtypes of anxiety have been shown to be related to an interpretive bias. Kolassa and colleagues (2007) presented spider phobics and controls with images of spiders morphed with flowers, and found a spider-related bias in the phobics. Davey, Menzies, and Gallardo (1997) found that agoraphobia and acrophobia were associated with a tendency to interpret ambiguous bodily sensations as threatening. Individuals with high social anxiety tend to interpret neutral facial expressions in a threatening manner (Richards et al., 2002; Yoon & Zinbarg, 2008) and have consistently been shown to interpret ambiguous social scenarios in a negative direction (Amir, Beard, & Bower, 2005; Brendle & Wenzel, 2004; Hertel, Brozovich, Joormann, & Gotlib, 2008; Wenzel, Finstrom, Jordan, & Brendle, 2005). There is also evidence that social anxiety is associated with a diminished positive bias, suggesting that such individuals lack positive on-line inferences, which is thought to typify non-anxious controls (Hirsch & Mathews, 1997; Hirsch et al., 2007). Many of these studies on different types of anxiety have relied on self-report measures, and so there may be an influence of response bias.

In sum, it appears that emotions are associated with a bias for reporting mood-congruent interpretations. However, these effects may be related to a response bias rather than an interpretive bias, per se. Depression appears to be associated with a response bias, but not an interpretive bias. By contrast, different affective states related to anxiety have been shown to produce robust effects on interpretation (e.g., social anxiety, phobias). The limited research examining disgust has revealed comparable effects to those found with anxiety. As we mentioned previously, this research has focused, by definition, on incidental affect, as the ambiguous stimuli in themselves do not clearly evoke a specific emotion. There appear to be close links between interpretation and attention processes, a point we come back to later in the discussion. However, we note that the robust effect of anxiety, and the absence of effect of sadness on interpretation parallel similar findings in the attention literature, where strong effects of anxiety, but not sadness, are observed. Given this specificity and these parallels, the effect of emotion on interpretation may be construed as an attentional focus on threatening information (the selective focus on threatening interpretation) modulated by anxiety, rather than as a more general mood-congruent effect. More work needs to be done to examine the effect of other emotions on interpretation, in particular positive emotions and anger, to evaluate this hypothesis. This future research should use some of the more sophisticated techniques that have been developed and used more recently in order to differentiate true interpretation bias from response bias, and to determine the mechanisms that underlie these effects.

## JUDGEMENT

While interpretation involves resolving the ambiguity inherent in a stimulus or a situation that is immediately present, judgement may be seen as the process by which participants cope with the ambiguity inherent in estimating the future. An additional distinction is that the interpretation literature has typically focused on the rapid on-line construction of meaning while judgement tasks usually allow participants time to think explicitly about the different possibilities and come up with a judgement of probability (how likely is it?) rather than a binary answer. Interpretation and judgement share a lot in common, and the early research on anxiety and interpretation, using ambiguous social vignettes, actually also included judgement tasks, where participants had to estimate the likelihood of positive and negative events (Butler & Mathews, 1987).

Judgement research thus examines how people estimate the likelihood of future events. The outcome of this process, the estimates, are key component ingredients of decision making. Whether or not you get your child vaccinated, buy insurance, or invade a foreign country all depend on how likely you judge different outcomes to be. A considerable amount of research has investigated whether affect influences risk perception, or how people estimate the likelihood of future negative or threatening events. In this section, we review the empirical studies that have documented affect-congruent judgement effects. We then explore different mechanisms (memory-based and heuristic) that have been proposed to account for these effects. Because a lot of the work has examined negative emotions generally, we finally explore whether affect-congruent judgement biases are emotion specific and whether judgement is affected similarly by all emotions.

## Empirical effects

Johnson and Tversky published a pioneering paper in 1983 in which they examined how incidental affect influences risk perception. They started from the premise that judgements about risk " ... seldom occur in an emotionally neutral context". Negative mood was induced by asking participants to read newspaper reports about different forms of death (leukaemia, homicide, or fire). These stories provided only anecdotal information and no information about probabilities. Participants then evaluated the likelihood of death resulting from a variety of causes. Relative to a control condition, participants who read accounts of deaths reported more negative affect. They also showed increased risk estimates generally, for all causes of death. Interestingly, this increase was independent of semantic similarity. Causes that were semantically similar (e.g., leukaemia and stomach cancer) were not perceived as more likely than causes that were semantically distant (e.g., tornadoes). This argues against the idea that the influence of affect (the increase in the estimated likelihood of negative outcomes as a result of negative affect) was simply a function of semantic priming (Forgas, 2006). Johnson and Tversky (1983) concluded that affect produces effects that are qualitatively different from cognitive priming, which is typically moderated by semantic distance.

Since this initial work, a number of studies have examined the influence of incidental affective states on estimates of likelihood, using similar paradigms. In these studies, mood is manipulated and participants' estimates of likelihood for different future events are measured (Constans & Mathews, 1993; Mayer, Gaschke, Braverman, & Evans, 1992). Many studies have contrasted negative and positive moods, sometimes including a control condition, and examined estimates for positive, negative, and neutral events. Results typically show that participants in positive moods estimate positive events (e.g., marriage resulting in long-term happiness) as more likely than participants in negative moods. Participants in negative moods show increased likelihood estimates for negative events (e.g., being a victim of crime). The effect generalises to non-student samples, including random community samples (Mayer et al., 1992). Although most studies are cross-sectional in nature, comparing positive and negative mood groups at one point in time, covariation between mood and estimates of likelihood has also been shown within participants over time (Mayer & Hanson, 1995).

In addition to variations in affective state, there is also strong evidence that high-anxious individuals perceive negative events as more likely than low-anxious individuals (Constans, 2001; Gasper & Clore, 1998; Zelenski & Larsen, 2002). Some findings suggest that this might be restricted to judgements that are self-relevant (Muris & van der Heiden, 2006), and that the anxiety-congruent judgements do not extend to events happening to others.

## Mechanisms

Two principal mechanisms have been proposed to account for the effects of mood on judgement. One, the availability heuristic, is based on memory processes. The other, the mood-as-information hypothesis, involves the strategic use of affect in the judgement process.

The availability heuristic describes the process by which participants form estimates of likelihood based on how easily they can retrieve instances from memory. Ease of retrieval, or availability, will generally correlate with actual probability (e.g., it is easier to retrieve an instance of a brown dog than a white dog from memory precisely because one has encountered a greater number of brown dogs, because there are indeed more brown dogs). However, there are factors that influence ease of retrieval without affecting actual probabilities. This is the case for incidental affective states. According to network theories, affective states prime the representations of mood-congruent concepts (Bower, 1981; Forgas, 2001, 2006). This has been confirmed empirically with numerous studies showing mood-congruent memory facilitation (e.g., Derry & Kuiper, 1981; Greenberg & Beck, 1989). Thus, if temporary incidental affective states prime mood-congruent exemplars and make those exemplars more accessible, this should lead to inflated estimates of likelihood, independently of actual occurrence.

MacLeod and Campbell (1992) provided evidence for the role of memory accessibility in affect-congruent probability judgements. They used a series of negative and positive events (e.g., a heated argument, a wonderful holiday) and measured how long participants took to retrieve a specific personal experience from memory as well as their estimates of probability for these events. Negative and positive mood inductions affected both measures in mood-congruent ways. For instance, when participants were in negative moods they were quicker to retrieve instances of negative events, and estimated the frequency of these events as higher. Crucially, there was a direct link between the effects of the mood manipulation on the two measures. The degree to which the mood induction changed participants' affective state was linearly related to the extent to which participants were quicker to retrieve mood-congruent items compared to mood-incongruent items, and the same differential impact was seen on probability estimates. This provides some evidence for the mediating role of retrieval in affect-congruent estimates of likelihood.

Another possible mechanism to account for affect-congruent estimates is the mood-as-information hypothesis. Clore and colleagues (Clore & Huntsinger, 2007; Gasper & Clore, 1998) suggested that participants use the information conveyed by affective states strategically during the judgement process. Participants ask themselves, "How do I feel about this?" and use the answer to provide a judgement about the target. When the feeling is evoked by a source other than the target, misattribution may occur. A crucial point is that this misattribution is reduced if participants are explicitly aware of the source of their feelings (L. Martin et al., 1992; Schwarz & Clore, 1983) or are asked to base their evaluations on facts rather than feelings. Thus, feelings may be used as a shortcut to produce a judgement on a given target, as long as the feeling is perceived (rightly or wrongly) to be evoked by the target object. In addition, there is evidence that the feelings also have to be perceived as relevant to the decision-making tasks (Pham, 1998) to influence judgement.

One interesting difference between the availability heuristic account and the mood-as-information account concerns the normative aspect of judgement. The mood-as-information hypothesis would predict that insofar as the affective state results from some aspect of the target, then affect will augment the normative accuracy of judgements. Thus, integral affect (but not incidental affect) should lead to more accurate judgements. Based on the availability heuristic account, however, mood will bias judgement, without a corresponding change in objective probabilities. Thus mood may inevitably lead to increased departure from normatively correct judgement. Based on the literature on emotion and memory, it may also be predicted that emotional events will be more memorable, without necessarily being more frequent, and hence will lead to overestimation relative to non-emotional events. There is, as yet, no empirical evidence to answer these questions but future research will surely shed more light on the mechanisms underlying the effects of mood on judgement.

While the availability heuristic and the mood-as-information accounts have both been developed in the context of the research on mood, they could also be extended to understand the effect of individual differences in trait anxiety on risk perception. However, an additional complication in the case of individual differences in trait anxiety is past experience. The fact that high-anxious individuals estimate negative events as being more likely could be due to increased personal experience of negative events. If judgements of likelihood are based on memory retrieval, and anxious individuals are anxious because of frequent negative past experiences, this would lead to increased estimates of likelihood of negative events. It would also imply that judgement itself is not biased in anxious individuals, but rather that their experience sample is skewed. However, this hypothesis is refuted, at least in part, by studies looking at monitoring of occurrence for threatening and neutral events. Kverno (2000) presented high- and low-anxious individuals with threat and neutral words. The frequency of presentation of each word was varied. The frequency of occurrence of threat words was generally overestimated, relative to neutral words, but this was even more pronounced in high-anxious individuals. This pattern suggests that increased risk estimates by high-anxious individuals may occur even under similar objective frequencies of occurrence of negative events. Consistent with this conclusion are results from a study showing that level of situational anxiety can be independent from objective levels of threat. The extent to which students were anxious about an upcoming exam was unrelated to later marks on an exam (Constans, 2001). Thus, increased risk perception in anxious individuals is possibly not related to objective increased likelihood of negative experiences, past, current, or future. Rather it seems to be a genuine bias in judgement.

## Specificity

Research is now mapping out the boundaries of the effects of affect on risk perception. In this recent literature, some work has examined the question of whether mood influences judgement only of events that are specifically related, or whether it has a more diffuse influence. Other research has examined whether all moods produce the same effects on judgements of risk. We examine these two strands of research in this section.

The initial findings by Johnson and Tversky (1983) suggested that mood produced broad-ranging effects, with negative affect increasing estimates of likelihood for negative events generally. However, other research has suggested that the effects of mood may be more circumscribed. For instance, students who showed increases in state anxiety as a result of an upcoming statistics exam showed an increase in risk perception for doing poorly on the exam only, and not for other domains of risk (Constans, 2001). In a different but related task, Niedenthal and Setterlund (1994) found that happy as opposed to sad participants made faster lexical decisions to happiness-related words but not to general positive words.

Some research examining different affective states of the same valence has also provided evidence for specificity. For instance, angry and sad participants show increased emotion-specific judgements (DeSteno, Petty, Wegener, & Rucke, 2000). Angry participants estimate the frequency of angering events as more likely and sad participants estimate the likelihood of sad events as more likely, but the reverse is not true. Thus, specific emotions increase estimates of likelihood of events that are thematically related, not negative events generally.

Furthermore, there is some evidence that different negatively valenced emotions may produce contrary effects on judgements of risk. Using the same task as used by Johnson and Tversky (1983), Lerner and Keltner (2000) found that fear increased risk estimates while anger reduced risk estimates. The authors suggest that this difference results from the appraisal patterns related to each emotion. Anger is related to certainty while fear is related to uncertainty. The suggestion is that the same appraisal dimensions that evoke the emotion in the first place also affect the judgement task, and bias estimates in the same way, in a kind of cognitive contamination. Fear is typically evoked in situations where the outcome is uncertain. The uncertainty that characterises the appraisal pattern influences judgements and increases risk estimates. Appraisal theory suggests that anger is evoked in situations with low uncertainty, and therefore reduces risk estimates.

Lerner and colleagues (Fischhoff, Gonzalez, Lerner, & Small, 2005; Lerner, Gonzalez, Small, & Fischhoff, 2003) examined this appraisal-contamination effect using a nationally representative US sample tested at different intervals after the terrorist attacks of 9/11 (from a few days to a year later). The researchers manipulated emotion by asking participants to describe what it was about the attacks that made them angry or afraid. Participants were asked to estimate future risks related to terrorist attacks. Participants primed to feel angry reported lower estimates of risk both for the country in general, and for themselves and other Americans, compared to participants primed to feel afraid, who reported higher estimates of risk.

To conclude, robust effects have been identified in judgement tasks whereby affect influences estimates of likelihood of future events. Although this has generally been shown mostly for negative moods and anxious personalities, effects of positive affect have also been shown. In addition, however, recent research has started to document differentiation between the effects of specific negative emotions that might be linked to appraisal patterns. These studies, looking for instance at the effect of fear and anger in relation to terrorist attacks, represent one introduction of the study of integral emotion, where researchers examine affective states that are linked with the contents of the cognitive task. In these studies, participants are induced to feel fearful or angry in relation to the attacks, and their estimates of related events are then measured. In these cases, results show effects that are emotion specific rather than valence based. Although strong conclusions would be premature at this stage, we observe that studies that have found valence-based effects have typically examined incidental emotions. In those cases, where affect was not linked to the judgement task, results have sometimes shown affect-congruent judgement effects that were general (positive/negative) and not linked to semantic similarity. When studies have examined integral affect, where the emotional state was linked to the target stimuli (e.g., what made you feel angry about the terrorist attack and then judge the likelihood of more terrorist attacks) they have tended to show specific rather than general effects (i.e., different effects of anger and fear).

Studies on incidental affect have, however, generally only compared positive and negative states, which makes it impossible to draw strong conclusions about the differential effects of incidental and integral emotions. An additional problem is that many of the studies on emotion-specific effects do not include a neutral mood condition, or estimates of the likelihood for neutral events. This makes it difficult to determine whether the emotion-specific component occurs in addition to a general effect related to valence, or whether the two effects are mutually exclusive. Future research will surely allow us to better integrate the insights provided by these different lines of research.

Altogether, though, the research on the impact of affect on judgement reveals robust effects (valence based or emotion specific) of a wide range of emotions, including anger, sadness, anxiety, and positive moods. This contrasts with interpretive effects, which are robust but generally restricted to anxiety. In the conclusions, we will suggest that this is a result of the different component mechanisms that underlie interpretation and judgement, with interpretation being closer to attention, and judgement being more heavily based on memory processes.

## DECISION MAKING

While research on judgement investigates how people estimate the likelihood of different outcomes, studies of decision making examine how people actually choose between different options. In the laboratory, gambling tasks are often used where participants are asked to choose between options that vary in value (outcome) and probability. Other studies examine self-reports of actual risky behaviours (e.g., not wearing a seatbelt, gambling, smoking, etc.). The key focus has been to examine whether mood and affective traits influence the propensity towards risk, that is, the extent to which outcomes with lower probabilities are sought in order to obtain outcomes of greater value.

We begin this section with an examination of decision making and incidental affective states. We then explore an example of research looking at integral emotion and decision making, the work on somatic markers, which examines how the emotional arousal induced in a decision-making task influences cognitive processes.

## Empirical effects

It has generally been shown that anxiety leads to risk aversion. Using laboratory tasks and self-reports, anxious individuals show more risk-averse behaviours than non-anxious individuals (Maner & Gerend, 2007). This has been shown for both trait anxiety and induced anxious moods (Västfjäll, Peters, & Slovic, 2008).

Risk aversion seems to be at least partly specific to anxiety, and not characteristic of all negative affective states. Patients with anxiety disorders are more risk averse than patients with other mood disorders, such as depression. In fact, some mood-induction studies show increased risk preference in sadness. Raghunathan and Pham (1999) used a paradigm where participants had to choose between two gambling options, or between two jobs. In both cases, there was a trade-off between risk and reward. Risk preference was highest for participants induced to feel sad, followed by controls, and anxious participants were most risk averse. This pattern was evident only when the decision applied to the self, not when participants were asked to chose on behalf of somebody else.

There is robust evidence that participants in positive moods are also risk averse, as are anxious participants. The work of Isen and colleagues has examined positive mood and gambling behaviour. In a game of roulette, participants in a positive mood were more risk averse than controls especially when the odds of losing were high (Isen & Geva, 1987; Isen & Patrick, 1983). While they may be risk seeking in low-risk situations, it seems that positive mood participants systematically become more risk averse than controls when the level of risk increases (Isen, Nygren, & Ashby, 1988). Similarly to what has been found with anxiety, risk aversion is more likely in positive moods when the situation is self-relevant (Isen & Patrick, 1983).

Overall, then, it seems that different emotions produce specific effects on decision making. Anxious states as well as positive states increase risk aversion, while sadness increases risk tolerance or even risk seeking.

## Mechanisms

The effects of anxiety and positive moods on decision making cannot easily be explained by one common mechanism. Because one of the ingredients of decision making is judgements of likelihood, the mechanisms that influence judgement should necessarily impact on decision making. This means that memory-based estimation processes as well as heuristic use of affect as information should influence decision making. If anxious participants perceive negative events as being more likely, this should increase risk aversion. In fact, the effects of anxiety on decision making are consistent with this hypothesis. However, the effects of positive mood are not. If positive moods increase the likelihood of retrieving positive instances from memory, or induce participants to assess the situation as safe, then positive mood should increase risk taking. We have reviewed research that shows that, actually, the opposite is the case.

One notion that may help account for the differential effect of positive moods on judgements and decision making is perceived utility. Decisions are based not only on estimations of the likelihood that something will happen (judgement), but also on estimates of the value of that outcome, which is termed perceived utility. For instance, although a contest might give fantastic odds of winning a slow cooker, if you already have this exact slow cooker, the utility of the outcome is quite low. Conversely, although the likelihood that a fatal car accident will occur may be relatively low, the consequences of this happening are so high that it is worth wearing a seatbelt.

Perceived utility, compared to estimates of likelihood, has been relatively ignored in the literature. However the few studies that have started to examine affect and utility judgements have found instructive results. This research shows that positive moods affect the perceived utility of negative outcomes (Isen et al., 1988). Losses are perceived even more negatively by happy participants than they are by control participants. Risk aversion in decision making may thus stem from an increased motivation to avoid losses that are perceived as being more consequential by participants in positive states, rather than an increase in the perceived likelihood of negative outcomes.

By contrast, fear seems to increase both the perceived consequentiality of negative outcomes (negative utility) and their estimated likelihood (Maner & Gerend, 2007). This effect may be fairly circumscribed, although the evidence on this is mixed. One study has found that anxiety affected the perceived utility of negative outcomes but not that of positive outcomes. However, another study showed anxiety was related to increases in the perceived probability and in perceived negative utility of negative events, as well as decreased probability and utility estimates for positive events (Ströber, 1997).

While much of the literature has examined interpretation, judgement and decision making separately, these findings on perceived utility illustrate how these concepts are intrinsically linked. There are some examples of investigations of judgement and decision making within the same paradigm, some with practical applications. For instance, Mittal and Ross (1998) examined the effect of mood on decision making in business settings. Participants considered a scenario about marketing strategy, and made decisions concerning marketing plans. The results showed affect congruent interpretations. Participants in a positive mood were more likely to interpret the scenario as a potential opportunity rather than a threat, relative to participants in a sad mood. In addition, however, positive-mood participants were more risk averse than sad participants. This also confirms that at least some of the general patterns observed in the laboratory do transfer to more naturalistic problem-solving areas where expertise and rich knowledge bases may be used.

To sum up, work on decision making finds that specific emotions have differential effects on risk aversion. Anxiety increases risk aversion, and so does positive mood. The effect of anxiety on decision making is consistent with memory-based affect-congruent priming or increased attentional bias towards threat, both of which could lead to increased perception of the probability of negative outcomes, and thus increased risk aversion. By contrast, the effect of positive moods, which also lead to risk aversion, cannot easily be accounted for by memory or attentional mechanisms. The risk aversion linked with positive mood seems to result from alterations of perceived utilities of negative outcome. This illustrates that motivational processes, possibly linked with mood-regulation strategies, influence decision making. Although there is some suggestion that sadness may increase risky decision making, the evidence is still preliminary at this stage.

The research on decision making reviewed so far has focused on incidental affect, looking essentially at induced mood and personality traits. This research has confirmed that positive and anxious mood states influence decision making. This is in conditions where the emotions are not evoked by the contents of the decision-making task. To examine research that has examined integral affect, we now turn to the literature on somatic markers.

## Specificity: Somatic markers

Another area of the decision-making literature has examined how affective reactions to the target stimuli influence decision making. A specific question of interest has been whether decision making is hindered or improved by affective reactions. The issue of rationality has been at the centre of the cognitive literature on decision making generally, and the emotion and decision-making literature specifically.

The work on somatic markers addresses the question of whether the experience of emotional arousal hinders or promotes normatively correct behaviour in decision-making tasks (Bechara, Damasio, Tranel, & Damasio, 1997; Damasio, 1995). The paradigm often used in this research is the Iowa gambling task, a decision-making task where participants must choose from different decks of cards, which involve immediate rewards, large or small, and unpredictable losses, also large or small.[1] Participants quickly learn to avoid the risky decks that lead to bigger losses. Measures of skin conductance responses (SCRs) show that participants not only produce SCRs when the outcome is revealed to be a loss, but that most, though not all, participants also develop anticipatory SCRs. These are SCRs that occur before the loss is revealed, when the risky option is being considered. This

---

1 The Iowa gambling task was first developed by Damasio (1995) at the University of Iowa to study complex decision making. It is a gambling task where participants are allocated play money and their goal is to maximise their wins and minimise their losses. There are four decks of cards and on each trial participants select from one of the decks. The cards are turned over to reveal a loss or a win. Decks have different odds of winning and losing, and offer different amounts. "Good decks" are those that maximise gains in the long term, with small losses and small wins. "Bad/risky decks" provide larger amounts of both wins and losses.

physiological response occurs before participants can verbalise an explicit appreciation of the likelihood of winning for each of the decks. Patients with damage to the ventromedial prefrontal cortex (VMPFC) are typically poor at this gambling task. They fail to learn to avoid the risky options, and typically do not develop anticipatory SCRs. These findings have led to the hypothesis that peripheral physiological reactions are used in the decision-making process and help individuals to avoid risky options by evoking a negative feeling at the time these options are considered. It has also led to the general conclusion that affect is beneficial for normatively correct decision making.

The research on somatic markers has generated an enormous amount of interest and there are now hundreds of studies that have examined decision making in gambling paradigms, although few have included an examination of peripheral physiological arousal. The somatic markers theory and associated research has been criticised on methodological and theoretical grounds (e.g., Dunn, Dalgleish, & Lawrence, 2006). Some of the main points of contention are the extent to which the physiological responses are independent from explicit knowledge, how to interpret the physiological data, and whether there are alternative, more parsimonious, interpretations of the findings. As an example, Maia and McCLelland (2004), using more-detailed measures of explicit knowledge have found that advantageous behaviour on the gambling task was only observed when participants had explicit verbal knowledge of the reward and punishment probabilities involved in the task. Tomb and colleagues (Tomb, Hauser, Deldin, & Caramazza, 2002) have provided some evidence that SCRs might actually reflect the variability in rewards associated with different decks, rather than their inherent safe or risky character. Another example of alternative explanation is the fact that the deficits observed in patients with VMPFC lesions may reflect impairments in reversal learning, which is necessary in the Iowa gambling task to learn to avoid the initially preferred risky decks, rather than somatic feedback (Fellows & Farah, 2003). Despite recent critical evaluations of the initial work and theory, the general idea that affective reactions to the target stimuli (integral emotion) may be beneficial for decision making, rather than a hindrance, has remained innovative and influential.

## REASONING

Similarly to the decision-making literature, a central question in the reasoning literature has also been that of rational thought, and the effect of emotion has been examined from this angle. Reasoning, like decision making, is often cited as an example of the human ability for sophisticated abstract processes. In the reasoning literature generally, as in the emotion and reasoning literature, a central issue has been to determine to what extent humans can use this ability optimally.

In 1946, Lefford published one of the first studies on the effect of emotion on reasoning, stating that:

> The disastrous effects of emotional thinking ... [are far reaching and] the problem is especially acute today, in a war-torn world, where only action based on objectivity of analysis and rationality of thought can lead to a successful solution of the social and economic problems ....
> (p. 127)

A starting point for this research seems to be the assumption that rational thinking should ideally be immune from the influence of emotion.

Much of the work on reasoning and emotion has been conducted using deductive-reasoning paradigms. In deductive-reasoning tasks, participants are asked to draw inferences from a set of premises, or to determine whether an inference is valid or not based on some premises. Performance can be compared to the norms of propositional logic (although this is not the only way to conceptualise these tasks, nor the only normative model available).

In this section, we first review the work that has examined whether emotion promotes or hinders normatively correct reasoning. This includes work on incidental emotion as well as integral emotion, emotion evoked by the reasoning materials. We later examine work that has asked whether different emotions promote different styles of reasoning, again looking at both incidental and integral emotions.

## Empirical effects

### Deductive reasoning and incidental emotion/mood

Lefford's early study (1946) included a syllogistic reasoning task where participants had to determine the logical validity of 20 emotional syllogisms (e.g., All Communists are believers in trade unions, therefore, all trade-unionists are Communists) and 20 non-emotional syllogisms (e.g., All members of Phi Beta Kappa must be college students ...). Lefford observed that participants made more errors when reasoning about the affective syllogisms, and concluded that "in dealing with subject matter which arouses an emotional reaction the subject does not retain his capacity for correct reasoning".

In the contemporary literature, results from studies on emotion and deductive reasoning have been surprisingly consistent with Lefford's original conclusions (1946) that emotion negatively impacts "correct reasoning" or logicality. A number of studies have shown that logicality is impaired by affective state, affective trait, and affective contents. For instance, Oaksford and colleagues (Oaksford, Morris, Grainger, & Williams, 1996) manipulated participants' mood using video clips. They found that both positive and negative moods impaired performance on a Wason selection task compared to participants in a neutral mood condition. Similar results have been found in other studies inducing both positive and negative moods, using other reasoning tasks (Melton, 1995; Palfai & Salovey, 1993). Consistent findings have been obtained in studies examining the impact of affective traits. For instance, high-anxious participants show impairments on verbal reasoning, relative to low-anxious participants, especially when the task demands are high (Derakshan & Eysenck, 1998). Depression produces similar effects. Participants who score higher on the Beck Depression Inventory (BDI) show impairments in syllogistic reasoning (Channon & Baker, 1994). Thus, a number of studies looking at different affective states of positive and negative valence, sampling different forms of deductive reasoning, show that heightened affect impairs logicality.

The same conclusion prevails when examining the impact of affective contents. Closer to Lefford's original investigation, studies have compared whether participants reason similarly about emotional and neutral contents (Blanchette, 2006; Blanchette & Richards, 2004; Goel & Dolan, 2003). Across different tasks, results show that participants are less likely to draw logically valid inferences, and more likely to endorse logical fallacies, when reasoning about emotional contents, compared to neutral contents. This is true for both non-clinical and clinical samples (Kemp, Chua, McKenna, & David, 1997). The effect has also been shown to be uniquely determined by the affective value of the materials and not any semantic confound resulting from the use of different words in the emotional and neutral conditions. For instance, some studies have used classical conditioning to manipulate the affective value of the reasoning stimuli through repeated association with emotional or neutral images (Blanchette, 2006; Blanchette & Richards, 2004). Using this methodology, the same words may be manipulated to become negative or neutral. Results show that both negatively and positively conditioned stimuli lead to more logical errors, suggesting that the affective value itself is producing effects on reasoning. Thus, two ways of manipulating incidental emotion, mood induction and classical conditioning, produce similar impairments in logical reasoning.

### Deductive reasoning and "integral" emotion

The studies reviewed previously adopt a similar approach in trying to examine the effect of emotion independently from the task. Such an approach is consistent with the study of incidental affect reviewed in the context of judgement and decision making. Whether the affective state is manipulated through a mood-induction procedure, or the affective contents manipulated through classical conditioning or other means, the goal is to isolate affect from semantic features and examine its independent impact on reasoning. A different literature on emotion and reasoning has focused on integral emotion, affect that is intrinsically linked to the semantic contents of the reasoning task; where the emotion stems from the target stimuli.

One way in which integral emotion has been studied involves examining the impact of intense emotional experiences on reasoning. While research in the laboratory has shown robust and consistent detrimental effects of emotion on logicality in deductive reasoning, recent studies examining how participants reason about emotional personal experiences demonstrate strikingly different results. A number of studies show that participants reason more logically about emotional than neutral contents. For instance, in one study British war veterans reasoned more logically about syllogisms with combat-related contents (e.g., All friendly fire incidents are accidents ...) than those with generally emotional contents (e.g., All priests are paedophiles ...) and neutral contents (e.g., All dentists are golf players ...; Blanchette & Campbell, 2005). Another study looked at reasoning in three different cities shortly after the London terrorist attacks of July 2005 (Blanchette, Richards, Melnyk, & Lavda, 2007b). Participants in London, UK, reported the highest levels of emotion, and they were also more accurate than participants in Canada when reasoning about syllogisms related to terrorism (e.g., Some Muslims are terrorists ...). Similar effects have been observed in patients suffering from obsessive-compulsive disorder and phobias (Johnson-Laird, Mancini, & Gangemi, 2006), who provided more normatively accurate answers when reasoning about topics related to their condition. A study on framing effects in decision making provides conceptually congruent evidence (Tanner & Medin, 2004). Participants were less affected by superficial aspects of the task, and thus showed evidence of increased normatively correct thinking when reasoning about "protected values", that is, issues that they felt very strongly about, relative to other more neutral issues.

There is evidence that these patterns cannot be accounted for solely by expertise. In some studies, experience was negatively related to the advantage in reasoning about emotional materials (Blanchette & Campbell, 2005). There is also recent work providing evidence of a direct link between the emotional impact of an event, namely sexual abuse (i.e., scores on the Impact of Event Scale; IES) and the advantage in reasoning about abuse-related contents in victims of sexual abuse (Blanchette, Lindsay, & Davies, 2008). Thus, there is a growing body of evidence suggesting that using intrinsically emotional materials, participants are not necessarily reasoning less logically about emotional contents. Indeed, in some cases, they may actually provide more normatively correct responses when reasoning about emotional materials.

## Mechanisms

The main mechanism that has been investigated in relation to the effect of emotion on reasoning is working memory. Investigators have suggested that processing affective content may take up working-memory capacity. Given deductive reasoning is highly reliant upon working memory (Copeland & Radvansky, 2004), any reduction as a result of affect would negatively impact upon the primary task. Channon and Baker (1994) provided evidence that the performance of participants in a negative mood was related to problem difficulty, with errors related to the integration of information. Similarly, anxious participants are particularly affected under conditions of high working memory load because anxiety leads to task-irrelevant processing of affective information, which depletes resources available for the primary task (Derakshan & Eysenck, 1998; Richards, French, Keogh, & Carter, 2000). Despite this, a number of studies have failed to find significant or robust effects of affective contents on working-memory capacity generally (Kensinger & Corkin, 2003) or effects on verbal short-term memory particularly (Lavric, Rippon, & Gray, 2003; Shackman et al., 2006), a component that would specifically support deductive reasoning. Oaksford and colleagues (1996) found that although a positive mood manipulation affected both reasoning performance and a measure of central executive function, there were no effects of a negative mood induction on executive function. Thus, while there is some suggestion that the effect of emotion on reasoning may be mediated through working memory, the evidence for this remains equivocal.

The proposed working memory depletion, however, would not explain why integral affect enhances logicality. By analogy to the research on incidental and integral emotion and memory (Laney, Campbell, Heuer, & Reisberg, 2004), it is possible to hypothesise that incidental emotion may focus attention away from task-relevant information while integral emotion may focus attention towards task-relevant information. This would improve normatively correct performance for integral emotion.

Hypotheses concerning the mechanisms underlying effects of emotion on deductive reasoning remain to be examined empirically. These mechanisms fall within the realm of memory (working memory, activation of counter-examples) or attention (attention to relevant or irrelevant information as a function of affect). Resolving the apparent paradox between the effects of incidental emotion, which seems to impair logicality, and integral emotion, which seems to facilitate logicality, represents an exciting avenue for future research.

## Specificity

The work reviewed previously stems primarily from experimental cognitive psychology and has focused mainly on comparing emotional and non-emotional conditions. This work has examined whether emotion affects the outcome of the reasoning process. Another line of research has examined whether different emotions promote different styles of reasoning. The question here has not been whether emotion makes people better or worse at reasoning, but rather whether specific emotions change the way in which people reason. As in the previous section, we first examine the work on incidental affect, which stems mainly from the field of social cognition, and then examine work on integral emotion, which originates in the clinical-psychology literature.

## Incidental emotion and reasoning style

Work by Worth and Mackie (Mackie & Worth, 1989; Worth & Mackie, 1987) initiated a novel line of research examining the impact of mood on systematic and heuristic processing. They presented participants with different essays on topical issues. Across conditions, the researchers varied the deep features of the messages. For instance, some messages included arguments judged to be strong or weak (by other participants). They also varied superficial features. The same messages could be presented as coming from an expert or a non-expert. In judging the validity of a message, systematic processing will lead to a reliance on deep features while heuristic processing will lead to a reliance on superficial features. Results showed that participants in a positive mood were less affected by the strength of the arguments (the deep features), and more affected by the source of the message (the superficial features) than participants in a neutral mood. This led to the conclusion that positive mood increases heuristic processing and decreases systematic processing.

The effect of positive moods on heuristic processing has been replicated a number of times. The mechanisms underlying the effect are not entirely clear. There is some evidence that positive moods deplete cognitive resources for processing the message (Mackie & Worth, 1989). Other studies have shown that happy participants do not necessarily have reduced cognitive resources available but rather are less motivated to process the message systematically (Bless, Bonher, Schwarz, & Strack, 1990; Bodenhausen, Kramer, & Susser, 1994a). Yet other research has shown that reduced message scrutiny as a result of positive mood may be modulated by strategic factors, for instance if the message is likely to improve or worsen mood (Wegener, Petty, & Smith, 1995).

While initial work focused on positive mood, additional work has shown the converse effect. Sad or negative moods seem to produce more systematic, careful, elaborative information processing, and less reliance on heuristic or top-down processing. This has been shown using different paradigms such as judgement formation, persuasion, covariation detection, and mock jury tasks (Bless et al., 1990; Edwards & Weary, 1993; Gold, 2002; Semmler & Brewer, 2002; Sinclair, 1988). In all cases, sad participants have been shown to process information more systematically and carefully, and be less affected by superficial features. This could be interpreted as being consistent with the literature on "depressive realism", which proposes that depressed individuals are less subject to certain judgemental biases and more accurate in their judgements than non-depressed individuals (Allan, Siegel, & Hannah, 2007; Alloy & Abramson, 1979, 1988). For instance, non-depressed individuals typically overestimate the degree of control over the environment they have, while depressed individuals tend to be more accurate. Although the depressive realism effect has been shown in different laboratory tasks, its robustness and the extent to which it generalises to more naturalistic settings has been questioned (Allan et al., 2007; Pacini, Muir, & Epstein, 1998). Nevertheless, it is consistent with the experimental evidence that induced negative moods bolster systematic processing.

Interestingly, sadness does not necessarily always improve normatively correct reasoning and judgement. The outcome may depend on the precise features of the task. In cases where systematic processing is likely to increase departure from normatively correct thinking, sadness can actually worsen performance. This has been shown in the case of the anchoring effect, which occurs when judgements are influenced by the initial value provided to participants. In one task, Bodenhausen, Gabriel, and Lineberger (2000) asked participants to make different estimates (e.g., How long is the Mississippi River?) after having provided high or low anchors in a previous question (e.g., Is the Mississippi River longer or shorter than 5000/100 miles?).[2] Sad participants were more susceptible to the effect of the anchor than were participants in a neutral mood. Conceptually similar effects have been shown in situations where increased processing leads to worse performance on a judgement task. Ambady and Gray (2002) studied "thin slice judgements", judgements that have to be made on the basis of very little information.[3] The tendency of sad participants to rely on more extensive processing actually led them to provide judgements that were more at odds with external standards than those of control participants. Thus, the effect of sadness on extensive or systematic processing seems robust and does not necessarily lead to increased normatively correct thinking.

While a large proportion of the research on reasoning strategies contrasts positive and negative moods, some work has investigated distinctions

---

2  The anchoring effect describes the tendency to rely heavily on initial information that is presented in judgement and decision making and compare other incoming information in relation to that. For instance, a pair of trousers now sold for £35 will seem cheaper if it was initially marked as £50 than if it was initially £36. This effect occurs even when the initial value is arbitrary.

3  Thin slice judgements refer to judgements that are based on very limited amounts of data, or very narrow samples, that nevertheless lead to accurate outcomes or evaluations.

between specific negative emotions. Bodenhausen, Sheppard, and Kramer (1994b) examined the differential impact of sadness and anger in guilt assessment and persuasion tasks. The extent to which individual exemplars fit a stereotype was manipulated, and the impact of this manipulation on reasoning was measured. A greater effect of the stereotype manipulation would reflect a greater reliance on heuristic processing. For instance, in one task, participants had to judge cases of student misbehaviour. The perpetrator was either stereotypically associated with the offence (e.g., a college athlete caught cheating on an examination) or not. Angry participants were affected by the stereotype manipulation to a greater extent than participants in sad or neutral mood conditions. Thus, anger may produce effects similar to those of happiness in increasing reliance on heuristic processing. Tiedens and Linton (2001) examined similar distinctions between emotions using the appraisal tendency framework. They found that participants primed to feel emotions related to certainty (e.g., anger, contentment, disgust) were more likely than those experiencing emotions related to uncertainty (worry, surprise, fear) to rely on superficial cues (expertise of the source, stereotypes) in the context of persuasion and judgement of guilt. This parallels some of the effects found in the judgement literature and demonstrates that emotions of similar valence may have different effects on reasoning.

Overall, research in social cognition has provided evidence that affective states influence the types of strategies that are used in reasoning and judgement tasks. There is robust evidence that positive moods increase reliance on heuristic processing. Anger and other emotions related to certain appraisals might produce similar effects. Sad moods by contrast have been shown to increase systematic processing, and this leads to increased normatively correct performance on a number of tasks that rely on extensive processing, but it may also decrease task performance when extensive processing is detrimental. The mechanisms underlying these effects of emotion on reasoning style may be related to working memory (depleted working-memory capacity in positive moods may lead to increased reliance on heuristics), strategic use of mood as information (negative moods signal that there is something problematic and information must be processed more carefully), or priming of knowledge structures (appraisal consistent effects).

### Integral emotion and reasoning style

While much research in social cognition shows that incidental affect influences reasoning style, another literature provides examples of how integral emotion also influences reasoning style. Work by de Jong, van den Hout, and colleagues (de Jong, Haenen, Schmidt, & Mayer, 1998; de Jong, Mayer, & van den Hout, 1997; de Jong & Merckelbach, 2000; de Jong, Weertman, Horselenberg, & van den Hout, 1997; Smeets, de Jong, &

Mayer, 2000) has examined the way that clinical and non-clinical samples reason about safety and danger rules. This research compares how participants reason about rules signalling danger (e.g., If mushrooms have brown stems they are poisonous) and safety (e.g., If mushrooms have brown stems they are edible). Results show that danger rules systematically induce rule-confirming reasoning strategies. When asked to verify whether or not a danger rule is correct (e.g., If brown stem, then poisonous), participants typically look for instances that will confirm the rule (i.e., brown stems and poisonous mushrooms). In fact, a normatively correct answer would be to try to find falsifying instances (i.e., non-poisonous mushrooms with brown stems), as these are the only ones that can determine whether the rule is being violated. The confirmation response can only determine that a rule is true, not that a rule is false. Safety rules, however (e.g., if brown stems then edible), typically do evoke falsification strategies, where participants look for instances that will disprove the rule (i.e., brown-stem mushrooms that are not edible). From a structural or logical point of view, danger and safety rules are identical (if p, then q) and thus should evoke the same reasoning strategies. Yet participants provide very different answers depending on the semantic information and how it relates to situations of danger or safety.

These findings on the impact of danger and safety rules are consistent with effects of expected utility on rule verification that have been noted in other areas (Smeets et al., 2000), a concept that links this reasoning literature with the work on decision making. Participants use the semantic contents of rules to guide choices about relevant information. The expected utility of information about danger is especially high. Participants will look for cases that lead to avoiding potential harm (e.g., poisonous mushrooms). This happens to coincide with the normatively correct responses for safety rules (not q = not edible), not for danger rules (not q = not poisonous). In both cases participants may essentially be adopting strategies that maximise expected utility, that is selecting cases that will tell them about dangerous outcomes. This is consistent with the results from experiments conducted by Perham and Oaksford (2005) where they examined participants' strategies when reasoning about danger and neutral rules (e.g., If you feel pain/have worked for 90 minutes, then you take a break). Participants' behaviour was significantly affected by the inclusion of threat-related information in the rule in a way consistent with the role of expected utilities. One possibility is that the expected utility of threatening information may be closely linked with the attentional bias towards threatening information. Exploring the link between higher level cognitive processes and basic component mechanisms may represent a fruitful avenue for further research.

Overall this burgeoning literature on emotion and reasoning has already demonstrated what important effects affective variables can have on higher level cognitive processes. There is evidence that emotion can both enhance and impair normatively correct responses, depending on the type of emotion examined, the features of the task, or the interaction between the reasoning style and the requirements of the task. Furthermore, as the work on danger and safety rules exemplifies, emotions might promote adaptive responses even though responses are not normatively accurate.

## GENERAL CONCLUSIONS

The literature on higher level cognitive processes and emotion is becoming complex and growing at a fast pace. It will shortly be impossible to review this literature together, as we have attempted to do here, given the amount of work being published in this area. The field is varied and somewhat disjointed with different areas originating from different traditions. Research on interpretive bias stems from clinical psychology where processing biases were observed in patients suffering from certain mood disorders. Judgement and decision making research stems from a social-cognition tradition. Reasoning has its roots in cognitive science, problem solving, and philosophy. In addition, the different areas have tended to focus on different levels of analysis, with, for example, interpretive research examining lower level processes and on-line processing with immediate responses whereas reasoning has investigated higher level cognitive processes and issues of rationality. Despite these differences, these areas all provide converging evidence on the importance of the relationship between emotion and cognition. We hope to have provided a relatively representative overview of these different perspectives. We had set two main goals. Our first goal was to determine whether there is an effect of emotion on higher level cognitive processes, specifically focusing on interpretation, judgement, decision making and reasoning. Our second aim was to try to identify the mechanisms that underlie the effect of emotion on each of these processes. In this conclusion, we first evaluate the evidence concerning the first question. We then propose that focusing on the underlying mechanisms provides a framework to unify some of the disparate findings in this field and highlights areas where more work is needed.

The main conclusion we draw from reviewing this body of work is that affective variables have an important influence on cognitive processes. This may appear to be a trivial conclusion, but we believe it should not be overlooked. Most of the research we have reviewed has been conducted in the last 20 years. This illustrates how the study of cognitive processes has until recently been conducted in a vacuum where affective processes were considered a source of noise that should be controlled, not an important set of variables that should be examined. The studies on the impact of affective variables on interpretation, judgement, decision making and reasoning have shown that not only can these variables be systematically studied using an experimental approach, but that they indeed can have a large influence on higher level cognitive processes. This conclusion has been established remarkably quickly and highlights how coming to a complete understanding of human cognition will necessitate a consideration of how it interacts with affective factors. In addition, there have been attempts to examine how these processes work in real-life situations to see if the effects observed in the laboratory are reflected in more ecologically valid domains. We believe that such research is essential in order to fully understand human cognition.

In this paper we have used a simple model where we examined the effect of affective independent variables on cognitive outcome processes. This model is too simplistic, and new models in cognitive science, experimental psychopathology, and cognitive neuroscience are proposing novel, more complex ways to understand the relationship between these sets of variables. The traditional distinction between "hot" and "cold" functions, referring to emotion and cognition respectively, is being replaced with a dynamic interplay between the two, with an acknowledgment that many brain structures are both "cognitive" and "emotional". Nevertheless, it is necessary and meaningful to attempt to delineate the processes involved in interpretation, judgement, decision making and reasoning in order to determine their appraisal and emotional components.

Showing that emotion has an impact on higher level cognition is an important starting point. Moving beyond this general statement though, it is clear that not all specific emotions produce the same effects on all cognitive processes. Extensive anxiety-congruent effects have been documented in interpretation, judgement, and decision making. Anxiety leads to more threatening interpretations, increases estimates of likelihood of future negative events, and risk aversion in decision making. This paints a portrait of anxiety as a state where information processing is geared toward identifying potential threats and minimising potential negative outcomes. Research on fear content and reasoning strategies is consistent with this pattern. The effects of sadness appear to be rather different. Sadness does not produce an interpretive bias, although less research has been conducted on the effect of sadness on judgement and decision making. Sadness does seem to induce more careful and systematic processing, which is sometimes beneficial and sometimes not. Positive emotions have been much less studied, but there is evidence for increased mood-congruent judgement, increased risk aversion, and reliance on more heuristic reasoning style. Using a different approach, research comparing emotional and non-emotional conditions has shown important differences on tasks examining judgement, decision making, and reasoning. These studies have often focused on integral rather than incidental affect, for example in the somatic marker and the reasoning literatures. Appraisal-based contamination effects have also been identified across reasoning and decision-making tasks. This represents a potentially powerful framework to start to look at the effect of specific emotions across different tasks.

Most of the research has focused on fear and sadness, possibly largely because these are the emotions implicated in the clinical disorders of anxiety and depression. Other emotions, such as disgust and anger have not received the same coverage. The effect of positive emotions has also received much less interest than that of negative emotions generally. Though the need to broaden research efforts to include all emotions is obvious, the research that has been conducted generally shows effects of most emotions. In fact, there is very little evidence of affective states *not* affecting higher level cognitive processes, with the exception of the absence of effect of sadness on interpretation. With the usual caveats about publication bias and null findings, it is nevertheless obvious that the literature is replete with examples of the effect of emotion on higher level cognitive processes.

The findings in this field of research are quite disparate and trying to integrate them is a daunting task. We do not propose a fully fledged theoretical model to incorporate this research, but our approach has been to try to focus on the component mechanisms that are involved in each of these higher level cognitive functions, and examine how common under-lying mechanisms may explain similar effects of emotion. Interpretation, judgement, decision making, and reasoning are complex processes that comprise a number of constituent mechanisms such as attention, working memory, semantic priming, processing contextual information, etc. Emo-tion may have different effects on each of these constituent mechanisms, and to the extent that each higher level cognitive function relies more or less heavily on each mechanism, it will be differentially affected by emotion.

We propose that emotion interacts with four types of constituent processes: basic attentional effects; priming of concepts and knowledge structures; computational capacity; and reflective processes. Attentional effects involve biases in the information that is preferentially processed. Priming effects are observed when certain concepts or knowledge structures are more strongly activated than others in semantic or autobiographical memory. Computational capacity refers to the cognitive resources available to process particular information. Reflective processes are the ways in which information is used strategically to orient further deliberative processing. All of these mechanisms are involved to different degrees in each of the four cognitive functions we reviewed. We now propose how emotion may affect each of these constituent processes and how this helps account for the effect of emotion on interpretation, judgement, decision making, and reasoning.

There is a large literature on the effect of emotion on attention showing in particular a strong effect of anxiety or threat on attention. Threatening stimuli are preferentially attended to, and this is especially pronounced in anxious participants (Bar-Haim, Lamy, Pergamin, Bakermans-Kranenburg, & van IJzendoorn, 2007). The effect of other emotions on attention is less clear, but it appears that anxiety has a greater effect on attention than other emotions, especially sadness/depression. This fits nicely with the literature on interpretation that shows strong effects of anxiety, and little evidence for genuine interpretive effects of sadness and other emotions. Furthermore, the research shows that anxiety leads to a selective preference for the threatening interpretations, rather than a differential generation of threatening and neutral interpretations. Thus, anxious participants seem not to be generating threatening interpretations more quickly than non-anxious participants, but rather focusing their attention on the threatening interpretation once this interpretation has been generated. Neurobiological evidence confirms that the effect of anxiety on both interpretation and attention rely on the same prefrontal–amygdala network, thus adding support to the suggestion that the two processes are linked. If this is the case, then interpretive biases can in fact be seen as a modulation of threat bias by anxiety, rather than a genuine mood-congruent effect. This means that we would not expect other emotions to produce genuine mood-congruent interpretive biases, at least not in tasks that measure rapid, on-line interpretation of ambiguous stimuli. A possible exception is disgust, which may produce the same attentional effects as fear.

This attentional bias towards threat may be linked to other effects we have reviewed, including some effects on risk perception and reasoning about danger and safety rules. If anxiety increases attentional focus on threat, this would increase estimates of probability for dangerous events (through the availability heuristic), which should lead to risk aversion. Similarly, when reasoning about safety rules, participants would focus on threat information, which would lead them to disconfirm, whereas focusing attention on the same threatening information in danger rules would lead to a confirmation bias, exactly the pattern that is observed. Both of these examples suggest that the early effects of fear/threat on attention will produce knock-on effects on higher level cognitive functions that allow for more time and deliberation. In all cases, we suggest that these are not mood-congruent effects, but rather threat focus modulated by anxiety.

A second level where emotion seems to be affecting constituent mechanisms is memory, specifically through priming of concepts of similar valence (affective priming) or priming of knowledge structures that are used in generating the emotion in the first place (appraisal contamination). These mechanisms operate through semantic and autobiographical memory. There is robust evidence for the existence of affective priming (Fazio, 2001), which leads to mood-congruent processing, and growing evidence for priming effects related to appraisal. These memory-based mechanisms take more time to operate than the very rapid attentional mechanisms linked to threat/anxiety. We would therefore not necessarily be able to observe these effects at the short delays used in interpretation tasks, but could observe them in tasks such as judgement, reasoning, and decision making, where the longer time frame would allow a greater influence of spreading activation.

In the literature we have reviewed there are mood-congruent effects that may be caused by such affective priming mechanisms. One example is the mood-congruent judgements, resulting from the availability heuristic, which lead participants to overestimate the likelihood of events that are consistent with their current mood state. Another example is sadness-congruent effects found in interpretation tasks that allow more deliberative processing (and response bias). Spreading activation to emotionally related materials may also increase access to counterexamples in logical verification tasks, which may account for the increased logicality in studies looking at integral emotion. In addition to priming specific concepts, emotions may also prime orchestrated knowledge structures in a similar way. Examples of these may be most evident in the work on appraisal contamination where, for example, emotions with appraisals related to uncertainty increase estimates of uncertainty in subsequent judgement and decision making.

Apart from interpretation, which has often been studied in tasks where elaborative processing is minimised, the cognitive functions examined in this paper may all rely heavily on working-memory resources. Judgement, decision making and reasoning can all be influenced to some extent by automatic parallel processing obviously, but they also allow for the involvement of more deliberate effortful processing. These processes are heavily reliant upon working-memory capacity. This is why we include computational resources as a third possible constituent mechanism on which emotion might have an effect. The findings on the impact of emotion on working memory are not yet conclusive and so any discussion can only be somewhat speculative at this stage. However, if emotion does, indeed, have an impact on working-memory capacity, this would reverberate and produce important effects on all higher level cognitive processes. So far, two effects have been proposed to be related to working memory, with some supporting evidence. One is the effect of incidental emotion on logicality in deductive reasoning, where induced positive and negative moods as well as anxiety and depression have been linked with lower working-memory capacity and impaired reasoning performance. Another is the effect of positive moods on reliance on heuristic processing, which may be partly linked to limited cognitive resources. There is conflicting evidence on the issue of mood and working memory, and the implications are not straightforward. If all moods impede computational capacity, then negative moods would be expected to increase heuristic processing as well, which they don't. Furthermore, we evoke here a simplistic model of working memory. A more realistic model would allow for more complex interactions between emotion and different structures of working memory. These points highlight the fact that further work is needed. A better comprehension of the effect of emotion on working memory will inevitably lead to a better understanding of the effect of emotion on higher level cognitive processes.

We notice a fourth level of influence in the literature we reviewed that we term reflective. This is the strategic use of affect as evidence that in itself orients further information processing. The effect of emotion on processing style is one example of reflective use of emotion. The mood-as-information hypothesis suggests that negative moods signal that something is amiss and that careful information processing is required, which leads the individual to engage in more elaborative processing. Similarly, positive moods may promote heuristic processing because the mood itself signals that the situation is benign and information processing may rely on habitual patterns. The effect of positive mood on risk aversion may also be interpreted as a reflective effect of emotion on information processing. When participants feel that losses would compromise the maintenance of their positive mood, they perceive the expected utility of negative outcomes as being increased and thus refrain from choosing risky options.

The work on somatic markers and on the effect of integral affect on emotion, both showing increased normatively correct thinking in emotional compared to neutral conditions, can also be interpreted as an example of a reflective effect of emotion on higher level cognition. In decision making, peripheral arousal is used as a cue concerning the level of risk associated with different options. In reasoning, emotional arousal may be taken as a signal that the situation is important, and insofar as the task is not trivial but is personally significant, this may encourage participants to mobilise cognitive resources to think through the problem carefully. These two domains do represent important exceptions in the field as they are the few studies that include an examination of physiological arousal. Although most models of emotion integrate peripheral physiological arousal as one important component of emotion, very few studies of the effect of emotion on higher level cognitive functions actually consider this dimension. This is despite the fact that arousal generally is closely linked to attention and processing capacity, which are directly implicated in higher level cognitive processes and so represent likely avenues of influence for emotion. We think the link between physiological arousal and cognitive processes represents an important area for future work.

Given that emotions can have simultaneous and contradictory influences through (at least!) these four different types of constituent mechanisms, the effect of emotion on higher level cognitive functions will inevitably be complex and impossible to summarise in a few sentences. This also means that there are numerous avenues that further research could explore. Given the state of the field and the current unanswered questions that are highlighted by our framework, we see a number of particularly exciting and useful research questions. One central issue is to systematically explore the effect of emotion and mood on working memory, and examine how this produces knock-on effects on judgement, decision making, and reasoning. While we have partial evidence that there might be an effect, findings are inconsistent and more work needs to be done, relying on more sophisticated models of working-memory function. Another important area that has received little attention is the role of peripheral physiological arousal in higher level cognitive functions. This must be studied to understand the interplay between arousal, attentional and processing effects, and higher level cognitive function as well to understand how arousal is used reflectively in guiding information processing in reasoning and decision making. More generally, integrating more diverse methodologies will inevitably enrich our understanding of these different issues. Although we have focused on the behavioural literature here, the use of neuroimaging methods should help identify the important constituent mechanisms for each higher level cognitive function. Recent technological advances have enabled sophisticated methodologies to become more accessible to researchers, allowing a more comprehensive analysis of information processing. Various methodologies such as functional magnetic resonance imaging (fMRI) and electroencephalography (EEG), event-related potentials (ERPs), and magnetoencephalography (MEG) in conjunction with sound behavioural paradigms and peripheral psychophysiological measures can highlight different aspects of the same process, and collectively have the potential to produce a more comprehensive understanding of the processes and constituent components than one methodology on its own. Identifying the constituent mechanisms of the interpretation, judgement, reasoning and decision making using behavioural and neurophysiological measures will help us understand the commonalities and differences between these processes, and the interactions between emotion and higher level cognitive functions.

## REFERENCES

Allan, L. G., Siegel, S., & Hannah, S. (2007). The sad truth about depressive realism. *Quarterly Journal of Experimental Psychology, 60,* 482–495.

Alloy, L. B., & Abramson, L. Y. (1979). Judgment of contingency in depressed and nondepressed students: Sadder but wiser? *Journal of Experimental Psychology: General, 108,* 441–485.

Alloy, L. B., & Abramson, L. Y. (1988). Depressive realism: Four theoretical perspectives. In L. B. Alloy (Ed.), *Cognitive processes in depression* (pp. 223–265). New York: Guilford Press.

Ambady, N., & Gray, H. M. (2002). On being sad and mistaken: Mood effects on the accuracy of thin-slice judgments. *Journal of Personality and Social Psychology, 83,* 947–961.

Amir, N., Beard, C., & Bower, E. (2005). Interpretation bias and social anxiety. *Cognitive Therapy and Research, 29,* 433–443.

Amir, N., Foa, E. B., & Coles, M. E. (1998). Automatic activation and strategic avoidance of threat-relevant information in social phobia. *Journal of Abnormal Psychology, 107,* 285–290.

Anders, S., Lotze, M., Erb, M., Grodd, W., & Birbaumer, N. (2004). Brain activity underlying emotional valence and arousal: A response-related fMRI study. *Human Brain Mapping, 23,* 200–209.

Atkinson, M. J., & Caldwell, L. (1997). The differential effects of mood on patients' ratings of life quality and satisfaction with their care. *Journal of Affective Disorders, 44*, 169–175.

Aviezer, H., Hassin, R. R., Ryan, J., Grady, C., Susskind, J., Anderson, A., et al. (2008). Angry, disgust, or afraid? Studies on the malleability of emotion perception. *Psychological Science, 19*, 724–732.

Bar-Haim, Y., Lamy, D., Pergamin, L., Bakermans-Kranenburg, M. J., & van IJzendoorn, M. H. (2007). Threat-related attentional bias in anxious and nonanxious individuals: A meta-analytic study. *Psychological Bulletin, 133*, 1–24.

Barrett, L. F., Lindquist, K. A., & Gendron, M. (2007). Language as a context for the perception of emotion. *Trends in Cognitive Sciences, 11*, 327–332.

Bechara, A., Damasio, H., Tranel, D., & Damasio, A. R. (1997). Deciding advantageously before knowing the advantageous strategy. *Science, 275*, 1293–1294.

Bishop, S. J. (2007). Neurocognitive mechanisms of anxiety: An integrative account. *Trends in Cognitive Sciences, 7*, 307–316.

Bishop, S. J., Cohen, J. D., Fossella, J., Caswey, B. J., & Farah, M. J. (2006). COMT genotype influences prefrontal response to emotional distraction. *Cognitive, Affective, Behavioral Neuroscience, 6*, 62–70.

Bishop, S. J., Duncan, J., & Lawrence, A. D. (2004). State anxiety modulation of the amygdala response to unattended threat-related stimuli. *Journal of Neuroscience, 24*, 10364–10368.

Bisson, M. A., & Sears, C. R. (2007). The effect of depressed mood on the interpretation of ambiguity, with and without negative mood induction. *Cognition and Emotion, 21*, 614–645.

Blanchette, I. (2006). The effect of emotion on interpretation and logic in a conditional reasoning task. *Memory & Cognition, 34*, 1112–1125.

Blanchette, I., & Campbell, M. (2005). *The effect of emotion on syllogistic reasoning in a group of war veterans.* Paper presented at the XXVIIth Annual Conference of the Cognitive Science Society, Stresa, Italy.

Blanchette, I. Lindsay, P. & Davies, S. (2008). *Conditional reasoning about highly emotional events: Victims of sexual abuse.* Paper presented at the Sixth International Conference on Thinking, Venice, Italy.

Blanchette, I., & Richards, A. (2003). Anxiety and the interpretation of ambiguous information: Beyond the emotion-congruent effect. *Journal of Experimental Psychology: General, 132*, 294–309.

Blanchette, I., & Richards, A. (2004). Reasoning about emotional and neutral materials. Is logic affected by emotion? *Psychological Science, 15*, 745–752.

Blanchette, I., Richards, A., & Cross, A. (2007a). Anxiety and the interpretation of ambiguous facial expressions: The influence of contextual cues. *Quarterly Journal of Experimental Psychology, 60*, 1101–1115.

Blanchette, I., Richards, A., Melnyk, L., & Lavda, A. (2007b). Reasoning about emotional contents following shocking terrorist attacks: A tale of three cities. *Journal of Experimental Psychology: Applied, 13*, 47–56.

Bless, H., Bonher, G., Schwarz, N., & Strack, F. (1990). Mood and persuasion: A cognitive response analysis. *Personality and Social Psychology Bulletin, 16*, 331–345.

Bodenhausen, G. V., Gabriel, S., & Lineberger, M. (2000). Sadness and suscept-ibility to judgmental bias: The case of anchoring. *Psychological Science, 11*, 320–323.

Bodenhausen, G. V., Kramer, G. P., & Susser, K. (1994a). Happiness and stereotypic thinking in social judgment. *Journal of Personality & Social Psychology, 66*, 621–632.

Bodenhausen, G. V., Sheppard, L. A., & Kramer, G. P. (1994b). Negative affect and social judgment: The differential impact of anger and sadness. *European Journal of Social Psychology, 24*, 45–62.

Bower, G. H. (1981). Mood and memory. *American Psychologist, 36*, 129–148.

Brendle, J. R., & Wenzel, A. (2004). Differentiating between memory and interpretation biases in socially anxious and nonanxious individuals. *Behaviour Research and Therapy, 42*, 155–171.

Butler, G., & Mathews, A. (1983). Cognitive processes in anxiety. *Advances in Behaviour Research & Therapy, 5*, 51–62.

Butler, G., & Mathews, A. (1987). Anticipatory anxiety and risk perception. *Cognitive Therapy and Research, 11*, 551–565.

Byrne, A., & Eysenck, M. W. (1993). Individual differences in positive and negative interpretive biases. *Personality and Individual Differences, 14*, 849–851.

Calvo, M. G., & Castillo, M. D. (1997). Mood-congruent bias in interpretation of ambiguity: Strategic processes and temporary activation. *Quarterly Journal of Experimental Psychology, 50A*, 163–182.

Calvo, M. G., & Castillo, M. D. (2001a). Bias in predictive inferences during reading. *Discourse Processes, 32*, 43–71.

Calvo, M. G., & Castillo, M. D. (2001b). Selective interpretation in anxiety: Uncertainty for threatening events. *Cognition and Emotion, 15*, 299–320.

Calvo, M. G., Castillo, M. D., & Estevez, A. (1999). On-line predictive inferences in reading: Processing time during versus after the priming context. *Memory & Cognition, 27*, 834–843.

Calvo, M. G., Eysenck, M. W., & Castillo, M. D. (1997). Interpretation bias in test anxiety: The time course of predictive inferences. *Cognition and Emotion, 11*, 43–63.

Calvo, M. G., Eysenck, M. W., & Estevez, A. (1994). Ego-threat interpretive bias in test anxiety: On-line inferences. *Cognition and Emotion, 8*, 127–146.

Cane, D. B., & Gotlib, I. H. (1985). Depression and the effects of positive and negative feedback on expectations, evaluations, and performance. *Cognitive Therapy and Research, 9*, 145–160.

Channon, S., & Baker, J. (1994). Reasoning strategies in depression: Effects of depressed mood on a syllogism task. *Personality and Individual Differences, 17*, 707–711.

Clore, G. L., & Huntsinger, J. R. (2007). How emotions inform judgment and regulate thought. *Trends in Cognitive Sciences, 11*, 393–399.

Constans, J. I. (2001). Worry propensity and the perception of risk. *Behaviour Research and Therapy, 39*, 721–729.

Constans, J. I., & Mathews, A. M. (1993). Mood and the subjective risk of future events. *Cognition and Emotion, 7*, 545–560.

Copeland, D. E., & Radvansky, G. A. (2004). Working memory and syllogistic reasoning. *The Quarterly Journal of Experimental Psychology, 57A*, 1437–1457.

Craig, A. D. (2002). How do you feel? Interoception: The sense of the physiological condition of the body. *Nature Reviews Neuroscience, 3,* 655–666.

Craig, A. D. (2003). Interoception: The sense of the physiological condition of the body. *Current Opinion in Neurobiology, 13,* 500–505.

Damasio, A. R. (1995). *Descartes' error: Emotion, reason and the human brain.* New York: Avon Books.

Davey, G. C. L., Bickerstaffe, S., & MacDonald, B. A. (2006). Experienced disgust causes a negative interpretation bias: A causal role for disgust in anxious psychopathology. *Behaviour Research and Therapy, 44,* 1375–1384.

Davey, G. C. L., Menzies, R., & Gallardo, B. (1997). Height phobia and biases in the interpretation of bodily sensations: Some links between acrophobia and agoraphobia. *Behaviour Research and Therapy, 35,* 997–1001.

de Gelder, B., Meeren, H. K. M., Righart, R., van den Stock, J., Riet, W. A. C., & Tamietto, M. (2006). Beyond the face: Exploring rapid influences of context on face processing. *Progress in Brain Research, 155,* 37–48.

de Jong, P. J., Haenen, M.-A., Schmidt, A., & Mayer, B. (1998). Hypochondriasis: The role of fear-confirming reasoning. *Behaviour Research and Therapy, 36,* 65–74.

de Jong, P. J., Mayer, B., & van den Hout, M. (1997). Conditional reasoning and phobic fear: Evidence for a fear-confirming reasoning pattern. *Behavior Research and Therapy, 35,* 507–516.

de Jong, P. J., & Merckelbach, H. (2000). Phobia-relevant illusory correlations: The role of phobic responsivity. *Journal of Abnormal Psychology, 109,* 597–601.

de Jong, P. J., Weertman, A., Horselenberg, R., & van den Hout, M. A. (1997). Deductive reasoning and pathological anxiety: Evidence for a relatively strong "belief bias" in phobic subjects. *Cognitive Therapy and Research, 21,* 647–662.

Derakshan, N., & Eysenck, M. W. (1998). Working-memory capacity in high trait-anxious and repressor groups. *Cognition and Emotion, 12,* 697–713.

Derry, P. A., & Kuiper, N. A. (1981). Schematic processing and self-reference in clinical depression. *Journal of Abnormal Psychology, 90,* 286–297.

DeSteno, D., Petty, R. E., Wegener, D. T., & Rucke, D. D. (2000). Correction to DeSteno et al. (2000). *Journal of Personality and Social Psychology, 78,* 707.

Dunn, B. D., Dalgleish, T., & Lawrence, A. D. (2006). The somatic marker hypothesis: A critical evaluation. *Neuroscience & Biobehavioral Reviews, 30,* 239–271.

Edwards, J. A., & Weary, G. (1993). Depression and the impression-formation continuum: Piecemeal processing despite the availability of category information. *Journal of Personality and Social Psychology, 64,* 636–645.

Eysenck, M. W., MacLeod, C., & Mathews, A. (1987). Cognitive functioning and anxiety. *Psychological Research, 49,* 189–195.

Eysenck, M. W., Mogg, K., May, J., Richards, A., & Mathews, A. (1991). Bias in interpretation of ambiguous sentences related to threat in anxiety. *Journal of Abnormal Psychology, 100,* 144–150.

Fazio, R. H. (2001). On the automatic activation of associated evaluations: An overview. *Cognition and Emotion, 15,* 115–141.

Fellows, L. K., & Farah, M. J. (2003). Ventromedial frontal cortex mediates affective shifting in humans: Evidence from a reversal learning paradigm. *Brain: A Journal of Neurology, 126,* 1830–1837.

Fernandez-Dols, J. M., & Carroll, J. M. (1997). Is the meaning perceived in facial expression independent of its context? In J. A. Russell & J. M. Fernandez-Dols (Eds.), *The psychology of facial expressions* (pp. 275–294). Cambridge, UK: Cambridge University Press.

Fiedler, K. (2000). Toward and integrative account of affect and cognition phenomena using the BIAS computer algorithm. In J. P. Forgas (Ed.), *Feeling and thinking. The role of affect in social cognition* (pp. 223–252). Cambridge, UK: Cambridge University Press.

Fischhoff, B., Gonzalez, R. M., Lerner, J. S., & Small, D. A. (2005). Evolving judgments of terror risks: Foresight, hindsight, and emotion. *Journal of Experimental Psychology: Applied, 11*, 124–139.

Foa, E. B., Franklin, M. E., Perry, K. J., & Herbert, J. D. (1996). Cognitive biases in generalized social phobia. *Journal of Abnormal Psychology, 105*, 433–439.

Forgas, J. P. (2001). Affect, cognition, and interpersonal behavior: The mediating role of processing strategies. In J. P. Forgas (Ed.), *Handbook of affect and social cognition* (pp. 293–318). Mahwah, NJ: Lawrence Erlbaum Associates, Inc.

Forgas, J. P. (Ed.). (2006). *Affect in social thinking and behavior.* New York: Psychology Press.

Forgas, J. P., Bower, G. H., & Krantz, S. E. (1984). The influence of mood on perceptions of social interactions. *Journal of Experimental Social Psychology, 20*, 497–513.

Furl, N., van Rijsbergen, N. J., Treves, A., & Dolan, R. J. (2007). Experience-dependent coding of facial expression in superior temporal sulcus. *Proceedings of the National Academy of Sciences, 104*, 13485–13489.

Gadsby, N., Arnott, W. L., & Copland, D. A. (2008). An investigation of working memory influences on lexical ambiguity resolution. *Neuropsychology, 22*, 209–216.

Gaskell, M. G., & Marslen Wilson, W. D. (2001). Lexical ambiguity resolution and spoken word recognition: Bridging the gap. *Journal of Memory and Language, 44*, 325–349.

Gasper, K., & Clore, G. L. (1998). The persistent use of negative affect by anxious individuals to estimate risk. *Journal of Personality and Social Psychology, 74*, 1350–1363.

Gernsbacher, M. A., & Faust, M. E. (1991). The mechanism of suppression: A component of general comprehension skill. *Journal of Experimental Psychology: Learning, Memory, and Cognition, 17*, 245–262.

Gifford, S., Reynolds, S., Bell, S., & Wilson, C. (2008). Threat interpretation bias in anxious children and their mothers. *Cognition and Emotion, 22*, 497–508.

Goel, V., & Dolan, R. J. (2003). Reciprocal neural responses within lateral and ventral medial prefrontal cortex during hot and cold reasoning. *NeuroImage, 20*, 2314–2321.

Gold, R. S. (2002). The effects of mood states on the AIDS-related judgements of gay men. *International Journal of STD & AIDS, 13*, 475–481.

Goldin, P. R., McRae, K., Ramel, W., & Gross, J. J. (2008). The neural bases of emotion regulation: Reappraisal and suppression of negative emotion. *Biological Psychiatry, 63*, 577–586.

Greenberg, M. S., & Beck, A. T. (1989). Depression versus anxiety: A test of the content-specificity hypothesis. *Journal of Abnormal Psychology, 98*, 9–13.

Grey, S., & Mathews, A. (2000). Effects of training on interpretation of emotional ambiguity. *The Quarterly Journal of Experimental Psychology, 54A,* 1143–1162.

Hadwin, J., Frost, S., French, C. C., & Richards, A. (1997). Cognitive processing and trait anxiety in typically developing children: Evidence for an interpretation bias. *Journal of Abnormal Psychology, 106,* 486–490.

Halberstadt, J. B., Niedenthal, P. M., & Kushner, J. (1995). Resolution of lexical ambiguity by emotional state. *Psychological Science, 6,* 278–282.

Hertel, P. T., Brozovich, F., Joormann, J., & Gotlib, I. H. (2008). Biases in interpretation and memory in generalized social phobia. *Journal of Abnormal Psychology, 117,* 278–288.

Hertel, P. T., Mathews, A., Peterson, S., & Kintner, K. (2003). Transfer of training emotionally biased interpretations. *Applied Cognitive Psychology, 17,* 775–784.

Higa, C. K., & Daleiden, E. L. (2008). Social anxiety and cognitive biases in non-referred children: The interaction of self-focused attention and threat interpretation biases. *Journal of Anxiety Disorders, 22,* 441–452.

Hirsch, C., & Mathews, A. (1997). Interpretive inferences when reading about emotional events. *Behaviour Research and Therapy, 35,* 1123–1132.

Hirsch, C., Mathews, A., & Clark, D. M. (2007). Inducing an interpretation bias changes self-imagery: A preliminary investigation. *Behaviour Research and Therapy, 45,* 2173–2181.

Huppert, J. D., Pasupuleti, R. V., Foa, E. B., & Mathews, A. (2007). Interpretation biases in social anxiety: Response generation, response selection, and self-appraisals. *Behaviour Research and Therapy, 45,* 1505–1515.

In-Albon, T., Klein, A., Rinck, M., Becker, E., & Schneider, S. (2008). Development and evaluation of a new paradigm for the assessment of anxiety-disorder-specific interpretation bias using picture stimuli. *Cognition and Emotion, 22,* 422–436.

Isen, A. M., & Geva, N. (1987). The influence of positive affect on acceptable level of risk: The person with a large canoe has a large worry. *Organizational Behavior and Human Decision Processes, 39,* 145–154.

Isen, A. M., Nygren, T. E., & Ashby, F. G. (1988). Influence of positive affect on the subjective utility of gains and losses: It is just not worth the risk. *Journal of Personality and Social Psychology, 55,* 710–717.

Isen, A. M., & Patrick, R. (1983). The effect of positive feelings on risk taking: When the chips are down. *Organizational Behavior & Human Performance, 31,* 194–202.

Johnson, E. J., & Tversky, A. (1983). Affect, generalization, and the perception of risk. *Journal of Personality and Social Psychology, 45,* 20–31.

Johnson-Laird, P. N., Mancini, F., & Gangemi, A. (2006). A hyper-emotion theory of psychological illnesses. *Psychological Review, 113,* 822–841.

Jones, G. V. (1984). Fragment and schema models of recall. *Memory & Cognition, 12,* 250–263.

Jones, G. V. (1987). Independence and exclusivity among psychological processes: Implications for the structure of recall. *Psychological Review, 94,* 229–235.

Kemp, R., Chua, S., McKenna, P., & David, A. (1997). Reasoning and delusions. *The British Journal of Psychiatry, 170,* 398–411.

Kensinger, E. A., & Corkin, S. (2003). Effect of negative emotional content on working memory and long-term memory. *Emotion, 3,* 378–393.

Kim, H., Somerville, L. H., Johnstone, T., Alexander, A. L., & Whalen, P. J. (2003). Inverse amygdala and medial prefrontal cortex responses to surprised faces. *Neuroreport, 14*, 2317–2322.

Kim, H., Somerville, L. H., Johnstone, T., Polis, S., Alexander, A. L., Shin, L. M., et al. (2004). Contextual modulation of amygdala responsivity to surprised faces. *Journal of Cognitive Neuroscience, 16*, 1730–1745.

Kolassa, I.-T., Buchmann, A., Lauche, R., Kolassa, S., Partchev, I., Miltner, W. H. R., et al. (2007). Spider phobics more easily see a spider in morphed schematic pictures [on-line journal]. *Behavioral and Brain Functions, 3*, 59.

Kverno, K. S. (2000). Trait anxiety influences on judgments of frequency and recall. *Personality and Individual Differences, 29*, 395–404.

Laney, C., Campbell, H. V., Heuer, F., & Reisberg, D. (2004). Memory for thematically arousing events. *Memory & Cognition, 32*, 1149–1159.

Laney, C., Heuer, F., & Reisberg, D. (2003). Thematically induced arousal in naturally occurring emotional memories. *Applied Cognitive Psychology, 17*, 995–1004.

Lavric, A., Rippon, G., & Gray, J. R. (2003). Threat-evoked anxiety disrupts spatial working memory performance: An attentional account. *Cognitive Therapy and Research, 27*, 489–504.

Lawson, C., & MacLeod, C. (1999). Depression and the interpretation of ambiguity. *Behaviour Research and Therapy, 37*, 463–474.

Lefford, A. (1946). The influence of emotional subject matter on logical reasoning. *Journal of General Psychology, 34*, 127–151.

Lerner, J. S., Gonzalez, R. M., Small, D. A., & Fischhoff, B. (2003). Effects of fear and anger on perceived risks of terrorism: A national field experiment. *Psychological Science, 14*, 144–150.

Lerner, J. S., & Keltner, D. (2000). Beyond valence: Toward a model of emotion-specific influences on judgement and choice. *Cognition and Emotion, 14*, 473–493.

Lucas, M. (1999). Context effects in lexical access: A meta-analysis. *Memory & Cognition, 27*, 385–398.

Mackie, D. M., & Worth, L. T. (1989). Processing deficits and the mediation of positive affect in persuasion. *Journal of Personality and Social Psychology, 57*(1), 27–40.

MacLeod, C. (1999). Anxiety and anxiety disorders. In T. Dalgleish & M. J. Power (Eds.), *Handbook of cognition and emotion* (pp. 447–477). New York: Wiley.

MacLeod, C., & Campbell, L. (1992). Memory accessibility and probability judgments: An experimental evaluation of the availability heuristic. *Journal of Personality and Social Psychology, 63*, 890–902.

MacLeod, C., Campbell, L., Rutherford, E., & Wilson, E. (2004). The causal status of anxiety-linked attentional and interpretive bias. In J. Yiend (Ed.), *Cognition, emotion and psychopathology: Theoretical, empirical and clinical directions* (pp. 172–189). New York: Cambridge University Press.

MacLeod, C., & Cohen, I. L. (1993). Anxiety and the interpretation of ambiguity: A text comprehension study. *Journal of Abnormal Psychology, 102*, 238–247.

Maia, T. V., & McClelland, J. L. (2004). A reexamination of the evidence for the somatic marker hypothesis: What participants really know about the Iowa gambling task. *Proceedings of the National Academy of Sciences of the United States of America, 101*, 16075–16080.

Maner, J. K., & Gerend, M. A. (2007). Motivationally selective risk judgments: Do fear and curiosity boost the boons or the banes? *Organizational Behavior and Human Decision Processes, 103,* 256–267.

Martin, L., Harlow, T. F., & Strack, F. (1992). The role of bodily sensations in the evaluation of social events. *Personality and Social Psychology Bulletin, 18,* 412–419.

Martin, M., Horder, P., & Jones, G. V. (1992). Integral bias in naming of phobia-related words. *Cognition and Emotion, 6,* 479–486.

Martin, M., & Jones, G. V. (1995). Integral bias in the cognitive processing of emotionally linked pictures. *British Journal of Psychology, 86,* 419–435.

Mathews, A., & Mackintosh, B. (1998). A cognitive model of selective processing in anxiety. *Cognitive Therapy and Research, 22,* 539–560.

Mathews, A., & Mackintosh, B. (2000). Induced emotional interpretation bias and anxiety. *Journal of Abnormal Psychology, 109,* 602–615.

Mathews, A., & MacLeod, C. (2002). Induced processing biases have causal effects on anxiety. *Cognition and Emotion, 16,* 331–354.

Mathews, A., Richards, A., & Eysenck, M. (1989). Interpretation of homophones related to threat in anxiety states. *Journal of Abnormal Psychology, 98,* 31–34.

Mayer, J. D., Gaschke, Y. N., Braverman, D. L., & Evans, T. W. (1992). Mood-congruent judgment is a general effect. *Journal of Personality and Social Psychology, 63,* 119–132.

Mayer, J. D., & Hanson, E. (1995). Mood-congruent judgment over time. *Personality and Social Psychology Bulletin, 21,* 237–244.

McClelland, J. L. (1987). The case for interactionism in language processing. In M. Coltheart (Ed.), *Attention and performance 12: The psychology of reading* (pp. 3–36). Hove, UK: Lawrence Erlbaum Associates.

Melton, R. J. (1995). The role of positive affect in syllogism performance. *Personality & Social Psychology Bulletin, 21,* 788–794.

Mittal, V., & Ross, W. T. (1998). The impact of positive and negative affect and issue framing on issue interpretation and risk taking. *Organizational Behavior and Human Decision Processes, 76,* 298–324.

Mogg, K., Bradbury, K. E., & Bradley, B. P. (2006). Interpretation of ambiguous information in clinical depression. *Behaviour Research and Therapy, 44,* 1411–1419.

Mogg, K., Bradley, B. P., & Hallowell, N. (1994). Attentional bias to threat: Roles of trait anxiety, stressful events, and awareness. *Quarterly Journal of Experimental Psychology, 47A,* 841–864.

Muris, P., & van der Heiden, S. (2006). Anxiety, depression, and judgments about the probability of future negative and positive events in children. *Journal of Anxiety Disorders, 20,* 252–261.

Niedenthal, P. M., & Setterlund, M. B. (1994). Emotion congruence in perception. *Personality and Social Psychology Bulletin, 20,* 401–411.

Nunn, J. D., Mathews, A., & Trower, P. (1997). Selective processing of concern-related information in depression. *British Journal of Clinical Psychology, 36,* 489–503.

Nygaard, L. C., & Lunders, E. R. (2002). Resolution of lexical ambiguity by emotional tone of voice. *Memory & Cognition, 30,* 583–593.

Oaksford, M., Morris, F., Grainger, B., & Williams, J. M. G. (1996). Mood, reasoning, and central executive processes. *Journal of Experimental Psychology: Learning, Memory, and Cognition, 22,* 476–492.

Ochsner, K. N., & Gross, J. J. (2008). Cognitive emotion regulation: Insights from social cognitive and affective neuroscience. *Current Directions in Psychological Science, 17,* 153–158.

Onifer, W., & Swinney, D. A. (1981). Accessing lexical ambiguities during sentence comprehension: Effects of frequency of meaning and contextual bias. *Memory & Cognition, 9,* 225–236.

Pacini, R., Muir, F., & Epstein, S. (1998). Depressive realism from the perspective of cognitive-experiential self-theory. *Journal of Personality and Social Psychology, 74,* 1056–1068.

Palfai, T. P., & Salovey, P. (1993). The influence of depressed and elated mood on deductive and inductive reasoning. *Imagination, Cognition and Personality, 13,* 57–71.

Pell, P. J. & Richards, A. (2009). *The ambiguity of unambiguous facial expression: A study of adaptation induced perceptual shifts.* Manuscript submitted for publication.

Perham, N., & Oaksford, M. (2005). Deontic reasoning with emotional content: Evolutionary psychology or decision theory? *Cognitive Science: A Multidisciplinary Journal, 29,* 681–718.

Pham, M. T. (1998). Representativeness, relevance, and the use of feelings in decision making. *Journal of Consumer Research, 25,* 144–159.

Pham, M. T. (2007). Emotion and rationality: A critical review and interpretation of empirical evidence. *Review of General Psychology, 11,* 155–178.

Phan, K. L., Fitzgerald, D. A., Nathan, P. J., Moore, G. J., Uhde, T. W., & Tancer, M. E. (2005). Neural substrates for voluntary suppression of negative affect: A functional magnetic resonance imaging study. *Biological Psychiatry, 57,* 210–219.

Raghunathan, R., & Pham, M. T. (1999). All negative moods are not equal: Motivational influences of anxiety and sadness on decision making. *Organizational Behavior and Human Decision Processes, 79,* 56–77.

Ray, R. A. D., Ochsner, K. N., Cooper, J. C., Robertson, E. R., Gabrieli, J. D. E., & Gross, J. J. (2005). Individual differences in trait rumination and the neural systems supporting cognitive reappraisal. *Cognitive, Affective and Behavioral Neuroscience, 5,* 156–168.

Richards, A., Blanchette, I., & Munjiza, J. (2007a). Contextual influences in the resolution of ambiguity in anxiety. *Cognition and Emotion, 21,* 879–890.

Richards, A., & French, C. C. (1992). An anxiety-related bias in semantic activation when processing threat/neutral homographs. *The Quarterly Journal of Experimental Psychology, 45A,* 503–525.

Richards, A., French, C. C., Calder, A. J., Webb, B., Fox, R., & Young, A. W. (2002). Anxiety-related bias in the classification of emotionally ambiguous facial expressions. *Emotion, 2,* 273–287.

Richards, A., French, C. C., Johnson, W., Naparstek, J., & Williams, J. (1992). Effects of mood manipulation and anxiety on performance of an emotional Stroop task. *British Journal of Psychology, 83,* 479–491.

Richards, A., French, C. C., Keogh, E., & Carter, C. (2000). Test anxiety, inferential reasoning and working memory load. *Anxiety, Stress and Coping, 13,* 87–109.

Richards, A., French, C. C., Nash, G., Hadwin, J. A., & Donnelly, N. (2007b). A comparison of selective attention and facial processing biases in typically developing children who are high and low in self-reported trait anxiety. *Development and Psychopathology*, *19*, 481–495.

Richards, A., Reynolds, A., & French, C. C. (1993). Anxiety and the spelling and use in sentences of threat/neutral homophones. *Current Psychology: Developmental, Learning, Personality, Social*, *12*, 18–25.

Russo, R., Patterson, N., Roberson, D., Stevenson, N., & Upward, J. (1996). Emotional value of information and its relevance in the interpretation of homophones in anxiety. *Cognition and Emotion*, *10*, 213–220.

Salemink, E., van den Hout, M., & Kindt, M. (2007). Trained interpretive bias: Validity and effects on anxiety. *Journal of Behavior Therapy and Experimental Psychiatry*, *38*, 212–224.

Schwarz, N., & Clore, G. L. (1983). Mood, misattribution, and judgments of well-being: Informative and directive functions of affective states. *Journal of Personality and Social Psychology*, *45*, 513–523.

Semmler, C., & Brewer, N. (2002). Effects of mood and emotion on juror processing and judgments. *Behavioral Sciences & the Law*, *20*, 423–436.

Shackman, A. J., Sarinopoulos, I., Maxwell, J. S., Pizzagalli, D. A., Lavric, A., & Davidson, R. J. (2006). Anxiety selectively disrupts visuospatial working memory. *Emotion*, *6*, 40–61.

Simpson, G. B. (1984). Lexical ambiguity and its role in models of word recognition. *Psychological Bulletin*, *96*, 316–340.

Simpson, G. B., & Burgess, C. (1985). Activation and selection processes in the recognition of ambiguous words. *Journal of Experimental Psychology: Human Perception and Performance*, *11*, 28–39.

Sinclair, R. C. (1988). Mood, categorization breadth, and performance appraisal: The effects of order of information acquisition and affective state on halo, accuracy, information retrieval, and evaluations. *Organizational Behavior and Human Decision Processes*, *42*, 22–46.

Smeets, G., de Jong, P. J., & Mayer, B. (2000). If you suffer from a headache, then you have a brain tumor: Domain-specific reasoning "bias" and hypochondriasis. *Behaviour Research and Therapy*, *38*, 763–776.

Somerville, L. H., Kim, H., Johnstone, T., Alexander, A. L., & Whalen, P. J. (2004). Human amygdala responses during presentation of happy and neutral faces: Correlations with state anxiety. *Biological Psychiatry*, *55*, 897–903.

Sprengelmeyer, R., Young, A. W., Sprenglemeyer, A., Calder, A. J., Rowland, D., Perrett, D., et al. (1997). Recognition of facial expressions: Selective impairment of specific emotions in Huntington's disease. *Cognitive Neuropsychology*, *14*, 839–879.

Stopa, L., & Clark, D. M. (2000). Social phobia and interpretation of social events. *Behaviour Research and Therapy*, *38*, 273–283.

Ströber, J. (1997). Trait anxiety and pessimistic appraisal of risk and chance. *Personality and Individual Differences*, *22*, 465–476.

Taghavi, M. R., Moradi, A. R., Neshat-Doost, H. T., Yule, W., & Dalgleish, T. (2000). Interpretation of ambiguous emotional information in clinically anxious children and adolescents. *Cognition and Emotion*, *14*, 809–822.

Tanner, C., & Medin, D. L. (2004). Protected values: No omission bias and no framing effects. *Psychonomic Bulletin & Review*, *11*, 185–191.

Tiedens, L. Z., & Linton, S. (2001). Judgment under emotional certainty and uncertainty: The effects of specific emotions on information processing. *Journal of Personality and Social Psychology, 81,* 973–988.

Tomb, I., Hauser, M., Deldin, P., & Caramazza, A. (2002). Do somatic markers mediate decisions on the gambling task? *Nature Neuroscience, 5,* 1103–1104.

Västfjäll, D., Peters, E., & Slovic, P. (2008). Affect, risk perception and future optimism after the tsunami disaster. *Judgment and Decision Making, 3,* 64–72.

Waters, A. M., Craske, M. G., Bergman, R. L., & Treanor, M. (2008). Threat interpretation bias as a vulnerability factor in childhood anxiety disorders. *Behaviour Research and Therapy, 46,* 39–47.

Wegener, D. T., Petty, R. E., & Smith, S. M. (1995). Positive mood can increase or decrease message scrutiny: The hedonic contingency view of mood and message processing. *Journal of Personality and Social Psychology, 69,* 5–15.

Weis, R., & Lovejoy, M. C. (2002). Information processing in everyday life: Emotion-congruent bias in mothers' reports of parent–child interactions. *Journal of Personality and Social Psychology, 83,* 216–230.

Wenzel, A., Finstrom, N., Jordan, J., & Brendle, J. R. (2005). Memory and interpretation of visual representations of threat in socially anxious and nonanxious individuals. *Behaviour Research and Therapy, 43,* 1029–1044.

Wilson, E. J., MacLeod, C., Mathews, A., & Rutherford, E. M. (2006). The causal role of interpretive bias in anxiety reactivity. *Journal of Abnormal Psychology, 115,* 103–111.

Worth, L. T., & Mackie, D. M. (1987). Cognitive mediation of positive affect in persuasion. *Social Cognition, 5,* 76–94.

Yiend, J., & Mackintosh, B. (2004). The experimental modification of processing biases. In J. Yiend (Ed.), *Cognition, emotion and psychopathology: Theoretical, empirical and clinical directions* (pp. 190–210). New York: Cambridge University Press.

Yiend, J., Mackintosh, B., & Mathews, A. (2005). Enduring consequences of experimentally induced biases in interpretation. *Behaviour Research and Therapy, 43,* 779–797.

Yoon, K. L., & Zinbarg, R. E. (2008). Interpreting neutral faces as threatening is a default mode for socially anxious individuals. *Journal of Abnormal Psychology, 117,* 680–685.

Young, A. W., Rowland, D., Calder, A. J., & Etcoff, N. L. (1997). Facial expression megamix: Tests of dimensional and category accounts of emotion recognition. *Cognition, 63,* 271–313.

Zelenski, J. M., & Larsen, R. J. (2002). Predicting the future: How affect-related personality traits influence likelihood judgments of future events. *Personality and Social Psychology Bulletin, 28,* 1000–1010.

Zhou, W., & Chen, D. (2009). Fear-related chemosignals modulate recognition of fear in ambiguous facial expressions. *Psychological Science, 20,* 177–183.

Correspondence should be addressed to: Isabelle Blanchette, Département de psychologie, Université du Québec à Trois-Rivières, CP 500, Trois-Rivières (Québec), Canada, G9A 5H7. Isabelle.Blanchette@uqtr.ca

The writing of this review was supported by the BIAL Foundation, grant number 68/04.

# Author index

# Subject index